D1095936

CHABOT COLLEGE-HAYWARD

2 555 000 023649 +

OLD MASTERS
OF RETAILING

OLD MASTERS OF RETAILING

by Philip J. Reilly

Fairchild Publications, Inc., New York

HF
5429
R375

Copyright 1966 ©
Fairchild Publications, Inc.

Second Printing 1967

All rights reserved. No part of this book may be
reproduced in any form without permission in writing
from the publisher, except by a reviewer who wishes
to quote passages in connection with a review
written for inclusion in a magazine or newspaper.

Library of Congress Catalog Card Number 65–27051

Designer: Ernst Reichl

Printed in the United States of America

CONTENTS

37643

INTRODUCTION

By Samuel Feinberg

Thomas Carlyle, the Scottish essayist-historian, once said:

"The true past departs not, no truth or goodness realized by man ever dies, or can die; but all is still here, and, recognized or not, lives and works through endless changes."

One hundred years later, Herbert Landsman, executive vice-president for divisional services of Federated Department Stores, advises:

"When you look back over the history of retailing, there have been quite a few major breakthroughs, and in every case they were made by the ability of a brilliant individual to look ahead of his immediate problems to foresee some great new trend of the future. In some cases, it was as simple as Marshall Field finding a manager arguing with a customer and asking him what he was doing. 'Settling a customer complaint,' said the manager. 'No, you aren't,' said Field. 'Give the lady what she wants.' In this simple way came the great discovery that satisfying the customer even when she is unreasonable can be the greatest single builder of customer confidence and affection—and, with it, sales. The same truth was arrived at by Fred Lazarus, Jr.'s, commonsense discovery that 'A shopper is like a baby who wants milk. When he cries for milk, he doesn't want a meal ticket. He doesn't want an argument or an excuse. He wants warm milk that is right for him—and he wants it at once.'"

Mr. Landsman might also well include Lincoln Filene who explained his preoccupation with the value of good employee relations and systematic training and development: "If we are to create contentment in front of the customer, we must first create contentment behind it. Many employees learn their manners of serving the public from the manner in which they are served by their managers."

Mr. Landsman continues:

"There was one common denominator to all these innovations . . . First, they were introduced by a brilliant owner or manager who sensed more or less instinctively the need for change, and who had the power to take the necessary risk in making it. Second, they arose from existing or anticipated—but always real—customer needs. Third, all had profits as their objective—and all did contribute mightily to the profitable growth of retailing.

"Today, these conditions are no longer quite the same. Then, the pioneer was also the owner, whose ideas came through daily contact with the customer, through seat-of-the-pants inspiration. These great innovating giants were few in number, as the tremendous mortality rate of department stores in the last half-century clearly shows. They were few to begin with, and today even the surviving pioneers are hard put to keep the old feel of daily intimacy because retailing has become so huge, management so large and so complex, and more remote from the customer. At the same time, enormous changes are overtaking our society, in fundamental ways which undoubtedly are creating equally great opportunities for expanding the horizons of retailing—the times are crying for innumerable innovations. Now, the burden of my argument is that today it is we in research and development who have got to do what the giants of old were doing."

In writing "Old Masters of Retailing", Philip Joseph Reilly had something similar in mind—to report major breakthroughs in retailing's history as precept and incentive for the current and future generations of leadership. He drew his material from a capacious portfolio of personal memories and accomplishments—as well as from the business records and family archives of associates and contemporaries. He carried out this long-nourished project, this labor of love, with simple eloquence and quiet humor.

Successively personnel advisor and research head of Retail Research Association and operating chief of Associated Merchandising Corporation for about a quarter century after World War I, Col. Reilly came into closer contact with important store executives than perhaps any other single individual. He was on intimate terms, and often consulted on mutual problems, with the Filenes, the Lazaruses, and many others in the Associated Merchandising fold of giant department and specialty stores of whom he writes. And, because of his signal position in the industry, he was able to obtain much inside knowledge for the book about other companies.

Col. Reilly's title, by which he was addressed until his death in 1963 at 77, stems from his having been commissioned a lieutenant colonel in charge of classification of enlisted personnel in the U.S. Army during World War I. A man of probing, restless mind, the colonel was as much an innovator in his own right as were the men who founded, inherited, bought, or supervised the top stores of America, Canada, and Britain. His special contribution was his pioneering effort in "selling" personnel management in the 1920s to a number of department stores as a desirable business philosophy and practice. In so doing, he elevated stores' consideration of employee well-being from "do-good-ism" and "welfare" into its modern definition as a sound, integral part of corporate operations. He was one of the first men in the high command of retailing to promote women beyond buying jobs. Col. Reilly was also a stalwart proponent of many merchandising advances.

This volume, then, is a guide to company and community service, a career-opportunity, and a history of men and institutions. As such, "Old Masters of Retailing" is a supplementary text for the student and novice in retailing, and in distribution in general as well as a source spring of memory, stimulus and pride for oldtimers.

FOREWORD

In this text, which attempts to impart not only the importance of retailing but also its romance and glamour, the term "Old Masters" designates the founders of 35 selected department stores. Necessarily, the emphasis is placed on these men and their descendants. These notable stores, in business from 75 to 100 years, are covered from A to Z—from Abraham & Straus in Brooklyn to ZCMI in Salt Lake City. Of course, not all of the fine stores in the nation are included because of the limitations of time and space. But the author has attempted to select a representative group, taking into account history, location, size, and contributions to merchandising.

All of the founders were men of integrity, industry, and imagination. They had above all the determination that established stores that have endured. Most of these men began with meager capital and little schooling, and achieved success despite fires, floods, depressions, and other serious setbacks. Many of these stores are at present being operated by descendants of the founders.

Some of the Old Masters not only established great stores, but also served their communities, their states, and the nation in other ways. In the course of their progress, they also earned the loyalty of their employees by establishing advanced personnel policies that are now commonplace in modern retailing.

How flexible and fluid retailing is was observed anew during the writing of this book when many significant changes were taking place in the organizations described.

Retailing offers certain unique advantages to those who remain in the field. Employees can move easily from one store to another, earn a premium beginning salary in addition to the benefits granted most occupations. A college education is not required, though it does speed promotion to high-paying executive positions.

For women, particularly, retailing has great advantages: Practically all executive positions are open to them. Marriage does not interfere with progress; even the bearing of children need not delay a career unduly.

For both men and women, there is in retailing the glamour of travel and the attraction of public service. Buyers make regular visits to the wholesale markets and many go also to the foreign markets with expense accounts permitting stops at the best hotels. It is hoped that the narratives in each chapter will be of sufficient interest to young men and young women to impel them to enter the retail field with the purpose of making it a career.

The author is familiar with nearly all of the stores covered in this book. His years in industry, before he became director of the Associated Merchandising Corporation, give weight to the opinion that more and more young persons should investigate the rewards of retailing.

Recognition must be given many people for their help in the preparation of this book. All the data and research material were furnished by the descendants of the founders, the staffs and executives, both past and present, of the stores mentioned. It has, therefore, been accepted as authentic and historically accurate.

Particular appreciation must be expressed to Walter N. Rothschild, Louise Towne, Lyman S. Ayres, David L. Yunich, Kenneth Collins, Frank I. Liveright, Albert D. Hutzler, Joseph E. Hansen, Harry A. Hatry, Philip Corrin, Hector Escobosa, Edward W. Carter, John J. Reilly, William C. Berwick, Howard

L. Schlesinger, John T. Pirie, Jr., J. Chalmers O'Brien, A. R. Mcgee, and Martha Douglas.

Also to George S. DeBonis, Gladys Lehning, Charles S. Hobbs, Frederic S. Hirschler, Reginald H. Biggs, Edward C. Lipman, William C. Bores, J. A. Brockie, Maurice Lazarus, Harold D. Hodgkinson, William S. Street, Beatrice Fox Auerbach, Samuel Einstein, Thomas J. Carroll, Ward Gardner, Bernard F. Gimbel, John R. Hager.

And from England and Canada, Sir Richard Burbidge, Bart, C. B. E., CDR.; Sir Robert Hobart, BT. R.N., personal assistant to Hugh Fraser; Sir Rex A. L. Cohen, K. B. E.; and F. B. Walker, Executive Assistant, Canadian Committee.

Thanks are also due to Walter A. Crow, Cameron S. Thompson, Fred Lazarus, Jr., Walter Hoving, Robert J. McKim, Samuel W. Reyburn, William F. Gekle, and Edmund P. Platt, as well as to Jack I. Straus, Walter J. Brunmark, Julia Coburn, J. L. Palmer, Ina C. Dorsey, Aaron M. Frank, Frank H. Neely, Frank M. Mayfield. And G. Stockton Strawbridge, Irving May, William B. Thalhimer, Jr., Richard C. Bond, Frank M. Folsom, Irene Wilhelm, Neil Petree, Harold H. Bennett, and Jerry Bergsman.

A special thank you to Michael F. Dowley, for encouragement in this project, and for information furnished for several chapters. And deep appreciation to my wife, Ethel, whose advice in presenting this material and editing the text was invaluable.

The Fairchild Publications, with emphasis on *Women's Wear Daily*, its staff, particularly Samuel Feinberg, also deserve special mention.

PHILIP J. REILLY

THE
BUYING OFFICE

The buying office plays an important part in modern retailing. As stores grew from small establishments to great volume businesses, it became necessary to organize to meet the growing competition, for the purpose of exchanging figures, and receiving daily firsthand information of the markets.

Following is the history of one of the first co-operative groups to organize. The author had firsthand knowledge of this fine group of stores for 25 years.

Retail Research Association, referred to as RRA, was created in November, 1916, by a group of independent department store principals who wished to establish an organization that would study scientifically problems of marketing and operation and provide a means of exchanging statistics on these problems. This group was organized by Lincoln Filene, the Boston merchant. The 19 stores originally represented were shortly increased to 21; at present, there are 28.

The successful accomplishments of these research functions by RRA encouraged the store principals to expand this association into an organization through which the member stores would be enabled to buy co-operatively. As a result, in March, 1918, an affiliated organization, Associated Merchandising Corporation, referred to as AMC, was established.

At first, RRA and AMC were separate corporations with the

same preferred stockholders, board of directors, executive committees, directors, and officers. The member stores from which both organizations drew their support were the same. The two organizations have since been merged into AMC with RRA merely a division of that corporation. However, their functions remain unchanged: RRA is an agency for research and the interchange of facts and figures on store operation and promotion, while AMC is essentially the buying division.

It must be kept in mind that this is a voluntary organization and not a centrally controlled group. The annual expenses are borne by the member stores based on the volume of their respective sales.

Another subsidiary, Aimcee Wholesale Corporation, was later formed to further the promotion and development of Aimcee brands, and to buy merchandise co-operatively to better advantage. L. F. Koranda is president and general manager of the Aimcee division.

The AMC export department not only serves its member stores but also buys in the United States for foreign stores located around the globe. The import department buys goods from the four corners of the world for member stores and for some noncompeting domestic stores. Throughout the world, AMC maintains offices in important cities where merchandise is purchased for domestic consumption.

A constant task of the import department is developing new markets. Norman Tarnoff, vice-president of AMC foreign operation with headquarters in Paris, administers the offices in Europe and the Far East.

The first managing director of RRA in 1916 was Alvin E. Dodd who, with a B.S. degree from the Armour Institute of Technology, was previously an instructor in several manual arts and industrial schools. He resigned from the retail group in 1921 to join the U.S. Chamber of Commerce.

Paul H. Nystrom, who succeeded Mr. Dodd as managing director of RRA and AMC, graduated from Superior (Wisconsin) State Teachers College in 1905; University of Wisconsin Ph.B. in 1909, Ph.M. in 1910, and Ph.D. in 1914. He clerked in stores before going to college and taught in high schools and colleges during his college years. His books on retailing were notably successful before he joined RRA and AMC. Dr. Nystrom resigned in 1925 to give full time to a professorship at Columbia University.

The author joined RRA July 1, 1919, as advisor on employee relations and personnel problems in member stores. In January, 1923, he was appointed managing director of RRA, and from January, 1926, to June 30, 1944, he was managing director of both RRA and AMC. The author started his business career with Dennison Manufacturing Co. as a young boy, after graduating from a business college in Philadelphia. He later attended night classes at Boston College. He was subsequently a divisional superintendent in charge of personnel, then advertising manager and employment manager. He was at one time president of the National Association of Employment Managers. During 1917, he was a member of the Committee on Classification of Personnel in the army and was commissioned a lieutenant colonel.

In 1944, following the resignation of the author, Joseph P. Kasper took over the reins of AMC, and was named president, a title with a little more glory though the responsibilities were the same. Mr. Kasper, who earned a B.A. degree from Middlebury College, Middlebury, Vermont, is a life trustee of the college. He came to his new position with a rich experience in retailing, having started in 1920 as a member of the original Macy training squad. Following this, he was an assistant buyer, buyer, merchandise manager, and for 11 years executive vice-president in charge of all home furnishings. For 14 years, he made annual trips abroad for Macy's, covering all European countries. In 1960, Mr. Kasper was named chairman of the board of AMC. He retired in 1962.

William T. French, a non-retailer who succeeded Mr. Kasper as president, attended the University of Pennsylvania, earning his B.B.A. degree in 1934 and an LL.B. from George Washington University in 1940. He was a lieutenant in the U.S. Navy and served as supply officer at the Philadelphia Navy Yard. Before joining AMC, Mr. French was president of the Pepsodent division of Lever Bros., New York, and before that had extensive experience in advertising, sales promotion, and marketing. He was with Vick Chemical Company, Curtis Publishing Company, Electrolux Corporation and National Dairy Products Corporation.

In 1929, under the brilliant leadership of Fred Lazarus, Jr., five members of AMC combined to form Federated Department Stores to diversify financial risks through common ownership of previously independent stores in various sections of the country. The number of operating subsidiaries has increased to 13 plus 60 branches, and Federated now leads the department store field in volume.

AMC, including Federated operating divisions, now includes 28 U.S. retailers and eight overseas.

Many men found the experience gained in RRA-AMC a valuable steppingstone to more lucrative positions in the retail field. James S. Schoff, for example, left AMC to join Bamberger's, Newark, as personnel manager; then, The Fair, Chicago, as president. He subsequently became president of Bloomingdale's, New York, of which he is now chairman of the board.

Stanley Roth, Sr., who assisted in many of the surveys made in the member stores, became personnel manager of L. S. Ayres, Indianapolis; then, one of its divisional merchandise managers. He left to become, successively, vice-president of Gimbel's, Milwaukee; vice-president of The Golden Rule, St. Paul; executive vice-president of Darling Stores, and president of Grayson-Robinson Stores. He now heads Apparel Buying Associates, which buys ready-to-wear and millinery for Woolco, F. W. Woolworth discount-store subsidiary.

B. Earl Puckett, employed by the author to supervise the RRA figure exchange and represent the RRA-AMC controllers' group, later went to Frederick Loeser & Co., Brooklyn, as controller and merchandiser of home furnishings. He became president of Loeser's, and a few years later was made head of Allied Stores Corporation, formerly known as Hahn Depart-

ment Stores, a heterogeneous group of some 40 subsidiaries
ranging from relatively small stores to the great Jordan Marsh
Co., Boston, and Bon Marche, Seattle. The group had been unprofitable, but in a short time under Mr. Puckett's able direction the stores with few exceptions were operating profitably.
The company now operates more than 100 units, and is the
second largest department store chain in volume.

Alfred C. Thompson followed Mr. Puckett in the RRA division, coming from Strawbridge & Clothier, one of the member stores. Later, Mr. Thompson was appointed a vice-president of RRA-AMC. He resigned to establish an independent
consulting service to other retailers. One of his clients was
Miller & Rhoads, Richmond, Virginia. He joined this store as
vice-president, and was there for 15 years. He resigned as
executive vice-president in 1963 to become president of
Frederick Atkins, Inc., another important co-operative group of
which he had previously been chairman of the board. He also
served in 1960 and 1961 as president of the National Retail
Merchants Association. Mr. Thompson died in the latter part of
1963.

Sidney R. Rosenberg, divisional merchandise manager of
AMC home furnishings, came from the Associated Dry Goods
Corporation, a centrally owned group of important department
stores. Mr. Rosenberg is now president of American Furniture
Associates, a co-operative buying group of leading furniture
stores.

This list would not be complete without mention of Sylvan
Gotshal, an ex-officio member, who has been attorney and
counsel for AMC from 1919 to the present time. He is the
senior partner of Weil, Gotshal & Manges.

For many years, Mr. Gotshal was president of the American
Arbitration Association. He also devoted much of his time to
curbing style piracy of both American originals and French
originals, using both personal appeals and arbitration. For his
efforts, the French Government bestowed on Mr. Gotshal the
rank of Officer of the Legion of Honor.

Frederick Atkins, Inc., patterned after AMC, is owned by

41 fine stores throughout the country. Four of them are included in this book: City of Paris; G. Fox & Co.; Luckey, Platt & Co.; and Scruggs-Vandervoort-Barney. This buying-research organization also serves three foreign members.

Specialty Stores Association is another important co-operative group. There are 18 members.

Many of the department store chains—Gimbel Bros. and Macy's, for example—maintain their own resident buying offices to furnish merchandising assistance to their store buyers.

In New York, there are about 165 paid buying offices representing all types of stores. Additional offices are located in Chicago, Los Angeles and other major cities. Individual, non-competing stores pay a certain fee for buying services as well as market information and reports. Usually, there is no exchange of figures between the stores, as in the more than 100 centrally owned or co-operative offices of independents and chains of all types. In addition, there are some 140 New York merchandise brokers—privately-owned offices whose fees are paid by manufacturers.

The organizational structure of a buying office corresponds to the divisions of a retail store, from a president or director, general merchandise manager, basement merchandise manager, divisional merchandise managers, buyers, assistant buyers, and secretarial staff.

CHAPTER 1

ABRAHAM & STRAUS

BROOKLYN, NEW YORK

"A Friendly Store"

When Abraham Abraham was 22 in February, 1865, he opened his first store, Wechsler & Abraham, in partnership with Joseph Wechsler. A century later, the firm—now Abraham & Straus— had an annual volume of more than $210 million in its main Brooklyn store and five suburban branches that occupy more than 2,300,000 square feet of space. The company is one of America's four largest department stores.

Abraham Abraham, born in New York City, the son of a Bavarian emigrant, left school at 14. He learned the retail dry goods business at Hart & Dettlebach, Newark, which also employed as clerks such future distinguished merchants as Benjamin Altman and Lyman G. Bloomingdale.

Abraham's first store on Fulton Street—barely 25 feet wide and 90 feet deep—was started on a capital of only $10,000, and Abraham did everything from sweeping floors to trimming windows. He believed a merchant should know his customers and he constantly walked through his store to greet old friends and make new ones. He encouraged his staff to create and maintain a pleasant atmosphere, and the firm today still counts its reputation for friendliness as one of its most important assets.

When the store required more space, Abraham found it in a large building known locally as "Wheeler's Folly" because it was some distance from what was then Brooklyn's shopping center. Abraham, however, believed that "when the Brooklyn Bridge opened, that part of Fulton Street could be made the trade center." And so, in 1885, amid the jeers of many local merchants, he moved into the five-story, two-basement structure of 145,000 square feet which still forms the core of the Brooklyn store. Annual sales for the second year in that location reached $2,500,000.

In 1893, two brothers, Isidor and Nathan Straus, and Charles B. Webster, partners in Macy's, bought out Joseph Wechsler, and the firm name was changed to Abraham & Straus. The purchase followed the lines of the Strauses' acquisition of the Macy financial interest: L. Straus & Sons, wholesaler of crockery, china and glassware, founded by Lazarus Straus, father of Isidor and Nathan, previously held prosperous concessions for this department at Wechsler & Abraham as at Macy's. Some central buying was done by A & S and Macy's from 1893 to 1903, the only direct business connection that ever existed between the two stores. The Abraham and Straus families became related when Edith Abraham, daughter of the Brooklyn retailer, married Percy S. Straus, son of Isidor and, later, Macy's president.

Since the Macy Strauses never became active in the management of A & S—in fact, they withdrew about 1913—it is ironic that the family name has been perpetuated in that of a firm they did little to develop, while it never appeared in the firm name of Macy's, which they and their relatives built into one of America's leading stores.

In that same year, Simon F. Rothschild, Abraham's son-in-law, became a partner. Two years later, his son, Lawrence Abraham, joined the firm. He became a vice-president and retired in 1933, shortly before his death. In 1896, Edward C.

Blum, another son-in-law, also became a member. By 1902, two new buildings had been added to the ever-expanding store. When the senior Abraham died in June, 1911, the store occupied 28 acres and had a $13-million-a-year sales volume.

Abraham Abraham had devoted much of his leisure time to local civic and humanitarian projects and, at the time of his death, New York Mayor William J. Gaynor said, "I never knew a more just and equitable man . . . always patient, always kind, always just and tolerant, prone always to overlook and forgive."

A & S helped found Retail Research Association in 1916. The affiliation initiated by Rothschild and Blum played an important part in A & S's future. Rothschild was president of A & S from 1925 to 1930, while Blum occupied that post from 1930 to 1937.

Rothschild, who moved up to chairman in 1930, died in 1936. He was a wise counselor and teacher. His son, Walter N. Rothschild, Sr., who became general manager in 1927 and was president from 1937 to 1955, followed his father's example. Blum, until his death in 1946, was also involved in many civic activities. His son, Robert E. Blum, became affiliated with the company in 1922, worked through all the divisions of the business, and became vice-president and secretary. Like his father, he was also active in the community. He retired in 1964 although he continues as a member of the management board.

Hugh Grant Straus, son of Nathan Straus, joined A & S in 1914 and became vice-president and treasurer in 1920. He resigned as treasurer in 1943 and as vice-president three years later. He was succeeded as treasurer by Kenneth C. Richmond, who had joined the firm in 1928 as assistant controller, becoming controller a year later, and vice-president in 1930. In 1964, he was named executive vice-president. He is on the firm's management board. For a number of years, he has been chairman of the board of the New York State Council of Retail Merchants and a member of the Merchants Advisory Council of the New York University School of Retailing, now its Institute of Retail Management.

In 1937, Edward Blum became chairman of the board, and

Walter Rothschild became president. The latter had joined A & S in 1913 after graduating from Princeton. He worked in various capacities, and was appointed vice-president and general manager in 1927. He became board chairman five years before his death in October, 1960.

When A & S went public in 1925, its annual volume was $25 million. In 1929, the store joined with Filene's, Bloomingdale's and F. & R. Lazarus to form Federated Department Stores.

Walter Rothschild, Sr., a sincere and perceptive humanist, established one of the first executive training courses to develop a reservoir of future leaders for the company. Candidates were chosen mainly from the staff but occasionally from the graduating classes of leading universities, thus encouraging competition for promotion on merit. In 1955, he instituted a plan, unique in retailing—annual scholarships providing from $500 to $2,000 a year for sons and daughters of employees who had been with the store three years or longer. Leading educators select the candidates who are free to choose their own fields of study.

Rothschild, a Navy lieutenant, junior grade, in World War I, was awarded the War Department's Medal of Freedom with bronze palm in 1947 for his services as vice-president of the National War Fund and as a member of the national executive board of the U.S.O. He was chairman of the Retailers' Protective Committee and was awarded the Tobe retailer-of-the-year award in 1956.

Sidney L. Solomon, a Harvard graduate, became chief executive officer of A & S after Rothschild's death in 1960. He rose to the chairmanship at the end of 1963. After acquiring experience at Filene's and Jordan Marsh in Boston and at Forman's in Rochester, he became basement merchandise manager of A & S in 1934. His presence was soon reflected in the growth and expansion of the basement division. Within three years, he was appointed main store manager, and in 1948 executive vice-president and general manager. He was named president in 1955, the first man outside the founder's family to hold that office. He, too, is active in community affairs.

Under the leadership of Rothschild and Solomon, the store

expanded rapidly. Its first and smallest suburban branch—an 80,500-square-foot store—was opened in 1950 in Garden City, Long Island. The next, now occupying 381,400 square feet, was opened in Hempstead, Long Island, in 1952 with 224,000 square feet. Babylon, Long Island, the third branch, opened in 1957 with 249,000 square feet. The fourth, a branch of 220,000 square feet, opened in Huntington, Long Island, in 1961. A fifth branch of 262,000 square feet was opened in Manhasset, Long Island, in May, 1965. Additional Long Island sites are being studied. The Brooklyn store has been expanded by some 60,000 square feet to give it 1,182,000 square feet, and with four warehouses a total of over 2 million square feet in that borough.

Sidney Solomon sponsored these pioneer moves in the department store industry:

In 1948, he separated responsibility for soft and hard lines merchandising, creating two general merchandise managers with the rank of vice-president. They report directly to the top and form a three-man team with the sales promotion director, likewise a vice-president. The basement is headed by a general merchandise manager-vice-president. Each branch store manager is directly responsible to the president in order to short-circuit conflicts that might otherwise arise between branch and parent. The A & S command-setup has been adopted by many other large-scale retailers.

A & S acts on the theory that true dominance may be attained and maintained only by competing against all comers. In 1950, it challenged Macy's 6 per cent price cut on fair-traded items, thereby precipitating a major price war. In 1957, it launched an aggressive counterattack against Korvette when that promotional department store opened opposite it on Fulton Street. A & S seeks at least to meet, preferably to beat, discounters' prices whether in Brooklyn or on Long Island.

Walter N. ("Bill") Rothschild, Jr., a Harvard graduate, obtained his preliminary store experience at Bloomingdale's and joined A & S in 1950. He was manager of the Hempstead branch store from the time it opened until 1955 when he became merchandise vice-president of the parent firm. In 1960, he was promoted to assistant general manager, and in 1964 to president.

In 1962, A & S's yearly dollar volume passed $100 million in the Brooklyn store. The company's total sales aggregated $187 million. At the end of 1964, estimated total volume rose to more than $210 million, with the headquarters store doing $110.5 million of this. Hempstead accounted for an estimated $50 million; Babylon, $21.5 million; Huntington, $20.5 million; and Garden City, $7.5 million.

CHAPTER 2

B. ALTMAN
& COMPANY

NEW YORK, NEW YORK

"The Lengthened Shadow of a Man"

Benjamin Altman, born in New York City in 1840, acquired his
early retail experience in the same Newark, New Jersey, store
where Abraham Abraham and Lyman G. Bloomingdale received their initial training. Son of a dry goods merchant, Altman opened his first store at 39 Third Avenue in 1865, when he
was 25 years old. The store was in a three-story building on a
lot 25 feet wide and 100 feet deep, and his one-year lease required a rental of $40 per month.

The store prospered from the outset. To accommodate growing trade, it moved in the early 1870's successively to larger
stores on Sixth Avenue between 21st and 22nd Streets, and in
1876 to Sixth Avenue and 19th Street where it remained 30
years.

With unusual foresight, Altman decided to open a store on
Fifth Avenue, the mecca for many other merchants of his day
who featured only merchandise of quality. The structure, at the
corner of 34th Street, was erected in two sections. The first,

eight stories high, opened for business in September, 1906. A 12-story addition was completed in 1914, and extensive interior alterations were made in 1938. The building occupies the entire square block bounded by Fifth Avenue, Madison Avenue, 34th Street and 35th Street. The architect, Goodhue Livingston of Trowbridge & Livingston, either alone or with his partner, designed many other notable buildings.

Benjamin Altman was described by Arthur Brisbane, then editor of the New York *Post*, as a "man who was never satisfied with products as he found them, he always strove to have them made better." Altman invited salesmen to visit him and suggested product improvements, sometimes pointing out the difference between a freak and a fashion.

A buyer who worked under Altman for many years said that the latter imbued his merchandisers with his own quality-mindedness, that the names of Altman and Tiffany were synonymous with "sterling" values. Altman believed that "the recollection of quality remains long after the price is forgotten."

Benjamin Altman died in 1913 at 73. A bachelor, he left his remarkable collection of paintings, statues, rugs, enamels, and tapestries to the Metropolitan Museum of Art in the largest gift ever made to the museum up to that time. His $20 million stock in the business was given mainly to the Altman Foundation. Income was to be used for philanthropic purposes at the directors' discretion. He also made generous provisions in his will for many employees. At the Altman funeral services, the officiating rabbi said, "Whatever he did, he did well. Call him the Prince of Merchants; call him a Prince among art collectors; but let me, who knew him well, call him a 'Prince among men!'"

Michael Friedsam, Altman's partner for many years before the new Fifth Avenue store was opened, was also born in New York City. Although he was 18 years younger than Altman, the two men had identical characteristics. Both were able merchants with good taste, interested only in the finest merchandise; both had the utmost consideration for their employees; both were art collectors. Exceptional service to customers also was paramount in the minds of both men. No wonder Friedsam, as president, was able to carry on the business without change after Altman passed away.

During World War I, Friedsam served as Quartermaster General of the New York State Guard. Even after he relinquished that post with the rank of colonel, he was still referred to as Colonel Friedsam.

The store's sales volume and prestige continued to increase under Friedsam.

When Michael Friedsam died in 1931, his will provided for the continuance of his philanthropies through the Friedsam Foundation. He, too, left his art collection to the Metropolitan Museum of Art.

John S. Burke, Sr., who became president after Colonel Friedsam died, was born in Norwich, Connecticut. He was graduated from Yale with an A. B. degree in 1912 and began as a clerk in the correspondence department at Altman's the same year. He later served as an investigator in the adjustment department and then became secretary to Colonel Friedsam. He was appointed a vice-president and assistant to the president in 1919, and in 1955 became chairman of the board. He died in 1962.

John S. Burke, Jr., who attended Yale for three years, then served in the Marine Corps in World War II, began work at Altman's in the receiving department in 1945. He served as a divisional merchandise manager, later as a suburban branch-store manager, and became president of the firm when his father stepped up to the board chairmanship.

Over the years, the store became known especially for its interior-decorating department which can furnish an unusual lamp for a bedroom table or outfit an entire ocean steamship. One contract to redecorate the White House in 1951 involved many intricate problems in manufacturing draperies, rugs, wall coverings, china, and other items which had to be close reproductions of the originals. In addition to redecorating many private homes and office buildings throughout the country, Altman's in recent years did the interior of the Executive Mansion of the State of New Jersey, Princeton, and the President's room in the Truman Library in Independence, Missouri.

Another department that has grown in volume and importance during the last decade is Altman's first-floor epicure and gourmet food section whose buyer spends about two months in Europe every year in search of suitable products. The chief domestic line of fine groceries is supplied by S. S. Pierce Co., of Boston.

One of the largest and best-known Oriental rug departments in the country contributes a three-million-dollar annual volume to the store. Credited with its development is James Archibald Keillor—"Archie," as his friends call him—who was born in Glasgow, Scotland, and came to this country when he was still a child. His first job at Altman's was in the shoe department in 1906, but he soon became assistant buyer in floor coverings, which was more to his liking, possibly because his father had worked for W. & J. Sloane, New York, one of the leading firms in the floor-covering and home-furnishing field.

Keillor became buyer of Oriental rugs within a few years, and in 1912 made his first buying trip to the Middle East. These trips were repeated each year and substantial orders were placed. Archie also pioneered in other foreign markets and, like the founder, helped manufacturers improve their products so Altman's could promote them profitably. He became general merchandise manager in 1932 and continued regular trips to the foreign markets.

He was responsible for building a staff of competent, quality-minded Altman representatives at strategic buying and shipping points in all of the foreign markets. The foreign staff assists other Altman buyers during their trips to the various foreign markets.

Keillor still has an office at Altman's although he has relinquished his duties as vice-president, general merchandise manager, and director to Randolph Stambaugh, previously divisional merchandise manager of home furnishings and housewares. However, the Keillor influence and name are destined to endure for a long time in Altman's merchandising plans, partly because Archie's son, James A., Jr., is a furniture buyer, and another son, Ronald W., is a buyer in the children's department and of several other items.

James D. Twiname joined Altman's in 1919, became secretary to John S. Burke, Sr., in 1924 and secretary to the firm in 1936. His 40 years' experience has been very helpful to other executives who needed essential information to carry out their jobs within the established policies of the firm.

Altman's policies toward employees and executives are the enlightened ones of all progressive stores. Executive positions are filled by promotions from within and not until the staff has been thoroughly screened is an executive obtained from the outside.

Many of the employees have been with the store for a great number of years; a paymaster served for 76 years before he died at 89 several years ago, and another employee was in his 69th year with the company when he retired in 1964.

Although the firm has a generous retirement plan, operative when an employee reaches 65, retirement at that age is not mandatory and employees may continue to work if they wish to and are able to.

Altman's regular staff for the parent store and three branches totals 4,000 employees, but during the holiday season reaches 6,000. The percentage of female employees ranges from 60 to 65 per cent of the total.

Altman's does not disclose its sales figures, but an estimate for 1964 places total annual sales at $86.5 million. The New York store accounts for $58 million; White Plains, for $13.25 million; Short Hills, New Jersey, for $8 million; and Manhasset, for $7.25 million. A fourth branch opened in St. Davids, suburban Philadelphia, in the fall of 1965.

When Emerson wrote, "An institution is the lengthened shadow of a man," he may well have had in mind a prototype of Benjamin Altman whose successors, by consistently following his basic policies, have operated in his shadow for a half century.

In a different sense, his shadow is providing esthetic pleasure to the multitudes who view his art collection at the Metropolitan. Thus, his name will be perpetuated for generations to come, which augurs well for the future of the exceptionally fine store he founded.

CHAPTER 3

L. S. AYRES
& COMPANY

INDIANAPOLIS, INDIANA

"From a Peddler to a Palace (of Trade)"

Like most pioneer retailers, Lyman S. Ayres learned his trade the hard way. Born on a farm near Oswego, New York, in 1824, he decided to strike out for himself when he was less than 20 years old.

He went to Montville, Ohio, and on foot started peddling maps, pictures, and frames. A year later, he changed his pack for a wagon loaded with dry goods and notions.

For five years he peddled his wares alone in the surrounding country, then took on a partner and opened a store at Chardon, Ohio. In 1864, he sold his share of the store to his partner and went to Geneva, New York, where he formed a new partnership with J. G. Thomas, remaining in the business until 1870.

Influenced by H. B. Claflin, an important wholesaler, Ayres in 1872 came to Indianapolis, then a city of 50,000, where he purchased the controlling interest in N. R. Smith's Trade Palace on Washington Street, thereafter known as N. R. Smith & Ayres. With commendable foresight, Ayres decided to act as the firm's resident buyer in New York, and soon many domestic and imported fashions and other items were flowing regularly into the store.

Smith retired in 1874, and Ayres returned to Indianapolis to assume full management. A year after he took over, he moved across Washington Street to a larger new building consisting of four floors and a basement, each 50 feet wide and 195 feet deep. It was the first local store to have gas lighting, at that time the newest in illumination.

The firm name was changed to L. S. Ayres & Company, the "Company" being J. G. Thomas, who held a quarter interest and was store superintendent until he retired in 1895, leaving Ayres sole owner.

Ayres had an innate interest in fine merchandise, whether it was an inexpensive calico dress, a $200 velvet cloak, or a $500 Paisley shawl. He taught his staff to give customers the best of service and to apply the Golden Rule in every transaction. On entering the store each morning, his custom was to speak to everyone. He was the first merchant to have stools placed behind the counters so that salespeople could rest when they were not busy. He was the first to announce, in 1870, an annual Fourth of July picnic for employees, prompting the local papers to urge other employers to adopt the same policy.

Ayres' first wife died a short time after their marriage. In 1862, he married Maria Helen Murray, a sister of his first partner, John Murray. When Ayres died in 1896, his son, Frederic Murray Ayres, who had graduated from Yale with a B.S. degree, succeeded him.

Frederic M. Ayres was an inspiring leader who quickly detected executive talent in his employees and promoted them; he was rated tops as a merchant and he also served his community, his state, and the nation without stint.

The old Trade Palace burgeoned quickly under his direction, and his ambition to make the store at the "Crossroads of America" the leading store in his state was accomplished in his lifetime.

The store inaugurated Saturday-afternoon closing hours

during the summer months in 1894. In 1899, Ayres Relief Association was formed, providing 13 weeks' salary during an employee's illness. In 1915, a store hospital with a registered nurse was opened and, in the same year, an employee lunchroom offered a complete meal for 16 cents.

A year later, Fred Ayres accepted an invitation from Lincoln Filene, Boston merchant, to meet with store heads from noncompeting cities. The result was the formation of the Retail Research Association of which the Ayres store became a charter member.

Fred Ayres continued to enlarge and modernize the store. A new eight-story building was erected in 1905 with a downstairs store called an "economy basement." Many changes in department layouts were made each year. Horse-drawn delivery wagons were gradually replaced by electric autos. In 1915, five and one half acres of floor space were added. Every modern time-saving device and customer comfort was installed as soon as it was available, including air-conditioning, escalators, indirect lighting, and the largest telephone exchange in the state.

Fred Ayres, although a modest man who preferred to remain in the background, never shirked the chance to further projects that were of benefit to other retailers. He organized the Indianapolis Merchants Association, headed the first committee of the local Chamber of Commerce, was active in the Indianapolis Board of Trade, and served as vice-president of the National Retail Dry Goods Association.

Commissioned a major in 1919, he was sent to Paris as Director of Property Operations under the European Commission of the American Red Cross to supervise the liquidation of its surplus supplies and material in Europe.

He died in 1940 after 44 years as head of Ayres. A bronze bust of the late president, a gift of 15 employees who had worked closely with him, was placed at the entrance to the executive offices.

Victor C. Kendall, who first went to work at the Trade Palace in 1882 at $8 a week selling piece goods, observed that the auditor of the store worked late every night. He offered to help him two hours daily and learned the job so well that, when the auditor was promoted, Kendall got his job. He became secretary in 1896, and later secretary-treasurer. In 1905, he was appointed to the board of directors and continued also as secretary-treasurer until he retired in 1943. He died in 1946.

William B. Wheelock, born in 1862 in Ogdensburg, New York, joined Ayres in 1893 after initial experience in a dry-goods store in St. Joseph, Missouri. He became store superintendent and first vice-president of Ayres and remained with the store 39 years. He became a director of the Merchants Association in 1918, was president for the 1921–22 term, and continued as a director until 1926. Wheelock died in 1936.

His son-in-law, Theodore B. Griffith, who became president in 1940, was born in Indianapolis and was graduated with an A.B. from Williams College in 1910. He came to Ayres in 1920 as research director, reporting directly to the president. He became assistant to the president in 1921, general merchandise manager and vice-president in 1923, and vice-president and general manager in 1929.

As general merchandise manager, Griffith had to come to grips with many challenging problems. One of the most important was the downstairs store which he reorganized, expanded, and built into a diversified and separate fashion and home-furnishings store.

In 1929, John R. Barrett was made manager of this division of the business. Growth of basement volume justified more and more expansion over the years. Today, the downstairs store occupies well over 100,000 square feet, making it one of the largest in the country.

Although Barrett started at Ayres in 1914 as a wrapper, his ability justified rapid promotion. In 1945, he was elected to the board of directors. His retirement in 1960 ended 46 years of service solely with Ayres.

Griffith directed the store during the period when it made some of its greatest strides. In 1940, a building was purchased and a service center was established to house the delivery, most of the workrooms required by the home-furnishings division, and additional reserve stock space for many of the selling departments.

In 1945, still another building was purchased for use by the display and purchasing departments; it was connected by a tunnel to the downstairs store.

In 1946, another building was acquired for additional warehouse space and, in 1947, the south building was extended to permit the opening of a complete and separate store for men on one floor.

In 1948, six additional floors were added to the main-store building for selling, office, and storage space.

Griffith was active in civic and public affairs. He was president of the Merchants Association of Indianapolis, vice-chairman of AMC, and trustee of the American Retail Federation. Theodore B. Griffith retired from Ayres management at the beginning of 1959 after 38 years with the store but continued to serve on the board of directors.

Lyman S. Ayres, elder son of Frederic M. Ayres, and grandson of the founder, became president in 1954. A graduate of Yale in 1930, he worked in various positions until he became divisional manager of ready-to-wear in 1938 and vice-president in 1940. He was commissioned Lieutenant USNR and served as executive officer on a PT boat in the New Guinea area. He became president in 1954 and chairman of the board in 1962. He was appointed chairman of the AMC executive committee in May, 1960.

When Lyman Ayres assumed the presidency, the store built its first branch, a 150,000-square-foot store in Glendale, Indiana. Another 60,000-square-foot store was built in Lafayette, Indiana, and the 90,000-square-foot John Bressmer Co. department store of Springfield, Illinois, was purchased. Bressmer's had been founded in 1868 and, like Ayres, carried fine merchandise and catered to the "carriage trade". Ayres also owns Murray Showrooms, wholesale furniture showrooms for decorators and dealers in Indianapolis and Cincinnati.

In April, 1960, Ayres added a downstairs store of 3,000

square feet across the mall from its main Lafayette branch. A second complete branch department store opened about seven miles south of the Indianapolis business section in Southwood Shopping Center in 1962. It has 125,000 square feet. In 1964, the Lafayette branch was enlarged by 15,000 square feet to be devoted to home furnishings.

Ayr-Way Stores, Inc., a self-service subsidiary, was opened in late 1961. It has five units in the 100,000-square-foot class.

Ayres' department for infants and toddlers is notable in that it has its own drug store, prenatal care items, layettes, toys, clothing for toddlers, a shoe store, a furniture section, and even a baby boutique where aunts, uncles and grandparents may select unusual gifts for new babies.

Ayres maintains a special orthopedic shoe department for children with deformed feet. Customers are sent to Ayres with doctors' prescriptions. The department has about 22,000 prescriptions on file and another 2,000 are added annually. A stock of $50,000 is carried and, if the shoe prescribed is not in stock, it is ordered from selected makers who manufacture special lasts when needed. Some of these shoes retail for $100 or more. This department is reputed to be the largest orthopedic shoe section in the Midwest.

Ayres employs more than 3,600 of whom 74 per cent are female. Record sales of $82.2 million and net earnings of $2.1 million were attained in 1964.

James A. Gloin, at 61, succeeded Lyman S. Ayres in 1962 and became the first man outside the family to become president and chief executive officer. Mr. Ayres is board chairman. Mr. Gloin joined Ayres as a researcher in 1925 after acquiring a master's degree in business administration from Harvard University. He became controller six years later, assistant general manager in 1937, treasurer in 1943, and executive vice-president in 1949. He is a director of AMC. In the tradition of the store, he maintains an active interest in civic affairs.

Ayres' 1966 plans include opening a 205,000-square-foot department store in Fort Wayne and an Ayr-Way store in South Bend.

CHAPTER 4

L. BAMBERGER
& COMPANY

NEWARK, NEW JERSEY

Still "One of America's Great Stores"

No department store has had such an impact on American retailing as Bamberger's. Still young compared to Altman's and
Lord & Taylor's, it became equally well known within a span
of two generations.

The store was established in 1893 by Louis Bamberger who,
with his brother-in-law, Louis M. Frank of Philadelphia, and
Felix Fuld of New York, bought the bankrupt stock of Hill &
Craig, a retail firm on Market Street, Newark. The sale of stock
proved profitable, and the three decided to continue in retailing as a partnership under the name, L. Bamberger & Company. Despite the report that the location was a major factor
in the failure of Hill & Craig, they continued the operation on
Market Street.

Bamberger and Fuld were able merchants, but obtaining
sufficient capital to finance their increasing purchases and expanding store proved difficult, undoubtedly because of the fail-

37643

ure of the Hill & Craig store. This problem continued for five years when their sales had reached $1,331,000.

Bamberger, 40 years old when he started the store, was reserved and unassuming almost to the point of shyness. However, he had all the other qualities required of a successful merchant, especially fair dealing with others.

Frank died in 1910 and his widow, Bamberger's sister, married Fuld eight years later.

Although Bamberger and Fuld had a most harmonious business relationship, they were formal with each other. Their offices adjoined and the door between them usually was open, but they addressed each other as "Mister".

Not even his business friends and equals called Bamberger "Louis", although he was a kindly man with the interests of his employees uppermost in his mind. He gave generously to all worthy causes, usually anonymously because he shunned personal publicity.

In contrast to Bamberger, Fuld was a good "mixer", and his host of friends outside the store called him "Felix". He had a dynamic personality, was unfailingly considerate of others, and had an uncanny success in judging other men. The story of Bamberger's is really that of Felix Fuld. Born in Germany where his father was a partner in a banking and brokerage house, Felix was a rubber-goods salesman before joining Bamberger's. He deferred to Bamberger's judgment when the two could not agree, but Bamberger never interfered on any matter Fuld had been deciding alone.

When the firm began making great strides, Fuld realized that outstanding executive talent had to be obtained:

Frank I. Liveright, employed in 1898 at $8 a week, was a nephew of Louis M. Frank and had a successful store in Danville, Illinois, before joining Bamberger's where he became one of the top executives.

Harry A. Hatry was hired in 1906 at $6,000 a year as women's wear buyer. Ultimately, he reportedly earned not only the highest salary ever paid any other Bamberger executive but one of the highest of any New York area store. Fuld rated Hatry as the equal of Paul Bonwit and Franklin Simon, then the two top executives in women's wear merchandising.

Bamberger's was a charter member of RRA-AMC, and Fuld a member of the executive committee.

Michael Schaap, married to Bamberger's niece, became personnel manager of the firm in 1917. He had practiced law in New York and was a member of the New York Assembly from 1913 to 1914. Fuld also hired Meyer Bloomfield on a part-time basis to advise Schaap. Karl Egge was named employment manager.

Under Schaap, Bamberger's became a leader in personnel administration. Starting wages were raised, initial training was intensified, periodic reviews of all employees were made, paid vacations were extended, illness benefits increased, discounts on goods for personal or in-store use rose, all terminating employees were interviewed in an effort to discover any management shortcomings, and labor turnover was reduced sharply. Promotions from within were numerous, but it still was necessary to add other executives to the store's operation division.

H. Norman Schwarzkopf, a graduate of West Point in 1917, became Bamberger's delivery superintendent. When he left in 1921 to organize the New Jersey State Police, Abraham Schindel, a store superintendent, became head of the delivery department.

In 1927, Bamberger's announced a public sale of $10 million preferred stock. Employees and executives were given the first chance to subscribe and the demand was so heavy the shares had to be allotted even before subscription books were opened to the general public.

By 1928, Bamberger's sales had reached $38 million. This represented the fourth highest retail volume in the nation, which would have ranked Bamberger's next to Marshall Field's, with Macy's first, and J. L. Hudson second.

Walter S. Moler joined Bamberger's as publicity director in 1903 when he was only 25 years old. His advertising ability soon was recognized and he devoted much of his time to institutional promotions. After receiving a letter describing Bam-

berger's as "One of America's Great Stores", Moler promoted
the phrase until it became inseparably linked with Bamberger's.
Largely inspired by advertising manager Ira Hirschmann, Moler
persuaded Bamberger's to launch radio station WOR in a room
off the furniture department in 1922. This became a valuable
asset to the store.

When Moler died in 1928 at the early age of 48, Bamberger's
lost an invaluable good-will ambassador.

Joseph E. Hanson, who had been advertising director for
Lionel Trains, succeeded Moler as publicity director. One of
his notable contributions was the idea of establishing, editing,
and publishing a magazine of women's fashions. *Charm* magazine became an almost immediate success and attained a circulation of 100,000.

Hirschmann rose to vice-president in charge of sales promotion, in 1931 went to Lord & Taylor where he was latterly vice-
president in charge of advertising and publicity, and then occupied vice-presidential positions at Saks Fifth Avenue and
Bloomingdale's. His brilliant career also encompasses diplo-
macy, public affairs, politics, the arts, and banking. He is cur-
rently a sales consultant to retailers and manufacturers.

Fuld died early in 1929 and, shortly thereafter, the second
era in Bamberger history began. In June of that year, Bamberger, then 76, arranged for a special board meeting on a busy
Friday afternoon, an unusual situation that caused speculation
beforehand. When Bamberger appeared at the meeting, he
stated, "L. Bamberger & Co. has been sold to Macy's."

The announcement came as a shock both to employees and
the public. Liveright claimed the public was stunned because,
"what many people in all walks of life regarded as the most influential institution in all New Jersey had passed out of the
hands of the founder after 36 years of unparalleled growth."

Hatry felt that Fuld's death had caused Bamberger to panic
and forget he was surrounded by able men and women trained
by Fuld. "Naturally," he said "we resented being 'sold down
the river' and I think the entire buying and management staff
probably resented Macy taking us over because Macy had

always been our arch-enemy and we fought many a price war."

Shortly after the sale, many of Bamberger's top executives went to other firms. Edgar Bamberger, who had joined the store in 1907 as Moler's assistant, bought an interest in a large Hackensack, New Jersey, firm. Hatry went to Bloomingdale's as vice-president and general merchandise manager, and Schaap became Bloomingdale's president and general manager. James S. Schoff, personnel manager and also a member of the management board, became president of The Fair in Chicago, then moved to Bloomingdale's. Hector Suyker, Bamberger's controller, succeeded Schoff as president of The Fair.

Liveright was the only top Bamberger executive to agree to remain with the store. In two years, he became general manager of the new Macy division. William J. Wells, who had joined Macy's in 1906, became president of Bamberger's.

Although Bamberger's was a charter member of RRA-AMC, its membership was dropped when Macy assumed control because of the competitive conflict Macy's posed for other RRA-AMC stores—Abraham & Straus and Bloomingdale's.

Both WOR and Charm were sold, but Macy's did not otherwise change the character of the Bamberger store despite rumors it would drop the charge accounts and begin a campaign of underselling other Northern New Jersey stores. The same type of merchandise and service was continued, but Bamberger's sales began to slump.

Macy's tried to earn the loyalty of Bamberger employees and re-establish customer good will, but morale was further upset when Hatry and Schaap, from their new jobs at Bloomingdale's, reopened the price war. Although the target was Macy's, shots reached into Northern New Jersey through advertisements in New York newspapers circulating there. Federated Department stores, of which A & S and Bloomingdale's are subsidiaries stopped the conflict, however, and it never was resumed.

Notable among competent Macy executives who moved to the Newark store was John C. Williams, who succeeded Wells as president and later became chairman of the board.

In 1954, David L. Yunich became president of Bamberger's at 37. A graduate of Union College and Harvard Graduate School of Business Administration, he had raised money for his tuition by playing baseball for Syracuse in the International League. After receiving his diploma, Yunich remarked, "I took a 400 per cent cut in my baseball salary when I went to work on Macy's training squad.

By his 27th birthday, Yunich was a vice-president at Macy's.

Bamberger's, under Yunich's eight-year reign, became America's fastest-growing department store. Seven branches were added. Volume jumped from $60 million to $141 million. The seven branches occupy a total of 1.4 million square feet, the Newark store alone 1.2 million square feet. For 1964, estimated volume was $175 million. The Newark store accounts for $54 million. Branches include Paramus, $37 million; Menlo Park, $27 million; Monmouth, $17 million; Morristown, $12 million; Cherry Hill, $12 million; Plainfield, $12 million, and Princeton, $4 million. Its estimated sales in Newark are more than the combined sales of the two stores regarded as its main local competitors.

In the late 1950s, Yunich separated buying and store operation functions. Buyers concentrate on buying, sales promotion, and development of resources, and a new group has taken over the vital job of store management. The multi-store program eliminates the parent-branch store relationship and treats each unit the same. The same procedure has been adopted at Macy's New York and a number of other larger retail companies. Thus, the old-line concept, established by department stores in 1927 —a concept that holds buyers responsible for both merchandising and operational functions—is giving way to an "equal store" plan as more and more single-unit retailers become regional chains.

Bamberger's also sponsors a three-shift selling-force arrangement. This provides adequate coverage for all stores, some of which are open six nights a week. Men with daytime office jobs have been found particularly good for night and Saturday selling.

When Yunich returned to Macy's New York in 1962 as president at 44, Herbert L. Seegal became Bamberger's president, and Arthur L. Manchee moved from the presidency of Macy's New York to chairman of the board at Bamberger's. Manchee joined Macy's in 1928 and became executive vice-president and general manager of Bamberger's in 1938. He returned to Macy's as a senior vice-president in charge of store operations in 1948 and became president of Macy's New York 10 years later. In early 1965, Seegal succeeded Manchee as chief executive officer in preparation for the latter's retirement.

Seegal, a 1937 graduate of the University of Michigan, first worked for R.H. White & Co. in Boston. He joined Thalhimer's, Richmond, Virginia, as assistant buyer in 1941 and was made merchandising vice-president eight years later. He joined Macy's in 1953 as merchandising vice-president.

Through all these changes, Bamberger's has remained "One of America's Great Stores."

CHAPTER 5

BROADWAY-HALE

LOS ANGELES, CALIFORNIA

Arthur Letts:
From Early Failure to Ultimate Success

After years of experience and difficulties, Arthur Letts founded The Broadway in 1896 when he was 34.

A native of England who became a naturalized American, Letts had been apprenticed to a drapery shop at 14. When he was 21, he went to Quebec, Canada, and worked for $7 a week with Robert Walker & Sons, the great clothing house of Ontario known as "The Golden Lion."

Within two years, the Indian Rebellion erupted and Letts served with the Queen's Own Rifles, later returning to the store for a year. In the carpet department of John Kay Son & Co., in Ontario, he increased his earnings to $75 a month but left in three years after his salary had reached $125 a month.

He went to Seattle, Washington, in 1889, took a job in a local store, and decided to begin on his own when a fire devastated the entire business section. He opened a men's store in a large tent and, after encouraging results, branched out into Spokane. That store, however, was unprofitable and closed in a short time.

The Seattle store grew, the stock was expanded, and new lines added. Then, city authorities ordered all tents removed from the business district. With a family of two daughters and a son, some of his stock stored and the rest sold at a loss, Letts moved on to Los Angeles in 1895.

An auctioneer with confidence in Letts as a merchant sold him the bankrupt stock of Karl Epstein for $8,167 on a small down payment. Using the store Epstein had vacated, Letts brought some of his remaining stock from Seattle.

The new store was a success and Letts paid off his Seattle and Spokane debts with interest. Shortly thereafter, he acquired another Los Angeles store that had failed, The Broadway Department Store at Broadway and Fourth Street.

In February, 1896, The Broadway reopened under Letts's management. Having acquired an intimate knowledge of merchandising, sales promotion, and store operation, Letts ultimately developed The Broadway into a spectacular success. A vigorous and imaginative promoter, he adopted the slogan, "Watch us grow," and grow the store did.

At that time, nothing less than a nickel passed for change in local stores, but Letts advertised his intention to give pennies as change. Customers usually left them on the counter, and that, of course, added up to additional profits.

He was the first locally to adopt fixed retail prices plainly marked and this increased customer confidence. He is also credited with being the first to employ a woman, a graduate of the Prince School of Retailing, Boston, as training director but he was slow to appoint women to other executive positions.

Letts helped to organize the Los Angeles Retail Dry Goods Association in 1910 and became its first president. Two years later, he was elected first vice-president and a year later president of the California Retail Dry Goods Association. He supported a national minimum-wage law to cover shop girls, having earlier endorsed a minimum wage law for California women.

Shortly after Letts opened The Broadway, John Gillespie Bullock joined the store as a floorwalker for $12 per week. The year was 1896 and Bullock, who had some retail experience in a dry goods store in Canada, was 25. Eight months later, Letts hired as cash boy at $2 a week Percy Glen Winnett, another Canadian, then 15 years old.

But a different and modern Broadway opened to the public in 1915. It contained everything then known in modern building construction, including air-conditioning and a complete sprinkler installation. Letts announced that the new store represented, "Truth, Courtesy, Liberality and Value in its foundations."

The business was incorporated in 1919, and Arthur Letts, Jr., was made president; Malcolm McNaghten, vice-president in charge of finance; and William H. B. Kilner, secretary-treasurer. Before joining The Broadway, McNaghten, a son-in-law of the founder, was an investment banker in Los Angeles. Kilner had joined the store as an assistant bookkeeper 19 years before.

In 1927, the founder died, leaving a $7 million estate. The story of Arthur Letts, great merchant and humanitarian, depicting his failures in Seattle and Spokane and his amazing success in Los Angeles, is one of the great epics in retailing. It should inspire the present younger generation as an older generation was inspired by Horatio Alger, Jr. It seems a pity that, due to his modesty, his first great store in Los Angeles did not bear his name instead of that of a street!

In 1926, Kilner wrote an informative biography of Arthur Letts, Sr. Unfortunately, it was issued in a limited edition for private circulation and has done little to perpetuate the memory of the great merchant who founded Bullock's as well as The Broadway.

Arthur Letts, Jr., retired from the store to devote his entire time to the Holmby Corporation and other affairs of his late father's estate, and McNaghten became president of The Broadway. Sales and profits continued upward. McNaghten retired in 1945 and died in 1959 at 69.

In 1946, Edward W. Carter, 34, joined Broadway after Blyth & Co., investment bankers, acquired controlling interest of the Letts family stock and invited him to become the president. The company then comprised three stores doing $30 million. With a degree in economics from the University of California, Carter went to work for Silverwood's, a men's wear store in Los Angeles, before entering Harvard Business School where he won the Shuman Award as top scholar in the class of 1936. Two years later, he joined May Co. in Los Angeles as assistant men's clothing buyer and had become divisional merchandise manager by the time he left in 1946.

During his first week at Broadway, he halted work on a Crenshaw branch, then under construction, and redrew plans to double space to over 200,000 square feet.

Hale Bros. of San Francisco (including Weinstock, Lubin, Sacramento department store bought by Hale in 1927) was merged with Broadway in April, 1951. Prentis C. Hale, of the Northern California store group, became chairman of the new Broadway-Hale corporation. Since then, Carter has forged the West's largest department store chain. He sees his greatest contribution as his concept of regional, similarly sized units, operating with centralized merchandising and advertising and decentralized selling and housekeeping.

Carter has always surrounded himself with other able men and given them the freedom to operate effectively. Among them:

Charles S. Hobbs, a vice-president and director of Broadway-Hale and former president of Hale, joined the firm in 1946 after an extensive background in merchandising. He gained his early experience with The Emporium, San Francisco's leading department store; was merchandise manager of J. W. Robinson Co., Los Angeles; president of James McCreery, New York; and a consultant on distribution with Booz, Allen & Hamilton, management engineers. He became president of Hale after serving as general merchandise manager of Broadway.

Dorothy Marshall, vice president for corporate planning, began with Broadway as a salesgirl in 1929 and was appointed to her present post in early 1965 after having been vice-president and general manager of Broadway.

Edmund P. Platt, who began at Broadway-Hale in 1946 as divisional merchandise manager of the home-furnishings department, left in 1952 to become general merchandise manager of Meier & Frank, Portland, Oregon; held an executive position with Montgomery Ward & Co.; and became president of William Hengerer, Buffalo, New York. He is a descendant of one of the founders of Luckey, Platt & Co., Poughkeepsie, New York.

Howard L. Schlesinger, son of B. F. Schlesinger, former general manager of The Emporium, operated his own resident buying office in Los Angeles. He joined Broadway-Hale in 1946 as divisional merchandise manager of ready-to-wear and is now a divisional merchandise manager in the Weinstock, Lubin division in Sacramento.

At the end of 1965, Broadway-Hale was composed of 27 department store units in three divisions—Broadway (18), Weinstock-Hale (7), and Korrick's of Phoenix, Arizona (2). Each division has its own president—W. Earl Miller, Broadway (including Marston Co. of San Diego); Norris B. Brisco, Korrick's; and Norman V. Wechsler, Weinstock-Hale. William J. Ahern is chairman of the last-named division.

In 1964, net profits were $8,216,447 on sales of $219,292,685.

The company has a 24 per cent interest in Emporium-Capwell with a January 30, 1965, quoted value of $34.2 million against a cost of $10.7 million.

In 1965, Broadway-Hale paid $16 million cash for about 300,000 shares of Meier & Frank stock, representing more than one-third ownership of the Portland department store. However, May Department Stores acquired the controlling interest. (This transaction is further discussed in the chapter on Meier & Frank.)

Two units were opened in the fall of 1965 in Downey and Huntington Beach. Several other units are being enlarged or renovated. In 1966, Broadway stores will be opened in Bakersfield and Las Vegas, Nevada, and a Weinstock, Lubin unit will open in Stockton. About 10 other locations are in the planning stage for 1967–1968.

Carter's civic endeavors are legion. He is chairman of the board of regents of the University of California, president of trustees of the Los Angeles County Museum of Art, a director of the San Francisco Opera Association, and a director of the Southern California Symphony Association. He was given UCLA's Alumni of the Year award in 1953 and the Tobe Award for distinguished services in 1960.

CHAPTER 6

BULLOCK'S, INC.

LOS ANGELES, CALIFORNIA

"This is the house that Jack built"

In 1906, a new seven-story department store was going up on the northwest corner of Broadway and 7th Street, Los Angeles, three blocks from The Broadway. Building operations were suspended when one of the partners died and Arthur Letts, head of The Broadway, signed a 50-year lease of the property because he wasn't then certain he could renew his store's lease on favorable terms. In the interim, he put John Gillespie Bullock, Broadway's general superintendent, in charge as president. Percy Glen Winnett, then holding an important merchandising post at the company, joined Bullock as vice-president and general manager. The new store was given Bullock's name and opened in 1907. Letts renewed Broadway's lease and decided to continue both stores. He gave Bullock and Winnett complete freedom. Bullock supervised accounting and store operation; Winnett, merchandising and publicity.

H. M. Bigelow, who had run a general store in Iowa, was named store superintendent. He and A. E. Woof, in charge of the accounting and general office, reported directly to Bullock. Holt and the buyers reported to Winnett, who operated as his own general merchandise manager. William A. Holt handled publicity and his brilliant work was a major factor in the store's subsequent success. Later, W. O. Sampson was elected secretary and treasurer and replaced Woof.

The store held a public nonselling preview on March 2, 1907, and two days later, in pouring rain, it opened for business. Its $1,310,000 first-year sales volume proved that Bullock's could sell quality merchandise in the higher price ranges. This led to the opening of 30-day charge accounts, although the original plan had been to operate only on a cash basis.

Letts never interfered with the store operation and, as he rarely visited the establishment, he was unknown to most of the Bullock staff. Bullock and Winnett went to Letts' office at The Broadway for their meetings.

In 1919, Bullock's began Saturday-afternoon closings, which were applauded by employees and competitors alike, but ten years later the store decided to remain open on that busy sales afternoon.

When Bullock's joined RRA-AMC in 1919, the third store on the West Coast to become a member, its sales totaled $10 million a year. In 1923, the May Co. purchased the Hamberger Department Store near Bullock's. Winnett instructed buyers not to purchase different merchandise to meet the May Co. price offerings and predicted the aggressive promotions would increase traffic to mutual benefit. He was right.

Letts died in 1927 and Bullock's, Inc., was formed as a publicly owned corporation to acquire the store from his estate. Bullock's was then doing over $22 million.

Bullock's opened its Wilshire store in 1929 in a specially designed building catering to the "carriage trade." Uniformed attendants greet customers driving to the rear entrance, park cars, and return vehicles when the patrons leave. Hollywood movie notables have become regular customers, many of them making it their favorite luncheon place. Luncheon customers view daily style shows, accompanied by lilting music. Other units were opened in Palm Springs in 1930 and Westwood in 1932.

Sales personnel were selected carefully. One of these, Patricia Ryan, a college student working her way through the University of Southern California, is now Mrs. Richard M. Nixon.

Bullock died of a heart attack in 1933 at the age of 62. He was recognized as an influential civic leader. He headed a committee promoting passage of a $200 million bond issue for the Colorado River Aqueduct, was president of the Retail Merchants Credit Association of Los Angeles, and was a trustee of the California Institute of Technology. Bullock, a practical idealist, gave the store a character it never lost and a bronze bust of him on the first floor of the downtown store reminds personnel of his admonition, "The ideals of this business must not be sacrificed to gain."

After Bullock's death, Winnett, known to his close friends as "Jack," assumed full responsibility for the store's operation but continued to concentrate on merchandising. Buyers were directed to comparison-shop stores while in the New York market and report their observations. Winnett also studied monthly merchandise figures of other RRA-AMC stores for leads to improve Bullock departments. Buyers spent as much time as possible on the floor to supervise and assist in sales.

Winnett, himself, observed selling-floor activities daily and held regular meetings to assist buyers. He was an "angel" to local manufacturers, encouraging the development of the local market by buying everything that showed promise, giving local manufacturers special consideration, and urging buyers to suggest helpful product changes. He persuaded other AMC stores to send buyers to the Los Angeles market and AMC opened a buying office there. The Los Angeles wholesale market today excels in such lines as beach wear, swim suits, and women's sportswear.

Winnett also departed from traditional buying procedure, using separate buyers for what other large stores regard as subdivisions of main departments. Under this plan, each buyer maintains closer contact with consumer desires and market trends. It has not been followed to any appreciable extent by other important stores, however.

Bullock's storewide August sale in the downtown store is its most notable annual event. Because Bullock's buyers are not permitted to wangle for special prices on regular merchandise in the markets during the year, regular vendors co-operate wholeheartedly for the August sale.

Bullock's opened a Pasadena store in 1947, complete in all lines except a lower-price basement. Walter Young, of Bullock's downtown, became general superintendent, and the main store controlled the merchandising. The Pasadena store was a success from the start and its reputation for fine merchandise spread far and wide as thousands of visitors to the Tournament of Roses shopped and lunched there. The store more than justified Winnett's initial $6 million investment.

Walter W. Candy, Jr., a director of the company since 1942, became president in 1950, the year Winnett, his father-in-law, became chairman of the board. A native of St. Louis, Missouri, Candy was vice-president of the family-owned Busy Bee Candy Co. there from the time he was graduated from Princeton until he came to Bullock's as divisional merchandise manager of the Wilshire store in 1935.

In 1942, the year in which he became a director, Candy joined the Navy, attaining the rank of commander and earning a Bronze Star and four battle stars. In 1945, he became assistant to the president at Bullock's. Active in civic affairs, he was president of the Los Angeles Welfare Federation and campaign chairman of the Community Chest.

Philip Corrin, who retired in early 1963 as vice-chairman of the board and a director, joined the firm in 1919 as a copywriter. Born in Northern Ireland, he began work at Bullock's under Holt and attended night school until he completed his college education. In 1932, he became publicity director and, with a prolonged publicity campaign to remove the impression that Bullock's was a high-priced store, attracted as customers many of the low- and medium-income residents who flooded Los Angeles from 1940 to 1950. He became manager of Bullock's Wilshire in 1942, general superintendent of the downtown store three years later, and general manager downtown in

1947. He was elected to the board of directors in 1946, became a vice-president in 1947, an executive assistant to the president in 1954, and vice-chairman of the board in 1958. With the exception of Winnett, he was with Bullock's longer than any other man in top management. Corrin also served as president and chairman of the board of the Downtown Businessmen's Association, chairman of the board of the local Better Business Bureau, and president and director of the California Retailers Association.

Ann Hodge, one of retailing's first outstanding women, came to Bullock's in 1912 after graduation from Mount St. Mary's College, Cincinnati. Eventually, she succeeded Corrin as manager of Bullock's Wilshire.

Mahlon E. Arnett, graduated from the University of Southern California, joined Bullock's as a copywriter in 1929. He rose to vice-president and treasurer and, later, to still higher office under Federated Department Stores' control.

Mrs. Mary Ann Magnin opened a small shop in San Francisco to sell notions and baby clothing she made herself. Born in Holland, she was the wife of Isaac Magnin, also of Dutch birth. They were married in London, England, and emigrated to this country with their six-year-old son, Emanuel John, in 1876. As the business grew, women's wear was added.

John (as he was to call himself) entered the business in 1887. I. Magnin & Co., as a name, came into being in 1900. Isaac Magnin was a wood carver who made picture frames for Gump's of San Francisco and never was active in the expanding family firm. John's younger brother, Grover A., started with the company in 1906. John, who had been in complete charge since 1892, became president in 1907.

John, who lived in New York, was responsible for buying. He made numerous trips to Europe and succeeded in having garments from leading Paris couturiers confined to Magnin's. Similarly with the finest things in the New York market. Grover supervised selling and store operations. Starting in 1912, he opened new Magnin stores. One was opened in Seattle in 1925, another in Oakland in 1931. Others were the shop in Pasadena opened in 1913 and replaced with a modern building in 1949, and a Wilshire unit in 1939.

Mrs. Magnin continued her interest in the business until her death in 1943 at 95. A few weeks later, Bullock's obtained control of seven-unit Magnin's, its chief competitor in fine-quality women's wear and accessories. John Magnin died at 74 in November, 1944, a month after he had resigned his presidency due to ill health. Grover succeeded him.

I. Magnin's acquisition was the most audacious move that P. G. Winnett had ever made. He was determined not to interfere with Magnin's established merchandising procedures. The Magnin executive organization remained intact. Magnin's continued its own New York buying office and foreign connections. Incidentally, this enabled Bullock's to avoid paying AMC annual dues on the additional Magnin sales.

Grover Magnin agreed to continue until the new Magnin San Francisco store, then merely in the planning stages, was open and the old store disposed of. The new Magnin San Francisco store on Union Square, opened in 1948, is one of the finest store buildings in America.

Meanwhile, in 1947, the Beverly Hills shop was moved to its present building and a new Magnin store in Santa Barbara began business. But even more important, a new Pasadena Magnin store opened in 1949 in a location directly competitive to Bullock's.

Grover Magnin retired in 1950. Hector Escobosa, who became president of I. Magnin & Co. and vice-president and director of Bullock's, Inc. in 1951, was born in Arizona but spent most of his life in San Francisco before receiving his B.A. from the University of Washington.

Escobosa was with Hale Bros., San Francisco, from 1926 to 1934, latterly as apparel merchandise manager, and was vice-president of Mercantile Stores Company, a chain of 18 department stores, with numerous units, from 1935 to 1938. From 1939 to 1951, he was executive vice-president and general merchandise manager of Frederick & Nelson, Seattle, a division of Marshall Field & Company, and a vice-president of Field's.

Escobosa was a frequent and welcome visitor to all of the foreign markets. Magnin's selections from the large first showings were often bought by other non-competing important American stores. He was awarded France's Chevalier of the Legion of Honor and Italy's Star of Solidarity for his services to the fashion industries of those countries. Escobosa died in 1963.

Both Bullock's and Magnin's have continued to expand. Bullock's Palm Springs opened in 1947, the Westwood store in 1951, and in 1958 the Santa Ana store, frequently called "Mister Candy's Store" because of the personal interest Candy has taken in this unit in the company-owned shopping center. Another new Bullock store opened in 1962 in Van Nuys in the San Fernando Valley. New Magnin shops opened in Sacramento in 1953, in La Jolla in 1954, in Fresno in 1955, in Palo Alto in 1956, in Santa Ana in 1958, in Carmel in 1960, and in San Fernando Valley and Portland, Oregon, in 1962. In 1965, Bullock's was operating eight stores; Magnin, 18.

More than 40 per cent of the regular Bullock and Magnin employees are members of the profit-sharing and retirement-benefit plans. Retirement at 65 is mandatory except at the option of the management.

Even in America, "The House that Jack Built" is an amazing business achievement for Jack Winnett. As William Dean Howells once said of someone: "He was in love with his work and he felt the enthusiasm for it which nothing but the work we can do well inspires in us."

In 1963, the last year before its acquisition by Federated Department Stores, the store group had sales of $196.6 million and net earnings of $9.4 million. The Bullock stores contributed two-thirds of the sales and profits; the Magnin group, the balance. About 25 per cent of Bullock's sales were cash and the remainder on 30-day charge and revolving budget accounts. Bullock's again posted record sales and earnings in 1964.

Bullock's became an autonomous operating division of Federated in August, 1964. Bullock's then had seven stores, I. Magnin 18. Bullock's-Magnin Co. is headed by former president Walter Candy, Jr., now chairman; and former executive vice-president Mahlon Arnett, now president. Winnett, who fought the merger, has retired. Two operating divisions have been formed: Bullock's, with Frank Gillett, previously vice-president for merchandising, now president; and I. Magnin, with William P. Keeshan continuing as president.

CHAPTER 7

CARSON, PIRIE,

SCOTT & COMPANY

CHICAGO, ILLINOIS

"A Century-old Store with Plenty of Verve"

Carson, Pirie, Scott & Company was founded late in 1854 by John T. Pirie and Samuel Carson, who had emigrated from Ireland eight months before. Pirie, born in Scotland, had been apprenticed to his uncle's dry goods store in Newry, Ireland, at the age of 15. There, he met Carson, of Scotch-Irish descent, also an apprentice. The two men continued to learn their trade at Belfast before sailing for the United States. They worked briefly at Beck's dry goods store in New York and then moved on to Peru, Illinois, where they obtained employment with Murray Brothers, whose family they had known in Ireland.

They began their store with $1,200 worth of stock in LaSalle, Illinois. After a brief period, they moved on to Amboy, Illinois, to a larger establishment in a vacated saloon. After a year in business and following a second move to still larger quarters in Amboy, the two men had a profit of $2,500.

In 1856, another family, the Scotts, whom the two men had known in Ireland, emigrated to the United States with 12 children. Two older brothers, George and Robert S. Scott, went to work in Amboy with Carson and Pirie and soon became partners.

Robert took charge of stores opened in Galena and Mendota in 1857. Another store was opened in Polo in 1858, and a fifth in Sterling in 1859. In that year, John E. Scott, a younger brother, became the firm's first errand boy at 15. He earned $50 a year plus room and board.

One other man, whose name never appeared in the store title, also joined the firm. He was Andrew MacLeish, born in Scotland and apprenticed to the dry goods trade at Glasgow. He arrived in Chicago in 1856, worked briefly for a dry goods store, taught school for a year, and tried various other jobs before joining Carson, Pirie & Company as a partner and first manager of the Chicago store that opened May 8, 1867, at 136 Lake Street. Three years before that, the firm had opened a wholesale division at 20 Lake Street, Chicago, to supply the stores in other Illinois towns. Samuel Carson died in 1869. A year later, the retail and wholesale divisions were combined at 118–120 State Street.

The Chicago fire of October, 1871 destroyed the building and much of the stock and nearly put the firm out of business. MacLeish saved $50,000 worth of goods by offering passing teamsters $50 a ton for every wagonload of merchandise hauled outside the fire zone. The salvaged goods finally were safely stored in a barn on Wabash Avenue near 16th Street. The firm reopened in a small building in West Chicago. The Scott name was added to the firm's signature in 1875. In 1876, a second retail store was opened eight blocks north of the Chicago River. Between 1876 and 1904, the business had many ups and downs, but the partners always obtained adequate credit. In good times, the store firmed its position with resources by paying bills before they were due in return for a small discount.

In 1883, the store bought Charles Gossage & Company on State near Washington for $800,000 and closed the Clark and Erie Street site opened after the fire. In 1887, the second store was moved downtown to Wabash and Adams, and Samuel Carson Pirie, son of the founder, became manager. Both were combined in 1890 at State and Washington.

In 1904, Carson's purchased the Harry Gordon Selfridge store. Selfridge, who had operated it only three months, had leased it from Schlesinger & Mayer, for which it was built. The 12-story building, at Washington and State, designed by Louis H. Sullivan, was considered one of the most beautiful stores in America. With the acquisition of this handsome structure, adequate for future expansion, the firm closed or disposed of outlets outside Chicago. The new store opened on September 19, 1904. Robert Scott died the following day, four years after his brother, George. The building was expanded by 50 per cent within two years. In 1907, John T. Pirie and John E. Scott, also a partner, retired. Scott died in 1913.

The business incorporated in 1919 with Samuel C. Pirie as the first president. He had started in the firm's New York office, managed a Chicago store, and later headed the New York office. He continued as president for ten years and served as board chairman from 1929 to 1938.

Carson's bought the wholesale dry goods firm of John V. Farwell in 1925, and two years later made Chicago's first air-express shipment. On July 18, 1927, the store opened a 15-story men's building connected to the State Street store.

Andrew MacLeish, who helped found the University of Chicago, died on January 14, 1928. John E. Scott's three sons continued in the business. In 1929, Samuel Carson Pirie became board chairman and the second John T. Pirie, who had been admitted to partnership in 1901, became president. He remained in that capacity until 1940 when he became chairman of the board but died within three months at 68.

Frederick H. Scott succeeded Pirie as president of the firm and no board chairman was named until after World War II. Scott attained that position in 1946. Bruce MacLeish became president then, and in 1952 succeeded Scott as board chairman. Frederick Scott served the company 55 years. The third John T. Pirie then became president.

When, in 1942, the United States Government took over the building that housed the wholesale division, Carson's disposed of all lines except floor coverings, moving this section to the Merchandise Mart. At the time Marshall Field closed its jobbing and wholesale division, Carson's was the only large department store continuing in wholesaling. The store explained that some manufacturers sell only to distributors and jobbers and, thus, Carson's was able to obtain merchandise direct. Carson's maintains a regular staff of 300 in the wholesale division. Having joined AMC in 1949, its customers include fellow members.

Under third-generation John T. Pirie, Jr., Carson's opened its first suburban unit in December, 1952. In 1956, it opened Edens Plaza, a shopping-center subsidiary in which it has 22 tenants besides its own store.

Pirie stepped up to chairman of the board in 1958 and C. Virgil Martin became the first president named outside the original owning families. He had come to Carson's in 1948, had risen to assistant to the president four years later, and vice-president and general manager in 1954.

In 1959, the firm bought the Rau Store in Chicago Heights, adding $3 million dollars to annual sales. On October 1, 1959, it bought the Block & Kuhl chain, thereby increasing its volume by $30 million. This chain, operating as the Peoria division, includes 12 stores in Illinois and one in Iowa. Carson's bought The Fair, Kankakee, Illinois, in 1960. During this period of expansion, substantial sums were also spent to make the parent store attractive and sales were promoted with vigor. An eight-story addition, which was begun in 1961, gave the State Street store 1,000,000 square feet of space. Carson's itself includes 10 branches in Illinois, and one in Indiana, and also the wholesale floor coverings business. The firm's volume in 1964 was $176,-300,000; its net profit, $3,219,000.

Carson's employs about 8,930. The store's merchandise staff has seven divisional managers and 84 buyers, of whom 50 are women. There is virtually no buyer turnover.

For years, Carson's has been concerned with the welfare of its employees. Martha Douglas, sister of Supreme Court Justice

William O. Douglas, is director of counseling and employee activities and devotes her full time to helping prepare employees for retirement. An annual interview is held with those 60 and over and a 10-lesson course on preparation for retirement is offered to those 45 and older.

Carson's still is virtually controlled by the founders' descendants who hold 80 per cent of the stock.

CHAPTER 8

CITY OF PARIS

SAN FRANCISCO, CALIFORNIA

"Since 1850"

The City of Paris, one of the oldest department stores on the West Coast, was established in 1850 during the Gold Rush that brought rapid population growth to Sacramento and San Francisco. Many of the newcomers, adventuresome men from all sections of the country, were a rough lot who congregated in San Francisco for diversion and became unruly after drinking too much at the numerous local bars. Vigilantes were organized quickly to deal summarily with them, and the worst trouble-makers were either hanged or jailed.

From far-away Paris, France, came two other "prospectors," Felix Verdier and his brother Emile, not with picks and shovels but with a diversified stock of the finest products that could be collected in France. These were brought in a chartered ship named *The City of Paris.* News of the impending arrival reached the miners before the ship docked, and a good-sized crowd with ready money was waiting. The entire stock was sold in short order at shipside.

The brothers sailed immediately for France to bring another more extensive collection. The second cargo consisted of gorgeous silks, shawls, laces, trinkets, vintage wines, gourmet goods and many other items not found in stores. The merchandise brought high prices from the money-laden prospectors because of its unusual appeal and because, for the first time, they could obtain for their wives and sweethearts items that could not be found elsewhere.

The Verdiers' first store, on Geary Street, became the most unusual store in San Francisco because of the wide diversity of direct imports. The brothers also operated a retail store in Paris, which promptly replenished the stocks of the San Francisco store. New items were also developed in the home markets.

Among those who shopped in San Francisco about the time the City of Paris opened was the Swedish Nightingale, Jenny Lind, and her concert tour manager, P. T. Barnum. Lotta Crabtree, who became a multimillionairess singing and dancing on the San Francisco stage, was one of the most loyal customers the store had for its French imports.

Gaston Verdier succeeded his father, Felix Verdier, as head of the store in 1870 and remained in that position until 1900. He successfully promoted some of the store's unusual departments and gave it a "Frenchified" image by increasing direct imports, including vintage wines, from France. The store prospered under his regime.

Paul Verdier, Gaston's son, took over the top job in 1900 and continued to promote French imports, including women's ready-to-wear as well as liquor and wines. Madame de Tassan, Paul's sister, joined the firm as a partner and a director.

City of Paris followed the ever-shifting center of business in San Francisco. In 1851, it was at 152 Kearney Street and later expanded into an adjacent store. In 1860, it was at 633 Clay Street, and ten years later it occupied a corner in the Occidental Hotel. By 1890, it had moved to the southeast corner of Geary and Grant. Six years later, it was located at its present site on Union Square. The great earthquake and fire of April 18, 1906, destroyed the store but it was rebuilt on the same site.

In 1926, the City of Paris came under the control of B. F. Schlesinger, the able, former head of The Emporium and at that time the best-known merchant in San Francisco. He used the City of Paris as his headquarters during the organization of his own West Coast group, B. F. Schlesinger & Sons.

This group went bankrupt in 1932, and control of the City of Paris reverted to Paul Verdier and Madame de Tassan. B. F. Schlesinger retired and died in 1959.

In 1950, a branch store was opened in San Mateo. Later, a branch was opened in Stonestown and, in 1964, another in Northgate Shopping Center in adjoining Marin County.

Georges S. DeBonis, who succeeded Paul Verdier as president in 1958, had joined the City of Paris in 1916, after having been with John Breuner Company of San Francisco, a home furnishings store about as old as the City of Paris.

The home store, with an area totaling 200,000 square feet, features many departments, including home furnishings, but it has no basement department offering low-price merchandise.

Of the total of about 36 buyers, 18 are women. The total staff of regular full-time employees numbers 600, approximately 80 per cent females, of whom 500 are engaged in selling.

In its earlier years, the City of Paris was noted for its wide variety of direct imports, including women's ready-to-wear. Now, only 3 per cent of its total sales are imports. This low percentage does not give the City of Paris any competitive pull from imports, since other important local stores feature imports totaling 6 per cent or more of their annual sales. Yet, the City of Paris has a very good buying office to cover the foreign markets.

Although the City of Paris is the oldest department store in California, age alone has not been sufficient to develop an enduring loyalty of customers. In 1948, annual sales were $15,-842,000; net profit, $445,543. In 1964, the company did an estimated $13 million downtown plus $5 million in the two branches. This was an increase of about $1 million, most of it gained downtown.

CHAPTER 9

THE T. EATON
COMPANY, LIMITED

TORONTO, CANADA

"The Irish Tradesman from Ballymena "

Timothy Eaton, founder of Canada's largest group of department and mail-order stores, now estimated to be doing over $1 billion, was born near Ballymena, Northern Ireland, in 1834. He was the youngest in a family of nine and his father had died shortly before his birth. At 13, Timothy, apprenticed to a draper, worked from dawn to dusk and slept under the counter of the store. At the end of his apprenticeship, he took his accumulated wages in a lump sum of £100, about $500, and went to Canada.

He was in his early 20s when he arrived there. He settled in St. Marys, near London, Ontario, and joined his brother, James, in the operation of a general store from 1860 to 1868. Eaton outgrew the limitations of the village and moved to Toronto where he entered into a partnership that lasted only a year.

On December 8, 1869, Eaton opened his own store, T. Eaton & Company, at the corner of Yonge and Queen Streets in Toronto, in a space 24 feet wide and 60 feet long. The staff was two men, a woman, and a boy.

Eaton's opening advertisement, which amused his competitors, announced: "We propose to sell our goods for cash only; in selling goods, to have only one price." These policies, along with the promise that goods could be returned if unsatisfactory, and money refunded, were revolutionary in Canada at the time. His competitors ceased to be amused when they suffered sales losses because of customers' increasing good will toward the new store.

The founder's cash policy endured until January, 1926, when the deferred payment plan was introduced in Toronto. A similar plan had operated in the Montreal store since April, 1925, as a continuation of a plan effective in Goodwin's, a department store purchased by Eaton's. Under this plan, customers could pay for certain types of goods—furniture, floor coverings, stoves, furnaces, clocks and radios—in 10 monthly instalments. Charge accounts were introduced in the Halifax store in 1931, in Toronto in 1936, and in all other Eaton stores in 1939. In 1904, deposit accounts were introduced. Customers could deposit money in an account and then buy goods up to the amount of their deposit.

Two other policies, regarded as old-fashioned, were put into effect when Eaton opened his store. One was to draw the shades on display windows each Sunday; the other was to prohibit selling tobacco or liquor in a retail store. Eaton did not use tobacco and he was a deeply religious man who would not even indirectly solicit trade on Sundays. A surprisingly large number of customers approved of these policies. Except for the adjustment in the cash policy, the original Eaton principles have been continued through the years.

Eaton's mail-order business started modestly with the distribution in 1874 of 40,000 handbills in Toronto. Ten years later, Eaton's circulated its first catalog, a 6-by-9-inch 32-page booklet, at the Toronto Industrial Exhibition. Today's great mail-order catalog contains 600 or more pages and goes to millions of Canadians.

Eaton's installed telephones in 1884. A switchboard was added in 1899. For many years, Eaton's had the world's largest telephone system devoted to retail selling. The Eaton downtown Toronto retail complex alone now handles as many as 100,000 calls a day.

In 1886, the first elevator was built into the Eaton store. A buying office was opened in London in 1893, in Paris in 1898, Manchester and New York offices in 1911, Leicester, Belfast, Berlin, and Zurich in 1913. Berlin and Zurich were subsequently closed. An office was added in Frankfurt, Germany, in 1957, and one in Florence, Italy, in 1963. The company has buying agents in California and Hong Kong, Japan.

Eaton's was incorporated as a limited company in 1891.

Timothy Eaton's eldest son, Edward Young Eaton, who was being trained to succeed his father, died in 1900 while still a young man. The elder Eaton continued as president until he died in 1907 at 72. Another son, John Craig Eaton, succeeded him.

After leaving school, John Eaton joined the store and worked in all departments. In 1905, he supervised the first great expansion in the west—the opening of a store in Winnipeg. In 1912, a 10-story building was opened in downtown Toronto. In 1919, a Maritimes mail order headquarters was established in Moncton, New Brunswick.

One of the primary concerns of Eaton's second president was the welfare of his staff. During World War I, he granted a special military service allowance to active Eaton servicemen and women at a cost of more than $2 million. In addition, staff positions were kept open until the employee returned from military service. John Craig Eaton's generous support of charitable, educational and welfare projects reached many hundreds of thousands of dollars. At the close of World War I, a chair of medicine, bearing the Eaton name, was endowed at the University of Toronto. He was knighted by King George V in recognition of his contributions during World War I and tribute was paid him as one of Toronto's leading citizens. Sir John died in 1922.

Robert Young Eaton, a nephew of the founder, succeeded his cousin as president and guided the firm for 20 years through some of its hardest times, including the depression of 1930 and the early part of World War II. During his presidency, the company took over and enlarged Goodwin's Montreal department store in 1925, opened stores in Regina in 1926, in Hamilton and Saskatoon in 1927, in Halifax in 1928, and in Calgary in 1929. Mail order facilities were expanded throughout the country in 1928. Despite the depression, the College Street Store was added in Toronto in 1930. This was the largest retail building in Canada devoted to home furnishings. The company also acquired the 21-unit Canadian Department Stores chain—20 in Ontario, one in Quebec—in 1928.

Before Robert Eaton stepped down as president in 1942, he had served the company 45 years. He died in 1956 at 81.

Sir John's son, John David Eaton, grandson of the founder, became president of Eaton's in 1942 at 33. He had 12 years' experience in the stores at home and in Eaton's foreign offices. In 1937, he was appointed a director, and four years later became vice-president. Under his management, the company has expanded into every province in Canada and now has stores from Newfoundland to Vancouver Island. In 1948, Eaton's purchased David Spencer's chain of eight stores in British Columbia. In 1955, Eaton's opened a store in Charlottetown, Prince Edward Island. In 1956, the company added its first shopping-center store in Oshawa, Ontario. In the same year, a huge service building and warehouse were opened in the Toronto area. A major addition was completed to the Calgary store in 1957. In that year, too, a store was opened in a shopping center in Gander, near Newfoundland's International Airport. In 1960, a 250,000-square-foot store was launched in the Wellington Square shopping center in downtown London, Ontario. The Hamilton and Montreal stores were enlarged. In 1962, an automotive center was established in downtown Toronto. Later, two shopping-center units were opened in the eastern and northeastern sections. About the same time, a store was opened in North York on Toronto's outskirts. In this location—Yorkdale Shopping Center—Eaton's operates its largest suburban store and the biggest department store—362,900 square feet on four selling floors—in any Canadian shopping center. There, Eaton's has been joined by Simpson's, marking the first time the two companies have had major branches in the same shopping center. Other units are planned to give Eaton's a department store in every major population center in metropolitan Toronto.

Still family-owned, Eaton's has become a merchandising giant, the largest in the Commonwealth. It reaches virtually every home in Canada through its retail stores, mail-order offices and catalogs.

Two of John David's four sons, John Craig and Fredrik Stefan, have joined the company.

Eaton's parent store in Toronto occupies most of a city block and is nine stories high. A notable feature is its Georgian Room restaurant, seating 400 and always well patronized.

In Toronto alone, Eaton's maintains 26 buildings devoted to retailing, warehousing, manufacturing, and maintenance service. The store has seven parking lots. Unconfirmed reports in May, 1965, were that Eaton's was planning vast redevelopment of its downtown holdings.

In Montreal, Eaton's joined First National Property Corp. in June, 1965, in ownership and development of some 20 acres in the heart of downtown at a cost of $125 million. The site comprises six city blocks of which Eaton's is one. In the first phase of development, Eaton's will erect a 12-story building at a cost of $12 million to contain 10 floors for parking 1,250 cars, plus two for Eaton office use above. Below ground will be 90,000 square feet of retail space which Eaton's will rent. Also subsurface will be pedestrian walkways and shopping areas connecting with the present Place Ville Marie shopping center— adding some 400,000 square feet of retail space.

Other key elements in the plan: Twin 34-story office towers, a retail and commercial center on two blocks with an enclosed two-level retail shopping area, another nearly 1 million square feet of commercial and office space, a street designed as a sky-lit gallery, and a network of pedestrian ways lined with shops and linked to the other major department stores in the vicinity.

The manufacturing end of the business, which started in 1890 with a single sewing machine turning out white goods, now includes fur coats and repairs, men's and boys' shirts, paja-mas, furniture-finishing, drapery, slipcover and curtain work-rooms, pharmaceutical products, candies, and ice cream.

Some of Eaton's branch stores in larger cities are as big as the parent stores of many American department stores. Eaton's, Winnipeg, for example, has a staff of 7,000. There are 14 build-ings in Winnipeg, four parking lots, and a six-story car park accommodating 600 cars. The Montreal store, a nine-story structure, occupies a city block. The staff there speaks both French and English.

Eaton's operates some 70 main stores and branches, 45 heavy goods stores, three catalog order centers, about 340 catalog sales offices, two factories, and 10 buying offices. Additional stores are planned. The company employs 40,000, about 6,000 of them on the mail-order staff.

Eaton's pioneered in the establishment of its own brands covering a substantial number of its regular items. Many were introduced to Eaton's customers 50 years ago and have become well known. Eaton's features merchandise made in Canada. The company maintains its own buying office in New York.

Eaton's employees are well cared for both during their active working years and when they retire. Regular employees receive a three-week vacation after five years, four weeks after 20, and a two-week bonus (making six weeks in all) during the 25th an-niversary year. The Eaton retirement annuity plan provides either a commuted value sum or monthly pension to retiring employees. It was established in 1948. Eaton's pays a percent-age of the regular employee's wages during illness, and a com-pany plan, at modest rates to employees, provides for medical and surgical expenses. Employees are granted a 10 per cent discount on most purchases and an additional 10 per cent during a two-week period before Christmas.

A bronze statue of Timothy Eaton was placed in the Toronto parent store in 1919 on the company's 50th anniversary. A reproduction of it was erected in the Winnipeg store from contributions made by the Eaton staff. Reviewing his life as a merchant and humanitarian, one must have an abounding admiration for a man who made the Golden Rule meaningful at a time when it was frequently forgotten in business transactions.

CHAPTER 10

THE EMPORIUM

SAN FRANCISCO, CALIFORNIA

The Big "E" of Northern California

In 1896, Adolph Feist, a promoter, pursuaded Mrs. Abby Parrott to build the Market Street store which opened as The Emporium, a group of individual leased departments.

The operation was not successful, and the present Emporium was incorporated in July, 1897, through the efforts of F. W. Dohrmann and Andrew Davis. Later it was consolidated with the nearby Golden Rule Bazaar, founded in the gold rush era of 1849, and was known as The Emporium and The Golden Rule Bazaar. Soon, the name was shortened to The Emporium and the leased-department policy was abandoned. By 1906, nearly all departments were controlled by The Emporium Company, under the policies originated by Dohrmann.

The big fire of 1906 destroyed all the records, including the accounts receivable. The store ran ads asking customers to pay what they owed and the response was such that there was very little loss from unpaid accounts. After the fire, the business was carried on in the home of one of the store's stockholders. In

1907, B. F. Schlesinger became general manager of The Emporium. He had grown up around his father's State Street store in Chicago—the Schlesinger & Mayer Store—and had been its general superintendent. He had attended Harvard for three years, intending to follow a medical career, but his studies were interrupted when his father sent him on a buying trip to Japan. On his return, B. F. Schlesinger decided to make retailing his lifetime vocation.

In 1904, the Schlesinger & Mayer store was sold to Harry Gordon Selfridge, who had been a partner of Marshall Field. Selfridge operated the store for only three months, and then sold it at a profit to Carson, Pirie, Scott & Company. B. F. Schlesinger successively was general superintendent of Selfridge's and Carson's, before going to The Emporium.

When Selfridge purchased Schlesinger & Mayer, Charles W. Steines became his general merchandise manager. Selfridge had known Steines when both of them had worked in Marshall Field's wholesale division. Carson's kept Steines on as general merchandise manager until 1906 when he joined Selfridge in London. Steines returned to the United States in 1909 as general merchandise manager at The Emporium.

In 1916, The Emporium became a charter member of the RRA-AMC group and Steines' London experience with Selfridge's was an invaluable help when the AMC decided to open its own foreign buying offices. With Louis E. Kirstein of Filene's, Steines opened the AMC foreign offices in 1920.

Schlesinger resigned from The Emporium in 1924 to become vice-president and general manager of The May Company in Los Angeles. He remained only a year before organizing his own group of stores under the name of B. F. Schlesinger & Sons, forerunner of Western Department Stores. He died in January, 1960.

C. W. Steines succeeded B. F. Schlesinger in 1924 as general merchandise manager of The Emporium and the store continued to prosper and expand.

In 1927, Steines had bought the H. C. Capwell Company, Oakland, California. A new building was erected and the store merged with The Emporium. Edward C. Lipman, an Emporium executive for many years, was placed in charge of the Capwell store.

After C. W. Steines died in 1930 at 63, the Emporium-Capwell stores were managed by A. B. C. Dohrmann, who was a director. "Mister Alphabet," as he was called, was the best-known merchant, and civic leader in San Francisco. He headed The Dohrmann Commercial Company, wholesale dealers in equipment and supplies for hotels, restaurants, and other users. They had operated a number of leased departments in The Emporium, and A. B. C. Dohrmann was thoroughly familiar with its methods. He was assisted in the management of the two stores by four co-ordinate vice-presidents: Reagan P. Connally, general merchandise manager; Haldane S. Fisher, in charge of buying and leasing outside properties for the stores; Roy Southworth, controller; and E. C. Lipman of Capwell's.

When A. B. C. Dohrmann died in 1936 of a heart attack at 68, he was a poor man, having lost his personal fortune some years previously in an outside business venture. Nevertheless, all the local papers devoted editorials to his 50 and more years as a merchant, humanitarian, and civic leader.

R. P. Connally and Roy Southworth left The Emporium at this time. Connally later became president of Interstate Department Stores. The Emporium-Capwell directors appointed Haldane Fisher to manage the two stores and their branches. Fisher came to San Francisco after a successful career in retailing in the East. He had intended to retire and play golf but agreed to supervise the construction of the new Capwell store instead.

Reginald H. Biggs, later to become president of The White House, San Francisco, was publicity director of Capwell's at the time of Fisher's appointment. Biggs wrote: "Mr. Fisher was a shrewd Yankee trader and performed a valiant service to the company and Mr. Dohrmann. He had a keen knowledge of helping business which was in trouble, and we were in trouble."

At Fisher's death in 1947, Edward C. Lipman was appointed president of the two stores and their branches. Born in Berkeley,

California, in 1893, he graduated from the University of California in 1914 with a B.S. degree and joined The Emporium that year. He was successively assistant general superintendent, general superintendent, divisional and assistant general merchandise manager, general manager of Capwell's, vice president and managing director of The Emporium, president of Emporium-Capwell Company, and chairman.

His training at The Emporium under both Schlesinger and Steines fitted him for the top position in both stores. He took a special interest in employee relations both inside and outside the store and was in demand as an arbiter during the period when the unions were getting a foothold in the local stores.

Lipman, although born into a well-to-do family, was exceedingly democratic. None of his predecessors had a more rounded experience in merchandising, store operation, and administration. His ability was highly respected and the stores continued to expand under his regime.

The world of retailing in general and the merchants of San Francisco in particular were stunned at his sudden tragic death at 68 in 1958 from injuries received in a traffic accident.

E. C. Lipman was a director of the local Credit Bureau, the State Chamber of Commerce and the State Retailers Association; and director of two other companies and of RRA-AMC. He also was consulting professor at Stanford University and a member of the Advisory Council of the University of California.

The directors of The Emporium-Capwell Company have always had a capable man standing by to meet any emergency and they appointed Frederic S. Hirschler to succeed his friend and mentor, Ned Lipman. A graduate of the University of California with a B.S. degree in business administration, Hirschler started at The Emporium in 1925 as a stockboy, went through various steps in nonselling and merchandising, and became sales promotion manager at Capwell's in 1937, general manager of Capwell's in 1948 and of The Emporium in 1954; president and chief executive officer of The Emporium-Capwell Company in 1958, and chairman of the board and chief executive officer in January, 1966. Ardern R. Batchelder, with the company since 1934, and executive vice-president since 1964, was elected president and chief operating officer.

The Emporium occupies 703,328 square feet and Capwell's 497,946. There are about 5,200 employees. In mid-1965 Emporium had six units, one being built, and two regional shopping center units in the planning stage, while Capwell had four stores and one planned.

In April, 1960, the store established an employee joint stock-purchase and pension plan, effective in July of that year. Prior to that, retirement income based on individual needs had been provided solely by the company. Under the stock plan, employees with at least three years of service and between 24 and 64 years of age may contribute from 2 to 5 per cent of their annual compensation toward stock purchases. The company contributes 4 per cent of its income before taxes and the total is used to buy stock for contributing employees at prevailing market prices.

In a report to stockholders, Hirschler said, "Of those eligible to participate, a vast majority elected to subscribe to the plan."

Hirschler is a director of AMC, California Retailers Association, and National Retail Merchants Association. He is also a director of the San Francisco Federal Reserve Bank and of the San Francisco Symphony Orchestra Association and is on the executive committee of the Bay Area United Crusade.

For 1965, the company had net sales of $165,668,641, and net profits of $9,191,376. Hirschler has given a good account of his stewardship as head of one Northern California's leading department stores.

CHAPTER 11

WILLIAM FILENE'S SONS COMPANY

BOSTON, MASSACHUSETTS

---

*"America's Best-Known Women's
Specialty Store"*

William Filene was born in 1830, the son of a ribbon salesman in Posen, then in Germany. He was sent to Berlin to study law, but abandoned his studies and emigrated to the United States when his father died. At 21, he opened his first store on Hanover Street in Boston.

The first store was unsuccessful and Filene opened a new one in Salem in 1856 and married in the same year. Two of his sons, Edward Albert, born in 1860, and Abraham Lincoln, born in 1865, became important figures in the store's history.

Between the births of these two sons, Filene worked in metal trades in New York, lost most of his money, and then opened two small shops at Lynn, Massachusetts. He developed a small chain with two more in Salem, Massachusetts, and Bath, Maine.

While his sons went to high school in Lynn, they also worked in the stores. Edward began full time in 1879 when his father became ill. Two years later, Filene and the two sons opened a store at 10 Winter Street, Boston, and sold the other properties. By 1890, the store had moved to larger quarters at 445 Washington Street and soon became the largest in Boston devoted to women's wear and accessories.

A year later, the two sons assumed the management of the store and inherited it in 1901 when their father died. They owned equal shares and became the best-known brother team in all American retailing. Edward proved to be a wizard at merchandising and Lincoln a genius in administration and management of the store staff.

The following year, the store trebled its space on Washington Street, but still more was needed and the Filene brothers employed Daniel H. Burnham, a leading architect, to design a new eight-story building with basement and sub-basement. The new building opened in September, 1912. So great was public interest that 715,000 persons went through the store in a week, and the year's sales leaped from $4,810,899 to $8,466,467.

In 1916, Lincoln Filene organized a group of noncompeting stores into the Retail Research Association and a year later formed a complementary group of the same stores into the Associated Merchandising Corporation. A separate chapter is devoted to the activities of these two associations.

When Edward J. Frost and John R. Simpson, two men of superior ability, joined the firm, they were given stock and appointed directors. Frost became controller. Simpson took charge of publicity, resigning in 1918 to re-enlist in the army where he became a colonel and won the Distinguished Service Medal.

Frost and Louis E. Kirstein became dominant figures in the management about 1925. Kirstein had joined Filene's in 1911 after giving up a top position with Stein-Bloch Co., Rochester, New York, men's clothing manufacturers.

After the organization was complete, friction developed between E. A. Filene, president, and Kirstein. This became so intense that Kirstein decided to oust E. A. Filene from management. With support from Frost, Lincoln Filene, and the other

directors, he succeeded. E. A. Filene retained his title as president but was stripped of all authority. As a result, he developed
many outside interests, some of which caused him to spend
much of his time in Europe. He died of pneumonia in Paris in
1937, leaving his $2 million estate to two foundations he had
developed: the Twentieth Century Fund and the Edward A.
Filene Good Will Fund, Inc.

No other member of management contributed so much to
Filene's success as E. A. Filene. A notable contribution was the
low-expense and self-service "automatic" bargain basement in
1909. Other important stores had low-price basements, but
none on automatic markdown provision. Initial markups were
fairly low but always profitable. After 10 days, the goods were
reduced 25 per cent and further reductions were made at stated
intervals until an entire lot was sold. Any remaining goods were
given to local charities.

Actually, very little was given away, but the provision created
a lot of good will. Buying scouts covered the domestic and foreign markets to keep the basement supplied with seconds,
close-outs and similar "distress" merchandise. Filene's bargain
basement continues to be one of the store's most profitable divisions.

E. A. Filene also established the first retail store credit union
to keep employees from borrowing money from loan sharks. He
successfully sponsored a law in Massachusetts to make such
unions legal and in 1921 established the Credit Union National
Extension Bureau.

Another notable achievement, largely due to E. A. Filene,
was the board of Filene employees organized as the Filene Co-
operative Association to arbitrate all grievances, including discharges. Louis D. Brandeis, Filene's attorney who later became
Supreme Court Justice, drafted the by-laws and management
was obliged to accept all decisions of the board. E. A. Filene's
book, *The Model Stock Plan,* was translated into five languages.
He was a leader in the Boston, national and international Chambers of Commerce. In 1954, he was elected to the retailing Hall
of Fame in the Chicago Merchandise Mart. In 1959, a monu-

ment to him was dedicated on Boston Common by the National Association of Credit Unions.

Nepotism did not exist in the Filene organization. Edward Albert Filene remained a bachelor. Lincoln Filene's two sons-in-law and the sons of Frost and Kirstein all found positions with other stores.

Filene's was in the forefront in providing pleasing hours of work, better wages, and sickness payments. During World War II, the store made up the difference between service and store pay.

For Lincoln Filene, who liked people and devoted much of his time to helping them, RRA-AMC provided an additional outlet. In the store, Lincoln influenced the selection and progress of many promising men who "graduated" from Filene's and pursued successful careers in other stores and organizations.

In the summer of 1929, Walter N. Rothschild, Sr., president of Abraham & Straus, invited L. E. Kirstein and Fred Lazarus, Jr., to spend a weekend with him on his yacht. They became close business associates and friends through RRA-AMC membership. Out of this came the formation of a corporation known as the Federated Department Stores. The development of the Federated chain is covered in the chapter devoted to the Lazarus stores since Fred Lazarus, Jr., was largely responsible for its success.

Kirstein died in 1942, Frost in 1944. When Frost passed away, Lincoln Filene remarked that he had never expected to outlive his partners, all of whom, with the exception of E. A. Filene, were younger than he.

The Charga-Plate, now widely used for credit accounts, was pioneered by Frost at Filene's. It was brought to his attention by Lawrence S. Bitner, Filene's store manager. After Bitner retired from Filene's, the Charga-Plate manufacturer employed him to promote the use of the invention in other stores.

As all retailers know, it costs more to carry charge accounts than to conduct business solely on a cash basis. Frost at one time decided to add 50 cents to each monthly bill issued to charge customers, but this proved to be a grave mistake. Customers would not pay the fee and many closed their accounts. The idea was dropped after a trial period of several months.

Bitner was recommended by the author for the Filene post of personnel manager. Frost gave Bitner a free hand and he soon earned the respect and admiration of the entire staff. He was a versatile man who wrote the lyrics and composed the music for all the annual shows produced by the Filene staff.

Harold D. Hodgkinson, a Yale graduate, came to Filene's in 1912, and was hired by Ernest Martin Hopkins, employment manager, who later became president of Dartmouth College. The new employee began by addressing envelopes. With a warm and friendly personality, he soon became manager of Filene's bargain basement. In 1956, when Lincoln Filene was made chairman of the board, Hodgkinson became president. When Filene died at 92 a year later, Hodgkinson succeeded him as chairman. He is now chairman of the executive committee.

The Lincoln and Theresa Filene Foundation, the post of Lincoln Filene Professor of Retailing at Harvard, and Filene Hall at Bates College were established in honor of Lincoln Filene.

Hodgkinson served from time to time on many boards and as president of RRA-AMC. In addition to his Yale education, he studied at Harvard Graduate Business School, which later awarded him the distinction of being the first Yale man ever to become a governor of the Harvard Club of Boston.

Maurice Lazarus, son of Fred Lazarus, Jr., chairman of the board of Federated, became president in 1958. He had been executive vice-president of Foley's, a Federated store at Houston, Texas, before joining Filene's. He rose to board chairman of the Boston company in 1964 and was succeeded as president by Harold Krensky, who joined Filene's in 1960 as executive vice-president and general manager. In 1965, Lazarus became a vice-chairman of Federated Department Stores and Krensky stepped up to the Filene chairmanship and chief executive officer. Richard G. Shapiro, 40, was appointed president.

Shapiro had risen at Lord & Taylor from a merchandise control assistant in 1948 to senior vice-president.

In recent years, Filene's has put added emphasis on wide assortments of medium-to-better price merchandise, instead of competing closely on a price basis. In this long-range trading-up program, the store is following the success formula of Bloomingdale's, New York, of which Krensky was formerly a senior vice-president.

Filene's had estimated sales of from $130 to $135 million in 1964. Its main Boston store, occupying 580,000 square feet, accounted for $80 to $85 million of this; the basement alone, for about $30 million. Eight Filene branches in Braintree, Peabody, Worcester, Chestnut Hill, Belmont, Wellesley, Winchester, and Hyannis were responsible for about $50 million, the Northshore (Peabody) unit for almost $10 million of this total. A Natick branch was added in 1965.

CHAPTER 12

G. FOX & CO.

HARTFORD, CONNECTICUT

"To build an institution that will never know completion" —MOSES FOX

The nationally known G. Fox & Co. began modestly in 1847, when Gerson Fox, a young man of vision from New York, opened a one-room specialty shop in Hartford. It was known as a "fancy" store because it stocked such items as buttons, cords, silk fringes, and tassels. Gerson's son, Moses, joined him in 1863 and at the father's death in 1880 assumed the management.

In January, 1917, the five-story building in which the store was housed was destroyed by fire. With it went nearly all the credit records, including the January bills that were ready for mailing. Although Moses Fox was 66 at the time, he announced that work would begin on a new 11-story establishment. Then, in one of the most heartfelt tributes in American mercantile history, many of Moses Fox's charge-account customers came to his temporary office and paid in full, from memory, bills for which there were no records. This included the large amounts due on Christmas purchases and totaled hundreds of thousands of dollars, providing ample funds for the new construction.

In the meantime, Moses Fox rented any space available in local buildings, including a vacant church. His reserve inventory, housed in a separate warehouse, had not been damaged. A year after the fire, the new store opened, prospered, and grew.

Moses Fox's daughter, Beatrice Fox Auerbach, began assisting her father in the store in 1929, replacing her husband, George S. Auerbach, who had died two years earlier. The management fell to her at the death of her father in 1938. As president and treasurer, she has devoted her life to seeing that the company retains its rank as one of the best stores in America.

Until the company's acquisition in late 1965 by May Department Stores Co., Mrs. Auerbach owned the majority of the stock. Her sister, Mrs. L. R. Samuels, was a minority stockholder and vice-president and secretary but was not active in the management. Mrs. Samuels is also secretary of Auerbach Company, Salt Lake City, Utah, which has no financial connection with G. Fox. Leslie R. Samuels, her husband, is president of the Salt Lake department store and of L. R. Samuels Company, Ogden, Utah, specialty store.

Samuel I. Einstein, who came from Macy's to Fox as controller in 1930, was appointed general merchandise manager in 1954. He was also vice-president until his retirement in 1965. Mrs. Auerbach's two sons-in-law are in the business: Richard Koopman, vice-president in charge of store planning, construction, and maintenance; and Bernard W. Schiro, vice-president, merchandise manager of children's and infants' wear, and also in planning. Other vice-presidents are Maurice H. Berins, with the company since 1929, who is superintendent of the store; and Solomon Katzen, active in the financial management.

There are seven divisional merchandise managers, including the manager of the lower-price basement. Amy Fagan, formerly fashion co-ordinator at Macy's, came to Fox in the same capacity and was later made divisional manager of ready-to-wear. Fifty-three main-store buyers plus nine basement buyers complete the Fox merchandising organization.

Divisional managers and buyers spend most of their Saturdays on the floor in order to supervise selling and have some direct contact with customers. This conforms to Mrs. Auerbach's concept of buyers as department managers who assume full responsibility for expense control and selling service. After important new items are purchased, the department managers hold staff meetings to discuss selling points of the new products.

Others in the top organization include the controller, publicity director, personnel manager, general superintendent and maintenance superintendent. All of these hold co-ordinate positions and each reports directly to Mrs. Auerbach as president and general manager. Having the personnel manager report directly to her reflects the deep interest Mrs. Auerbach has in good employee relations.

The extent of the organization is reflected in these figures: A staff of 80, all of them specialists, work in the maintenance department. The maintenance men handle 300 to 400 trouble calls a day, two of them just changing light bulbs. Two-way escalators are safety-checked daily and firemen make daily inspection trips to eliminate fire and accident hazards.

In one of the store's unusual departments, 15 registered pharmacists are employed to fill and triple-check the 3,000 prescriptions compounded every week.

Six registered nurses assist customers and employees. Two operate the four-bed ward for women; two, the two-bed ward for men and the treatment and waiting rooms; another helps new mothers select layettes; and the sixth assists women in corset selection. The nurses also check by telephone or pay a personal visit to employees on sick leave for three days. Hospital records show nearly 14,000 treatments and visits a year.

The Fox beauty salon, one of the largest in the country, employs 45 experienced operators. The women's alteration department employs 63.

While most large department stores have only one public restaurant, the Fox store has three. Style shows presented during the luncheon hour provide good publicity. Price tags are visible from a distance and customers are encouraged to stop the models for closer inspection of the garments. Resulting sales often include the accessories shown. The store also provides services not found in many American department stores. These include an optical department, travel bureau, post office, radio repair, shoe repair, jewelry and watch repair. A special photo service shows brides-to-be in their Fox-furnished bridal gown and extra photos are furnished free for the society pages of local newspapers.

Although the store is closed on Mondays, telephone orders on the 90-place board are accepted and relayed to the selling departments to any one of 48 order clerks. A busy day brings 20,000 calls, requiring the full-time services of 14 experienced operators. Twenty per cent are collect calls, accepted by the store from anywhere in the state. Mail orders from former customers living out of state or even in foreign countries reflect patrons' loyalty to the store.

The store's far-ranging public relations efforts are symbolized by Centinel Hill Hall, on the top floor, seating 1,100, as well as by adjoining clubrooms. The facilities are offered free to charitable, educational, civic, and cultural groups. The store provides attendants, furnishes models for fashion shows, and prepares meals in an adjacent kitchen.

The air-conditioned Fox store puts its main emphasis on quality merchandise and superior service. It does not dwell on low prices, although it makes every reasonable effort to meet local competition. Five experienced shoppers check daily items featured by other local stores and make purchases for comparison with their own merchandise. Markdowns are made immediately, if warranted.

Nearly every year, Mrs. Auerbach makes a trip abroad. She knows most of the important foreign department stores and visits them. Moreover, she usually places some orders with foreign manufacturers through her buying representatives. These have included items for the Fox boutique shop, gloves from Italy, glass from Yugoslavia, mats from India, sweaters from Sweden, and a variety of items from South Africa. During her absences, Sam Einstein serves as general manager.

When Mrs. Auerbach returns, she usually tells her staff about

the highlights of her trip and local newsmen are granted interviews in which she stresses the modes of living of the people
and some of the major problems their respective governments
are facing. Generally shunning personal publicity, this is about
the only time the local press is permitted to interview her for
direct quotation.

The regular daily routes of the Fox fleet of 147 delivery vans
cover most of Connecticut, Holyoke, Northampton, and Springfield in Massachusetts, and parts of Rhode Island and New
York State. Two million packages are handled annually. The
store also enjoys a large mail-order volume. Free parcel post is
given on orders sent anywhere in the New England states as
well as to New York, New Jersey, Pennsylvania, Delaware,
Maryland, and Washington, D. C. Free express and freight
shipments are provided for customers in Connecticut, Massachusetts, and Rhode Island. Fox is believed to be the only store
in the country offering such liberal free-delivery service.

G. Fox & Company employs 2,300 full-time workers and
1,200 part-time extras, many of them former regular employees,
for holiday seasons and special sales. About 75 per cent of the
total staff is female, and three-fourths of the regulars are in
nonselling departments. New employees are put through a
two-week course, during which they spend half a day in class
learning policy, procedure, and organization and the other half
day on a selling floor. Labor turnover is extremely low. Those
who show above-average ability go on to the junior-executive
training course so that management can continue to promote
from within.

The selling staff handles 21,000 transactions a day. These
range from a few minutes required to complete a sale of notions
to an hour or more that may be needed to conclude a sale of
major household appliances or furniture.

Daily, 16 employees are invited to lunch at a special Family
Circle table in the employee cafeteria. Store executives host the
table Tuesdays through Fridays; Mrs. Auerbach, on Saturdays.
She leads luncheon discussions and often obtains useful suggestions for improving departments.

In addition to pay based on periodic reviews of their job performance and seniority, Fox employees receive many fringe benefits. Discounts on items purchased for store use are liberal. All employees are given a 20-minute break in mid-afternoon for a snack. They buy their lunches at actual cost and the food is of the same high quality served in the store's public restaurants. Employees may obtain loans from the Theresa Stern Fox Fund. No interest is charged and payments may be as little as $1 or $2 a week.

Employees are eligible for retirement at 65 but may remain until 70. Those who remain usually are members of the Moses Fox Club for employees with the store 25 to 50 years. Mrs. Auerbach presides at a dinner given each January for this group. A 25-year pin and watch are given new members, appropriate gifts to the 50-year members. Those who do retire can draw from a retirement fund wholly financed by the management. A personal letter written by Mrs. Auerbach is sent each month with the pension checks. Veteran retired employees are also remembered in other ways. The store's nurses check on their condition from time to time and visit those who are hospitalized. At Christmas, Mrs. Auerbach visits as many retired employees as her time permits.

Since Fox was founded in 1847, there have been constant additions and changes. The chapter covering Harrods of London reveals its many striking similarities to G. Fox & Company. Both were established about the same time. Both stores had fires that destroyed the stores and merchandise. Both rebuilt and opened larger stores. Both provide numerous services not found in other stores. Both operate three public restaurants. And, finally, both have been managed by three generations of the same family—Fox by Gerson and Moses Fox and Mrs. Auerbach; Harrods by the Burbidges, the first Sir Richard, his son, Woodman, and Woodman's son, the second Sir Richard Burbidge.

Thomas J. Carroll, retired vice-president and general manager of Frederick Atkins, buying office for the Fox store, remarked: "G. Fox & Company is one of the country's distinctive and progressive family-owned stores. The store is quality-minded in all areas of merchandising and is eager to be the first with the new and important trends and items.

"The tradition of integrity, fair dealing with customers as well as resources, community service, and employee welfare are the guide lines that make this store dominant on a statewide basis and even beyond. Mrs. Beatrice Fox Auerbach, president, is the dynamic and creative personality behind the growth and development of G. Fox & Company. Complacency is not in her vocabulary or in the minds of her associates. There is a sense of 'go' and direction toward building a stronger image in the years ahead."

Until now, the company has had no branches because Mrs. Auerbach doesn't believe that little department stores all over the place give the kind of service the customer requires. She veered from this policy some years ago when the first of a planned series of roadside Fox-Marts was opened, but this venture was soon discontinued. However, branches are likely to be opened under May ownership.

Most persons interested in retailing feel that an "image" of a store is not complete without knowing the annual sales of the store under review, yet many important stores do not reveal their sales. Others, such as Marshall Field and Macy's, lump the annual sales of their parent stores with their branches and other stores they operate under separate names. Fox's volume exceeds $60 million, largest of any department store in New England outside of Boston where only Jordan Marsh and Filene's precede it. Within the past few years, over a half-million square feet have been added to the store, more than doubling its space. The company also operates a 500,000-square-foot warehouse for reserve stock.

Since 1936, G. Fox has owned Brown-Thomson Company, which directly adjoins the Fox establishment and is separately operated. Volume is $6 million.

For the fiscal year ended January 30, 1965, Fox's earned $2,042,287 on sales of $61,807,836. Mrs. Auerbach and her family exchanged their privately held stock for 720,000 shares of May common stock with a market value at the time of the transaction of about $41 million. Mrs. Auerbach continues as president and is also a vice-president of May.

CHAPTER 13

FREDERICK &

NELSON

SEATTLE, WASHINGTON

"Fredericks-Division of Marshall Field & Co."

Donald E. Frederick left his father's cotton plantation at Marshallville, Georgia, to grow hops in the West and founded a leading department store in Seattle instead.

In Colorado, he met two men who became his close friends and partners. They were Nels Nelson, a native of Sweden, who had spent his boyhood in Chicago and was then engaged in mining ventures and the cattle business, and James Meecham, a quiet, industrious plumbing-supply man who wanted to travel farther west.

Meecham, the first to reach Seattle, developed a prosperous plumbing business with second-hand stoves as a side line. Frederick was next to arrive and, with a $500 investment, became Meecham's partner. Soon, Nelson joined them, worked in the store, and finally bought out Meecham.

It was in 1890, in a Seattle with a population of 43,000, that Frederick & Nelson was formed. Business boomed under the two partners and, soon, second-hand furniture became more important than stoves. In 1891, the partners moved to larger quarters and began to sell carpets and new furniture. They continued to add new lines and even during the 1893 depression had small sales gains. Many sales were on a barter basis, the partners accepting baled hay, shingles, gold dust, and other items in payment.

When additional capital was needed, a man named Silas Munro supplied it and became a partner. The firm name was changed to Frederick, Nelson & Munro in 1893.

The depression vanished almost overnight with the discovery of gold in Alaska, and Seattle was the focal point for the great influx of prospectors. When the ship, *Portland,* docked in 1897, loaded with miners and $1 million in gold, Seattle became one of the most famous seaports in the world. In the 10 years since Frederick arrived in the city, the population had nearly doubled and the store with 90 employees was expanding rapidly.

Munro felt that it was growing too quickly and in 1900 sold his interest to the other two partners. Again, the store name became Frederick & Nelson.

The partners added piece goods and men's and women's wear, and the home furnishing store became a department store. In 1906, they assumed the lease of an adjoining dry goods company on Second and Spring. This gave the company the entire Second Avenue frontage. Upper stories of First Avenue buildings were connected to other structures with overhead bridges.

A year later, Nels Nelson died at sea while returning from a European vacation, but Frederick decided that Nelson should be part of the firm name as long as he remained in business.

With his usual foresight, Frederick planned to acquire property and erect a model department store large enough to meet the needs of his growing business for decades to come.

After studying various locations, he chose Pine Street between Fifth and Sixth Avenues, far from the retail center of 1916. It was dubbed Frederick's Folly. Old buildings on the site were razed and work on the excavation and foundation had been done when World War I scarcity of building materials interrupted construction. The building, completed in 1918 on the site it occupies today, was regarded as the most beautiful department store in the West.

On opening day in July, 1918, more than 25,000 persons went through the store. Letters, telegrams, and cables came from all parts of the world. Masses of flowers turned the store into a garden. Frederick stood on the first floor, greeting old and new friends. In its new location, the store made impressive gains and other retailers began to relocate in order to share in the traffic the department store attracted.

Frederick & Nelson joined RRA-AMC. In October, 1929, on the way home from a meeting held at Old Point Comfort, Virginia, Frederick stopped in Chicago where the sale of Frederick & Nelson to Marshall Field & Company was arranged. Frederick was 69 years old, had no male heirs to manage the store, and the sale made it possible for him to retire as he wished to do. He apparently reached an understanding with Field's to continue the firm name of Frederick & Nelson and to make only minimum changes in the top organization. The Seattle store was then doing $12 million.

William H. St. Clair, who had been with Frederick & Nelson for four years, was named president and general manager. A newcomer, William S. Street, became assistant general manager. A native of Oakland, California, he had begun his retailing career with Hale Bros., San Francisco, in 1923.

Thomas J. Carroll, who had been representing Frederick & Nelson at RRA-AMC headquarters, transferred to Field's New York buying office and shortly was appointed as its head. Later, Carroll became vice-president and general manager of Frederick Atkins, Inc., a co-operative buying office for a group of outstanding stores.

An office was set aside for Frederick's sole use, but the founder spent most of his time playing golf, fishing, hunting, and riding. He died of pneumonia at 77 at his Seattle home in July, 1937. At his death, the Seattle *Post Intelligencer* said:

Seattle lost one of its most distinguished citizens and one of the best known. Paradoxically, he also was one of the least known. His department store made the name Frederick's . . . almost a household word but his aversion to personal publicity kept him entirely out of the public eye.

Frederick & Nelson's advertising, direct-mail pieces and catalogs are reminders that the store is a division of Marshall Field & Company. But its customers and the public know the store only as Frederick's and will probably call it so to the end of time. A very modest man unwittingly perpetuated his name by erecting one of the most beautiful stores in the nation.

St. Clair retired in 1943 and Street succeeded him as president and general manager but was transferred to Chicago almost immediately as general manager of Field's and its branches. Street left Seattle reluctantly and only with the understanding that he would return at the end of the war emergency. St. Clair came back to act as president, and Hector Escobosa, who had joined the store in 1939, was made general merchandise manager.

In December, 1943, St. Clair died. Charles C. Bunker, a vice-president of Field's, was appointed president of Frederick & Nelson and Escobosa became general manager of the store. Two years later, when Bunker retired, Street finally returned to Frederick & Nelson.

Street and Escobosa, working together in complete harmony, had many postwar problems to solve. One was to overcome the prolonged shortage of merchandise that develped during World War II.

In April, 1946, Frederick & Nelson played host to 36 of the nation's top designers, heralding the return of fashion merchandise in Seattle. That same year, a new suburban store was opened in Bellevue, and Escobosa made the first buying trip abroad since before the war. With amazing speed, American ingenuity achieved the tremendous task of supplying consumer commodities to meet five years of unfilled demands.

In June, 1949, Field's board of directors met for the first time in Seattle and approved plans presented by Street and Escobosa for enlargement of the store. Five new stories, added at a cost of $6,250,000, gave the store 12 floors and increased space by 50 per cent. An adjoining parking garage was constructed later.

In 1951, Escobosa left to become president of I. Magnin & Company, San Francisco. Street retired in January, 1962, and C. J. Byrne, who had worked for Mandel Brothers and the May Company before joining Frederick & Nelson in 1946, succeeded him as president and general manager. Byrne had been a vice-president of both Marshall Field & Company and Frederick & Nelson.

In 1963, M. L. Storhow was named vice-president and general operating manager of Frederick & Nelson downtown, the larger Bellevue store, opened in 1956, and the Aurora Village unit. Beginning as a salesman in the book department in 1927, he had become general manager of Bellevue in 1956 and of Aurora Village when it opened in 1963.

Frederick's sales are not broken down from those of Marshall Field but an estimate is that the Seattle subsidiary is in the $35 to $40 million range.

CHAPTER 14

GARDNERS

WALLA WALLA, WASHINGTON

"The Oldest Department Store in the State"

Three brothers, Abe, Louis, and Sigmund Schwabacher, in 1860 founded the store now known as Gardners. This was two years before Walla Walla was incorporated as a town and 29 years before Washington became a state. The three, originally from San Francisco, operated a flourishing store in Seattle before opening the Walla Walla establishment on a much-traveled Indian trail that later became the city's main street. Gardners to this day occupies the original site. The Schwabachers treated both Indian and white fairly and, as a result, Indians as well as whites became loyal customers.

The brothers opened additional stores in Boise and Idaho Falls, Idaho, and at Colfax and Dayton in Washington about the time of the Civil War—undoubtedly the first department store chain in the Far West, if not in the entire country.

An extensive grain and milling business in the 1880's with connections in the East and in San Francisco, then the marketing outlet for the Pacific Coast, enabled them to handle sales of oats, wheat, and brewing barley for local growers. Most of the merchandise for the store came from San Francisco. Whatever came from Seattle was unloaded at Walula, about thirty miles from Walla Walla, and delivered overland by wagons or pack mules.

The barter system was prevalent. Customers traded butter, eggs, and other local products to the store for merchandise. Even butter unfit for table use was accepted and processed with other ingredients and converted into a profitable lubricant for farm use.

J. M. Fitzgerald and H. A. Gardner joined the Schwabacher Walla Walla store in the 1880's. After 25 years, both men became partners and the firm name was changed to Schwabacher & Company.

Fitzgerald, born in the north of Ireland, was a bachelor who lived in a small basement room in the store. He was a good "mixer" and well liked by everyone, particularly children to whom he gave candy or gum. He was a hard worker, living only for the store where he stood at the entrance to greet and chat with customers.

Gardner, a native of Maine, developed a reputation as a shrewd but fair "Yankee Trader." In 1910, when the Schwabacher brothers decided to operate their store and grain business from Seattle, Fitzgerald and Gardner acquired the Walla Walla outlet. Gardner became president and Fitzgerald vice-president and the firm name became Gardner & Company. Enlarged immediately, it became the largest store in northeastern Washington. The store had first occupied an existing building. In 1862, a two-story brick structure was erected and a still larger store was built in 1876. In 1910, old buildings were razed and a new one built of steel and stone. This structure was remodeled and modernized in 1953.

Gardner's son, Ward, joined the firm in 1912, and in 1928, two years after Gardner died, Ward became president, a position he still holds. Fitzgerald died in 1931.

In 1942, Ward Gardner and his two sisters, Mrs. William Steel and Elizabeth Gardner, purchased all the store's stock. Sixteen years later, Ward Gardner became sole owner. At the time he became president, he decided to make Gardners the headquarters in Walla Walla for nationally advertised brands.

Schwabacher had made a beginning in this direction as far back as 1898 when the store promoted men's clothing and shoes by name. As brands became important, Gardner had certain ones confined to his store. Now, most of the best-known brands can be found locally only at Gardners.

The firm has operated a profitable grocery department since the business opened. Although staple grocery sections were found in most large department stores 50 years ago, they became unprofitable and were closed when self-service groceries emerged on a cash-and-carry basis. But low overhead expense is the principal reason for the growth of supermarkets. In supermarkets, it is only about 16 per cent of sales, while for the average department store it is 33 per cent.

Gardners, nevertheless, has been able to operate the grocery department profitably even though the goods are delivered daily and carried on the regular monthly charge account. The department is in a wing with a separate street entrance and a rear entrance leading to the main store. Phone orders are encouraged and two telephone lines are in constant use. Customers who like the convenience of telephone grocery shopping often add items from other departments to their list.

Gardners constantly reminds customers the store is home-owned and not a member of a chain. Descendants of Washington pioneers find added pleasure in shopping at Gardners because many daughters of pioneers are employed in the store.

The store staff totals 80, and most of the extra help for busy periods are former employees. The average length of service is more than eight years and labor turnover has not been a problem.

Gardners is a junior department store because its limited space does not permit china, glassware, housewares, beds, bedding, furniture, or major household appliances. Sales lost by not carrying these items are made up in part by the grocery department volume. There are no "loss" departments in the store and total annual sales reach over $1 million.

In addition to being sole owner and president, Ward Gardner serves as his own general merchandise manager and buys for two departments. He employs six buyers, each of whom spends much time supervising and assisting in the selling. This constant direct contact with customers enables the buyer to understand customer merchandise preferences.

Gardner, one of Walla Walla's most highly respected citizens, has served as president of the Chamber of Commerce and of the Washington and Idaho Clothiers and Furnishers Association.

The late Al Jolson remarked that residents of Walla Walla must love their city because they named it twice. To this could be added that most of the residents would think twice before shopping other local stores for items carried by Gardners, Walla Walla's friendly home-owned store.

CHAPTER 15

GIMBEL BROTHERS, INC.

BROADWAY & 33RD STREET
NEW YORK CITY

Adam Gimbel: "Had Gun—Did Travel"

Twenty-year-old Adam Gimbel began his retailing career with a stock of merchandise on his back and a rifle for protection. He had arrived in New Orleans, Louisiana, four years earlier in 1835 from his family's farm in Bavaria. In New Orleans, he worked on the docks unloading cotton bales, and saved enough money to buy his first stock.

Indians, Creoles, farmers, and woodsmen were Gimbel's early customers. A horse and wagon enabled him to extend his trading area. As a result of paying a tribal chief the equivalent of $30 for furs and building a reputation for fair dealing, Gimbel was permitted to trade on tribal hunting grounds. The rugged young man also was respected by his white customers, many of whom invited him to remain overnight.

At first, Gimbel replenished his stock at New Orleans, but later increased the variety of his offerings through buying trips to Philadelphia. On his first trip to Philadelphia, Gimbel met Fridoline Kahnweiler, a dry goods merchant's daughter, whom he later married. Their seven sons were born in Vincennes, Indiana, where Gimbel established his first store in 1842, the beginning of a group of department and apparel specialty stores that now reach from coast to coast.

The first store prospered and additions were made to keep pace with an increasing trade. When, in 1887, Gimbel decided to open a new department store in Milwaukee, the Vincennes store was closed.

Seven years later, through the *Saturday Evening Post,* a magazine published in Philadelphia and having an extensive national circulation even then, Adam Gimbel announced the opening of a Philadelphia store. But he died that same year, and his sons, Jacob, Isaac, Charles, Daniel, Ellis A., Louis S., and Benedict continued the firm. Isaac became president and in 1909, Isaac's son, Bernard, became vice-president at 24. A year later, the New York City store opened at its present location.

Locating the new Gimbel store so near Macy's 34th Street location was an audacious move. Macy's had convinced a large segment of the public that its prices were at least 6 per cent lower than those in other local stores. But Gimbels felt that its strongly promoted low-price bargain basement would enable it to meet competition.

Although Gimbels became a public corporation in 1922, a member of the founding family has always been at the helm. An organization of top-flight executives was developed to complement the Gimbel management in each store. In 1923, Gimbels acquired the then 21-year-old Saks store at 34th Street and Broadway. Under the new management, the specialty shop continued to carry medium to better merchandise.

Before Saks Fifth Avenue opened in 1924, its founder, Andrew Saks, died and his son, Horace, developed it with Adam Long Gimbel, son of Charles Gimbel, as his assistant. Adam Gimbel became president when Horace Saks died in 1926. Adam Gimbel's wife, Sophie, is the designer of exclusive fashions sold only in Saks stores.

Gimbels acquired the Kaufmann & Baer department store in Pittsburgh, in 1925, and later its name was changed to Gimbel Brothers.

Bernard F. Gimbel, son of Isaac Gimbel, aptly referred to as a "merchant prince," has never lost the "common touch." In 1945, *Fortune* magazine extolled him as top merchant of that year. In the article, Bernard Gimbel summed up his success by saying: "As a young man, many years ago, I learned a great deal about human relations in a very practical way from my father. . . .

"I never heard him reprimand or say anything unpleasant to one person in the presence of another. It was his habit to call the individual to his office, and first tell him about something he had done well. Then he would take up that part of the job that had not been up to standard. I believe that we must constantly encourage and help those around us from the top all the way down the line."

Bernard Gimbel became chairman of the board in 1953 and his son, Bruce, became the fourth generation Gimbel to head the business. Born July 28, 1913, Bruce joined the firm in 1935 and was vice-president of Saks for seven years prior to heading Gimbel Brothers, Inc. The fifth generation is represented by Bruce's son, Robert, who in 1965 was made manager of active sportswear at Saks Fifth Avenue after having been manager of Saks' branch in Surfside, Florida.

Gimbel Bros. and Saks Fifth Avenue are operated as separate subsidiaries of the parent corporation.

There are 18,000 employees in the 49 stores of the group which includes 23 Gimbel stores and 26 Saks Fifth Avenue stores. Saks-34th's main store ceased operations in the summer of 1965 and three branches became Gimbels New York units. These are in Massapequa Park and Commack, Long Island, and Stamford, Conn., and do an estimated $7 million. A 217,000-square-foot store is opening in 1966 in King of Prussia in the Philadelphia region as a branch of the main store in that city.

In addition to the Kaufmann & Baer store, Gimbels purchased the capital stock of Lockhart's in St. Louis, Missouri, in

1956, and the assets of the four Ed Schuster & Co. stores in Milwaukee, Wisconsin, in 1962.

Gimbel Brothers' volume for the 12 months ended January 31, 1964, was $536,008,000; its net profit, $14,913,000. Saks Fifth Avenue does $160 million, more than half of it in the New York metropolitan area.

CHAPTER 16

HAGER & BRO., INC.

LANCASTER, PENNSYLVANIA

"One of the Oldest Department Stores in America"

Hager & Bro., Inc., of Lancaster, Pennsylvania, one of the oldest department stores in America, was founded by Christopher Hager in 1821. It is still located at the original site and is under the management of the fourth and fifth generations of the founding family.

At the time Hager founded the store in a 20-by-25-foot room, the town already had a long history. Incorporated three years before, it had served as the capital of Pennsylvania from 1799 to 1812, as the site of William Penn's treaty with the Indians, and as meeting place for the Continental Congress in 1717 when the Congress was driven from Philadelphia by the British.

The original Hager stock included groceries, dry goods and china, offered at "the most reduced prices." Four times a year, Hager went to Philadelphia to replenish his stocks.

Customers were granted credit for six months to a year, depending on the sale of their crops, and the store prospered from the start.

Christopher's son, John C. Hager, began working in the store at 14 years of age. In 1848 when he was 22, he was made president. The founder died in 1868 in his 69th year. John C. Hager continued as president until 1897, when his son, William H. Hager, Sr., was made president, continuing as head of the organization until 1939.

To name all the Hagers who contributed to the store's development would be more confusing than informative. William H. Hager, Sr., towered above all the rest. He joined the store in 1885, after his graduation from Franklin & Marshall College, and became a partner in 1890.

In 1911, a new building was constructed with a basement and four selling floors. With an addition in 1925, the building still houses the store. The firm was incorporated as Hager & Bro., Inc., in 1926.

In 1932, when a group of leading Pennsylvania retailers was called together to form a statewide organization to prevent re-enactment of a retail sales tax, William Hager, Sr., was elected the first president of the Pennsylvania Retailers Association. Re-elected for 11 successive terms, he resigned in 1943 because of ill health. He was also a founder of the National Retail Dry Goods Association and a trustee and treasurer of the American Retail Federation when it was founded in 1936. Upon his resignation in 1943, the Federation cited Hager as an outstanding example of the finest kind of merchant, a symbol of the right kind of co-operation between merchants.

Edward T. Hager, a son of William H., Sr., served as store president from 1939 to 1956, and William H., Jr., from 1956 to his death in 1962. The last-named was president of the Pennsylvania Retailers from 1959 to 1962 during which time the organization actively opposed Sunday shopping. Nathaniel E. Hager succeeded his brother, William H., Jr., as president and general manager. At the same time, John C. and Redmond C. Hager, two other brothers, were respectively elected first vice-president and general merchandise manager and second vice-president as well as a divisional merchandise manager. John R. Hager, son of John C., is treasurer and store manager. William

H. Hager III, son of William H., Jr., is secretary and a divisional merchandise manager.

The store has its own garage in which customer parking is validated for an hour on a $2 purchase.

The store's basement is used for delivery and reserve stock as well as selling space for appliances, television, radio, china, housewares, toys, and garden supplies. Stock rooms also are located on each selling floor.

The store has some private brands, most of them developed by Arkwright, its New York buying office. A number of nationally advertised brands are confined to Hager's in the area.

The store offers two-week paid vacations to regular employees after one year and three weeks to executives and members of the quarter-century club. Employees receive a 20 per cent discount on most purchases. Promotions are made from within when possible. When an employee reaches 65, his work is evaluated very closely on a year-to-year basis, but Hager's has no compulsory retirement age and no formal pension plan. Full-time employees number 200, and 70 per cent of these are female. The Hager store carries all lines and has 24 buyers, 16 of whom are women. Being privately owned, Hager & Brother does not disclose figures, but sales are estimated to be in the $4 to $5 million bracket.

CHAPTER 17

HARRODS

LONDON, ENGLAND

"The Three Knights from Knightsbridge"

Harrods, the English department store known the world over, began under its present name when Henry Charles Harrod, in 1849, took over a little grocer's shop on Brompton Road in Knightsbridge, at the same site as the present store. At the time, Harrod, who had been a wholesale tea merchant, was 49 and had no ambitious plans to develop the grocery.

In 1861, his son, Charles Digby Harrod, took over the business and changed the name to C. D. Harrod, Grocer. Charles, then 20, was soon in trouble because of his honesty. He refused to continue the ancient custom of bribing the gentry's servants for their patronage and he didn't give credit. The business, like those of every small shopkeeper, was threatened by the rise of Co-ops, supplying civil servants and their friends with articles of all kinds at the lowest wholesale prices. To combat this, Harrod advertised goods at "cooperative prices."

About 1868, a cousin, William Kibble, joined Harrods and the store began to stock perfumes, stationery, and patent medicines. Brompton Road gentry also discovered that the fresh fruit and vegetables Kibble obtained from Covent Garden were as good as those bought in Piccadilly.

Sales increased and a two-story addition was erected in 1873. The company began selling cooked meat and game, china, confectionery, and flowers. Two adjacent shops were acquired by lease and more goods were added. A delivery van replaced the two boys who had delivered goods in baskets or hand-drawn trucks.

In 1870, when Harrods circulated a 65-page catalogue, there were 16 employees. In ten years, the staff numbered nearly 100, and by 1914 there were 6,000. As the store's reputation for quality was established, lower prices ceased to be emphasized.

On December 6, 1883, the premises, fully stocked for Christmas, were destroyed by fire. But, within three days, Harrod was again in business. With co-operation from both staff and suppliers, the store exceeded all previous records for Christmas business.

By September, 1884, a new store was opened with many departments enlarged and such new ones as brassware, silverware, saddlery, and trunks added.

In 1885, the cash policy was abandoned and limited credit was granted approved customers. This was the beginning of the large "sanction" office in Harrods' basement. By 1939, there were 100,000 account customers.

Henry Charles Harrod, the founder, died in 1885 at 85. Four years later, Charles, nearing 50 and in ill health, decided to retire. The business was turned into a limited liability company with capital of £140,000 in 1889. Charles received £120,000 for the firm. Alfred Newton, later Sir Newton, Lord Mayor of London, became chairman.

Shortly after Harrod stepped down from active management, there was an alarming drop in sales. Charles was asked to give up retirement temporarily until a general manager could be hired. When Richard Burbidge was induced to accept this position in March, 1891, Charles Harrod finally was able to retire to Sussex where he died in 1905 at 64.

Burbidge had earned a high reputation at the Army and Navy stores, at Whiteley's, and later at the West Kensington stores. When he accepted the Harrods position, he was 44. He gave fresh impetus to the store. He abolished the fines that had been imposed on tardy employees and reduced their working hours. As early as 1894, Burbidge set the store closing at 7 P.M. every night except Thursdays when the closing was at 4. He was thus a pioneer of early closing long before London shop hours were fixed by law. His consideration for the well-being of his staff began during a period in class-conscious England when women salesgirls were not rated very highly.

Through the 1890s, Harrods expanded rapidly. The store's cable and telegraphic address, "Everything, London," registered in 1894, is in use today. In that same year, all the frontage on Basil Street was acquired. By 1911, the entire block site belonged to Harrods. It covers 4½ acres. The store contains 588,-260 square feet of selling space in 200 departments. The basement is used only for the delivery department and reserve stock. At the top is another floor not used for selling but containing high-class "flats" known as Hans Mansions. The apartments have entrances separate from the store.

In 1898, Harrods installed its first escalator from the ground (main) floor to the "first" (in America, the second) floor. It handled 4,000 customers an hour. An attendant at the top was prepared to comfort with free cognac anyone flustered by the ride. Eventually, the escalator was extended to the fifth floor and 32 "lifts" (elevators) were installed.

By 1905, Harrods' sales had reached £2 million (nearly $10 million) annually.

In 1913, Harrods received from Queen Mary the first of its two royal warrants, the most prized award a British tradesman can receive. Later, another came from the King. The warrants read: "By appointment, suppliers of China, Glass and Fancy Goods, to her Majesty the Queen" and "By appointment, grocers and provision merchants, to his Majesty the King." These covered most of the items Harrods sold and added immeasurably to the store's prestige.

Harrods' Buenos Aires, Limited, was founded in 1913 and later incorporated the South American stores of Gath & Chaves. It is no longer connected with the London firm. Harrods acquired Dickins & Jones Ltd., London, in 1914; Kendal & Milne & Co., Manchester, in 1919; D. H. Evans & Co. Ltd., London, in 1928; John Walsh Ltd., Sheffield, in 1946; J. F. Rockhey Ltd., Torquay, in 1948; William Henderson & Sons Ltd., Liverpool, in 1949; and Rackhams Ltd., Birmingham, in 1956.

Richard Burbidge's son, Woodman, became general manager of the store in 1901 and managing director in 1917. He put all his energy and experience into the war effort and, because of his work between 1914 and 1918, was made a C.B.E., knighted commander of the Order of the British Empire, in 1919. In addition, he received high Belgium and Rumanian decorations for his wartime efforts in behalf of those countries.

Richard Burbidge, who had been granted a baronetcy in 1916, died May 31, 1917, and the second Knight of Knightsbridge, Sir Woodman Burbidge, assumed the management of the business.

The years immediately following the end of World War I were lean for all London stores. On top of that, Harrods had suffered a heavy financial loss over the failure of a project in Belgium, Harrods Continental Limited.

In 1919, Woodman's son, Richard, prepared for his future work in London by going to the United States for two years, working in selling and nonselling departments of several large stores and finally at Wanamaker's in New York. About the same time, Harrods opened an office in New York to sell its own ladies' handbags and other small leather goods, luggage, and English plum puddings for Christmas gifts. The office closed in about two years, chiefly because of the high import duty but also because style changes in handbags and lighter luggage made the domestic items better sellers in American stores.

In 1920, Sir Woodman attended an RRA-AMC meeting in St. Louis, Missouri and, as a result, Harrods became affiliated with the group.

Sir Woodman arranged a three-month leave for the author to

make surveys of Harrods' various store activities. This London assignment was the highlight of the author's 25 years of association with RRA-AMC. In 1925, he made a second survey at Harrods and one of his recommendations, approved immediately, was the sending of Harrods' training director to complete a course at the Prince School of Retailing at Simmons College, Boston.

Richard Burbidge was invaluable to AMC with the help he gave foreign offices. Harrods operated on the Continent through the AMC offices from their establishment in 1920. Harrods buyers go to Manchester for cottons, Sheffield for steelware, Ireland for linens, and Scotland for knit goods. These buyers make available any information concerning important developments in the English markets to the AMC London office and to visiting AMC buyers.

This co-operation has been helpful not only to the AMC but to English resources as well by increasing their export volume with AMC and other noncompeting American stores.

Harrods' buyers purchase for more than one department. There are no divisional merchandise managers to come between the buyer and general merchandise manager. In addition, they spend more time in the wholesale markets than do American buyers. From 1921 until his death in 1945, Woodman was chairman of Harrods. His son, Richard, became general manager in 1927 and managing director in 1935. He continued as managing director even when he became chairman, after his father's death.

It fell to Richard to ask for territorial troops at the time of Munich and the staff of Harrods responded magnificently, providing volunteers for all three services, and the Harrods detachment of special constables was the largest of any retail store in London. Because of his noteworthy contributions to the war effort, Sir Richard, the third baronet, was awarded the C.B.E. in the Honours List of 1945. The store fortunately escaped severe damage from World War II bombings. Harrods' "Estate" office, which sold and rented houses and managed estates for absent owners, was the only company property destroyed. It was in a detached building opposite the store on Brompton Road.

Woodman initiated some unusual provisions for the comfort and happiness of the staff during a period when other London stores gave such matters little thought. The staff had its own council, and a kind of parliament of representatives elected by individual departments held regular meetings during store hours. Through the council, the staff freely voices suggestions or recommendations which are considered carefully by the management.

A pleasant staff restaurant is maintained along with sitting and smoking rooms, a health clinic, and rooms for voluntary evening classes held without charge. Thrift clubs, co-operative banking, and a credit union also were established. The staff's sports club at Barnes offers varied recreational facilities.

A visit to Harrods is an interesting and rewarding experience for Americans. As in Selfridge's, the first store in London inviting visitors to browse around, Harrods' assistants (sales personnel) do not importune visitors to buy.

Harrods' perishables department, with a nationwide reputation, has fresh fruits and vegetables in season, and out-of-season produce from the Continent.

Unusual gifts, many of them imports from the Old World countries, are found in great variety.

Harrods has a women's beauty salon, separate barber shops for children and men, car hire, catering for parties, china and glass repairs, shoe repairs, ticket reservations for concerts and plays, a travel agency, and post office. Orders are taken for piano tuning, for coal and wood, and for moving and storage of household furnishings. The store arranges funerals, sells real estate and insurance, and hires out servants.

Harrods won't supply a full-dress suit or tuxedo, but an assistant in men's wear will tell where one may be obtained and inform the visitor what dress is required at various functions and events. Work shops, in a separate building, turn out such products as leather goods, saddles, and printed stationery on special order.

In 1959, when two of England's department and specialty store giants, Debenhams and House of Fraser, fought for financial control of Harrods, the stock reached fantastic highs. On August 25, 1959, the House of Fraser gained control and became Britain's No. 1 department store organization. The honor cost Hugh Fraser $80 million. The Harrods group volume was estimated at $90 million at the time, of which the main store contributed about $50 million. Harrods employs 5,200 persons.

When Hugh Fraser assumed control, several Harrods directors resigned and others were deposed. Sir Richard Burbidge was induced to remain temporarily to have a stabilizing effect on the store staff during the transition period. He retired at the end of January, 1961, and became director of British Home Stores, Ltd., a chain of variety stores with outlets throughout England. His son, John Burbidge, who had joined the store in 1952 and become general merchandise manager in 1957, continued at Harrods as sales manager. Sir Richard died in February, 1966, at 68.

Alfred Spence, at 45, became managing director of Harrods in 1961. Spence had joined the Fraser organization when he was 19 after beginning as a junior salesman in a Perth, Scotland, store when he was only 14. He became general manager of a Fraser store, Arnott Simpsons, Glasgow, when he was 23. In 1948, he became a director of the House of Fraser when it changed to a public company with authorized capital of £1,-000,000.

House of Fraser, which has 75 department and specialty stores in the group and employs 30,000, began in 1849 with a shop on Buchanan Street, Glasgow. Hugh Fraser and James Arthur were partners in the firm of Arthur & Fraser, Arthur concentrating on the wholesale business and Fraser on the retail. In 1859, they separated, Fraser continuing at the head of Fraser & Sons until 1877 when he died at 55. His son, the second Hugh Fraser, continued to develop the business and, in turn, his son, now Sir Hugh Fraser, entered the retail firm in 1920, becoming chairman when his father died in 1926. House of Fraser's annual sales are in the $300 million range. The Har-

rods group—four in London, four in the provinces—probably
account for one-third of that of the entire chain. The Harrods
store in London's exclusive Knightsbridge—only one to carry
the name—does more than $50 million, which makes it the No.
1 volume-producer for a single retail unit in the British Isles.
Besides Harrods' main store, House of Fraser's six leading stores
include Wylie & Lochhead Ltd., Glasgow; Rackhams Ltd.,
Birmingham; Patrick Thomsons, Edinburgh; John Barker & Co.
Ltd., London; Kendal Milne, Manchester; and Binns Ltd., Sun-
derland.

CHAPTER 18

D. H. HOLMES
COMPANY, LTD.

NEW ORLEANS, LOUISIANA

"Sell to Others as You Would Buy for Yourself"

D. H. Holmes Company, Limited, another of America's earliest department stores, perpetuates the name of its founder, Daniel Henry Holmes who, in 1835 at 20, left Ohio to settle in New Orleans.

He opened his first small shop on Magazine Street three years later, operating it only five months a year. In April, 1842, he moved to Chartres Street, opened a larger store and employed five clerks. Although New Orleans had only 10,000 residents when the young pioneer tradesman decided to locate there, the population of the city increased rapidly, and the store's sales rose. So did the number of employees whom he urged to "Sell to others as you would buy for yourself." Holmes also believed "Good merchants make small profits and many sales."

Holmes' opening stock included fashions, linens, laces, and piece goods, most of them imported. There were no beauty shops and no cosmetics and the sewing machine had not been invented, but Holmes' store had a sewing section where piece goods were put together by hand and the customer finished the garment at home.

The store attracted customers and within four years moved to a much larger store on Canal Street. The same building, with many additions, is still occupied and Canal Street has become the busiest thoroughfare in the city. By 1860, Holmes was a full department store.

Holmes instituted many firsts in local store operation, several of them as wartime necessities:

During the Mexican War in 1845, he became the first to provide free delivery, using his own carriage driven by his own coachman. This service was started to provide army wives at Jackson Barracks, south of New Orleans, with merchandise they feared to carry personally through a wooded area alive with thieves.

During the Civil War, Holmes became the first to employ women as clerks when men went into military service. Eighty per cent of the store's employees still are women.

He was also the first to sell goods on a satisfaction-guaranteed basis but, when he felt himself victimized by a customer, he returned the individual's money with the request that he trade elsewhere.

Even in his first store, Holmes was partial to fine merchandise from foreign markets, much of it selected by him personally. Later, he opened his own buying office in Paris. His imported merchandise became a notable feature and established the firm early as a "quality" store. Until 1927, he also maintained a New York office and was thus in position to compare domestic-made goods with imports from England and the Continent.

There were several periods of adversity: Overflowing levees made some streets impassable for days, fires interrupted business, depressions had to be overcome. An epidemic of yellow fever in 1897 brought trade to a standstill, and shipments of merchandise from Northern wholesale markets were shut out during the Civil War. But Holmes never lost his faith in the future of his store.

In the 1880's, he took in as partners Samuel Geogehegan, who ran the office, and James T. Waller, who took charge of the buying operation in New York. Each received 25 per cent of the profits.

When Holmes died in 1898 at 83, Geogehegan took charge of the business. When he retired, it was operated by Dr. C. H. Thomas, a son-in-law of Holmes, and by Daniel H. Holmes, Jr. The firm incorporated in 1905 and Geogehegan returned to run the business until he died in 1906. There are no descendants or relatives of the partners in the business today.

The image the Holmes store projects locally is that of a friendly, quality store endeavoring to hold its customers and attract new ones by giving superior service. Its salespeople, for instance, are required to speak both English and French.

Of the 2,200 regular Holmes employees, 75 per cent are stockholders. And 95 per cent of all the stockholders live in Louisiana or Mississippi, retaining most of the firm's earnings in the areas it serves.

Hugh McC. Evans, who joined the store in 1934 and was successively a salesman in the men's department, assistant buyer, buyer, and merchandise manager, became the president and general manager in 1948.

In 1955, the Dalton Company, a department store in Baton Rouge, Louisiana, was purchased and its name changed to Holmes Downtown. Two smaller branches, Holmes Bon Marche and Holmes Delmont Village, also were opened in Baton Rouge, the state capital. In March, 1960, the largest of the Holmes suburban stores opened in Lakeside Shopping Center near New Orleans with the Halloway House cafeteria-restaurant under a leased arrangement.

In that same year, Holmes also opened a service building a block from its main New Orleans store and connected to it. The structure contains a freight dock that accommodates eight trucks and eliminates all sidewalk deliveries. Bulk merchandise goes on the first floor and the rest is moved by conveyer belts to the upper floors. The latest labor-saving appliances permit the automatic movement of goods, speed up procedures, and reduce labor costs. With their aid, women are able to move heavily laden trucks without any undue exertion. By pushing buttons, merchandise previously checked and marked is moved to the selling floors, to a reserve stock room, or set aside for a branch store. This building ranks Holmes as a pioneer in advanced methods of receiving, marking and distributing incoming merchandise.

Holmes also is a leader in insuring charge-account customers. The customer pays a nominal premium for a policy ranging from $250 to $2,000. On the death of the insured, the store deducts the amount owed it and pays the balance to the beneficiary.

The main store is a four-story structure, without basement, of 270,000 square feet.

The store's merchandise organization includes a general merchandise manager, five divisional merchandise managers, and 52 buyers who purchase all the merchandise, both domestic and foreign, for the main store and its branches.

Direct imports, it is estimated, constitute 3 per cent of the store's gross sales. Net sales for the fiscal year ended August 1, 1964 were $31,489,000 and net income was $614,000.

Since 1958, Holmes has been represented in New York and foreign countries by Frederick Atkins, Inc.

CHAPTER 19

HUDSON'S BAY COMPANY

WINNIPEG, CANADA

"The oldest chain store on the North American Continent"

The Hudson's Bay Company was established May 2, 1670, as "The Governor and Company of Adventurers of England Trading into Hudson's Bay" under a charter granted by King Charles II of England to Prince Rupert, the first governor. It is the oldest chartered trading company in existence. English settlers in 1607 had opened small shops in Jamestown, Virginia. These moved to Williamsburg, in 1698, but all were closed when Williamsburg ceased to be the capital of the British colony.

Hudson's Bay Company is a complex engaged not only in retailing but also in real estate, manufacturing, wholesaling, shipping, fur trapping, fur breeding, importing, and exporting. It is referred to by most Canadians as "The Bay." Canadian headquarters is Hudson's Bay House, Winnipeg.

About 80 per cent of the shares are owned by United Kingdom Proprietors, with principal administrative headquarters in Beaver Hall, Garlick Hill, London, England. Approximately 93 per cent of Hudson Bay's profits are earned in Canada. The board of governors meets regularly in London. Among its members until his death was Sir Winston Churchill, whose ancestor, John Churchill, Duke of Marlborough, was the company's third governor from 1685 to 1692.

During its early years, the company had to contend with Indians, white trappers, and French mercenaries from Montreal who constantly contested the exclusive trapping and hunting rights granted The Bay by the charter. It survived all these attacks, ultimately winning the confidence and support of the Indians by fair dealing.

For its first 200 years, the company was occupied solely in the fur trade. Toward the end of the 19th century, some trading posts were enlarged to general merchandise stores carrying foods, hard lines, and farm implements. As populations increased in towns and cities, some of these emerged as department stores. Today, retailing is the company's most important activity.

Although Hudson's Bay operated mainly in western Canada, a merger with Henry Morgan & Company, Ltd., in 1960, also gave it department stores in the eastern part of the country. With these, it operates 10 department stores, more than 30 smaller stores and 185 northern stores and fur-trading posts. A wholesale department operates another 17 branches.

Each manager of the combined trading posts and general merchandise stores maintained in the Arctic is provided with a completely furnished and heated six-room house rent-free, and for a nominal monthly sum may order food from the company's nearest supply depot. In addition, free government-sponsored correspondence courses, textbooks, and toys are provided children up to 10 years of age. For those between 10 and 17, the company pays the fare and $350 a year toward tuition in the nearest urban school.

The posts have two-way radio equipment and, often, radio-telephone facilities. The company's three airplanes and a dozen ships take personnel and supplies to the posts and return with furs, a trip made in earlier times with dog-drawn sleds.

The importance of furs in the history of Hudson's Bay Company is reflected in the name of the London headquarters and the company's coat of arms that depicts both beaver and elk and carries the motto, *Pro Pelle Cutem*—"A man risks his own skin for the skin of an animal."

The risks of hunting and trapping rose not from the animals but from poachers and those who challenged the company's trapping and hunting rights. Many of the company's employees and trappers were killed during these conflicts.

When it became obvious that the Canadian West would be opened to new settlers, and the company would have to surrender some of its unique privileges, the Dominion of Canada Act of 1867 provided for a deed of surrender under which Hudson's Bay gave up its governmental powers for $1½ million from the Canadian Government. The company retained three to five thousand acres around each trading post and was allowed seven million acres for sale to settlers. The company also retained all the mineral rights, and the coal that is mined is sold in a number of The Bay stores.

As a shortage of skins developed because of over-hunting and trapping, Hudson's Bay resorted to breeding and supplemented this with extensive imports of skins, which are sold at auctions in Montreal, New York, and London.

Hudson's Bay Company faced a modern crisis with the depression beginning in 1930. Sales in all divisions took a sharp drop and Sir Patrick Ashley Cooper, chosen governor in 1931, came to Canada to conduct an investigation. He found the Winnipeg management handicapped by too many London controls and recommended more autonomy for the Canadian store. Philip Alfred Chester, who had joined the company in 1923 as an accountant in London, was transferred to Winnipeg in 1924, became chief accountant in 1925, general manager in 1930, a director in 1941, and managing director in 1952. He decided the retail division had the brightest prospects, and hired Francis F. Martin, an American, to supervise The Bay's retail stores. Martin had been research director and controller for William Taylor Son & Company, Cleveland, Ohio, for 10 years, and the choice proved a happy one. At The Bay, he was promoted successively to assistant general manager and, in 1935, to general manager.

In the meantime, Chester concentrated on the company's other divisions and all began operating profitably. He also was granted the use of the AMC New York buying office service.

Sir Patrick retired in 1952 after 21 years as governor. His successor was William Johnston Keswick, who had been deputy governor since 1946.

Chester retired in 1959 after serving the company in London and Canada for 36 years. Martin died suddenly in 1957.

In early 1962, The Bay decentralized the supervision of its main retail operation into four major regional areas.

E. W. H. Brown, with the company 27 years at the time, became general manager of the Quebec region and president of Henry Morgan & Company, Ltd.

H. H. Abramson, general manager of retail stores in Winnipeg, became general manager of the British Columbia and Alberta divisions. W. G. Spalding, stock management controller at Winnipeg, became assistant general manager in charge of the central and Ontario region. H. W. Sutherland was named general manager of the Northern stores.

When the Morgan stores were acquired in December, 1960, it was Hudson's Bay Company's first invasion of northern Canada which had been dominated by Eaton's and Simpson's-Sears. Morgan's was established in Montreal in 1845 when the city had a population of only 45,000. Its founder, the first Henry Morgan, came from Scotland and four generations of Morgans controlled all the shares until 1954 when stock first was sold to the public. Morgan's always catered to the carriage trade.

At the time of the acquisition, Hudson's Bay operated six large stores in Winnipeg, Saskatoon, Edmonton, Calgary, Vancouver, and Victoria as well as its smaller stores and trading posts. Morgan's operated main stores in Montreal, Toronto,

Ottawa and Hamilton, including three shopping center sites in Montreal, two in Toronto, and one in Hamilton. It also ran specialty shops in Toronto, Montreal, and Ontario.

With Morgan's acquisition, the number of full-time employees has increased from 9,000 to about 12,500.

The Bay's Winnipeg store is the largest of the group. The late J. Gordon Dakins, executive vice-president of the National Retail Merchants Association, was at one time credit manager of that store. In Winnipeg, the company stocks such items, not usually found in American department stores, as staple groceries, canoes, and cut flowers. The store once sold 6,000 dozen daffodils in one day. Among the store's wide assortment of dolls are some made especially to please Eskimo children. This idea was developed by the Winnipeg store's toy buyer who noticed that Eskimos did not buy the traditional doll. He devised one and dressed it to resemble an Eskimo child, and 1,400 were sold the first year.

The Bay's own brand blanket is known and used by many American housewives. The store's Scotch whiskey, known as "Best Procurable", is imported in bulk, bottled, and distributed at the better clubs, bars, and hotels in America.

Two weeks' vacation with pay are provided after one year of service, with longer periods for additional years of service. Extra pay is given for holidays that occur during a vacation. After 15 years of service, no one may be discharged without the approval of the Canadian management committee. There is no compulsory retirement age.

In 1964, David E. Kilgour was named chairman of the Canadian Committee of the board, succeeding J. E. Woods who retired after 20 years with the company. Two executive deputy managing directors were chosen for the first time: H. W. Sutherland and R. E. Sheen. Both are also directors.

Lord Amory was elected the 32nd governor, succeeding Mr. Keswick, at the 296th annual general court of the company in London in May, 1965. Lord Amory had been deputy governor. Mr. Keswick remains on the board.

The Montreal store is engaged in a $5.4 million expansion including a 700-car Parkade for completion in 1967. Modernization has been completed in stores in Toronto and Hamilton shopping centers. The newest unit—a $6 million development —is planned for downtown Regina. With this store, the company will have a large department store in each of the seven largest cities in Western Canada. Eleven stores in Eastern Canada are operated under the Morgan name. In addition, there are 30 medium-size Bay department stores and 200 northern stores and fur trade posts in smaller communities across the country.

In the year ending January 31, 1965, Hudson's Bay Company recorded retail sales of $287.5 million, compared with some $103 million in 1952. Another $104 million was contributed by consignment sales of the three fur auction houses in London, Montreal and New York and by furs bought in Canada and traded for the company's own account. The value of the company's 22 per cent equity share in Hudson's Bay Oil and Gas Company is over $75 million. The company received a 1964 dividend of $1,400,000 on its $10 million capital investment in this venture.

Hudson Bay's 1964 profit after taxes was $11,277,000 as compared with $10,728,000 the previous year, and up 320 per cent from 1952.

CHAPTER 20

THE J. L. HUDSON COMPANY

DETROIT, MICHIGAN

"If there is a way, I'll find it;
if none exists, I'll make one."

—GUIDING MOTTO OF J. L. HUDSON

When Joseph Lothian Hudson decided to open his own men's and boys' clothing and furnishings store in Detroit in 1881, he had no idea he was establishing what would vie closely with Marshall Field as the department store with the second largest volume in the United States. J. L. Hudson was born in 1846 the third of seven children in Newcastle-on-Tyne, England. His grandfather, James Hudson, was a marine stores dealer, out-fitting ships that carried the proverbial coals from Newcastle. His father, Richard Hudson, a religious man who sometimes preached in the Methodist Church, was apprenticed as a young man to the grocer's trade.

Richard Hudson migrated to Hamilton, Ontario, Canada, in 1853 and his family followed two years later. Eight years later, they went to Pontiac, Michigan, where Joseph, 15, was ap-prenticed to Christopher R. Mabley, a men's clothing merchant who loved competition. For five years, young Hudson learned from Mabley and soon was running the store during the owner's absence.

In 1886, with Mabley as a backer and silent partner, Hudson and his father opened a small general store in Ionia, Michigan. The new store flourished under the aggressive direction of Joseph Hudson, then only 20 years old.

Could Hudson have foreseen the impending crash of 1873, he might not have rushed headlong into an expansion of his Ionia business. Caught in a financial squeeze after three years of trying to ride out the storm, Hudson went bankrupt. Although he was allowed to settle his obligations legally for 60 cents on the dollar, Hudson subsequently paid every creditor not only in full but with compound interest. This gesture gave him a virtually unlimited letter of credit with suppliers for the rest of his life.

The business was being re-established when C. R. Mabley, who by then was running the largest men's and boys' clothing store in Detroit, asked Hudson to run his store. Hudson left his brothers in charge of the Ionia establishment and went to Detroit in 1877. He not only ran the Mabley store but introduced some of his own ideas. Sales volume rose substantially.

Mabley gave Hudson a one-quarter interest in the business, a $7,500-a-year salary, and the title of general manager. This generous arrangement lasted only a few years. By January, 1881, they parted. Mabley's name survives in Mabley & Carew, Cincinnati, now a unit of Allied Stores Corp.

Hudson was 35 and his aggressive ideas clashed with those of the aging Mabley. Hudson had saved $60,000 from his salary and share of the profits and was now in a position to open his own men's and boys' clothing store. He started with a store in Toledo and within a year leased the old Detroit opera house just vacated by Newcomb–Endicott.

A business rivalry such as Detroit had never seen arose between Hudson and Mabley. It was a pitched battle of competition for customers, conducted so aggressively that both firms profited handsomely.

In 1887, the Hudson store moved to the Henkel Building on Woodward Avenue. Soon afterward, with Campbell Symington as a partner, Hudson added furniture and floor coverings. Four years later, Hudson launched a department store in an eight-story structure built on a site for which he paid $110,000. Although it was off the beaten track, the store was so attractive, its values so enticing, that customers came. Within ten years, Hudson's became Detroit's "big store," occupying the second tallest building in town. Only the 10-story Hammond Building erected in 1889 was taller. He also owned stores in other cities and was doing more than $2 million a year in men's and boys' clothing.

The panic of 1893, however, brought a serious setback to Hudson. Banks were closing all over the country. The Third National Bank of Detroit, of which Hudson was an inactive director, was extremely shaky. Sensing the danger, Hudson went to Washington with the State Bank Examiner and secured permission to liquidate the bank as soon as sufficient funds could be pledged to make this possible. Believing that many had deposited money in the bank because he was a director, Hudson promised that he personally would insure that no depositor should sustain a loss. In the end, Hudson and a Captain William H. Stevens raised the money.

Hudson's personal loss totaled $265,000, and in 1896 he had to ask for an extension of credit up to 24 months. This request brought a flood of letters and telegrams granting the extension and even offering additional time if needed. He sold or closed all but the Detroit store.

Hudson's sales showed no marked increase between 1892 and 1905, but reached $1 million in 1906 and grew to 3½ million by 1912. In 1911, a 10-story addition was opened.

In failing health, Hudson visited his homeland in the summer of 1912, and died there in July at 66.

During his lifetime, Hudson performed a prodigious amount of work of lasting benefit to his community and state. His personal response to any need had always been instant and generous, without regard to color, creed, or race. As chairman and one of the organizers of Detroit's Associated Charities, he blazed the trail for our modern-day community campaigns. His intense personal zeal, his unsparing energy for whatever task, his forthright attitude toward his fellow men were reflected in the business to which he dedicated his life. His cherished motto was: "If there is a way, I'll find it; if none exists, I'll make one."

J. L. Hudson never married, but the business stayed in the family. By 1910, four of his nephews were devoting full time to their various company jobs in preparation for their future executive responsibilities.

After Hudson's death, his nephew, Richard H. Webber, became president. A few years later, Oscar Webber, who had graduated from the University of Michigan as a Phi Beta Kappa, became vice-president and general manager. Joseph L. and James B. Webber, twins, better known as "Tom and Jerry," became vice-presidents and merchandise directors. This able quartet of brothers developed the department store into its present enviable position.

Carlos B. Clark, controller for 33 years, proved one of the ablest men in his field. He originated and used at Hudson's the "contribution plan" of expense proration. Certain departments in many large department stores, notably some in the home furnishings group, are regarded as "loss" departments. These are carried, however, as essential to complete the store's representation of all lines. Buyers of such departments suffer from frustration since their income is influenced by the department's profits. Clark's plan relieved them, to a large extent, of the burden imposed on their departments by the traditional plan of expense proration, and thus increased their morale. He died in 1947, a year after his retirement.

Irish-born Michael F. Dowley also made important contributions to Hudson's. He left Ireland and obtained work with Wanamaker's New York in July, 1905, remaining there only briefly. He was with Altman's from 1905 to 1914, left to work in Minneapolis and Denver stores, and then returned to Altman's. In 1917, he became general manager of the Edward

Wren store at Springfield and two years later joined Hudson's as New York office manager, a position designed to prepare future executives.

He left to become merchandise manager and director of Arnold Constable & Co. and rejoined Hudson's in 1919 as assistant divisional merchandise manager of home furnishings. He became general merchandise manager in 1923, and continued in that post until his retirement in 1946.

Joseph B. Mills, another "natural" for Hudson's, converted the public's image of the store into a beloved Detroit institution. He had an abundance of audacity and imagination and was not so much concerned with day-to-day results as with building enduring good will. He was at his best planning institutional projects in harmony with Hudson's traditions. Hudson's Thanksgiving Day parade, one of his projects, attained nearly as much national prominence as Macy's parade. Mills died in 1947.

George E. Preston, manager of Hudson's basement store (two selling floors), was a man of few words, who never lost his temper or raised his voice. In many large stores, the basement manager reports to the general merchandise manager, but Preston, reporting directly to the owners, had a free hand. No restrictions were imposed on his open-to-buy, price lines, types of merchandise, fashion, or style. He also had his own advertising staff. Consequently, Hudson's basement was constantly expanding and many of the departments became more profitable than their main-store counterparts.

The basement store was able to act so swiftly that its offerings could almost saturate the local trading area by disposing of large quantities of timely items before other stores could obtain the merchandise. This resulted in fast turnover and few markdowns.

In 1954, Oscar Webber said, "We are sure that the sales of Hudson's basement store are by far the largest basement store sales in the world, exceeding $35 million annually. It is interesting to note that practically all customers walk from the street level into the basement store since it is served by only one passenger elevator and there are no escalators from the street level . . ." By 1960, the basement store was said to be doing about 25 per cent of the company's sales or more than $56 million. Preston retired in 1949 and died in 1950.

Herman G. Petzold, Preston's assistant, was the son of William A. Petzold, who had started as a parcel boy on the original staff and retired as secretary-treasurer in 1951 after 70 years' service. Herman Petzold succeeded Preston as basement store manager and became a vice-president and general manager in 1954. He died in 1955.

Walker T. Wright, general superintendent of Hudson's, got his previous training at Gimbels, New York. Wright's assignment covered all rank and file personnel with the exception of those under C. B. Clark. Wright reported directly to Oscar Webber. Wright's job also covered store maintenance, workrooms, store protection, delivery, and warehouses. Hudson's maintained and operated its own delivery service that involved a fleet of 450 vans by the 1960's.

Wright usually patrolled a part of the huge store daily and was meticulous about having it clean from top to bottom, especially after workmen finished an alteration. He supervised a well-organized and alert protection staff. Shoplifters soon learned to shun Hudson's because of the fear of prompt detection, apprehension, and prosecution. Wright died in 1947.

When Hudson's joined RRA-AMC in 1916, its annual sales were $8,425,000. After World War I, sales increased so rapidly that the store was regarded as the most important member of the group. Hudson's continued to maintain a New York office and foreign buying connections until AMC established its foreign offices in 1920. From the very beginning of the association, Oscar Webber devoted more of his time and talents to RRA-AMC than any other member.

As a member of the executive committee, he attended every meeting. He actively participated in the studies conducted in each member store. Later, he succeeded Louis E. Kirstein as chairman of the AMC foreign-office committee. He was chairman of the New York office committee which decided the amount of each annual budget the two associations would work under. Budgets approved by Oscar Webber for both domestic and foreign activities were rarely questioned. Other members knew Hudson's, as the largest individual company in AMC, would pay a greater sum in dues than any of them.

In the early 1950's, a long-range shopping-center program was developed. Location, size, and timing were determined by the company in consultation with architect Victor Gruen and economist Larry Smith.

Hudson's Northland opened in March, 1954, in Southfield, Michigan, about 12 miles northwest of downtown Detroit. The branch contains 574,000 square feet of the center's total space of 1,100,000 square feet. Parking is available for 9,820 cars. A second branch, Hudson's Eastland, opened with 480,000 square feet in July, 1957, at Harper Woods, about 10 miles east of Detroit. The store occupies about half of the rented area. The center has parking space for 8,460 cars. Both branches, as large as many parent department stores in other large cities, are the focal firms in attractively landscaped shopping centers, controlled by Shopping Centers, Inc., a J. L. Hudson Company subsidiary.

Although Northland has about 80 other tenants, Hudson's sales account for 57 per cent of the total volume at the center. Eastland has some 70 other tenants and Hudson's volume represents 63 per cent of the total. All stores are air-conditioned. Customers can reach each store by walking under a cover.

Hudson's has reserved space at both centers for future expansion.

Main-store buyers do all the purchasing for the branches, but most of the merchandise is shipped to them directly. Furniture and related items, however, are warehoused until needed at the branches.

The main store of 2,124,316 square feet is located on 49 acres in Detroit's downtown and boasts a 25-story tower. It has 9,000 employees, 7,200 of them full time. About 80 per cent are female. The upstairs store has 96 departments and the basement, 45, and each has its own buyers.

James Benson Webber, Jr., son of Jerry, joined Hudson's in 1936, became vice-president and general manager in 1948, and president in 1954. When he died at 44 in 1956, Oscar and Richard Webber, who had virtually retired, returned to direct the store. Oscar is board chairman; Richard, honorary chairman.

Joseph Lothian Hudson, Jr., president, is a grandson of the original J. L. Hudson's brother, William H. Hudson. During the summers of 1950 and 1951, Joseph L., Jr., was employed by the store in receiving, the comparison bureau, research, and selling. After obtaining his degree from Yale in 1953, he joined Hudson's as an executive trainee in the employment department. Later, he served in the toy buying office and in basement women's dresses. He was in the army from 1954 to 1956. Upon his return, the Webbers plucked young Hudson out of the lower-echelon and exposed him to intensive managerial training. In 1956, he was made assistant to the general manager. The following year, he was appointed executive vice-president and general manager. In 1961 at 29, he became president when Oscar Webber moved up to chairman of the board.

Other than the family, there are about 150 stockholders consisting of the financial and social elite of the Motor City and a sprinkling of company executives.

An enduring tie that binds Hudson's executives and other employees to the firm is a pension plan that is one of the most liberal provided by any store. It is noncontributory and covers all regular full-time employees and even those part-time employees who work regularly 25 or 30 hours a week. Any employee reaching the age of 65 with a minimum of 20 years' service is eligible to receive benefits. Hudson's mandatory retirement age of 65 applies to executives only; others may work as long as health permits.

In addition to the pension plan, Hudson's has an employees' retirement income plan, designed primarily for supervisors and executives who have had five or more years' service. About 1,400 employees participate in this plan, contributing 30 per cent, the firm the other 70 per cent of the cost.

The store pays up to 10 weeks' wages during illness, and in extreme cases a second 10 weeks.

Being privately owned, Hudson's does not reveal its annual sales. It is estimated, however, that the company did about $280 million in 1964, and realized net earnings of 2.25 per cent of sales versus a typical figure in the $50 million and up bracket of 2.74 per cent. Estimated breakdown of sales by units; $121.1 million, Woodward Avenue headquarters; $83 million, Northland; $53 million, Eastland; $5.2 million, Dearborn; $5.2 million, Madison Heights; $5 million, Lincoln Park; $4.5 million, Pontias; $3 million, Warren warehouse outlet. Westland Regional Mall Shopping Center opened in July, 1965, and a Southland center is slated for the 1970–75 period. In addition, Hudson's has scheduled a store opening every 18 months until 1970.

CHAPTER 21

JORDAN MARSH CO., ALLIED STORES CORP.

BOSTON, MASSACHUSETTS

Jordan Marsh Company of Boston traces its beginnings to 1851 when Eben Jordan and Benjamin L. Marsh became partners with $5,000 capital.

A century later, Jordan Marsh Company was the largest store in New England and the biggest in the Allied Stores Corporation chain, accounting for about $155 million of the chain's $893 million volume in 1964.

Eben Dyer Jordan left his native Danville, Maine, in 1836, when he was 14, and went to Boston with $1.25 in his pocket. There, he became a hired hand on a farm for $4 a month.

At 16, he was an errand boy for the William P. Tenney & Company dry goods store. Three years later, he launched a career of his own when a merchant, Joshua Stetson, financed the youth in a store at 168 Hanover Street. His first sale was a yard of cherry-colored ribbon to a friend, Louisa Bareiss.

A year after Eben Jordan and Benjamin Marsh formed a partnership, Charles Marsh also joined the firm, then on Milk

Street, and it became Jordan Marsh & Company. In 1853, Jordan made his first trip to Europe to obtain stock on credit.

The store's first expansion came in 1856 when it moved to 18–20 Pearl Street. A business panic gripped Boston a year later, and Jordan, armed with the credit he had obtained in Europe, cut prices in half to move merchandise. Although losses were suffered, the store survived and Jordan Marsh began to departmentalize.

By 1859, it had moved into a six-story building in Winthrop Square. In 1861, the year the Civil War began, the retail business of George W. Warren & Company at 450 Washington Street was purchased. Then with Warren was Edward J. Mitton, a 14-year-old errand boy born in London. Mitton, his son, and grandson, all became presidents of the firm.

The store moved its retail business to the brownstone building on Washington Street, retaining a wholesale operation at Winthrop Square.

Nine years later, when fire damaged an adjacent theater on Washington Street, the firm leased the ruins and moved its wholesale operation there. This was a fortunate move because, in 1872, fire was to destroy the former home of the organization at Winthrop Square.

In the meantime, Jordan Marsh was buying adjacent private homes and small-store buildings on Central Court and Avon Street. In 1880, it bought the corner of Avon and Washington Streets, built a tower there, and installed an outdoor clock. That is the store's location today.

In that same year, at 23, Eben Dyer Jordan, Jr., son of the founder, joined the firm. He succeeded his father as president 15 years later in 1895 when the founder died at 73. About the same time as this first changeover in the store's management, the Marsh family left the firm.

When Eben, Jr., became president at 38, Edward J. Mitton became vice-president. He had served as silk salesman, silk buyer, wholesale business director, and finally had become a member of the firm.

The founder's son continued as president for 16 years until 1911. Mitton, who succeeded him for two years, died in 1913 and Eben, Jr., three years later.

Meanwhile, the store had continued to expand. In 1898, Jordan Marsh built an eight-story white brick building at Avon, Chauncy, and Bedford Streets. A marble-lined subway under Avon Street connected it with the main store. In 1901, the firm name was changed to its present style.

Six years later, flames leveled a neighboring structure on Avon Street and the retail firm bought the ruins. On this site, a nine-story building was completed in 1911 and connected with the 1898 structure, doubling the selling space of the store. The new building stood on top of two basements in which the firm began its first basement store.

Edward Mitton's son, George W. Mitton, became president in 1916 and continued in that capacity until 1930. He had begun work in 1888 as an 18-year-old stockboy in the wholesale department, had served as a traveling salesman, supervised the purchase of wholesale dress goods, and had been in charge of merchandising.

Jordan Marsh, in 1947, announced plans for a new building of 14 stories and two basements, covering the Washington, Chauncy, Summer and Avon Streets block. The structure was to have 2,015,071 square feet, air conditioning, automatic doors, radiant-heated sidewalks and block-long show windows.

Jordan Marsh began its first branch operation in 1951 at Shoppers' World, Framingham, about 20 miles from Boston. This suburban operation within a decade was the Allied chain's top suburban store in terms of sales per square foot.

In 1954, Jordan's opened a second branch at Malden, and in 1958 another in the Northshore regional shopping center at Peabody, since considerably enlarged.

For 1964, sales for the main store were estimated at slightly over $100 million. The branches in Framingham and Peabody had an estimated volume of about $25 million and $27 million, respectively. The Malden unit accounted for another $4 million. A fourth branch is proposed for Springfield, Massachusetts.

George Mitton served as chairman of the board from 1930 to 1943. His brother, Richard, succeeded him as president.

Edward R. Mitton, George's son, became president in 1937. After attending Harvard, he started with the firm as a sales clerk in 1917 and served later as divisional merchandise manager and general merchandise manager. He became a director of the corporation in 1924 and was merchandise vice president from 1931 until he became president. He was president of Jordan's until February, 1962.

In 1905, Jordan Marsh had begun a voluntary association for mutual aid of employees. A credit union was established in 1931. Employees still receive emergency treatment from a staff of nurses and free medical and dental care. The store has also developed an executive training course.

Allied Stores Corp. actually began in 1928 as Hahn Department Stores, a merger of 22 retail companies, big and small, doing over $100 million. Lew Hahn, who had been managing director of the National Retail Dry Goods Corporation, was Hahn's president and general manager for two years and chairman of the board for two years thereafter. He later returned to the retailers' association as president and general manager. B. Earl Puckett, who retired as chairman of the board in 1963, took charge of the chain in 1933 after its sales had slipped $42 million from a 1929 peak of $112 million.

By 1934, the chain had 31 stores with sales of $82 million. A year later, when volume had recovered to almost $90 million, the name was changed to Allied Stores Corp. By 1940, there were 60 stores with a sales volume of $121 million. Firms added during this period included Dey Brothers in Syracuse, New York, the four Pomeroy stores in Eastern Pennsylvania, and the 23-store C. C. Anderson Company chain in the Rocky Mountain States.

Five years later, there were 70 stores with a $281.6 million volume. The chain now also included B. Gertz in Jamaica, Long Island, New York. In 1950, the company numbered 73 stores and volume had nearly doubled to $439.9 million. Sterling-Lindner-Davis, Cleveland, had been acquired and new stores were built in Houston, Texas, Spokane, Washington, and St. Petersburg, Florida.

The total number of stores remained the same through 1954 although 16 smaller stores were closed as the corporation's operations were consolidated. A Jordan Marsh store was opened at San Diego, California, but was closed by 1958. Meanwhile, the chain had bought Stern Brothers in New York and D. M. Read Company in Bridgeport, Connecticut.

By 1957, Allied numbered 87 stores with 20,660,428 square feet of space and sales of $632,814,000. There were 31,000 regular employees and the work force of the chain reached 40,000 during peak periods.

In February, 1962, Cameron S. Thompson succeeded Edward R. Mitton as president of Jordan Marsh, the first change in 25 years. Mitton became board chairman. He continues on the Allied board. Thompson, who had joined Jordan Marsh as a stock boy in 1921, had taken the executive training course and later served as a buyer and merchandise manager. He became a vice-president and general merchandise manager in 1937, and a vice-president of Allied in mid-1963. He is also a director. In January, 1966, Thompson became vice-chairman of Jordan's. He was succeeded as president and chief executive officer by William P. Reed, a product of the company's executive training program.

As 1962 drew to a close, Earl Puckett, under whom the nationwide Allied chain had developed, stepped down from the helm. Puckett had been president of Frederick Loeser & Company of Brooklyn from 1927 to 1933 and went to Allied Stores as a vice-president in 1933. He retired as chairman of the board in 1963. Charles E. McCarthy, a vice-chairman of the board, who had been Puckett's right-hand man for 35 years, also retired before the year's end.

Theodore Schlesinger, now president of the corporation, started with Allied in 1929. He was assistant to the president from 1939 to 1945, served as vice-president from 1945 to 1959, and as director since 1955. He became president and chief executive officer of Allied in 1959.

Allied reached a crossroads in the early 1960's. It was behind Federated Department Stores in volume and behind both Federated and May Department Stores in profits.

Allied entered the discount field in 1961 with its Almart units, the first of these formed by converting Peck's store at Kansas City, Missouri, a department store the chain had purchased in 1939. In 1963, Allied closed that operation. Another Almart unit was formed from a retail store in Lynchburg, Virginia. Two others opened in November, 1962, at Bethlehem, Pennsylvania and Wilmington, Delaware. A third was added in Albany, New York. Estimated sales of the four units were $18 to 20 million. A second Wilmington Almart opened early in the fall of 1965.

During the early 1960's, Allied also bought Mabley & Carew, an 84-year-old Cincinnati apparel specialty store, the first purchase since the acquisition of the Cain Sloan store in Nashville, Tennessee, five years before. The Mabley & Carew purchase gave Allied two major stores in Cincinnati. The other was Rollman's Department Store, which took on the Mabley name.

In 1962, Allied paid $15 million for William H. Block Company, a 66-year-old family-owned operation at Indianapolis.

In 1961, Allied bought The Fair, a nine-unit chain in Fort Worth and Dallas, Texas. The Fort Worth stores were liquidated in 1963, and three Dallas units and one in Arlington, Texas, were converted to branches of Titche-Goettinger Company.

At the end of 1964, Allied had 3½ million square feet of shopping center space. A vigorous expansion program is underway throughout the 35 divisions which now number over 100 units.

Vice-presidents of the corporation include:

Rex L. Allison, with Allied stores since 1931, a vice-president since 1950, and now a senior vice-president. He has been chairman of the board of the Bon Marche, Seattle, since 1957 and is vice-president of Allied's Northwest Division, and an Allied director.

James H. Reedy, vice-president of the Central Division, was merchandise manager of Allied from 1934 to 1941, managing director from 1941 to 1948, group manager in 1948, vice-president and director since 1951, and now a senior vice-president. He has been chairman of the board of Dey Brothers since 1952.

W. Earl McCormick, senior vice-president and director, joined the store analysis division of Allied in 1929. In 1937, he became general merchandise manager of Polsky's, Akron, and in 1945 managing director. He became a corporate vice-president in 1947 and was elected director two years later. He is president of Allied Purchasing Corporation and of Metasco, Inc., respectively the domestic and foreign buying subsidiaries.

Theodore R. Brouillette, vice-president of the Twin Cities Division, became a vice-president, director, and group manager of Allied in 1948.

Also on the board is Charles McCarthy, who retired in 1962 but continues as a director and a member of the executive and finance committees. He is also chairman of the marketing department and a full professor at the College of Business Administration, St. John's University, Brooklyn and Queens, New York.

Other vice-presidents are John J. McGrath, vice-president in charge of executive development and organizational planning since 1959, Max Heller, who also serves as group manager of all Allied units in Pennsylvania; Robert Macht, group manager of all units in Florida, Cincinnati and Columbus, Ohio, and Nashville, Tennessee; Thomas M. Macioce, in charge of finance; Andrew L. Murphy, in charge of real estate; and Alfred Eisenpreis, in charge of planning and research.

For the year ended January 31, 1966, Allied's sales aggregated $955,490,000 and net profits reached $22,255,000.

CHAPTER 22

F. & R. LAZARUS & COMPANY

COLUMBUS, OHIO

JOHN SHILLITO COMPANY

CINCINNATI, OHIO

"The Customer Is Not Always Right"

—FRED LAZARUS, JR.

Simon Lazarus arrived in Columbus, Ohio, from Germany in 1850 and the following year opened a small men's and boys' clothing store in which he invested his entire savings of $3,000. By 1963, it had mushroomed into a 52-acre institution with 166 departments.

The first expansion step was taken in 1860 when Lazarus bought an adjacent boot-and-shoe store. His slogans from the start were "Strictly one price" and "It fits or you don't pay."

Simon Lazarus' two sons, Frederick and Ralph, began working in the store after school hours. At their father's death in 1877, the name of the firm was changed from S. Lazarus & Sons Company to F. & R. Lazarus & Company.

When Ralph Lazarus, a bachelor, died in 1903 at 52, Frederick assumed full responsibility. Two of his sons, Simon and Frederick, Jr., were active at the time of Ralph's death, Simon beginning work in 1901 and Frederick, Jr., in 1902. Robert entered the firm during World War I; Jeffrey, in 1919. The four brothers were referred to as "the Lazari." Simon gave his attention to store personnel and operation; Fred, Jr., to finance; Robert, to merchandising; and Jeffrey, to research. Fred, Jr., emerged as the ablest of the four brothers, and in later years was still regarded as one of the top-flight merchants in the nation.

Fred Lazarus, Sr., died in 1917, and Simon became president. The firm had built a new six-story building in 1909 and doubled its size in 1926 when it emerged as a full department store. Two years later, the organization acquired the then 98-year-old John Shillito Company in Cincinnati.

Meanwhile, Fred, Jr., fed ideas to the store. On a trip to Paris in 1927, he found women's dresses grouped by sizes rather than price lines, the practice in the United States. Customers thus found more quickly a wider selection in their sizes and frequently bought more expensive dresses than was their intention. The idea, adopted in the Lazarus store, was a success.

Fred, Jr., also was watchful of expense, keeping it as low as possible without impairing service. The store always was able to meet any low-price competition of other local firms.

Once, in an attempt to stop waste resulting from needless returns, Lazarus kept a record of all multiple returns from charge customers and, as a result, closed many accounts. Most of these customers, however, continued to buy at the Lazarus store on a cash basis, eventually requesting the reopening of their accounts with the promise to stop making needless returns. Thus it was proved, "The customer is not always right."

The Shillito store, long the prestige outlet in Cincinnati, had dropped from first to fourth place in the city in sales and was unprofitable at the time the Lazarus organization acquired it in 1928. Jeffrey Lazarus was assigned to run it and Leonard R. Minster, later chairman of the board, became his assistant. Within 11 years, it was again the top store in Cincinnati with $40 million in sales in 1939. In 1964, estimated volume was about $80 million, reflecting the first full year of operation of its 179,000-square-foot Western Woods branch. The downtown store has about 500,000 square feet of selling space. Shillito's opened its first shopping-center store in 200,000 square feet at the Tri-County regional development. Another site for a 250,-000-square-foot branch is being held in abeyance.

Fred Lazarus, Jr., played a dominant role in the formation and expansion of Federated Department Stores. The plan originated in a discussion aboard the yacht of Walter N. Rothschild, Sr., of Abraham & Straus. Also among the guests was Louis E. Kirstein, of Filene's. The retail companies which these men headed had been charter members of Retail Research Association and Associated Merchandising Corporation since 1916. The three agreed to organize primarily as a holding company in 1929, although later the individual corporations were dissolved and each company became an operating division of Federated. Stock of Federated Department Stores became the only one listed on the Stock Exchange. The new corporation, comprising Abraham & Straus, Filene's, Lazarus, and Shillito's, was formed to diversify capital investments and afford a wider field for promotion and assignment of promising executives and other employees. Fred Lazarus, Jr., pledged that members of the group would not expand into any selling area covered by other RRA-AMC stores. Federated developed a confidential figure exchange to supplement the RRA exchange.

Federated embarked on a dynamic expansion plan by acquiring, on long-term leases, stores in all parts of the country.

Bloomingdale's joined Federated soon after its formation in 1929, but the first significant addition came in 1945 when Foley's of Houston was purchased. In that year, Federated's central office was established in Cincinnati. The Boston Store, Milwaukee, joined in 1948; Sanger's, Dallas, in 1951; Burdine's, Miami, in 1955; Goldsmith's, Memphis, and Rike-Kumler Co., Dayton, in 1959; and A. Harris Co., Dallas, in 1961. When Harris joined, it merged with Sanger's to become Sanger-Harris. A Fedway Stores division, now consisting of eight main stores and two branches, was established in 1952. Bullock's-Magnin Co. was added in 1964 as Federated's 13th division.

The Federated chain comprised some 90 stores occupying 18 million square feet at the end of 1965. With $1,215 million volume in 1964, it led its closest competitor, Allied Stores Corporation, by $322 million and rolled up $64,469,000 net profit. For 1965, net profits totaled $70,517,333, a gain of 9.4 per cent.

Simon Lazarus, eldest of the four brothers, died in 1947 and Robert succeeded him as president, later becoming chairman of Lazarus. Charles Y. Lazarus, son of the late Simon, is Lazarus's president.

Fred Lazarus III is chairman of Shillito's, Jerome F. Swartsberg, president, and Jeffrey Lazarus, honorary chairman and consultant. Fred III was previously Shillito's president. Swartsberg joined Federated as a vice-president in 1964 after 31 years with Allied Stores. He assumed his present position in 1965.

Fred Lazarus, Jr., serves as chairman of Federated's board and executive committee. His son, Ralph, is president of Federated. In February, 1966, Fred, Jr., at 81, relinquished his position as chief executive officer to Ralph but retains the position as chairman of the board and executive committee. Another son, Maurice, was elected vice-chairman of Federated in 1965 after having been board chairman of Filene's. J. Paul Sticht, formerly executive vice-president and before that vice-president of Campbell Soup Company, is also a vice-chairman.

There are also two executive vice-presidents: Herbert S. Landsman, for divisional services including research and planning; and Richard L. Knight, for finance, real estate, and similar central services. Mr. Knight, formerly president of James Talcott, industrial finance company, joined Federated in early 1965 as successor to John Lebor, who retired at the end of the year. A third executive vice-presidency—one for executive development—has been set up, and an extensive search was begun for the person to fill that post.

No group of men comparable to members of the Lazarus family has emerged on the American retail scene. No other man has shown such organizing ability as Fred, Jr., who developed Federated into the largest department store chain in the nation. He was one of the founders of the Ohio State Council of Retail Merchants. He was granted the honorary degree of doctor of law by Ohio State University and of doctor of commercial science by the University of Cincinnati. He and Oscar Webber of Hudson's, Detroit, are largely responsible for the success of RRA-AMC.

CHAPTER 23

LORD & TAYLOR

ASSOCIATED DRY GOODS

CORPORATION

"The recollection of value remains long after price is forgotten." —JOHN T. LORD

Lord & Taylor was founded in 1826 at the lower end of the Bowery in New York by 23-year-old Samuel Lord, a native of Yorkshire, England, who had had no previous retailing experience. Before coming to the United States, he was a master molder at James Taylor's foundry in Marsden, England.

He borrowed $1,000, and with this opened his first store. By the end of the first year, the store was enlarged and his wife's cousin, George Washington Taylor, became a partner. In 1838, the partners bought a four-story structure at 61–63 Catherine Street.

With wealth obtained in the business, Taylor retired to Manchester, England, in 1852, and Lord resumed full control. A year later, Lord moved once again, this time to the corner of Grand and Chrystie Streets, and in 1860 added a building at Broadway and Grand Street. There, the "carriage trade" became a symbol of the firm. Throughout its career, Lord & Taylor has retained its "quality" label, paying no attention to the competition of other local stores offering lower price merchandise.

In 1860, Lord took as partners his son, John T. Lord, and his confidential clerk, John S. Lyle, the son of a Nova Scotia sea captain. At 12, Lyle was the firm's first messenger boy. He remained with the firm until his death in 1912.

When the Civil War ended, it became apparent that the new shopping area would be established between 14th and 23rd Streets. At this time, Samuel Lord and his son retired and the founder's younger sons, George Washington Lord and Samuel Lord, Jr., succeeded them. To retain its carriage trade, Lord & Taylor moved to a new four-story iron-frame building at Broadway and 20th Street in 1872.

Edward P. Hatch, who had had sole responsibility for management since 1857, was made president when the firm was incorporated in 1904. When Hatch died six years later, Louis Stewart bought his interest and became chairman of the board. J. H. Emery, with the store for 25 years, succeeded Hatch as president.

In 1914, Lord & Taylor relocated at its present site at 38th Street and Fifth Avenue in a 10-story building which had a basement and sub-basement. No expense was spared but the building soon proved to be too small to handle both the wholesale and retail sections. In addition, Lord & Taylor was having financial difficulties.

In 1914, a committee of New York bankers and Colonel Michael Friedsam, B. Altman & Company vice-president, chose Samuel W. Reyburn, a Little Rock, Arkansas, banker, to serve as treasurer. He spent the remainder of his retailing career with Lord & Taylor and Associated Dry Goods Corporation, becoming president of both in 1916 and continuing until 1936.

Associated Dry Goods was formed in 1914 when H. B. Claflin Company failed. Claflin, a large wholesaling business, had had considerable capital invested in department stores, including Lord & Taylor.

Reyburn salvaged those stores worth saving and formed them into a federated group called Associated Dry Goods Corporation. He closed Lord & Taylor's wholesale division, paid off the $5 to $6 million owed to 24 New York banks, and put Lord & Taylor on a profitable basis. He devoted most of his efforts to maintaining a superior degree of service that brought enduring good will to the store. Lower-price items never were sold at Lord & Taylor.

Samuel W. Reyburn died at 90 in 1962 in Sarasota, Florida.

Walter Hoving, a native of Stockholm, Sweden, succeeded him as president of Lord & Taylor, continuing in that position until 1945.

Hoving brought rich experience to Lord & Taylor, having spent four years with Macy's and four more with Montgomery Ward & Company in executive posts. Although his background was with stores featuring medium and lower prices, he was quality-minded. He originated many successful promotional projects for Lord & Taylor. He later became president of Bonwit Teller.

Meanwhile, Oswald W. Knauth had succeeded Reyburn as president of Associated Dry Goods Corporation in 1936, remaining in that post until 1943. All Knauth's experience had been with Macy's where he became treasurer in 1933. He started a drastic expense reduction at Associated and closed the New York buying office in 1939. Robert J. McKim, who succeeded Knauth as president of Associated in 1943, reopened it.

Dorothy Shaver, introduced to retailing by Reyburn, a distant relative, joined Lord & Taylor in 1924 as head of the comparison department. In 1931, she was elected a vice-president, and in 1937 first vice-president in charge of fashion and sales promotion. She succeeded Hoving as president in December, 1945, an unusual position to be held by a woman in a well-known store. Miss Shaver, who opened seven branches for Lord & Taylor, died in June, 1959. She was succeeded by Melvin E. Dawley, who joined the store as a buyer in 1936, became vice-president ten years later, and was appointed to the board in 1947. In the meantime, McKim, as head of Associated, provided dynamic leadership to the corporation. He became the first chairman of the Associated board in 1959. He continued as chief executive officer.

Lewis P. Seiler, who joined Associated as a drapery buyer for J. N. Adam Company, Buffalo, New York, in 1936, and moved up through various positions, succeeded McKim as president.

Associated, under McKim's leadership, had expanded for the first time since Reyburn was in charge. McKim added the J. W. Robinson Company store in Los Angeles, the Diamond at Charleston, West Virginia, and the Erie Dry Goods Company, Erie, Pennsylvania. He closed the James McCreery store in New York and the J. N. Adam store in Buffalo. Both had been unprofitable.

Recent additions include H. & S. Pogue Company, Cincinnati, Ohio; Stix, Baer & Fuller, St. Louis, Missouri; Goldwaters, Phoenix, Arizona; and Denver Dry Goods Company, Denver, Colorado. Other stores in the Associated chain include Hahne & Company of New Jersey; William Hengerer Company, Buffalo; Powers Dry Goods Company, Minneapolis; Stewart & Company, Baltimore; Stewart Dry Goods Company, Louisville, Kentucky; and Sibley, Lindsay & Curr, Rochester, New York.

Lord & Taylor stores are in Manhattan; Manhasset, Long Island; Eastchester, Westchester County, New York; Millburn, New Jersey; West Hartford, Connecticut; Bala-Cynwyd and Jenkintown, Pennsylvania; Garden City, New York; and Chevy Chase, Maryland. The firm plans to have 12 branches by 1967.

In 1964, Associated Dry Goods Corporation had nine divisions operating 46 stores with total sales of $459 million and net profits of $16,763,000. The Lord & Taylor Fifth Avenue store had an estimated volume of $44 million. Its Westchester store contributed $10 million; Garden City, $7¾ million; Millburn, $7½ million; and Manhasset, $6 million to make a New York metropolitan-area total of $75¼ million. The West Hartford unit does some $8 million; the Chevy Chase store in the Washington environs, an estimated $10 million; Bala-Cynwyd, about $6 million; and Jenkintown, about $5 million. Another branch opened in Falls Church, Virginia, in the fall of 1965.

CHAPTER 24

LUCKEY, PLATT

& COMPANY

POUGHKEEPSIE, NEW YORK

"Leading Department Store of the Hudson Valley"

In 1944, Luckey, Platt & Company officially celebrated its 75th anniversary. The store's establishment, however, can actually be traced back as far as 1835.

At that time, Isaac Dibble and Robert Slee were partners in Dibble & Slee. Later, it became R. & J. Slee and it was for this firm that Charles P. Luckey began to work. Slee and Luckey became partners in 1860.

After Slee retired, Luckey took in two partners and the store became Luckey, Vail & Mandeville. On March 22, 1869, the date observed as the official beginning of Luckey, Platt & Company, Edmund P. Platt, who had been clerking in another store, bought the interest of Vail and Mandeville and the firm name became Luckey & Platt.

To purchase the part interest, Platt, just turned 21, had borrowed $1,000 from his father, the publisher of the Poughkeepsie *Daily Eagle*. The Platt family had early beginnings in the region. Zephaniah Platt founded Plattsburgh in 1784 and brought a colony with him.

Smith L. DeGarmo became a partner in 1872 and the firm became Luckey, Platt & Company. It was the first store in Poughkeepsie to install plate-glass windows.

In 1875, the firm began a carpet and oil-cloth department. Three years later, telephones were installed to accept orders and merchandise was delivered in and around Dutchess County. In 1888, the store erected nearly 300 "mile stones," which related the mileage to the store within tenths of a mile. Arrows pointed out the direction the traveler must take to reach the firm.

Charles P. Luckey, whose foresight and integrity were largely responsible for the success of the business in those early years, died in 1896, and two new members were admitted to the firm: Howard Platt, just out of Yale, and William DeGarmo Smith, a nephew of S. L. DeGarmo.

In 1901, a boys' department, millinery and furniture departments were added and the store became a department store.

In 1912, Luckey, Platt & Company was incorporated with Edmund P. Platt as president, S. L. DeGarmo as vice-president, and W. D. Smith as secretary and treasurer. Platt died in 1913, and in 1915 DeGarmo became president and Smith vice-president. DeGarmo died the same year, and his nephew became president. At the same time, Edward F. Carey, who joined the business in 1911 to establish a statistical department, became vice-president.

William M. Smith, president and general manager, is the third generation of his family at the helm. He succeeded his father, William DeGarmo Smith, in 1948. S. L. DeGarmo was a great-uncle of the current head. David DeGarmo Smith, William's brother, vice-president and secretary, also merchandises home furnishings.

The Smith family owns 100 per cent of the stock. Until 1965, 50% of the stock was owned by the Platt family. Edmund G. Rawson, Jr., grandson of founder E. P. Platt, retired as vice-president and general superintendent in 1965 after 40 years' service.

F. Bennett Cody, with the company since 1959, is second vice-president and treasurer.

Luckey's advertising director is William F. Gekle, Jr. His originality in copy devoted to clearance sales was praised by the late Kenneth Collins in *Women's Wear Daily*. For example:

Gloves in an odd assortment of colors and sizes that look as if they might have been picked up the day after Custer's Last Stand. Matter of fact, they were, one of our buyers happened along.

Sweaters of orlon, wool and dust. The orlon and wool are supposed to be in them; the dust naturally accumulated over the years. No extra charge.

Luckey's has five floors and basement of 150,000 square feet, 90,000 for selling. Last expansion was in 1924. The store has undergone extensive renovation. Privately-owned Luckey's sales are in the $5 million range. It has some 200 full-time employees, about 50 part-timers, and from 30 to 35 in leased departments. The store employs 16 buyers, 6 of them women. Luckey's is a charter member of the Frederick Atkins office.

A namesake and grandson of the original Platt, Edmund P. Platt, worked in Luckey's during his school and college years. He was furniture buyer for William Hengerer & Company from 1936 to 1943; divisional merchandise manager of The Broadway, Los Angeles, in the home furnishings group from 1946 to 1953, and then merchandise manager and assistant general manager of Meier & Frank, Portland, Oregon. Later, he was West Coast regional director and vice-president of Montgomery Ward & Company and finally returned to Hengerer's as president. He was on the board of directors of Luckey, Platt & Company.

CHAPTER 25

R. H. MACY
& CO., INC.

"The Greatest Store in the Nation"

Rowland H. Macy entered the New York retailing complex inauspiciously in 1858 after indifferent success and, sometimes, failure in other areas.

Some believe his New York success was predictable because his business ideas were made for the large metropolitan market rather than for the small areas in which he developed them. In any case, Macy became a specialist in fancy dry goods when he opened his first New York establishment on Sixth Avenue near 14th Street.

The seed he planted there was to sprout from coast to coast. One hundred years after the beginning, Macy's corporate sales reached $456 million and net income $6½ million. In 1964, volume passed $600 million.

Today, Macy's New York carries 400,000 items in 168 selling departments. Traffic averages 150,000 customers a day in the Herald Square store alone and is twice that during peak seasons. Regular employees throughout the Macy organization number

28,000 on a steady basis, with 10,000 more as temporary workers during peak periods.

With low prices and heavy advertising, Macy gradually shifted from specialized to diversified merchandise and the store grew rapidly.

By 1869, it had 12 departments. Eight years later, there were 22, and in 1887 there were 30. The founder began expanding his selling area in 1863 when frontage was added on 14th Street. The increase in store space was continuous. In 1887, Macy's sales reached $5 million and the store was among the largest retail establishments in New York.

Rowland Hussey Macy, born in 1822, was of the eighth Macy generation on Nantucket Island, Massachusetts. He was a Quaker and a descendant of Thomas Macy, the first white man to settle on the island sometime between 1659 and 1661.

When Macy was 15, he joined a whaling ship that left New Bedford in December, 1837, and returned four years later. In 1844, when Macy was 22, he opened a thread-and-needle store in Boston and, two years later, a retail dry goods store in the same city.

In 1847, Macy went to work for his brother-in-law, George W. Houghton, a dry goods retailer in Boston. Shortly, however, Rowland and his brother, Charles, went to California with the Forty-Niners.

With his brother Charles, Charles B. Mitchell, and Edward R. Anthony, Macy formed a partnership as Macy & Company in July, 1850, at Marysville, California. The partnership was dissolved within two months.

Returning east, Macy opened a store in April, 1851, in Haverhill, Massachusetts, under the name, R. B. Macy, the initials of his brother, Robert, who had entered the dry goods business in Boston. It was at Haverhill that Macy pronounced many of the principles he later took to New York, advertising his "buy and sell for cash" policy and the one-price concept. He also gave notice of attempting to undersell all competition in 1853.

Macy remained in business in Haverhill for four years, and went briefly to Superior City, Wisconsin, as a money and real-estate broker. In the fall of 1858, at 36, he turned to New York and opened an 11-foot-front store selling ribbons, laces, embroideries, artificial flowers, feathers, handkerchiefs, hosiery, and gloves. First day's sales were $11.06. By the end of 1859, when he had been in business about 13 months, Macy's sales totaled $90,000.

His shift to diversified merchandise began early. Within a month after he opened his shop, Macy began selling gloves and hosiery for men. By the following spring, he was offering housekeeping goods and ready-to-wear.

In 1860, Macy opened a department devoted to French and German fancy goods, including pocketbooks, handbags, tea sets, china, games, and toys. A year later, soaps, perfumes, and toilet extracts were added, and in 1864 came jewelry. Four years after that, clocks and silverware were being sold and, in 1869, house furnishings, books, and candy gave the store 12 departments.

Expansion of the store's physical facilities closely paralleled the diversification of goods offered for sale.

Macy made his first buying trip to Europe in 1870. He introduced private-label hoopskirts in 1860, and his five-pointed red-star symbol two years later. He established a mail-order department in 1874.

As Macy entered this growth period, he was given assistance by a distant relative, Margaret Getchell, a schoolteacher who went to work in the store about 1860. She served first as cashier, later as a bookkeeper and then as superintendent. Her husband, Abiel T. LaForge, became Macy's first partner in 1872.

LaForge, born in Fishkill, New York, in 1842, had been commander of a company in the Union Army in which Rowland, Jr., served during the Civil War. He joined Macy's in 1869 as a buyer of laces, embroideries, handkerchiefs, and trimmings. In June of that year, he married Miss Getchell.

In 1875, Macy took a second partner, his nephew, Robert Macy Valentine, who had worked in the store four years, succeeding LaForge in 1872 as buyer of laces and books. Volume then had passed $1½ million.

The founder died in Paris early in 1877 at 54.

A year later, Rowland, Jr., died in Boston. In the interim, LaForge and Valentine had purchased Macy's share of the business. LaForge became the senior partner with 55 per cent control. But he died in Florida in 1878 and Valentine bought his share. A few weeks later, Charles B. Webster, a distant cousin of both the founder and Valentine, entered the firm as a partner. A year later, Valentine died.

Webster, who now controlled 55 per cent of the business, took into partnership Jerome B. Wheeler, Valentine's brother-in-law. The two remained partners to the end of 1887.

In March, 1874, Nathan and Isidor Straus, sons of a German immigrant, began a glassware department in the store basement. This department became the most profitable in the store. On January 1, 1888, when Wheeler left the firm, they became Webster's partners. In 1896, they assumed full control.

The Straus story begins in 1852 when Lazarus Straus, a farmer and grain trader in Germany, emigrated to the United States. He opened a store in Talbotton, Georgia. Two years later, he brought his wife, three sons and a daughter from Germany. At the outbreak of the Civil War, 16-year-old Isidor began to help in the store. When the Civil War ended, the Straus family moved to New York and began L. Straus & Sons, a wholesale business in crockery, china, and glassware, with Nathan the salesman and Isidor active in the administrative end.

They decided to centralize their business and opened the glassware department at Macy's in 1874. Macy supplied the selling space and retail expenses and Straus bought and maintained the stock and supervised the operation. The department became an important part of the Macy setup.

After Isidor and Nathan became partners, they and Webster bought into Wechsler & Abraham in Brooklyn in 1893. The store later became Abraham & Straus. The two firms never came into direct competition until both entered the Walt Whitman shopping center in Huntington, Long Island, in 1962.

In 1896, Webster sold his interest in Macy's to the Straus

brothers who thereupon gained complete control. Jesse Isidor and Percy S. Straus, two of Isidor's three sons, soon entered the business.

In the meantime, the lines Macy's carried continued to expand. Although Macy had experimented with and then dropped a picnic department in the 1870's, a complete line of staple and fancy groceries was installed in 1893. A furniture department began three years later. By 1902, Macy's had 65 departments.

Jesse and Percy selected a new site for the store a mile uptown from the 14th Street establishment. On November 3, 1902, the old store closed, ending 43 years in the original location. Sales had advanced beyond $10 million. Four days later, Macy's opened its Herald Square store.

The new building—nine stories high—occupied a half block between Broadway and Seventh Avenue and 34th and 35th streets. It had a basement and sub-basement. To pave the way for its construction, 32 buildings and the Koster & Bial's Theater had to be removed. The store contained 33 elevators, four escalators, a built-in vacuum-cleaning system, and a power plant.

In 1910, two stories were added. Expansion continued a decade later. A new 20-story building west of the existing structure was completed in 1924 and two more additions were made in 1928 and 1931. By then, with the exception of two small corners, the store covered the entire city block from Broadway to Seventh Avenue and 34th to 35th Streets. It contained over two million square feet of floor space, the largest store under one roof.

In 1912, Isidor and his wife lost their lives when the Titanic went down at sea.

A year later, Isidor's brother, Nathan, sold his share of the business to his three nephews, Jesse, Percy, and Herbert, Isidor's sons. The three continued as partners from 1912 to 1919, when the business was incorporated with all the stock continuing under the control of the Straus family. In 1922, shares were offered to the public.

In November, 1959, stockholders approved the first change

of authorized common stock since 1928 by permitting an increase from 2½ million to 4 million shares.

During the second generation of Straus family operation, Macy's launched an expansion program that continued at an accelerated pace under the third generation, Jack Isidor Straus, Jesse's son.

Jesse, who served as president from 1919 to 1933, became ambassador to France for three years from 1933 to 1936. Percy, who had served as vice-president under Jesse, became president in 1933 and continued in that capacity until 1939 when he became chairman of the board. Herbert served as secretary-treasurer from 1919 to 1929, as treasurer from 1929 to 1933, and as vice-president from 1922 to 1933.

Jesse's son, Jack, born in 1900, joined the Macy organization in 1921 and became a director in 1928, succeeding his uncle, Percy, as president.

Macy's New York started its Thanksgiving Day parades in 1924.

Jack Straus, a graduate of Harvard, became vice-president under Percy in 1933 and served in that position until his elevation to acting president in 1939 at the age of 39. He was made president in 1940 and continued in that station until 1949. He moved up to chairman of the board in 1956, a position he still holds.

Richard Weil, Jr., Jack's cousin, became Macy's president in 1949. He joined Macy's in 1928, went with L. Bamberger & Co. in 1936, and served as its vice-president from 1939 to 1945. He returned to R. H. Macy & Co. as a vice-president in 1945. Weil became president in 1949 and served until 1952. He died in 1958.

Wheelock H. Bingham, the current corporate president, while a student at Harvard, took a summer job as a sales clerk at Macy's. He did not return to college but continued in retailing. Within three years, at the age of 22, he was made buyer of men's furnishings. By 1940, when only 33, Bingham became executive vice-president in charge of four merchandising divisions.

During World War II, he was a lieutenant in the Navy. From 1945 to 1952, he was president of Macy's San Francisco. In 1952, he became president of Macy's New York, and in 1956, president and director of R. H. Macy & Company. He also served on the board of directors of the Bank of America and as trustee of the Community Service Society.

Beardsley Ruml, who was chairman of the board from 1945 to 1949, succeeding Jesse Straus, went to Macy's as treasurer in 1934. He conceived the idea of withholding federal income taxes, a concept that became law in 1943.

Kenneth H. Straus, a fourth-generation member of the family and the board chairman's son, became merchandise vice-president of men's and boys' wear at Macy's New York in 1963, having served in a similar capacity at Bamberger's. John W. Straus, Herbert's son, is vice-president in charge of drug and cosmetics marketing and manufacturing for the corporation. Edward K. Straus, John's brother, is president of Garden State Plaza Corporation, which operates Garden State Shopping Center, a Macy subsidiary. Ralph I. Straus, Percy's son, is a director and former officer.

In 1962, David L. Yunich, at 45, was named president of Macy's New York. Yunich, a graduate of Harvard Graduate School of Business Administration, joined the Macy training program in 1940. He became merchandise administrator at Macy's New York in 1946, merchandise vice-president a year later, and senior vice-president in 1950. He was named president of Bamberger's and a director of R. H. Macy & Company in 1954.

A training department for employees was established in 1915, and an executive training course in 1919. Eight years later, the firm established its own bureau of standards.

It was in 1923 that Macy's acquired a controlling interest in Lasalle & Koch Company, Toledo, Ohio. Two years later, it bought into Davison-Paxon, Atlanta, Georgia, and in 1929 bought the common stock of L. Bamberger Company, Newark. O'Connor Moffat & Company, San Francisco, was purchased in 1945, and John Taylor Dry Goods Company, Kansas City,

Missouri, in 1947. The West Coast company is now called Macy's California; the Midwest firm, Macy's Missouri-Kansas.

Macy's first leap into the suburbs came in 1941, when a branch store opened in Parkchester in the Bronx. After that branch proved successful, Macy's began to go farther in suburban areas.

In 1947, Macy's opened a Jamaica store, a year later one in Flatbush, Brooklyn, and in 1949 another at White Plains. All were about 120,000 square feet. The White Plains store later was doubled in size and the first branch at Parkchester was enlarged to 197,000 square feet.

A branch was opened at Roosevelt Field, Long Island, New York, in 1956 with about 340,000 square feet, later enlarged to 370,000 square feet.

Macy's 44th branch, a 320,000-square-foot store, opened near Bay Shore, Long Island, in 1963. A store was opened in downtown New Haven, Connecticut, 80 miles from the mid-Manhattan base, in the fall of 1964. A 400,000 square-foot branch in Rego Park, Queens, New York, opened in the fall of 1965. A 250,000-square-foot store is slated to open in a regional shopping center in the Albany-Troy-Schenectady triangle, 150 miles up the Hudson from Manhattan in mid-1966. A 285,000-square foot unit is planned for New Rochelle. Other units of Macy's New York are spotted for Rockland and Dutchess Counties. The last will be the 11th unit of Macy's New York.

Each of the other R. H. Macy divisions across the country has also established branches.

Throughout Macy's history, many of the founder's business ideas remained. This store was the first to step up its advertising budget from 1 to 3 per cent of volume. However, the Macy cash policy was altered slightly in 1939, when a cash-time credit plan-depositor's account system was launched. This required DA customers to make deposits in advance of purchases. The credit policy was liberalized in 1959 when the DA was changed to mean dual accommodation and gave customers the choice of paying within 10 days of the statement without a service charge or paying monthly instalments plus a service charge.

Annual sales for the year ended July 31, 1965, were over $668 million; net profit, $15,431,928.

In 1964, the New York division rolled up an estimated $327 million, the Herald Square store leading the way with $176 million. Estimated volume of other New York-area units: Roosevelt Field, $42 million; White Plains, $31¼ million; Huntington, $18½ million; Bay Shore, $18 million; Parkchester, $16 million; Jamaica, $14¼ million; Brooklyn, $11 million.

Macy's 48 stores contained more than 11 million square feet at the beginning of 1965. This was expected to increase to 52 stores with 13 million square feet by 1966.

CHAPTER 26

MARSHALL FIELD & COMPANY

CHICAGO, ILLINOIS

"The World's Best-Known Department Store"

Marshall Field, who founded the internationally known store bearing his name, was born in 1834 in Conway, Massachusetts, quit school at 17, and took a job at $10 a week in a dry goods store owned by Henry G. (Deacon) Davis, a scrupulously honest merchant in Pittsfield, Massachusetts. Field was frugal and, after five years with Davis during which he had saved $400, he moved to Chicago where he felt there would be more opportunities for success in the mercantile business. He joined Cooley, Wadsworth Company, as a jobber and wholesaler of dry goods, was soon a traveling salesman, and became a junior partner in 1860 at 25.

From 1860 to 1864, the firm name was successively Cooley, Farwell & Company and Farwell, Field & Company. A year later, Field and Levi Z. Leiter, also a partner in the firm, bought an interest in Potter Palmer's wholesale and retail dry goods store, and the firm name became Field, Palmer & Leiter.

Up to this time, Field had concentrated on the jobbing and

wholesale divisions. In 1867, however, the co-partnership was dissolved and Field, Leiter & Company was formed in a building owned by Palmer, whose name is perpetuated in the Palmer House.

Twice, the business was destroyed by fire, once in 1871 and a second time in 1877. Four years after the second fire, Leiter retired, and Marshall Field & Company was born.

The present mammoth store with 2,235,000 square feet was built at State and Washington in 1906.

Field is credited with introducing and incorporating into his policies many ideas that have become traditional in retailing. Among these are: The customer is always right; satisfaction guaranteed or money back; sales on approval and freedom to return without a time limit; all goods plainly marked and sold at one price; a lower-price basement; women shoppers to help men select items for their women folk; free delivery; a restaurant in a retail store; and the importation of merchandise directly from the foreign markets. Some students of early retailing, however, credit most of these advances to Harry Gordon Selfridge, who was an executive in the Field store.

Although Field was never a "mixer", he did in the early days stand near the main entrance and, wearing white gloves, greet customers as they entered. When he died in 1906 at 70, he left a fortune, but only a small part of it came from his retail and wholesale business. The bulk of it was derived from sagacious investments in Chicago real estate and in railroads and utilities. In the Retailing Hall of Fame in the Chicago Merchandise Mart, a statue of Field stands with those of John Wanamaker; George H. Hartford, founder of the Great Atlantic and Pacific Tea Company; and Frank W. Woolworth, founder of the five-and-ten-cent-store chain.

No manager of Marshall Field's retail store had a greater impact on its balance sheet and operating statement than had Harry Gordon Selfridge, who was hired by Field at $7 a week and started in the wholesale division. He was soon promoted to traveling salesman and quickly learned there was some disparity between what Field's had to offer merchants and what they wanted.

In addition, he picked up some helpful ideas on merchandise display and proper lighting. Transferred to the retail store at his own request, Selfridge became its manager in 1887. Field continued to be more interested in his jobbing and wholesale business, gave Selfridge a free hand in the retail store, and in 1890 made him a junior partner.

Selfridge essentially was a promoter and personally wrote much of Field's advertising. He displayed talent in interior and window displays, tying them in with his newspaper advertising or with some interesting local event.

Selfridge used to walk rapidly through the store every day and soon earned the nickname of "Mile-a-Minute Harry." Nothing that needed correction ever escaped his attention.

The Chicago World's Fair in 1893 gave Selfridge full scope for his showmanship, including eye-catching window and interior displays and unusual lighting effects. These, together with several million dollars' worth of imported merchandise, lured hordes of Fair visitors to the store and Field's business boomed to new highs. By 1904, the year Selfridge left Field's, the store's retail profit was a record one of $1,445,000. Selfridge left the firm after 25 years because he felt he had earned more than merely a junior partnership and Field showed no appreciation of his achievements.

When Selfridge told Field he had bought the close-by Schlesinger & Mayer store and intended to operate it under his own name, Field took the news quietly. He then began placing more confidence in men around him, notably in John G. Shedd, head of the wholesale division. Before a Congressional committee on tariffs, Field said that Shedd was "the greatest merchant in the United States." It was the first compliment Field ever paid a subordinate.

Selfridge opened his first store with theatrical flourish, but he felt he was about to compete with his own people at Field's and soon decided to dispose of the store.

The idea of opening a store in London under his own name was beginning to take form. On his trips to London, Selfridge had been disappointed not to find some usable ideas in that nation of shopkeepers and he had observed many shortcomings in customer service.

Shedd, always a friend, helped Selfridge sell the Schlesinger & Mayer store at a fair price to Carson, Pirie, Scott. Selfridge was nearly 50 years old when he established Selfridge & Company in London in 1906. His progress there is recorded in the chapter devoted to Selfridge's.

Field died in 1906 at 70. Shedd succeeded to the presidency and, in turn, was succeeded by James Simpson in 1923, who had risen from an office boy. In 1930, John McKinlay, who had started as cash boy, became president and Simpson stepped up to board chairman. In 1935, beset with continuing losses in the wholesale division, the directors hired James O. McKinsey, management consultant and at one time professor of accounting and marketing at the University of Chicago, to come up with a solution. He recommended that wholesaling and manufacturing operations be discontinued. He was appointed board chairman and McKinlay resigned.

Field's opened suburban branches in Lake Forest and Evanston in 1928, and one in Oak Park in 1929.

Disposing of the wholesale business also meant selling the Field-owned Merchandise Mart, the largest mercantile building in the world. McKinsey saw clearly that more and more retailers would be buying direct from manufacturers through their buying offices and that, even with the expense of sending their buyers to the wholesale markets, the merchandise could be purchased at lower cost. Therefore, the future of large wholesalers was dim, since the smaller stores could not provide sufficient volume to make it a profitable operation for Field's.

McKinsey was urged to remain in the organization and make his recommendations effective. He died, however, in 1937 before the task could be finished.

Frederick D. Corley was president from 1937 until his retirement in 1943.

Hughston M. McBain, with Field's since 1922 and once John Shedd's office boy, then became president. James L. Palmer, graduate of Brown University and professor of marketing at the University of Chicago before he came to Field's in 1937, became first vice-president. The two instituted merchandising, promotional, and operating procedures that substantially improved prestige and profits. In 1949, McBain became chairman, and Palmer president. McBain had joined Field's in 1922 as a bill adjuster in the retail store. He became general manager of the Merchandise Mart in 1932 and general manager of wholesale and manufacturing divisions in 1935. In 1938, McBain became a director and was appointed general manager of the retail store in 1940, and president of Field's in 1943.

While McBain was curtailing the wholesale activities, his chief concern was to find jobs for the 1,000 employees connected with the Mart and the jobbing division. Palmer, then vice-president, was McBain's aide on problems that developed in disposing of the mills and the Merchandise Mart. The latter was finally sold in 1946 to Joseph P. Kennedy, father of the late President John F. Kennedy, for $18 million, less than its cost.

Palmer, a native of Waterboro, Maine, has an A.B. degree from Brown University and an A.M. from the University of Chicago. He also is a C.P.A. He became director of sales promotion at Field's in 1925. In 1940, he became executive vice-president and director. McBain retired in 1958 and Palmer became chief executive officer. The chairmanship, as a separate function, was discontinued. Palmer retired in 1964 and was succeeded by Gerald A. Sivage. He had joined Field's as a clerk in the wholesale division in 1931, became a vice-president in 1954 and then was named, successively, general operating manager and general manager of the Chicago stores division and executive vice-president before he assumed the presidency. David W. Davidson, executive vice-president, was previously a senior vice-president and general merchandise manager and assistant general manager of the Chicago stores division.

A branch was added in Park Forest, Illinois, in 1955.

For the fiscal year ending January 31, 1964, Field's sales were

$280,105,000. Net earnings reached $12,441,000. This includes the volume of six Chicago-area units, one in suburban Milwaukee, and the three Frederick & Nelson, Seattle, stores. The two main stores and branches give Field's total gross area of 4,738,-000 square feet.

Shopping center stores, opened in Old Orchard, Skokie, Illinois, in the fall of 1956 and since expanded; in Wauwatosa, suburban Milwaukee, Wisconsin, in early 1959, and in Oakbrook, Illinois, in 1962 were reported in the 1964 financial report to have "attained new sales levels." The Old Orchard and Oakbrook units are in the $20 million plus class; the suburban Milwaukee branch, in the $12 to $15 million class.

Field's is planning another Chicago branch in the southeast suburban area to "complete a ring of regional shopping centers."

CHAPTER 27

MEIER & FRANK

CO., INC.

PORTLAND, OREGON

"A Northwest Retail Institution"

When Portland, Oregon, was still a frontier town of 1,300 residents, Aaron Meier, a 26-year-old immigrant, opened a dry goods and general merchandise store in a 35-by-50-foot area. The year was 1857. The store was at 137 Front Street, a site on which an expanding establishment would remain for 41 years.

One hundred and five years after the founder opened his first store, Meier & Frank Company, Inc., owned the two largest stores in the state. The company grew with the West. Sales for 1964 reached $71,076,681; net earnings, $2,219,738.

Sixteen years after the store was founded, the worst fire in Portland's history leveled 20 buildings in a business-center block. Meier & Frank suffered a $60,000 loss, and the family had to pool its resources to get back into business.

A flood in 1894 failed to faze the store operators. With the main floor three feet under water, Meier & Frank remained in business by building walks above the regular sidewalk level, raising the counters inside the store, building walkways around the counters, and taking customers down the main aisle of the store in rowboats.

Aaron Meier, born in Bavaria, came to the United States in 1855 when he was 24 and spent his first two years at Downeyville, California, where he worked in a store with his two brothers, Emanuel and Julius. Aaron then opened his own store in Portland, 2 years before Oregon became a state, which he operated for 13 years before the Frank family joined in the enterprise.

Meier returned to Germany in 1863 to marry Jeanette Hirsch. Returning to the United States, he bought merchandise for his store from A. T. Stewart & Company in New York. He reopened his store in Portland in July, 1864.

Six years later, in San Francisco, Meier met Emil Frank, who became a clerk in Meier's store and remained there until 1888 when he left to enter a drug firm. Emil's brother, Sigmund Frank, 23, married Fannie Meier, daughter of the Aaron Meiers. Shortly thereafter, the store became Meier & Frank.

In the 1880's, farmers and their wives came to Portland by steamer from downriver. Before shopping, the men sat around a stove, smoking store-supplied tobacco in store-furnished clay pipes. Employees were given 15- or 20-minute lunch hours and, if goods had to be shipped on the river steamer, they worked late labeling and delivering the merchandise.

It was during this period that Portland began to grow. The store in the early 1880's had 20 employees, nearly all of them related. But the transcontinental railroad that made Portland a western terminus in 1884 had a big impact.

Ludwig and Leon Hirsch, brothers of the founder's wife, went to work in the store in the 1880's. Ludwig brought ready-to-wear dresses to Portland, and went to Europe in 1892 to buy hosiery, gloves, and china for the store. Leon became the men's clothing and furnishings buyer and later was purchasing agent and secretary of the corporation.

In 1885, Meier & Frank opened a two-story building at 185–187 First Street that ran to Second Street.

Six years later, in 1891, a store at the corner of Second and

Yamhill was added and Meier & Frank opened on all four sides of the block, at First, Second, Yamhill, and Taylor.

At this time, Sigmund Frank was in charge of the store, assisted by the founder's two sons, Abe and Julius Meier. Aaron Meier had died in 1889 at 58, just 32 years after he founded the firm. Both of Sigmund Frank's sons, M. Lloyd and Aaron M., were to enter the business at a later date.

In 1893, the store was incorporated and that same year, Meier & Frank bought a half block on Fifth Street for $165,000.

In 1898, a five-story building, with a basement, opened on the Fifth Street site. By this time, the store had 250 employees. Two years later, the population of Portland was recorded at 90,000, and a decade after that, in 1910, the city had mushroomed to 207,000. The store had joined in the growth.

The first three floors of the store on Fifth Street were reserved for the retail business. The basement was utilized both for storage and the grocery and crockery departments. The fourth floor was for the wholesale department, the fifth for manufacturing and receiving sections.

In 1903, the corner lot at Sixth and Alder, behind the Fifth Street building, was bought, and a year later an adjoining lot was purchased. Construction began on a 10-story annex on this property in 1908. It opened in 1909.

A year later, death came to the second of the founders, Sigmund Frank, but the planned expansion went on under his successor, Julius L. Meier, son of the founder. In 1913, the old five-story building on Fifth Street was dismantled and construction began on a new 14-story structure on the same site. While it was being erected, Meier & Frank used both its 10-story annex and a rented 12-story building across the street.

The new building, then the largest store west of Chicago, opened in 1915. It had two basements, five elevators for customers, two more for employees and two for freight. It contained the first escalator on the Pacific Coast. Inside the steel-frame, reinforced-concrete structure was a power plant and central vacuum-cleaning system.

Five years later, a $1 million warehouse was opened on the block of Northwest Everett, Flanders, and 13th Streets.

In 1925, a 99-year lease was obtained on a building at the only corner left in the Meier & Frank store block, and in 1931 a 14-story building went up. The store opened in 1932, the year of the firm's 75th anniversary.

Aaron Meier's brothers-in-law and, later, two of his nephews, Leopold and Max Hirsch, played an important role in the store's beginning. Leopold, who had come to work in 1884, began the carpet and drapery department. Max became credit manager, general superintendent and, eventually, assistant to the president. Other members of the Hirsch family helped found White Stag Manufacturing Company.

In 1930, a friend, George Joseph, the Republican nominee for governor, died several weeks before the election. Julius Meier won the election and served as governor from 1931 to 1935. He died in 1937.

Aaron M. Frank succeeded Julius Meier as president and general manager of the firm in 1937. Born in 1891, he received a law degree from the University of Oregon in 1913, and went to work in the store in 1914.

Also of importance in the firm's history was Reuben R. Adams, hired by Meier & Frank in 1913, to set up a central receiving system. Adams was general manager from 1918 to 1923 when he left to become general merchandise manager at Nugent's, St. Louis, Missouri. From there, he went to May Company, Cleveland, as general merchandise manager, then served as president of Hahne & Company, Newark, New Jersey. He returned to the Portland store in 1931 as assistant to the vice-president and general manager. He became vice-president, assistant to the president, and general manager in 1937.

Egil Krogh, born in Oslo, Norway, went to work for Meier & Frank at the age of 57 in 1959. He had been divisional manager of Frederick & Nelson, Seattle, and president and general manager of Sibley, Lindsey & Curr Company, Rochester, New York. Leaving there in 1958 as chairman of the board, he went to Meier & Frank and was elected to its board of directors in 1962 but died the same month.

Charles E. Snell, who joined Meier & Frank in 1928, succeeded Krogh as general merchandise manager. He went to the Portland firm after graduation from the University of Oregon. He left in 1934 to become general merchandise manager of the Jones Store, Kansas City, Missouri. Then, in 1940, he became resident manager of the New York office of May Department Stores Company. Three years later, he returned to Meier & Frank as assistant general merchandise manager. He left the firm again in 1951 to become executive vice-president and general manager of the W. & J. Sloane Company, San Francisco, returning to Meier & Frank in 1955 as assistant general merchandise manager, a post he held until promoted to fill Krogh's position.

The third generation of the Meier and Frank families, Julius (Jack) L. Meier, Jr., and Gerald W. and Richard S. Frank, also were active in the business. Jack Meier became vice-president and secretary in 1958. Gerald Frank was manager of the Salem store from its opening in 1955 until 1964. He was named vice president in 1958. Richard Frank, Aaron's son and Gerald's brother, was vice-president and treasurer when he died in 1962 at 43. Leslie Sherman, son-in-law of M. Lloyd Frank, Aaron's older brother, became merchandise manager and manager of the Lloyd Center store and a director.

In 1964, dissension between the Meier and Frank families, which together owned about 80 per cent of the company stock, resulted in removal of Aaron Frank as president and general manager by his cousins and other relatives in the Frank branch and their allies in the company. The Meier contingent felt Aaron Frank had held the reins too tightly, too long, and wanted to sell out to May Department Stores. Until then, Aaron Frank had retained control because he had the voting rights to a block of about 20 per cent of the stock, owned by his brother, Lloyd, and held in trust for the latter's two daughters after his death in 1959. Lloyd Frank's children took over the stock in

early 1964. Aaron Frank and his son, Gerald, at that point controlled only 20 per cent of the stock, and Aaron was no longer
in command. Jack Meier, board member-chief counsel Abe
Eugene Rosenberg, and Leslie Sherman opposed the Aaron
Frank interests. Aaron and Gerald Frank resigned and sold
their shares to Broadway-Hale. Jack Meier was elected president and general manager. Roger L. Meier, who had been a
divisional merchandise manager at Lipman Wolfe & Company,
Portland department store, and whose father, Allen, Sr., had
been Meier & Frank's treasurer, was appointed manager of the
Salem store, succeeding Gerald Frank.

By April, 1965, May had acquired voting control of Meier &
Frank. Broadway-Hale, which bought more than one-third of
the Meier & Frank stock for $16 million, said it planned to hold
on to it as a long-term investment.

At Meier & Frank's annual meeting in June, 1965, Jack Meier
was reelected president and general manager; Sherman, vice-
president and secretary; and Lloyd F. Eckhardt, treasurer and
assistant secretary. A new post of executive vice-president was
created and given to William C. Miller, general merchandise
manager. Holdover directors are Jack Meier, Rosenberg, Sherman, and Eckhardt. New directors, replacing Aaron and Gerald
Frank and Allen Meier, Jr., San Francisco importer, are Roger
Meier, Harold W. Heller, vice-president, Bradley's Frozen
Foods, grandson of Abe Meier, first cousin of Roger, and second cousin of Jack; and Herbert A. Mack, assistant counsel,
May Co.

Jack Meier and Rosenberg were elected members of the
board of May Department Stores Company at the annual meeting in June, 1965.

CHAPTER 28

RICH'S, INC.

ATLANTA, GEORGIA

"The Spirit of Rich's"

With $500 borrowed from his brother, William, 20-year-old Morris Rich, born in Kashau, Hungary, opened his first retail store in 1867 in Atlanta, Georgia, still under the severe burden of Civil War reconstruction. The store comprised 1500 square feet. It had five employees.

Atlanta was rebuilt, prospered, and grew. Rich's also thrived and became the largest department store south of the Mason-Dixon Line.

Morris Rich, later joined by two brothers, Daniel and Emanuel, opened his shop with liberal credit and return policies, a one-price guarantee, and a promise of service to the customer.

The merchandising slogan of the founder was: "The success of any sale is measured by our customer's complete and final satisfaction. At Rich's, the customer makes her own adjustment. Merchandise from Rich's must be satisfactory; it must please you today and please you that much more tomorrow. The good name of an old institution stands behind our every transaction.

We believe in you, in your sense of fair play. Believe in us when we say you are always right at Rich's."

In later years, the store called itself a Southern Institution and officials said, "We never sell an article, we sell the institution."

Rich's weathered a financial panic in 1873, and in 1880 moved to a two-story building in Whitehall Street. It sported the first plate-glass show windows in Atlanta. The interior of the shop was done in black and gold and had elaborate gas chandeliers.

The first of the founders, Emanuel Rich, died in 1897 at 48. He had gone on the store's first European buying trip 10 years earlier and was on the board of directors of the Cotton States and International Exposition. His son, Walter, later was to serve as president of the store for 21 years.

A year after the turn of the century, the store built a six-story north annex at 52–56 Whitehall Street. That doubled the space in which was contained Rich's first elevator.

In 1906, the name of the firm was changed to M. Rich & Bros. Co.

M. Rich & Bros. Co. in 1919 leased the southwest corner of Broad and Alabama Streets. Five years later, it was to be the site of a six-story $1½ million steel, Indiana-limestone, and Normandy-tile store building.

In 1920, the second of the founders, Daniel Rich, died at 77.

In 1924, the year Rich's moved to the Broad and Alabama Street location, Lucian W. York, the store's general manager, died. He had begun with the firm as a teen-age stock boy and eventually secured an interest in the business. He was succeeded as general manager and secretary by Frank H. Neely, who was 40 when he joined Rich's. Entirely without retail experience, Neely came from 10 years of reorganizing and managing seven plants of the Fulton Bag and Cotton Mills. At Rich's, he promptly established one of the first merchandise stock-control systems.

Two years after Neely began working for the store, Morris Rich retired as president and became chairman of the board.

He died in 1928 at 81. Walter Henry Rich, Emanuel's son, succeeded his uncle as president in 1926.

Walter, who had been attending Columbia University when his father died, had left the school and joined the firm. In 1906, he was named treasurer; in 1920 vice-president, and, later, president. He received the fourth annual Tobe award shortly before his death in 1947.

He established the Rich Foundation which has provided the Emory School of Business Administration with a sustaining professorship, equipped the out-patient ward of Georgia Baptist Hospital, built the Rich Computer Center at Georgia Institute of Technology and inaugurated classroom lessons by radio and television throughout the Atlanta school system.

When Walter died, Neely assumed the presidency. He became chairman of the board in 1949, serving until 1961, when he was named to the store's executive committee. Neely has held many offices outside the company. He was the first chairman of the Georgia Department of Commerce, and a director and vice-president of the National Retail Dry Goods Association. For his contributions to the science of management, he received the Gantt Medal in 1952 and the Taylor Key in 1958.

In 1929, the firm reached corporate status as Rich's, Inc., but M. Rich & Bros. Co. continued as the real estate holding corporation. The two merged in 1957 to become Rich's, Inc.

In 1937, air-conditioning was installed, and the third floor of the store was redesigned as a fashion floor with 13 specialty shops.

In the Christmas of 1939, a $1 million expansion program was announced. Escalators were installed, and a new warehouse was built across the street. The program included six new floors, an addition to the selling basement, and new shipping rooms. The project was completed in 1940. In 1942, the store had 363,391 square feet. By 1949, the size had been expanded to 435,000 square feet.

There were 24 show windows in the main building and four air-conditioning plants. In 1948, a new Store for Homes was connected to the building by a four-level, 35-foot-wide, glass-enclosed bridge. A six-floor parking garage for 1,250 cars is next to the Store for Homes and affords direct access to all selling floors. The store is actually four separate units—the Store for Fashion opened in 1924, the Store for Homes opened in 1948, the Store for Men added in 1951, and the huge Basement Store.

When Neely moved up to board chairman, the presidency was assumed by Richard H. Rich, the founder's grandson, who joined the store in 1923 when it was doing $5 million. A graduate of the University of Pennsylvania's Wharton School, Richard Rich was the son of a daughter of Morris Rich. Richard legally adopted the Rich name at the suggestion of his uncle, Walter, in order to preserve it into the third generation.

With Ben R. Gordon as executive vice-president, a three-man executive team functioned. Gordon had joined the store in 1925 upon graduation from Georgia School of Technology, also Neely's alma mater. Gordon got his first job on the strength of an A-plus he received for a thesis proving that Rich's location was much more desirable than any other—then, a highly debatable issue. In 1955, Gordon left Rich's to become president of City Stores Company. He later became vice-president of Allied Stores Corporation and president of Stern's, New York, and in 1963 of The White House, San Francisco, which in 1964 ceased operations.

Richard Rich—employees call him Mr. Dick—succeeded Neely as chairman of the board in 1961 and continues in that position.

Richard Rich served as a special assistant to the American Ambassador to Brazil in 1943. He was president of the National Retail Merchants Association in 1957 and 1958 and received that organization's annual Gold Medal award in 1963.

When Rich stepped up to board chairman, Harold Brockey, who had worked for Macy's New York for 20 years, became president and chief operating officer. He had joined Rich's in 1950 as general merchandise manager of the homes and fabrics divisions, become general merchandising manager in 1955, and executive vice-president and general manager in 1958.

Rich's began to expand in 1954 when it acquired S. H.

George & Sons, Knoxville, Tennessee. The branch was built in a new location in 1955 and sold in 1961 to Miller's Inc., when Rich's centralized its holdings in the Atlanta area.

In 1959, Rich's opened a branch at Lenox Square Shopping Center, 10 miles north of the main store in Atlanta. The second branch opened at Belvedere Plaza Shopping Center east of the main store in 1959, a third at Cobb County Center in 1964, a fourth in the North DeKalb shopping center in 1965, and a fifth in the Greenbriar shopping center in the latter part of the same year. As of the beginning of 1966, the downtown store boasted 1,500,000 square feet; the branches, 763,000 square feet.

In the year ended February, 1965, sales had reached $116,-014,000, and net profit came to $5,628,000.

With the two new stores, there are about 9,000 employees during the summer or slow period; 10,000, during the peak fall and holiday periods.

The store has many traditions. Its liberal returns policy has become renowned as a complement to the "customer is always right" philosophy. The store has no complaint department and the sales clerk makes the adjustment.

Once a customer, after eight years, brought back two pairs of draperies because the color wasn't right. The store allowed the return. Another customer complained that a wedding cake, already eaten at the reception, had white instead of yellow layers and the store presented her with another cake. Rich's returns ratio runs between 13 and 14 per cent, admittedly greater than that of any other store of its size. Richard Rich calls an easy returns policy "the basis of our image."

In difficult times, the store liberalizes rather than tightens credit. When a peach crop was ruined by a freeze, the store ran a full-page advertisement announcing that Rich's could wait for its money. In 1930 when the City Council was unable to meet the schoolteachers' payroll, the store cashed $645,000 in scrip for the salaries without any obligation.

Rich's runs special trains to bring customers from outlying areas for shopping trips during "Rich's Days." The lighting of a tree on Thanksgiving brings 100,000 people to watch. At Easter, a farm with small animals is set up in the store's window. On "One Enchanted Evening," models show spring clothes during a concert.

For its employees, the store provides a cafeteria, nursing services, discounts on purchases, fashion shows, a library, and monthly bonuses for topping their sales quotas.

Customers use store facilities as meeting places for various clubs, and the store's nursery for children six months to six years old. Newcomers to the city are greeted at welcoming luncheons.

Said Richard Rich in 1963: "Our formula is to concentrate on fashion leadership and customer service. We are setting professionalism and high quality standards against mere price appeal . . ."

And Neely said in an address to the Newcomen Society of North America at a banquet in Georgia in 1960:

"The name Rich's, and even the title, a Southern Institution, doesn't convey our most precious asset, an intangible known wherever we serve as The Spirit of Rich's. This quality was present even at the founding of the business in 1867."

CHAPTER 29

SCRUGGS-VANDERVOORT-BARNEY DRY GOODS CO.

ST. LOUIS, MO.

"The Fashion Authority of St. Louis"

Two Virginia men, Richard M. Scruggs and his friend, M.V.L. McClelland, traveled west to St. Louis, Missouri. With capital supplied by McClelland's uncle, they founded a small dry goods store on Fourth Street in 1850. This was the year fire destroyed the city's business district and cholera brought death to 5,000 of its 74,439 people.

Scruggs, a native of Richmond, Virginia, began clerking in a dry goods store at Lynchburg, Virginia, at the age of 15 and later became its bookkeeper.

Spurred by the westward movement for which wagon trains formed in St. Louis, McClelland, Scruggs & Company grew with the city into what is now Scruggs-Vandervoort-Barney.

The original store, between Locust and St. Charles streets, moved in 1854 to larger quarters at the southeast corner of Fourth and St. Charles.

In 1860, William L. Vandervoort, a New Yorker, bought into the firm, having decided against accepting an executive position with A. T. Stewart in New York. He had entered the retailing business with a Baltimore store at the age of 12 for $1 a week and meals.

During the Civil War, Scruggs withdrew temporarily from the operation, the firm's name was changed to W. L. Vandervoort & Co., and Vandervoort continued in control.

In 1864, Scruggs returned and the store's name became Scruggs, Vandervoort & McClelland. McClelland retired in 1868. Two years later, the store moved to the Mercantile Library Building at Broadway and Locust streets.

In 1872, it was incorporated as Scruggs-Vandervoort-Barney Dry Goods Company. Incorporators included the founder, R. M. Scruggs, G. A. Scruggs, Vandervoort, and Charles E. Barney, who had been employed by the store in 1860 and had become a junior partner prior to the incorporation. He died in 1898; Vandervoort, two years later.

The store moved again in 1888, this time to the corner of Fifth and Locust streets. By 1895, St. Louis had exploded to a city of 600,000 people.

A year before the turn of the century, two men who worked at McCreery's in New York City—Hanford Crawford and Robert Johnston—acquired an interest in the business. Irish-born Johnston had been in the silk business before he emigrated in 1892 to New York.

In 1905, when the founder, Richard M. Scruggs, died, Crawford became the store's president; Johnston, the vice-president and secretary. H. B. Claflin Company bought the business from the founder's estate. Claflin also was in control of Associated Dry Goods and Mercantile Stores Corporation.

In 1911, Melville LeVaunt Wilkinson, who worked for Claflin and was in charge of both Hengerer's and J. N. Adam in Buffalo, was transferred to Scruggs-Vandervoort-Barney as president, and Crawford left the firm. In the fall of that same year, Claflin's failed and Wilkinson and a group of St. Louis businessmen bought the firm's common stock.

Wilkinson, who was born at Maysville, Indiana, went to work for Knisely Bros. Dry Goods Co., Butler, Indiana, in 1880 when he was only 15. He moved on in 1898 to Root & Mc-Bride Co. and later to William Taylor Sons & Co. in Cleveland, Ohio. He became president of William Hengerer Co. and J. N. Adam Co. of Buffalo and Thomas Watkins Son & Co. of Hamilton, Canada, in 1906. Five years later, when he was 46, he joined Vandervoort's as president and remained until his death in 1925 at the age of 60.

Under Claflin, the firm in 1906 incorporated the Scruggs-Vandervoort-Barney Bank for the convenience of customers and purchased the retail stores of Simons Hardware Co. and Georgia-Stimson Furniture and Carpet Co.

The following year, Scruggs-Vandervoort-Barney made a daring move. It left Broadway, a desirable shopping street, for a virgin location in the Syndicate Trust Building at 10th and Olive streets. In 1913, the firm added a seven-floor store in the Century Building on the square block bounded by Ninth, Tenth and Olive and Locust streets, its present site.

After World War I, the store expanded rapidly, acquiring Mermod-Jaccard & King Jewelry Co. in 1917; L. L. White Dry Goods Co., Columbus, Ohio, five years later; and, in 1924, Denver Dry Goods Co., Denver, Colorado.

At Wilkinson's death, Frank McConnell Mayfield, born in Cleveland, Tennessee, in 1887, became president in 1925 at 38. He continued in that office until 1954 when he was named chairman of the board. He also served as president of Mermod-Jaccard & King Jewelry Company and chairman of the board of Denver Dry Goods and Emery-Bird-Thayer of Kansas City, Missouri, a store the firm bought in 1945.

By 1940, Vandervoort's occupied eight floors of the Syndicate Trust Building and seven floors of the Century Building. It had 12 acres of space in the main store and 1,500 employees selling 400,000 items in 150 departments. There was also a warehouse on Locust Street, directly across from the store; a garage at 11th and St. Charles Streets with space for 500 cars; and a trade-in store on 12th Street for buying and selling new and used furniture.

In 1935, Vandervoort's began its downstairs store with 25 budget departments. It had established a mail-order department in 1884 and was the first department store to instal a travel bureau. By 1915, its delivery department was 20 per cent mechanized and, 10 years later, the last horse was sent out to pasture. In 1920, the store built the Vandervoort Music Hall inside the establishment and offered free recitals, lectures, and Shakespearean programs. A series of specialty shops opened in 1959.

Vandervoort's, calling itself the fashion authority of the Midwest, employs a stylist to plan fashion shows that include weekly tearoom showings. In 1960, it presented the first teen-age fashion show and offered a Chargette plan for 15-to-19-year olds. The Bride's Shop specializes in services that range right up to planning an entire wedding.

Laurence Edward Mallinckrodt, a native of St. Louis, was named president in 1954 at 45. He received a master's degree from Harvard in 1932, the year he joined Vandervoort's. He was divisional merchandise manager and assistant general merchandise manager from 1932 to 1943, became treasurer in 1946, a director in 1948, and served as vice-president and general merchandise manager from 1952 to 1954.

He has also been a director of the Metropolitan Planning Association of St. Louis, the Social Planning Council of St. Louis, president of the Council of St. Louis University, and vice-president and director of the National Retail Merchants Association.

Frank M. Mayfield, Jr., a director, was elected president of Emery-Bird-Thayer in 1959, succeeding Herbert H. Wilson. He went to the Kansas City store as vice-president and assistant to the president. He had been a secretary of Vandervoort's and a director of the parent firm as well as of Mermod-Jaccard & King Jewelry Co.

Although sales for the three-city corporation were up slightly to $65,509,763 for the year ended July 31, 1963, they still were below the $67,647,610 peak in the year ending in mid 1960.

On October 1, 1963, Marshall Wells Company, a wholesale distributor of hardware and related lines and 80 per cent owned by Larchfield Corporation, a holding company, acquired 96 per cent of the common stock of Vandervoort's and assumed control.

Hyman J. Sobiloff, chairman of both Marshall Wells and Larchfield, became chairman of Vandervoort's, succeeding Mayfield who was elected to a new post of vice-president. Sobiloff, born in Fall River, Massachusetts, in 1912, is a financier. He entered the retail scene in 1950 as a member of an investment group that acquired Frederick Loeser & Co., Inc., a Brooklyn, New York, department store. His investments carried him into other retail firms—first, W. & J. Sloane in 1955 and, later, Barker Bros., a West Coast home furnishings company. These have since been sold. Sloane is now a subsidiary of City Stores Company, while Barker is a subsidiary of City Products Corporation.

Under new management, Mallinckrodt was re-elected president of Vandervoort's. Frank Mayfield, Jr., resigned as president of the Kansas City subsidiary in 1963 and became a corporate representative of Marshall Wells. He died at 41 in late 1964. Denver Dry Goods Company was sold in December, 1964, to Associated Dry Goods Corporation.

Vandervoort's first branch was opened at Clayton, Missouri, in 1950 and expanded in 1964, its second in the Crestwood Plaza, St. Louis in 1958, and its third in a 150,000-square-foot store in Northwest Plaza in the fall of 1965.

Estimates of 1964 volume: downtown, $13 million; Crestwood, $6 million; Clayton, $3 million; Mermod-Jaccard & King, $2½ million. The $24½ million total is believed ahead of the previous year.

CHAPTER 30

SELFRIDGE'S LIMITED

LONDON, ENGLAND

The "Earl" of Oxford Street

When Harry Gordon Selfridge arrived in London in 1906, he was a man near 50 who already had had a successful career in America. But the new project of building a department store in London, incorporating all the best features of successful American businesses, had wholly possessed his mind for three years.

Selfridge began working for Marshall Field's wholesale division in Chicago, Illinois, in 1879 as a stockboy and salesman for $7 a week. He remained with the firm for 25 years. He became general manager in 1887, was made a junior partner three years later, and left the firm in 1904. He bought a competing Chicago store—Schlesinger & Mayer—but sold it within a short time, and eventually moved to England.

On his previous trips to London, Selfridge had noticed that many potential customers hesitated to enter stores unless they were ready to buy a specific item. "Lookers" were not encouraged to browse around as was the custom in America. London shoppers were expected to make selections from price-marked products in display windows. Newspaper advertising was not used extensively.

Selfridge hoped to change this as well as many other traditional practices of the London shops. His store would be an inviting place for all, including browsers, and no one would be importuned to buy. His floorwalkers would be affable, courteous hosts, trained to greet visitors with a smile.

Selfridge did not have sufficient capital to lease property or to erect the type of store he had in mind. Samuel Waring, later Lord Waring, became his partner. Waring was head of Waring & Gillow's home furnishings store on Oxford Street and also of Waring & White, building contractors.

On June 19, 1906, a company was registered as Selfridge & Waring Ltd., with capital of £1,000,000. Waring & White was to build the store, but plans that Selfridge had drawn by Chicago architects did not meet London regulations. Finally, after a wasted year, the plans were redrawn by London architects, old structures were razed, and excavations were begun at an Oxford Street site.

Even after ground was broken, however, Selfridge continued to change his plans, giving no thought to the additional expense. When Selfridge made newspaper headlines by hiring a band to speed the builders' pace, the conservative Waring withdrew. Work was stopped until Selfridge could obtain additional capital.

John Musker, of Home & Colonial Stores grocery chain, gave him a guarantee of £250,000, and the new firm was registered March 5, 1908, as Selfridge & Company. It had a capital of £900,000.

Selfridge called the cornerstone-laying ceremony the greatest moment in his life. Before the store opened, he laid plans for an advertising campaign and began hiring personnel. He planned a series of institutional advertisements that left the heads of other London stores aghast. He arranged for a group of full-page drawings by 38 of the leading British black-and-white artists. He wrote the copy himself, avoiding direct selling of goods and stressing instead his store policies and the unusual services it would offer. Selfridge spent £30,000 on these pre-opening advertisements.

Although competing stores were reluctant to adopt what amounted to a change in traditional London retail procedures, they did attempt to minimize the effect of the Selfridge ads by buying more space than usual themselves. Selfridge's display advertising represented a major departure in this field in England and, as a result, he and his activities were thereafter prime subjects of news columns. The American-type store had an enormous impact on British retailing.

Percy A. Best, who had been a salesman for a soft goods firm, was hired as staff manager and personnel director. He was instructed to obtain key personnel by paying slightly more than the starting rates prevailing elsewhere and by offering salesmen a small commission on every sale as well. Three key men were brought from Chicago, but Englishmen were employed for all other important executive posts.

Charles W. Steines, with Marshall Field's wholesale for many years, became Selfridge's first general merchandise manager, with complete freedom to select his own buyers and to choose the merchandise needed for the opening. He gave preference to resources in British markets but also sent buyers to America. It was not the practice in London to have divisional merchandise managers and none were hired.

W. Oppenheimer, store layout specialist whose work had contributed to Field's reputation as the most beautiful store in America, went to work for Selfridge. So did E. A. Goldsman, Field's display manager, who had made the Chicago store's window displays the talk of the town as well as of the display managers throughout America.

On March 15, 1909, a Monday, the store finally opened. It had 1,800 employees and £100,000 worth of goods in 130 departments.

Selfridge invited King Edward VII and Queen Alexandra to the opening although friends in high Court circles told him the idea was preposterous. The invitation was on a vellum scroll inscribed by a master craftsman and enclosed in a silk-covered casket. Although the King and Queen did not attend, Sir Dighton Probyn, a member of the Royal Household did, and the resulting publicity was good.

Despite cold weather and snow flurries, the crowd in front of the store by opening time numbered several hundred. Flags of 20 nations, the Union Jack in the most prominent position, flew from the store's roof. At precisely 9 A.M., the Selfridge house flag was unfurled as an army trumpeter heralded the store's opening. At the same time, curtains parted in each of the 21 display windows to reveal a series of fashion tableaux. Selfridge, with his son Gordon, wore formal daytime clothes and top hats.

The store interior was palatial. The aisles were spacious and the floors were covered with velvet carpets. Music came from hidden orchestras stationed on each floor. Each visitor received a miniature silver key, signifying Selfridge's wish for them to "feel at home."

New crowds assembled daily, and by the end of the first week an estimated million persons had passed through the store.

London reaction to the new store was mixed. The trade press was critical, accusing Selfridge of putting temptation in the shopper's way by displaying goods so they could be handled and by employing every art to lure the feminine public into extravagances that might bring misery and ruin to many households. Important newspapers, however, praised the store, predicting that it would cause a revolution for the better in English retailing. Competing firms counterattacked with special sales during Selfridge's opening week.

Selfridge expressed complete satisfaction with the "house warming," but the opening week's sales of £3,000 must have been a disappointment. The public had taken him at his word and went mostly to look.

Until sales reached a profitable level, Selfridge was faced with refinancing. The outlay for the opening had been enormous. He was committed to a £120,000-a-year payroll; a £35,000 rental; a heavy advertising schedule; and interest on Musker's mortgage. After three months, he succeeded in floating a new £1,-300,000 stock issue.

Selfridge never missed a chance to gain publicity for his store: In May, 1909, he held an Empire Day service on the store roof, with a ceremonial salute to the flag and patriotic speeches by notables. The monoplane of Louis Bleriot, who succeeded in the first channel flight from France to England in July, 1909, was placed on display at the store the morning after the flight.

At the end of six months, Selfridge was delighted with his store's progress. Competing merchants noted that the additional traffic created by Selfridge's exploits also brought more customers their way.

Business continued to improve that first year, but in 1910 all London tradesmen had difficulties. People were talking of the war to come with Germany and King Edward VII died that May. A mourning populace was in no mood to shop. Selfridge hung black crepe in his windows and filled his advertising space with eulogies to the deceased king.

When the period of national mourning came to an end, Selfridge and other retailers experienced a gratifying lift in trade. Selfridge and Goldsman prepared to make the store one of the focal points of the parade route for the Coronation of George V in the summer of 1911. Nephews and nieces of the King and Queen Mary were invited and agreed to watch the royal procession from the store's main balcony. The College of Heralds co-operated in the preparation of large shields and other display emblems that depicted events associated with the British Crown.

When the Royal Coach reached the Selfridge store, the King and Queen smiled and bowed to the children on the balcony as thousands watched. It was a triumph that even Selfridge's rivals had to concede, if not admire.

A bargain basement was started in 1912 "to provide a place where the thrifty housewife could shop to her advantage." It was a pioneer step, successful from the day it opened. Within a few years, its volume was £2,000,000 annually. At the same time, some of the main store departments were expanded. There now were 160 departments.

During the early years, Selfridge's, unlike other important local stores, did not encourage charge accounts.

Much of the increased sales in the main store could be traced to the creative merchandising Steines introduced to English retailing. Customers discovered many items that could not be found elsewhere: velveteen-bound Books of Common Prayer; a special printing of the Bible, Shakespeare, cook books, encyclopedias, dictionaries and world atlases. The store was the first to offer men's shirts in quarter neck sizes and with sleeves in proper proportionate lengths. It carried women's hosiery for five shillings a pair in a wider variety of colors, sizes, and shades than any other store. Women's shoes also were available in a larger variety of styles and sizes.

The cosmetics department was the first to display rouge and lipsticks, and Selfridge's own lily-of-the-valley perfume was responsible for a turnover that reached £250,000 a year. He was also the first to offer "specials" from opening until noon on Saturdays and promoted these so effectively that the otherwise slow Saturday morning hours produced a £2,000,000 annual volume.

The Selfridge impact on British retailing was tremendous. He profited handsomely from the word-of-mouth publicity that came from many pleased customers.

Selfridge introduced to English retailing open counters, new window-dressing ideas, and a new system of merchandise control that other merchants were happy to adopt.

Competitors regarded Selfridge as an alien interloper who had become a menace by disturbing the traditional procedures of British retailing. But Selfridge never fought back and went out of his way to get along with those he considered opponents rather than competitors. He even offered to reveal the reasons behind his practices and to furnish other merchants with forms covering merchandise control and other procedures.

For Selfridge, living in England was an exciting and challenging experience. He was supremely confident now that his store was on its way to becoming one of the most important ones in England. He felt that no problems could arise with which he could not cope successfully.

In 1917, Selfridge wrote a book, *The Romance of Commerce*, which told of the great merchant princes of the Middle Ages. It was given much newspaper space and Sir Woodman Burbidge found in it "something of the vision splendid."

Between 1918 and 1920, the store was very successful attracting customers even when neighboring firms lost sales. The store was refinanced for further expansion to complete long-deferred plans. And Selfridge began acquiring well-established smaller stores in the provinces. Known as Selfridge Provincial Stores, many continued to operate under their original names.

In 1926, Selfridge established the Gordon Selfridge Trust to acquire the ordinary shares of Selfridge & Co. Ltd. The trust had a capitalization of £2,000,000. The investing public responded and the shares were floated easily.

At the time, Selfridge, who was nearing 70, said he wanted to have his affairs in order when he died. "I do not want this great business to disintegrate; I want it to stand forever. With this trust, that will now be possible."

The Trust was followed quickly by an issue for £3,300,000 for Selfridge Provincial Stores Ltd. to assume control of the 17 stores acquired since 1918. Selfridge's son, who had been supervising the out-of-town establishments, became managing director of the new group.

The year 1927 was important in Selfridge's career for other reasons. Trade figures warranted a dividend of 20 per cent on ordinary shares for the Selfridge shareholders and Selfridge acquired William Whiteley's Ltd. at Bayswater, a department store founded in 1863.

The changing character of the Bayswater area had adversely affected Whiteley's profits and the owners were having difficulty paying dividends. Selfridge paid £140,000 to the directors for cancellation of their management agreement that included their salaries, commissions, and dividends. For the other Whiteley shareholders, he guaranteed a 25 per cent dividend for three years. When an elderly woman who reminded him of his mother asked Selfridge if he could not do better, the new owner immediately extended the guarantee to 15 years.

That was the greatest blunder in his business career. Despite every effort, Whiteley's earnings never justified the high dividends. During the first few years, he managed to pay them by robbing Peter to pay Paul—diverting dividends due Oxford Street shareholders to Whiteley's—but this became increasingly difficult.

At the same time, Selfridge increased his own earnings from the Oxford Street store from £40,000 to £100,000 annually to support his extravagant mode of living that included escorting well-known women of stage fame. His absences from the store became more frequent and prolonged. He kept a chartered plane busy flying him to Paris and he was often seen at gambling casinos.

In a nine-year period, Selfridge's lavish expenditures were estimated at £2,000,000. This included the maintenance of a yacht he rarely used and blooded race horses that never won a race.

Dividends to Selfridge shareholders were reduced or passed entirely. The oppressive guarantee to Whiteley stockholders had cost Selfridge £500,000 and still had four years to go. Selfridge owed £250,000 in taxes and his unpaid personal account in his store stood at £118,775. At 83, he had reached the end of his financial resources.

In October, 1939, the Midland Bank, his principal creditor, appointed H. A. Holmes, a financier with a reputation for putting new life into sick businesses, to take over the Selfridge holdings. Selfridge was retired with the courtesy title of president but did not hold a seat on the board. Originally, Selfridge was given a £6,000-a-year pension, but this later was reduced to £2,000.

Holmes became chairman of the board, and A. E. Cowper, senior director and managing head of Whiteley's, was appointed president of Selfridge's.

Gordon left the store because of a difference with Holmes

over reducing buyers' salaries. He went to America and, after a short time, left the retail field.

Harry Gordon Selfridge, died in his sleep at 91.

Holmes and Cowper reorganized the business. The Gordon Selfridge Trust was liquidated and the Selfridge Provincial Stores gradually were sold. The Whiteley dividend was reduced to a figure Cowper felt it could earn and, later, the business was sold to another company. The John Lewis & Company partnership acquired most of Selfridge's Provincial Stores. All were sold by 1940.

Lewis's Investment Trust Ltd. (L.I.T. Ltd.), operator of 11 large, successful department stores in Liverpool, Manchester, Birmingham, Glasgow and other British cities, took over control of Selfridge's in 1951. S. H. Leake, O. B. E. (Officer of the Order of the British Empire), became chairman of Selfridge's. Sir Rex A. L. Cohen, K. B. E. (Knight of the British Empire) succeeded him as chairman on January 1, 1959.

Cohen, born in Liverpool, was the fourth generation of his family to be connected with the management and ownership of Lewis's Ltd.

Cohen was also chairman of the Lewis Investment Trust of which Selfridge's is a subsidiary. Publicly-owned, L. I. T. was controlled by Cohen and Woolton family interests and the directors. Selfridge's estimated sales of some $45 million in 1964 accounted for a fourth of the group's total sales of about $185 million.

Despite the closing of the bargain basement in 1939 and the resultant loss of considerable volume, Selfridge's annual sales run close behind Harrods' main store, conceded to have the largest turnover in England.

Considering only selling area under one roof, however, Selfridge's is the largest store in England, if not in all Europe. It has 820,000 square feet, a third larger than Harrods. The main store has a 500-foot frontage on Oxford Street. An expansion program is in progress.

The store owns a contiguous, seven-story, 1,000-car parking

structure and runs it in partnership with a leading garage operator.

The Selfridge staff totals 4,000, 70 per cent of it female. Six of every 10 employees are directly involved in selling. There are 89 buyers, of whom 33 are women. The store has its own buying staff, controller, and advertising manager. Central buying and receiving for the Lewis stores are done at a headquarters building joined by several bridges to Selfridge's.

In November, 1965, Chester Clore, head of a shoestore-engineering-car distribution complex, bought Sir Rex's holdings and won control of Lewis Investment Trust.

CHAPTER 31

STRAWBRIDGE

& CLOTHIER

PHILADELPHIA, PENNSYLVANIA

"The Quaker Store"

Strawbridge & Clothier began as a wholesale and retail dry goods firm at the northwest corner of Eighth and Market Streets in 1862. Nearly 100 years later, the firm is still on that block, now in a 13-story building constructed in 1932.

In 1790, before either of the founders was born, the office of the United States Secretary of State, Thomas Jefferson, was at that location and, in 1949, a marble memorial to him was unveiled in the store.

Justus Clayton Strawbridge actually began the firm in 1862 in a three-story building. At 16, Justus had begun in the retail trade as a clerk with Joshua Bailey, dry goods. At 24, with his brothers, George and Benjamin, he began his own business, J. C. Strawbridge & Co.

The other founder, Isaac Hallowell Clothier, was following a similar pattern. A graduate of the Friends' School in Philadelphia at 17, he joined George D. Parrish & Co., a dry goods importer. He remained there six years, then formed a partnership with George Morris and Edward Lewis as Morris, Lewis & Clothier, woolen dealers. This firm continued for eight years.

Clothier's father-in-law, William Jackson, was the owner of the land which the Strawbridge store occupied and this apparently led to a meeting of the two founders.

In any case, in 1868, the two 30-year-old men formed a partnership. The original three-story structure was torn down that same year and a new building twice as large was constructed. This was the first of two reconstructions that left the firm in the same location.

Strawbridge had five sons, and all but one joined the firm. Edward Richie, the oldest, entered the firm directly from school and became a partner in 1895 when Clothier retired. Frederic Heap Strawbridge and Robert Early Strawbridge became partners in 1900 when their father retired. Francis Reeves Strawbridge entered the firm in 1903 when his brother, Edward, died. He retired as vice-president in 1927 but continued as a director until his death at 88 in 1965.

Two of Clothier's sons also entered the firm as others retired. Morris Lewis Clothier, who became a partner when his father retired in 1895, became senior partner when Edward Strawbridge passed on eight years later. Isaac Hallowell Clothier, Jr., joined the firm that same year, 1903, when his uncle, Clarkson Clothier, retired.

Justus Clayton Strawbridge died in 1911 at 73. Clothier, the other founder, who died in 1921 at 84, said of the firm, "The Quaker store was built on foundation stones of integrity and character."

When the store first opened, only the first floor and basement were used but, in 1875, the firm began expanding, adding 33 feet on Eighth Street. Three years later, the store frontage on Market was increased by the addition of three more buildings. By 1887, the store had 155 feet of frontage on Market and 250 on Filbert. There were other additions through the years. Construction of a new 13-story building began in 1928. By 1930, the cornerstone was laid and the building was dedicated in 1932. It was the first air-conditioned store in Philadelphia.

Strawbridge & Clothier joined Associated Merchandising Corporation in 1921.

During these same years, the firm became a pioneer in branch store development when two were established in Montgomery County. The Ardmore store opened in 1930, and the Jenkintown branch began business in 1931.

After the turn of the century, the firm made constant changes. In 1905, it installed a counter-to-customer telephone system. Five years later, belt conveyors for packages began operating. In 1911, the store introduced its seal of confidence.

The year 1922, marked a change for the firm. Not only did it start a radio broadcasting station and a budget department in its basement, but it was also incorporated. Morris Clothier became president of the new corporation at 54.

Morris, son of the founder, had begun work with Strawbridge & Clothier in 1890. He became the senior partner in 1903. He was the first president of the corporation in 1922 and became chairman of the board in 1927, a post he held until his death in 1947.

When Morris became chairman of the board, Herbert J. Tily, who began working at Strawbridge & Clothier when he was 13, rose to president.

English-born Tily came to the United States when only an infant and in 1879, at 13, began work at Strawbridge & Clothier. In 1905, he was made general manager, became a partner in 1918 and a vice-president when the business incorporated. He served as president from 1927 to 1946, and became vice-chairman of the board in 1947. He died a year later.

Tily organized in 1905 the Strawbridge & Clothier chorus which won widespread fame with its annual Christmas show. He also organized the Noon Day Club, formed to prepare employees for advancement in the store.

When the firm incorporated, Isaac H. Clothier, Jr., and Francis Strawbridge both were vice-presidents along with Tily, and Frederick and Robert Strawbridge were directors. Isaac H. Clothier, Jr., who had relinquished his vice-presidency in 1955, died in 1961.

Tily succeeded Morris Clothier as president of the firm in 1927 and Robert E. Strawbridge succeeded Clothier as chairman of the board in 1947. Strawbridge continued in that position until 1955.

Robert Strawbridge began work in the store in 1890 after two years at Haverford College. He became a partner ten years later, a director in 1922 when the firm incorporated, and a vice-president in 1927.

Dwight Goss Perkins succeeded Tily as president in 1947, continuing in that position until 1955 when he succeeded Robert Strawbridge as chairman of the board. When Perkins left the presidency, G. Stockton Strawbridge, son of Francis R. Strawbridge, and a third-generation Strawbridge in the firm, became president.

Perkins, a buying executive with Daniels & Fisher Stores Co. from 1916 to 1924, came to Strawbridge & Clothier as divisional merchandise manager of notions, ribbons, laces, neckwear, and art needlework in 1926. He remained in that capacity until 1944 when he became general merchandise manager. In 1946, he became a vice-president and director. From 1947 to 1955, he served as president and director and then became chairman of the board.

G. Stockton Strawbridge began with the firm in 1935 as a clerk and sales manager, becoming successively assistant buyer, assistant to the merchandise manager of ready-to-wear, divisional merchandise manager, and vice-president for merchandising and publicity. He served as executive vice-president from 1935 to 1955, became a director in 1948 and president in 1955. He also is on the board of Associated Merchandising Corp. During World War II, he served for four years as a Naval aviator in the Naval Air Transport Service.

(Justus) Clayton Strawbridge, son of Frederic Heap Strawbridge, joined the store in 1917 as a clerk and later was purchasing agent and transportation manager. He became a director in 1938, secretary in 1944, and vice-president in 1946. In 1947, he became a member of the executive committee.

In the postwar years, the firm again began to branch out. In

1950, the Ardmore unit was enlarged to 111,000 square feet. A new branch was constructed at Wilmington, Delaware, in 1952, and the Jenkintown store was enlarged to 157,000 square feet two years later.

A new 215,000-square-foot store was erected at the Cherry Hill Shopping Center near Camden, New Jersey, in 1961. In 1963, the firm added a 200,000-square-foot branch at Springfield, Pennsylvania. Another 200,000-square-foot store is scheduled for the Plymouth Meeting area of Pennsylvania in the spring of 1966.

In 1964, Strawbridge's main downtown store and its four branches had a total volume of $105.3 million. Of that, $44 million was realized in the downtown store. The Cherry Hill branch had sales of $17.5 million in its third year. The Ardmore branch volume was $9.5 million; Jenkintown, $11.3 million; Wilmington, $9 million; and Springfield, $14 million. The company has about 4,500 employees.

Strawbridge & Clothier still is largely controlled by descendants of the founding families. When ground was broken for the Cherry Hill branch in 1960, three generations of the founding families were present.

Other officers include Randall E. Copeland, executive vice-president who became general superintendent in 1948, a director in 1954, and vice-president in 1955; Francis R. Strawbridge, Jr., brother of the president, who became affiliated with the store in 1930, a director in 1946, and a vice-president in 1947; Donald C. Mills, treasurer and vice-president, who entered the firm as controller in 1946, became a director the same year, treasurer a year later, and vice-president in 1955; Frank R. Veale, vice-president, who became a director in 1954; and Isaac H. Clothier III, a grandson of the founder, who joined the store in 1926, became a director in 1946, and a vice-president a year later.

CHAPTER 32

THALHIMER

BROTHERS, INC.

RICHMOND, VIRGINIA

"Thalhimer's of Richmond"

Thalhimer Brothers, Inc., of Richmond, Virginia, was opened in 1842 by 33-year-old German-born Wolf Thalheimer. He later became known as William and dropped the "e" from the last name.

He emigrated from the Port of LeHavre in 1840 and landed in New Orleans. With two friends, Thalhimer headed for Pittsburgh, Pennsylvania, by way of the Mississippi, but landed in Petersburg, Virginia, instead.

One of his friends, Lewis Rosenstock, remained there. The other, Louis Stern, one of the founders of Stern Brothers, traveled on to New York.

In 1842, William Thalhimer arrived in Richmond, and started a dry goods store on North 17th Street, between Main and Franklin Streets. The one-room, 18-by-60-foot store, had living quarters above. He married two years later, and he and his wife had five sons and two daughters.

Through these early years, the business prospered. It expanded in 1848 to 18th and Main where it remained during the Civil War.

As the war began, Richmond, an important port and commercial center, was both the capital and largest city in Virginia. It had a population of 38,000. Unfortunately, as it turned out, Richmond also became the capital of the Confederacy. During the war and in the reconstruction period, times were difficult, and the Thalhimers suffered along with the rest of the South. Their savings disappeared, and the store was burned during Sherman's march.

As the war ended, the Thalhimers were faced with starting anew. William went to New York and the store was given credit by two firms there. He returned home via Baltimore where two more firms extended credit. Thalhimer was back in business. In 1875, the store moved again, this time to Fifth and Broad Streets, a block from its present location.

Although all the sons worked at one time or another in the business, only two of them, Isaac and Moses, remained. In 1877, William Thalhimer turned the firm over to them and its name became Thalhimer Brothers.

Dominated by the personality of the brothers, the business continued as a dry goods and notion store. Isaac's quick appraisal of the new features of cloaks, suits, and dresses made in factories gave the store the best name and reputation in Richmond for ready-made clothes. Thalhimer's recognized the importance of ready-to-wear early and coupled it with a continuing interest in both style and quality.

Isaac's son, William, began work in the family store at 16. Later, against family wishes, he went to Chicago where he worked briefly as a stock boy in Carson Pirie Scott. When the Chicago firm expanded and moved to State Street in 1907, William returned to Richmond and the family store.

In 1910, he began buying toilet articles. Later, he bought nearly all the lines except ready-to-wear and piece goods, two categories his father, Isaac, continued to purchase.

During that same year, William began the separation of infants' and children's items from the duties of the ready-to-wear buyer. It was considered radical then to have these departments on separate floors.

By 1915, sales had grown to more than $400,000. In that year, William, then only 27, purchased a part interest in the business from his father and uncle, Moses, who retired.

In 1922, the store incorporated and moved from the location where it had been for 47 years. The new store was one block east on Broad Street, between Sixth and Seventh Streets. The eight-floor building, with a basement and sub-basement, has 450,000 square feet.

In 1930, William B. Thalhimer, Sr., became president of the firm. His son, William B. Thalhimer, Jr., joined the firm four years later and became president and general manager in 1950. The father stepped up to the chairmanship. Another son, Charles G. Thalhimer entered the business in 1947 and is now senior vice-president. Irving May, Isaac Thalhimer's nephew by marriage, became secretary-treasurer in 1922.

May, who had a private law practice, joined the retail establishment in 1922, the year the firm incorporated. He was successively vice-president and treasurer, executive vice-president and, in 1947, became president. He was elected vice-chairman of the board in 1950. He died in 1964 at 72.

William B. Thalhimer, who in 1965 entered his 60th year in retailing, continues as chairman of the board and his son, William, Jr., as president and general manager.

Thalhimer's joined Associated Merchandising Corp. in 1937.

Herbert A. Leeds, vice-president and general merchandise manager, joined the firm in 1960. He was formerly with Lord & Taylor, and with Boston Store and Schuster's in Milwaukee. Newman Hamblet, vice-president, has been with the store since 1953. He was formerly with Lord & Taylor. Daniel Schiller, vice-president and treasurer, joined the store in 1942. Alex W. Parker, secretary, and a partner in Christian, Barton, Parker, Epps & Brent, has been general counsel since 1943. Walter M. Fisher, vice-president and controller, joined the store in 1946. Other vice-presidents are John W. Christian, Morris Goldstein, and Howard Klugman.

Among the board members are E. Claiborne Robins, a Richmond pharmaceutical manufacturer who became a director in 1955, Walter V. Moffitt, a New York investment banker who became a director in 1948, and Ralph A. May, son of Irving, who joined the board in 1964.

Thalhimer's branch store expansion began in 1949 when it opened in downtown Winston-Salem, North Carolina. That store was expanded to 80,000 square feet in 1958.

No further branch expansion came until 1955 when the L. Herman Co. (32,000 square feet) downtown Danville, Virginia, store was purchased.

By 1963, Thalhimer's had 12 branch stores. Besides the downtown Winston-Salem and Danville stores, the branches include:

The store in Riverside Shopping Center at Danville, Virginia, opened in 1960. The Ellis Stone department store in downtown Greensboro, North Carolina, purchased in 1957. A Young World Shop in Friendly Shopping Center in that city, and a store in Summit Shopping Center. The 62 year-old McCargo-Baldwin store in South Richmond, purchased in 1959 and known as Thalhimer's Hull Street. Besides the downtown Winston-Salem store, a 400-square-foot shop was opened on Wake Forest campus in 1956. In Durham, North Carolina, an Ellis Stone store downtown and a shop in Lakewood Shopping Center both opened in 1962.

After continued studies of suburban population, Thalhimer's opened two branches in 1960 in its home city: A Young Virginian Shop, 10 miles from the parent store, in the River Road Shopping Center, and a second branch in the warehouse and service building at Westmoreland.

An 18th unit will be opened in Petersburg, Virginia, in the fall of 1966.

Thalhimer's sales volume for 1964 totaled $45,659,000, and profit reached $1,825,000. The company employs 1,600 in its main store and another 1,000 in its branches.

CHAPTER 33

WANAMAKER'S

PHILADELPHIA, PENNSYLVANIA

---

*"A Great Store Built on Honor,
Truth & Integrity"*

Four days before the volley at Fort Sumter that began the Civil War, John Wanamaker opened a men's and boys' clothing store in Philadelphia in partnership with his brother-in-law, Nathan Brown.

On that Monday—April 8, 1861, the day Lincoln notified the Confederacy he would not evacuate the fort—the receipts from Wanamaker & Brown totaled $24.67, with all but the change spent for the advertising. Total sales for the first year were under $25,000. One hundred years later, the annual sales volume of Wanamaker's Philadelphia store and its branches was estimated at $105 million.

In an informal survey of top retail executives, conducted by Fairchild News Service in 1962, Wanamaker was nearly everyone's choice to be named one of the six greatest merchants in United States retailing history. The same year, he was placed on a similar list compiled by Malcolm P. McNair, professor of retailing at Harvard.

John Wanamaker, son of Nelson Wanamaker, a brickmaker, was born in Philadelphia in 1838. He left school at 14 to become an errand boy at Troutman & Hayes, a publishing house on Market Street, where he earned $1.25 a week. In 1856, Wanamaker embarked on what was to be a great retailing career when he went to work in a retail clothing store at Fourth and Market Streets for $2.50 a week.

He later worked for Joseph M. Bennett of Tower Hall, at the time the largest clothing store in Philadelphia. He stayed there about two years except for a brief trip to Minnesota in 1857 for his health.

Although Wanamaker was to return to stay in the retailing business, in 1858 he was elected secretary of the Young Men's Christian Association at Philadelphia and became the first salaried YMCA secretary in the United States.

This work was to exert a lasting influence on Wanamaker's life. He later served for eight years as president of the YMCA. In 1858, he also organized the Bethany Sunday School.

Wanamaker was rejected for army service in 1860 because of a lung condition and then helped organize the Christian Commission, which worked with the Sanitary Commission to aid the sick and wounded soldiers of both sides.

At 22, Wanamaker married Mary Erringer Brown. Before he reached his next birthday, Wanamaker and his wife's brother, Nathan Brown, opened Oak Hall, clothing store, at Sixth and Market Streets at 6:30 A.M. April 8, 1861. The partnership was to last until Brown died seven years later.

The first store was only 30 by 80 feet. Within ten years, its size would double. Within 16 years, when Wanamaker was only 38, he had opened in a new location the largest retail men's store in the nation.

The very first summer it was in business, Wanamaker & Brown used outdoor posters.

In 1866, a money refund was offered if merchandise was unsatisfactory. Two years later, just before Christmas, Wanamaker & Brown guaranteed its prices to be 10 per cent lower than elsewhere.

By 1869, a branch store was opened at 818 Chestnut Street. Wanamaker closed the store 16 years later.

Wanamaker announced an advertising principle of "accuracy in word and print," and in 1873 gave five reasons for his success:

1—We advertise what we have for sale.

2—We have for sale what we advertise.

3—The people come to see that it is so.

4—The people buy our cloth because they are pleased with the guarantee we make.

5—The people are satisfied that they get full value for the money they leave with us and they come again and send their friends.

Wanamaker also instituted his one-price system in 1871.

Nathan Brown had died by the time Wanamaker took the first big step toward his future success in the development of the department store. He purchased in 1874 the old Pennsylvania Railroad freight station at the corner of 13th and Market Streets, then outside the downtown business district.

On May 6, 1876, the Grand Depot at the new location opened and Wanamaker was operating the largest men's and boys' clothing store in the nation. That autumn, women's and girls' shoes and coats were added. The same year, a mail-order business was started. The following spring, Wanamaker's opened "The new kind of store," adding other women's fashions and merchandise for the home.

From then on, additions to the stock were rapid. In 1878, hosiery, china, and children's departments were included. Two years later, Wanamaker's began its bargain basement. In 1881, an optical section and gas stoves were added. Paris lingerie and corsets were sold in 1892. By that time, the store covered 16 acres of floor space.

Wanamaker in his day was renowned as an advertising genius. He bought his first full-page of newspaper advertising in December, 1879.

By 1885, the Grand Depot had become known generally as Wanamaker's. Occupying an entire block from Market to Chestnut and from 13th Street to City Hall Square, it was one of the largest retail stores in the nation.

But Wanamaker also had an interest in politics. For a four-year period from 1889 to 1893, he was Postmaster General under President Benjamin Harrison. He was credited with establishing sea post offices and rural delivery, organizing the postal service of the Pacific Slope, and supporting parcel post, a system not instituted until he had been gone from the administration for two decades. Nevertheless, Wanamaker and his son, Rodman, launched the system. Wanamaker in Philadelphia and Rodman in New York each mailed the first parcel-post packages at 12:01 A.M. Jan. 1, 1913, and the first free parcel-post deliveries were made the following day.

Shortly before the turn of the century, Wanamaker entered the New York retail field in what was to be his greatest blunder. In 1896, he purchased the A. T. Stewart store at 10th Street and Broadway in Manhattan even though the store was decadent and all signs indicated that its one-time customers were trading elsewhere. He opened a few weeks later with three million dollars' worth of stock. Taking a toll of the new Wanamaker store was the already evident uptown movement of better stores. To compound his error, he built a 14-story building alongside the Stewart store in 1907.

By 1952, the Stewart store was closed. The New York Wanamaker, alongside it and connected to it by three subway passages and a double-deck bridge, closed two years later.

However, Wanamaker still has an interest in New York. A junior department store, John Wanamaker Liberty Street, Inc., opened in 1943, still operates in Manhattan's financial district. The Wanamaker organization owns a half interest and Frank L. Kellogg, the store president, owns the other half. Kellogg joined Wanamaker's Philadelphia in 1946, was named vice-president in 1950, and took over the operation of the Liberty Street store in New York in 1955.

At the time Wanamaker entered the New York field, the combined sales of the two stores—Philadelphia and New York—placed it among the five largest in annual sales in the department store field. That year, there were 1,100 persons employed in the

Stewart store. When Wanamaker had been in business 50 years —in 1911—he employed 13,000 in the Philadelphia and New York stores.

About the time he was constructing his New York store, he also was busy rebuilding the Philadelphia establishment on the same site. Ground was broken in 1902. Formal opening of the first section was in 1906. By 1910, the store, with 45 acres of floor space, was completed.

On the capstone, which completed the new Philadelphia store in 1910, the founder inscribed these words:

"Let those who follow me continue to build with the plumb of honor, the level of truth and the square of integrity, education, courtesy and mutuality."

In the Grand Court of the store was a 2,500-pound eagle purchased from the St. Louis Exposition of 1904. In 1911, a grand organ, also erected for the St. Louis fair, was installed.

When Gen. Ulysses S. Grant, who had commanded the Union Army, visited the store in 1877, he was reported as saying, "It takes as much generalship to organize a business like this as to organize an army."

Wanamaker was in the forefront in many retail developments, either as a pioneer or close behind.

On the day after Christmas of 1878, he installed electric lighting. Two years later, pneumatic tubes to carry cash were put into use. In 1882, he added elevators and ventilating fans. In 1884, a bureau of information, post office, telegraph and phone offices were established.

Two years later, Wanamaker offered employees summer vacations with pay, and in 1887 he instituted a profit-sharing plan, later succeeded by a commission and bonus plan. Saturdays were made half holidays, and in 1914 Saturdays in July and August were made full holidays.

In 1900, the store began closing at 5 P.M. in the summer months and at 5:30 in the winter. By 1918, the 5 P.M. closing was extended the year around. By 1911, Wanamaker had 67 cars in use for deliveries, and by 1919 the last horse was sold and the delivery fleet was made up entirely of automobiles.

In 1920, the John Wanamaker Foundation was established to provide pensions, insurance, co-operative savings, sick relief, and first aid for employees.

Wanamaker's was the first store in the world to receive Marconigrams for transmission. Wireless stations were installed on the roofs of both the New York and Philadelphia stores in 1907. The station on the roof of the New York store was the first in America to receive news of the Titanic disaster. The Wanamaker wireless operator was David Sarnoff, later president and chairman of the board of Radio Corporation of America and chairman of the board and director of National Broadcasting Co.

Wanamaker died in 1922 at 84. His son, (Lewis) Rodman Wanamaker, who had served as resident manager of Paris stores for 10 years, became president of Wanamaker's Philadelphia and New York, serving in that capacity until his death in 1928.

The founder's other son, Thomas B. Wanamaker, was also associated with the firm. Robert C. Ogden, an associate in developing the Philadelphia store, later served the New York store until his retirement in 1907. Joseph Herbert Appel, John Wilberforce Appel, Jr., and Grover A. Whalen were also in the New York store.

Joseph Appel, a lawyer, went to Wanamaker, Philadelphia, in 1899 as director of advertising and publicity. He remained in that post until 1912 when he left for the New York store. He became executive manager of the New York store in 1934 and continued in that capacity until he was made a director in 1936, a post he held until 1940. He was a director of the Advertising Federation of America from 1930 to 1938. He authored several books, two of them on the Wanamaker store, *John Wanamaker, A Study*, in 1927, and *Business Biography of John Wanamaker, Founder and Builder*, in 1930.

John Appel was associated with Wanamaker's New York store from 1906 to 1932. He became president of Stern Bros., New York, in 1932.

Grover Whalen was general manager of Wanamaker's New York store from 1924 to 1934. He had been secretary to New York Mayor John F. Hylan in 1917, and was police commissioner from 1928 to 1930. He had for years the unofficial title of New York's greeter and was president of the New York World's Fair of 1939.

After Wanamaker's son, Rodman, died, William Latta Nevin became president and served for nine years until 1937.

Charles Raymond Shipley was president from 1937 until he resigned in 1947. He had been a partner in a retail dry goods firm in Charleston, West Virginia, from 1903 to 1913 and an associate of United—later Associated—Dry Goods Corp. from 1913 to 1931. He became merchandise manager of H. Batterman & Co., of Brooklyn in 1913 and continued there for two years, moving to J. N. Adam & Co., of Buffalo as merchandise manager. He stayed there until 1917. Shipley became first vice-president and a director of Lord & Taylor and Associated Dry Goods Corporation from 1928 to 1931, moving then to Wanamaker, Philadelphia, as general merchandise manager. He became president and director of Wanamaker's Philadelphia and New York stores in 1937.

John E. Raasch, executive vice-president, succeeded Shipley as president in 1947 and became chairman in 1952. Now board chairman of the Grand Union Company, he still serves on the board of John Wanamaker Liberty Street. He had served as executive vice-president of Wanamaker's New York from 1935 to 1947. He became a director of the firm in 1945, later president, and chairman of the board in 1953.

Richard C. Bond, who joined the Wanamaker organization in 1948, became president four years later, succeeding Raasch. John Rodman Wanamaker, great grandson of the founder, was elected chairman of the board in 1955. He joined the family firm in 1939, and served in various departments until 1943. He became a director in 1945, a vice-president in 1947, and then chairman of the board.

Under Bond and the founder's great grandson, the firm began to enter the branch store field. In 1950, Wanamaker opened its first branch, Wilmington, Delaware. Ten years later, the store was expanded from 167,000 to 200,000 square feet.

Other branches opened in Wynnewood, Pennsylvania, in

1954; Yonkers, New York, in 1955; Jenkintown, Pennsylvania, in 1957; Moorestown, New Jersey, in 1963, and King of Prussia, Pennsylvania, in 1965. The company bought a 300,000-square-foot building at B Street and Allegheny Avenue, Philadelphia, for $1.1 million to centralize warehouse operations.

Bond began his business career as a stock boy at Strawbridge & Clothier, another Philadelphia store, in 1934. He was soon made assistant buyer and, a year later, buyer. In 1938, he became assistant merchandise manager.

He moved to Marshall Field in Chicago in 1941 as merchandise manager of the budget store, and two years later became merchandise manager of ready-to-wear accessories at Frederick & Nelson in Seattle. He became assistant general merchandise manager of the Seattle store in 1946 and moved back to Marshall Field with the same title a year later.

He began his association with Wanamaker as vice-president and general merchandise manager in 1948, and three years later was executive vice-president. He became president in 1952.

Active in many community affairs, Bond lives up to the beliefs he expressed in a talk he gave in January, 1959, when he said: "The day is gone forever when the retailer, the manufacturer or the banker can limit his interest to just the techniques of his immediate job. In his own self-interest, he has a duty to participate in his community's civic affairs."

Richard Bond has brought Wanamaker from No. 4 position in Philadelphia after World War II to No. 1. Not only has he built and expanded branches but he has also sharpened the company's quality image and completed a long-range modernization of the center-city store.

In 1964, Wanamaker's corporate volume rose to about $122 million. The downtown Philadelphia store accounted for $68.5 million. The Wilmington branch did $11.6 million; Jenkintown, $9.8 million; Yonkers, about $11.5 million; Wynnewood, $10.8 million; and Moorestown, $9.6 million. The company employs about 7,500.

CHAPTER 34

WEINSTOCK, LUBIN
& COMPANY

SACRAMENTO, CALIFORNIA

"Failure at the Summit"

Weinstock, Lubin & Co. began in 1874 in California's capital city. Its founders were David Lubin and his half brother, Harris Weinstock, two forward-looking and able merchants who had only meager capital. The store was a one-story building, the rear of which the partners used as sleeping quarters.

The store, only 10 feet wide by 12 feet deep, was separated from a Chinese laundry by a thin partition. The first sign read, "D. Lubin, One Price," later changed to, "One Price—Mechanics Store," and to "Weinstock-Lubin & Co." when the shop moved to larger quarters.

Lubin had difficulty convincing his customers that the store really sold merchandise at "one price." Other local shops permitted haggling and some out-of-town customers had been accustomed to having home-town merchants give them "lagniappe" with their purchases. One customer, after selecting $50 worth of merchandise, refused to complete the purchase because Lubin would not throw in a 50-cent penknife free.

Later, however, Lubin stated: ". . . a crowd stopped in front of my store. 'There he is' their leader shouted, pointing to me; 'he's the only honest storekeeper in Sacramento. Let's buy him out.' It was the fellow I refused to dicker with a few days before. And sure enough, by the time they got through with their purcases, there was not much left of my stock." After that, other local merchants adopted the one-price plan.

The store was a success, and by 1877 adjoining buildings had been taken over and connected to the main store by a series of bridges.

Just prior to the turn of the century and through the mid-1920's, Weinstock, Lubin & Company instituted several benefits for its employees. Among them was a special lunch and kitchen, and a school for those under 18.

At the turn of the century, two smart, ambitious young men were brought into the business. These were Harry Thorp, who merchandised apparel and related lines, and S. Warder McKim, who handled all the other departments.

When both the founders became inactive in the store, Harry Thorp was appointed president and S. W. McKim, vice-president. These two men not only spurred consistent increases in the retail sales, but also developed a profitable and extensive mail-order business.

After Thorp retired, S. W. McKim became president and continued in that office until the death of David Lubin. Simon Lubin, son of David, then took entire charge of the business as president and another son, Jess, became vice-president.

Several who worked for Si Lubin described him as "a dreamer and sort of a mystic in many ways; not a merchant; a man with a lot of grandiose ideas."

Three moves made by Si Lubin, however, stand to his credit: he joined RRA-AMC in 1916, he surrounded himself with very able merchants, and he "dreamed" into actuality a modern new store.

His group of merchants consisted of Frank M. Folsom, Edward B. Krehbiel, Robert McKim, Neil Petree, and Irene M.

Wilhelm, to mention the outstanding ones. Unfortunately, however, Si Lubin did not permit any of them to exercise much of their own judgment and each in turn left Weinstock's for far more rewarding positions in retailing.

Irene Wilhelm, a native of Los Angeles, was shirt-waist buyer at Weinstock's from 1904 until 1916, when she moved on to Bullock's, eventually opening the AMC buying office in Los Angeles. She retired in 1946.

Folsom joined Weinstock's in 1914 as a buyer of books and toileteries, but found the job a frustrating one in this store. He went to Hale Brothers, San Francisco, as merchandise manager in 1923, became vice-president and a director of Montgomery Ward in 1932, and was executive vice-president and general manager of Goldblatt Brothers, Chicago, from 1940 to 1941. He joined Radio Corporation of America in 1944, became president in 1949, and, since 1957, has been chairman of the executive committee.

Krehbiel joined Weinstock's after a successful career as a history professor at the University of California and Stanford University During a sabbatical year, Krehbiel made a study for Lubin, found that he was more interested in retailing than teaching, and became publicity manager for Weinstock's from 1919 to 1921 and general manager from 1921 to 1925.

Though Krehbiel earned the respect and co-operation of all the buyers and other top executives, Lubin did not allow him the latitude he needed to operate with full effectiveness. He left to join J. L. Hudson Co. in 1925, later becoming general manager and treasurer of Black, Starr, Frost, & Gorham, in New York.

Robert J. McKim, a nephew of S. W. McKim, joined Weinstock's in 1915 as basement manager, an operation that was highly successful under his direction. He left in 1923, and 20 years later was president of Associated Dry Goods Corporation where he had a free hand to apply his knowledge of finance and personnel administration.

Neil Petree, one of Krehbiel's promising students, joined

Weinstock's in 1920 as buyer of boys' clothing and furnishings. He later became president of Barker Brothers, Los Angeles, the leading home furnishings store in the Far West.

The achievement records of Folsom, Krehbiel, McKim and Petree, after leaving Weinstock's, attest their respective abilities.

Weinstock's was one of the major mail-order operations in the West prior to World War I. In 1919, a visitor from Chicago told Si Lubin that he had been a "consultant" for a large mail-order company there, and that its business had been considerably improved by following his recommendations. He said that, although Weinstock's mail-order volume was impressive, it could be greatly expanded by separating the mail-order operation from the retail, by offering lower-price merchandise, and by issuing a more complete catalog than Weinstock's had been using.

Si Lubin hired the gentleman to take complete charge of the mail-order division. In due course, the stocks were bought and new catalogs mailed to old customers and to many others. The immediate response in orders was gratifying to Si Lubin.

Then, the new mail-order venture collapsed. Under Weinstock's traditional "money back if not satisfied" policy, the returns of merchandise were appalling.

Customers, used to receiving mail order merchandise identical to that personally selected on their visits to the store, would not keep the cheaper "stuff," and Weinstock's quickly lost its former profitable mail-order volume. Fortunately, the retail good will was not permanently impaired.

Si Lubin, who neither sought nor accepted advice from the able merchants around him, had previously made plans for building a new store in a new location. Subsequent years proved that the move was a wise one, but the financing for the new store and the losses from the mail-order business forced Si Lubin into bankruptcy. He was even unable to pay his RRA-AMC dues and had to resign.

Hale Brothers, Sacramento, took over Weinstock's in 1927, retaining the old and honored name. Lubin was provided with a modest income and an office in the store. Here, he "dreamed" away the remaining years of his life.

Mrs. Marion Armstrong became president of Weinstock, Lubin in 1951, when Lawrence Ellis, who had been in that office for 25 years, was made chairman of the board. Mrs. Armstrong, who was with the firm for 40 years served as advertising copy writer, fashion coordinator, sales promotion director, general merchandise manager, executive vice president, and a member of the board of directors. She retired at the end of 1964 to be succeeded by Norman V. Wechsler, formerly vice-president and general merchandise manager of Halle Brothers, Cleveland.

Weinstock, Lubin, with three units, is now part of the Weinstock-Hale division of Broadway-Hale.

CHAPTER 35

ZIONS COOPERATIVE MERCANTILE INSTITUTION

SALT LAKE CITY, UTAH

America's First Department Store

"This is the right place" —BRIGHAM YOUNG

Brigham Young, who founded Zion's Cooperative Mercantile Institution, was best known as the inspired leader of the Mormons and a great colonizer. He was also one of the most versatile men ever connected with retailing.

He was an expert carpenter, cabinet maker, glazier, and painter. He knew enough about surveying to plan and lay out a city. He became a manufacturer, wholesaler, newspaper publisher, and banker.

This peace-loving pioneer lived a turbulent life, but his fame and name have been perpetuated. His statue, sculpted by a grandson, Mahonri Mackintosh Young, is side by side with other notable Americans in Statuary Hall, Washington, D.C.

On July 24, 1847, when Brigham Young first saw the site that was to become Salt Lake City, he exclaimed, "This is the right place." He was riding in the lead wagon of a train of ox-drawn prairie schooners, carrying 147 of his followers in search of a place to make a permanent settlement. They had traveled 1,000 miles over hazardous and uncharted territory from Council Bluffs, Iowa, to their new haven.

Within a month, Young had laid out and named Salt Lake City. It was done so well that the downtown streets are wide enough to handle six lanes of automobile traffic and still permit curbside parking.

Stores were established to serve the growing population, but some non-Mormon traders contrived to purchase all available stocks of scarce goods and corner the market. Sugar often sold for $1 a pound, flour for 75 cents a pound, and other essential but scarce goods proportionately as high.

Young met with a group of leading retailers, and the formation of ZCMI followed in 1868, with Young as president. Zion was made part of the name because it was a community enterprise, founded by settlers to whom the area was a Zion or refuge where they hoped to find peace and security.

Because some of the new directors were familiar with the co-ops of Europe, it was agreed to make the new venture a co-operative one with a stock issue. Young asserted, "In regard to this co-operative institution . . . it is our duty to bring goods here and sell them as low as they possibly can be sold and let the profits be divided with the people at large."

Soon, there were six noncompeting stores displaying the ZCMI sign and featuring merchandise at uniform prices. Three others were added later, and by 1871 ZCMI had branches or departments under separate managers, selling clothing, dry goods, drugs, groceries, produce, shoes, trunks, sewing machines, wagons, and machinery. It was thus a department store from the very start. The branch managers were under the supervision of a secretary, treasurer, and general store superintendent who, in turn, were directed by the president and directors.

ZCMI claims to be America's first full-fledged department

store at birth. In addition, ZCMI in 1870 also became the first incorporated department store in America.

The co-operative was among the first stores to employ women as sales clerks. Women managed many of the remote "co-ops" being established in other areas, and consequently also attained executive status.

Mormons in other parts of Utah Territory opened branches, once ZCMI was functioning smoothly. Ultimately, 146 of these were established. All were co-operatively owned and operated by local citizens, and all were dependent on the parent Salt Lake City store for most supplies.

To supply these outlets, ZCMI started wholesale depots at various centers, including Logan and Ogden in Utah, and Soda Springs in Idaho. Later, most of the co-op stores outside Salt Lake City became privately owned but continued to use ZCMI wholesale divisions as their principal suppliers.

ZCMI also opened factories, and in 1872 became the first department store in America to make its own clothing—house dresses, underwear, overalls, and duck and flannel clothing. In 1870, it purchased a tannery to manufacture boots and shoes, and began importing merchandise and advertised crockery from England.

In 1873, Young founded a Mormon bank, which later became Zion's First National Bank. In April, 1960, the Church of Jesus Christ of Latter-day Saints sold the bank to private businessmen.

Young gave his unremitting attention to ZCMI, its factories and its wholesale activities. The stores were enlarged and attractive new buildings were erected.

Mark Twain wrote in 1861 that Salt Lake City not only was beautiful but also so healthful that it had only one doctor who occasionally was arrested for "having no visible means of support."

Young's services to Utah Territory and to the nation are matters of record. In 1861, he pledged the state's allegiance to the Union in the first message sent east over a newly completed overland telegraph line. A year later, at President Lincoln's request, Young armed and equipped a company of cavalry to protect the Western mail lines.

Young died in Salt Lake City in 1877, but ZCMI continued to expand under strong leadership. By 1946, the combined retail and wholesale volume exceeded $30 million.

In 1926, Harold H. Bennett joined ZCMI, of which his father, John F. Bennett, was manager. Young Bennett started in the general accounting office and was successively controller, assistant treasurer, secretary-treasurer, and general manager. He was appointed executive vice-president in 1946 and became president 12 years later. He also is a director. In 1960, he won the Gold Medal Award of the National Retail Merchants Association and in 1962 became that organization's president.

When Bennett took over ZCMI, he and the other directors decided to liquidate the remaining wholesale divisions and confine their efforts to expanding the retail operation. The wholesale food division had been sold in 1949.

But a store that has been engaged in large-volume wholesale activities cannot get out overnight. ZCMI directors, in fairness to friendly local merchants, decided not to liquidate by disposing of large inventories to their own retail stores for spectacular low-price sales. Instead, the co-operative decided to sell the stocks to other wholesalers. Drugs and hardware went in 1959, the rest in the following year. ZCMI arranged to have many of its wholesale employees continue with the new owners and most others were absorbed into the co-operative's retail stores.

One of Bennett's merchant friends from the East, during his first visit to Salt Lake City, said, "So this is America's oldest department store. Well, it certainly looks it!"

As a result, at an estimated cost of $4½ million, a projected program of face-lifting, redecorating, and revamping of many departments was speeded up. Expansion added one-third more selling space in the store. A branch was opened in 1962, about 12 miles south of the parent store, and locations for other branches are under consideration.

Most of the ZCMI employees are Mormons because that is the faith of the majority of residents of the area, but the question of religious affiliation does not enter the store's employment policies. ZCMI employs about 1,100, about one of five being part-time workers. The store has pioneered in paying fair wages and providing fringe benefits for all employees.

Unlike most other department stores, ZCMI carries bakery goods from its own ovens, groceries, fresh produce, health foods, and meats. No liquor or tobacco is sold. Food products are carried on 30-day charge accounts, telephone orders are accepted, and the store offers free delivery if the order totals $5. Otherwise, a 25-cent delivery fee is charged.

ZCMI has a larger assortment of well-known brands confined to it than other local stores. In 1954, it was selected as the brand-name retailer of the year in the department store field.

There are about 1,400 stockholders, the church among them.

Sales promotion is handled by Ted Bushman, who joined ZCMI in 1950, bringing with him a lot of advertising "savvy" acquired in five years with an advertising agency in the Northwest and 12 years with other department stores.

ZCMI is the largest newspaper advertiser in the city. Its direct-mail pieces keep customers in the outlying areas abreast of store developments.

Bushman also uses the local television stations to promote important and timely items. Brief commercials are tied in with a 15-minute evening news broadcast. ZCMI is the only local store using TV.

Weekly fashion shows are held in the city's finest hotel and in the store tearoom. Thousands of teenagers and younger people are attracted to the annual back-to-school fashion presentation on top of the store's parking terrace.

This five-story parking space, opened in 1954, handles 510 cars without double parking. Each floor, except the top, is covered to protect customers and their cars from inclement weather. Direct entrances lead to the store from each of the enclosed floors. Parking is free with a $2 purchase.

ZCMI total sales took an expected nose dive when the wholesale divisions were discontinued. For years, however, its retail sales led in local average percentage gains. Volume was $21,-463,652 in 1964, about $5 million over the 1961 showing. Net profit in 1964 was $528,851.

The Lost Panoramas of the Mississippi

THE LOST
PANORAMAS OF THE

Alton Ill.

MISSISSIPPI

By *John Francis McDermott*

THE UNIVERSITY OF CHICAGO PRESS

CONTRA COSTA JUNIOR COLLEGE
DISCARD
MARTINEZ, CALIFORNIA

SEP 1 2 '62

F
353
M2

Library of Congress Catalog Number: 58-5682

THE UNIVERSITY OF CHICAGO PRESS, CHICAGO 37
Cambridge University Press, London, N.W. 1, England / The University of Toronto Press, Toronto 5, Canada

© *1958 by The University of Chicago. Published 1958*
Composed by THE UNIVERSITY OF CHICAGO PRESS, *Chicago, Illinois*
Printed by PHOTOPRESS INCORPORATED, *Broadview, Illinois, U.S.A.*

TO THE MEMORY OF *Rolla Martin Kendrick*, MY FATHER-IN-LAW

AND TO *Martin Kendrick McDermott*, HIS NAMESAKE AND GREAT-GRANDSON, MY GRANDSON

PREFACE

Five times during the 1840's pictures were painted of the Mississippi River that measured from four hundred and forty yards up to twelve hundred and fifty in length by four in height. Exhibited as moving newsreels or travelogues in St. Louis, Cincinnati, Louisville, New Orleans, and in many another city on their way to the eastern seaboard before they were carried to Europe, they entertained and instructed vast audiences and some of them earned considerable fortunes for their producers. They enjoyed a place in theatrical history and in the educational uses of art well recognized in their day, but long since they have been almost completely forgotten. Except for a few contemporary prints and a handful of recent articles, hardly a thing is known today of this once popular form.

Many long years ago my interest was aroused in this subject by the numerous accounts I found of the pictures in the St. Louis newspapers of the period, for all of the artists had career connections with St. Louis, two of the panoramas had been painted there, and three of them exhibited in the home town. In 1946 and 1947 I had the fortunate experience of correspondence and personal interview with members of the families of three of the artists.

I wish to acknowledge my very real indebtedness first of all to the late Miss Edith Banvard, youngest daughter of the artist, who not merely wrote numerous letters in answer to my questions and read my account of her father's life, but most generously lent me a collection of rare pamphlets describing her father's work, a number of these titles being ones I could not find elsewhere. I also had the pleasure of an evening's talk with Miss Banvard in September, 1947, and then examined sketches by the artist, clippings related to his work, and other Banvardiana of considerable value. Other members of this family have likewise been of assistance: Miss Esther W. Bates, a cousin, very kindly supplied me with an interesting picture of Banvard in costume, painted in London in 1849, as well as information concerning the artist and his family; James G. Banvard, a grandson, gave me useful information.

Henry Lewis, who left no descendants, lived in Düsseldorf the last fifty years of his life, but fortunately for me the children of his brothers lived in the Mississippi Valley. I have had the pleasure of talking with John A. Lewis of St. Louis, who visited his uncle in Germany in the 1880's and who gave me ready access to letters and drawings that came to him from the artist. Mrs. Myron B. Chapin of Ann Arbor has written me of her granduncle and sent me the photograph of the Irving portrait of Henry Lewis. She has also permitted me to transcribe many letters from Lewis and has given me permission to publish them. Mrs. Emelie K. Greenough of Upper Montclair, New Jersey, a niece, and Miss Elizabeth Hittle, a grandniece, have shared Lewis correspondence with me. Wallace Wilson of Jefferson City, Missouri, a grand-nephew, has been kind enough to answer my queries. Emerson L. Conselman, Wilson Lewis, Mrs. N. K. Ross, Mrs. Edgar Stehli, and Miss Margaret Sobolewski have all been interested and helpful.

Although Leon Pomarède lived sixty years in St. Louis, his family became widely scattered after his death. I was fortunate enough, however, to meet three of his grand-daughters in New Orleans in the spring of 1946 and to have reached by correspondence another granddaughter in South Africa. I am particularly in debt to Miss Pauline Pomarède and Mrs. Alec O'Donnell as well as to Mrs. Robert Townsend for firsthand impressions of and information about their grandfather, his life and work. Mrs. Langton Thornhill, their cousin, of Dunottar, Transvaal, has also written me of the artist.

Naturally, there are many others who have answered my many questions, suggested lines of investigation, furnished me with pictures, or read my manuscript. Special thanks go to Miss Bertha L. Heilbron, editor of *Minnesota History*, both as a generous friend and fellow worker among panoramas and as a member of the Minnesota Historical Society staff. Stanley Pargellis, director of the Newberry Library, put me onto the Henry Lewis press-cuttings book in my own backyard and Thomas T. Hoopes, curator of the City Art Museum of St. Louis, has allowed me free use of it. Charles van Ravenswaay, director of the Missouri Historical Society, has always been more than generous in sharing his knowledge of art in the Mississippi Valley. Clarence E. Miller of the St. Louis Mercantile Library is the very model of all librarians as far as I am concerned. Harry J. Owens of Chicago called my manuscript to the attention of the University of

ix

Chicago Press. Stanley W. Walker of New York, too, has been particularly kind.

Other helpful friends and strangers include Miss May Davenport Seymour of the Museum of the History of New York, J. Alden Mason, curator of the American section of the Museum of the University of Pennsylvania, Philip D. Jordan of the University of Minnesota, Paul Rice North, chief of the Reference Department of the New York Public Library, Matthew W. Stirling, chief of the Bureau of American Ethnology, R. P. Tolman, formerly director of the National Collection of Fine Arts, Smithsonian Institution, Robert C. Albrook of the Watertown, South Dakota, *Public Opinion*, Perry T. Rathbone, formerly director of the City Art Museum of St. Louis and now director of the Museum of Fine Arts, Boston, Mrs. Odille Stewart, librarian of the City Art Museum of St. Louis, Walter Harding, secretary of the Thoreau Society, the late Wolfgang Born, Victor W. von Hagen of Westport, Connecticut, Joseph S. Schick of the State Teachers College, Terre Haute, Stephen T. Riley, librarian of the Massachusetts Historical Society, Miss Laura Bell Everett of Oroville, California, Miss Marjorie Douglas, curator, Mrs. Brenda Gieseker and Miss Barbara Kell, librarians, of the Missouri Historical Society, Henry J. Regnet, S.J., formerly librarian of St. Louis University, John A. Bryan of the National Park Service, St. Louis, Edward H. Dwight, director of the Milwaukee Art Institute. I want to call special attention to the work being done by J. Earl Arrington of New York: he is compiling a checklist of panoramas painted and exhibited in the United States in the nineteenth century which will prove a very revealing study and he is planning to write a history of panoramas.

For special courtesies in the use of materials I am truly

obligated to the Missouri Historical Society, the Mercantile Library, the Washington University and St. Louis University libraries (all of St. Louis), to the Newberry Library of Chicago, the University of Chicago Library, the Chicago Historical Society, the Wisconsin Historical Society, the Minnesota Historical Society, the Historical and Philosophical Society of Ohio (Cincinnati), the New York Public Library, the New-York Historical Society, the American Antiquarian Society, the Boston Athenaeum, and the Library of Congress. I wish to acknowledge also the assistance furnished me years ago by the long defunct National Youth Administration, which supplied me with typists who transcribed a vast amount of material from the St. Louis newspapers of the 1840's. Some portions of the material in this volume have previously been published in *Antiques* and *Bulletin of the Institut Français of Washington;* I am grateful for consent to use them again here.

Finally, my best thanks to Mary Stephanie McDermott, my wife, for typing the adventures of the panoramists and for the index that is so important to the usefulness of any history.

JOHN FRANCIS McDERMOTT

CONTENTS

List of ILLUSTRATIONS

NEWSREEL *Old Style*

Imagine a man who declared that he had painted a picture three miles long and a rival artist who announced a few months later that *his* painting was four miles in length! They were liars, of course, but what magnificent lies! Try, if you will, to conceive a third man saying that his new picture of the same region was to be three times as long as that of the first producer, a fourth informing the public that he would paint a picture on one hundred thousand square feet of canvas, and a fifth intending to use twelve thousand square yards. These lies were no less than colossal and supercolossal. Clearly the men were doubly artists: they were both painters and press agents. Such claims may now seem fabulous; but this was in the 1840's, and of all the astounding things in that age of enterprise the most incredible were the monster panoramic paintings of the Mississippi River which were unrolled night after night before an eager public.

Although the Mississippi pictures excelled everything that preceded them, the panorama was already old theatrical fare, for it had been invented half a century before. Report declares that a portrait painter of Edinburgh, in prison for debt, one day held a letter up to read it against a small stream of light that shone down from a crack near the ceiling of his dungeon and so discovered the principle of the panoramic display. However that may be, this young man, Robert Barker, did obtain a patent in 1787 and built a semicircular exhibit that was not successful. Five years later he presented his first satisfactory panorama in a building erected for the purpose in Leicester Square, London. This displayed the English fleet at anchor between Portsmouth and the Isle of Wight. He followed that popular show with a view of London, then a *Naval Battle of June 1, 1795*, the *Baths of Brighthelmstone*, and the *Environs of Windsor*. In 1798 he showed two pictures in the same house, one above the other. The first of these was the *Battle of Aboukir*. After viewing this violent and bloody combat the spectator could mount to a higher platform and calm his soul with the peaceful *Baths of Margate*.

Shortly after Barker built his first rotunda in London, Robert Fulton, who had come to England in 1786 to study painting under Benjamin West, became interested in the new production. In 1796 he went to Paris at the call of Joel Barlow and there he obtained the exclusive right to show panoramas in France, but for the lack of capital he could not proceed. Fulton sold out, abandoned painting, and took up the study of mechanics.

His rights were bought by a James Thayer and his wife, who built the two circular halls on the Boulevard Montmartre. In the first of these they exhibited in 1800 a *Vue de Paris*, as taken from the central dome of the Tuileries, painted by Jean Mouchet, Denis Fontaine, Pierre Prévost, Constant Bourgeois, and Charles Marie Bouton. The second

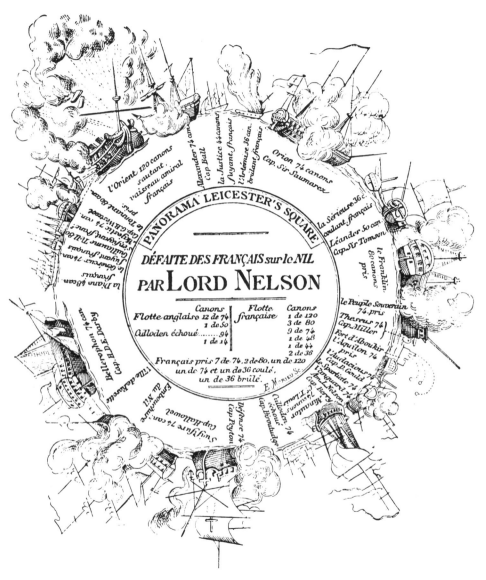

Inside the illustration (circular diagram), reading around the ring:

PANORAMA LEICESTER'S SQUARE

DÉFAITE DES FRANÇAIS sur le NIL

PAR LORD NELSON

Canons	Flotte	Canons
Flotte anglaise 12 de 74	française	1 de 120
1 de 50		3 de 80
Culloden échoué 94		9 de 74
1 de 14		1 de 48
		1 de 44
		2 de 36

Français pris 7 de 74, 2 de 80, un de 120
un de 74 et un de 36 coulé,
un de 36 brûlé.

E. MORIEU Sc.

Labels around the ships (clockwise):

Alexander 74 can. Cap. Ball

la Justice 44 canons Fuyant, français

l'Artémise 36 can. brûlant, français

Orion 74 canons Cap. Sir Saumarex

la Sérieuse 36 c. coulant, français

Léander 50 can. Cap. Sir Tomson

le Franklin 80 canons pris

le Peuple Souverain 74 pris

Theseus 74 Cap. Miller

Fort d'Aboukir

l'Aquilon 74 l'Audacieux 74 Cap. D. Gould

le Spartiate 74

le Timoléon 74

le Vanguard 74

le Conquérant 74

le Mercure 74

Mutator 74 Cap. T. Louis

Culloden 74 échoué Cap. Troubridge

le Heureux 74

Minotaure 74 Cap. Hirwaladge

Défense 74 Cap. Peyton

Swiftsure 74 can. Cap. Hallowell

Embouchure du Nil

l'Ile dévastée

la Diana 48 can. Fuyant, français

le Généreux 74 can. Fuyant, français, sauvé

le Guillaume Tell 74 can. Cap. G.B.H. Villeneuve

le Tonnant 84 can. pris

l'Orient 120 canons sautant vaisseau amiral français

Bellerophon 74 can. Cap. H.D.E. Darby

Caption below illustration:

*Diagram of Barker's Panorama of the Battle of Aboukir, London, 1798
(Bapst, ESSAI SUR L'HISTOIRE DES PANORAMAS, 1891)*

Thayer's Two Circular Halls on the Boulevard Montmartre, Paris, 1802 (Bapst)

rotunda was occupied by the *Evacuation de Toulon par les Anglais en 1793*, painted by Prévost, Bourgeois, and Bouton. This pair of panoramas earned for the painters eight thousand francs apiece.

About this time Barker took his pictures to Germany, where, under the pretentious name of "Nausorama," he exhibited his *English Fleet at Portsmouth* at Hamburg in 1799 and his *View of London* the next year at Leipzig. The first German to do panoramas was Breysig of Magdeburg, who, with the painters Tielker and Kaaz, produced a *View of*

Rome, which opened in July, 1800. The idea spread very rapidly and proved tremendously popular. A *View of Vienna,* twenty-seven meters in diameter, executed by Jausche and Postl, earned fifteen thousand florins. In 1805, Prévost, who had become the leading painter of panoramas in Paris, exhibited a *Camp de Boulogne* and a *Vue d'Amsterdam;* at this time Barker in London was offering a *Battle of Trafalgar;* and in Berlin the *View of Vienna* was being shown. These and other pictures in rapid succession met with acclaim from amusement seekers and from the critical. To one of the pictures of Prévost, the renowned David took his pupils and exclaimed, "Truly, gentlemen, it is here one must come to study nature." There could be no doubt that the newsreel was thoroughly established in public favor.

The panorama, in its early form, was a circular painting so arranged that the spectator, placed in the center of the room, saw only the subject portrayed. The frame around an ordinary landscape or historical scene constantly reminded one that he was after all looking at a picture. The panorama, inclosing him, made him feel that he was in the midst of the scene about him. He was not standing before a work of art but in the very "presence of nature." Nothing existed but the picture and the spectator. To achieve such an effect the showman needed a circular hall with a conical roof. The first in London (Barker's) was forty-five feet in diameter and sixteen feet high; the pair on the Boulevard Montmartre in Paris were seventeen meters in diameter and seven high. Later buildings were often fifty yards and more in diameter and fifteen high. In the center of such a room there was provided a platform on which the spectator was placed in order that he might be kept at an even distance from the painting. An opening in the lower part of the roof permitted the light to fall from above and behind on the painting, while a shelter over the head of the spectator allowed him to see the full picture but nothing above it. To accustom him to the change from the outside world the spectator was taken through a dark passage so that the reality of the picture might be doubly effective. The new rotunda built in Paris in 1807 was entered by a passage fifteen meters long; 150 people could view the picture at once.[1]

The effects possible in the panorama were increased by another invention. In 1822 Bouton and Daguerre opened their first diorama. They used the *rotonde* as an auditorium that turned on a pivot before huge stationary pictures! These exhibitions were, however, limited to two pictures, each twenty-two meters wide by fourteen high. Of greater importance in the development of this art were the dioramas *à double effet* that Daguerre began showing toward 1831. A typical example was his *Midnight Mass at Saint-Etienne-du-Mont.* The first view of this picture, daylight, showed an empty church. Gradually day gave place to twilight and then to night. The sanctuary lighted up and the church was seen crowded with people. All this was done within one frame and on one piece of canvas.[2] The effects were achieved by painting the clearer picture on the right side of the canvas and the second on the back, and by careful manipulation of the lighting. Effects of sky and distance, and sometimes of fire and of moonlight, could be obtained also by another device: the use of two or more transparent surfaces on separate frames placed a short distance apart. Sometimes part of these surfaces might be cut away to create highlights.[3]

The remaining step necessary for the huge panoramic shows of the 1840's was the devising of machinery for the moving panorama. As early as 1829 "a moving panorama of the southern bank of the Thames" was exhibited in London. "It was a very long picture," a contemporary account informs us, "of which only a part was sent at a time gliding slowly across the stage." This movement was achieved by unrolling the canvas from an upright roller and winding it up on another. It was now possible to produce a picture of any length, for, though there would be a limit to the amount of canvas that could be handled on one set of rollers, the only limit to the number of reels would be the length of time available for a showing.[4]

The newsreel, or travelogue, then, is no invention of the twentieth century. It is now more than one hundred and fifty years old and has settled down to a regular but modest place in our lives. By the 1840's it had already attained a noble maturity. It had grown to a length that required an audience to sit for two or three hours while hundreds of yards of colorful canvas were slowly unwound from one cylinder and wound onto another. Even then it had the characteristics of the successful newsreel: it entertained and instructed its audience by presenting vividly and faithfully scenes and actions that the spectators could not otherwise see. It did not talk, but an elaborate program and a commentator in person offered all necessary explanation, and a handsome young lady rendered appropriate accompaniment on the pianoforte. To the traveler it gave the additional personal pleasure of checking by his own experience the accuracy and skill of the painter. It strove also with the function of news; no sooner did an exciting event occur than an enterpriser placed it on canvas. Furthermore, many of the descriptive pictures—the educational newsreels—were of places about which the spectators had read only the usual literary ac-

7

NEWSREEL—
OLD STYLE

counts. "The love of travel is inherent in mankind," one producer pointed out. "He, therefore, who by means of panoramic exhibitions makes travellers of those who would otherwise tarry at home, is no ordinary benefactor to his fellow creatures."[5]

As early as 1790 one of these more-than-ordinary benefactors showed New Yorkers a panorama of Jerusalem. Westminster and London were displayed on canvas five years later. The bombardment of Fort McHenry was reported in a newsreel. In 1818 Vanderlyn built the Rotunda in City Hall Park to house his painting of Versailles. A few years later New York was treated to a "mechanical" panorama of "pictures of town and country, with artisans and servants at work, with boats plying in and out of harbours, &c." A "peristrephic" panorama covering twenty thousand square feet of canvas, depicting Waterloo, St. Helena, and the funeral of Napoleon, shown in 1831 (even though it almost certainly did not attain this huge size) must have been a moving picture. The Liverpool and Manchester Railway was in 1835 the subject of another newsreel. The rapidly growing popularity of such exhibitions (of which only a few have been cited) is illustrated by the New York season of 1839–40 during which Catherwood's *Jerusalem* and panoramas of Thebes, Lima, Rome, Bunker Hill, and the Bay of Islands in New Zealand as well as Daguerre and Sébron's dioramas of Jerusalem, the Crucifixion, and Calvary, provided instructive entertainment.[6]

To realize fully the vigorous early development of this theater art in America one has only to consider the variety of subjects that reached the frontier public in St. Louis as early as one hundred and twenty-five years ago. This prosperous and rapidly growing western town had some six thousand inhabitants in 1830; ten years later about sixteen thousand; and by 1850 seventy-five thousand. During those decades it was the westernmost town for road shows, and what St. Louisans gazed upon was a fair sampling of the newsreels that were being shown outside the biggest producing centers in the East.

One of the earliest of such panoramic shows[7] was that advertised on August 12, 1830, by Mondelli, scene artist at the local theater. The announcement in the St. Louis *Beacon* of his benefit promised that, after other items on an extremely generous bill of fare, there would be exhibited "a very exact panoramic view of the city and port of New Orleans, with ships and steamboats under weigh, coming in and going out of port, the steam escaping, etc., forming an exact and living representation of the city and its bustle."

Mondelli was no niggard; this was merely part of his show. "At the request of several persons of this city, he would also present a view of MOUNT VESUVIUS (for the last time,) a view of the Bay and City of Naples, the ERUPTION OF THE VOLCANO, forming a magnificent and imposing sight." To conclude his program he offered "a representation of the expedition of the AMERICAN FLEET AGAINST TRIPOLI; the American and Tropolitan [*sic*] fleets will meet, and begin the fight; the Tropolitan vessels are burned, their forts blown up, and the depot of the enemy, increases the glory of the American family, and gives immortality to the glorious heroes, Decatur, Preble, and to the host of other brave men who seconded their efforts in the memorable campaign of 1803–4." All these views apparently were the work of Mondelli himself.[8]

That evening with Mondelli no doubt provided lively and interesting entertainment, but it hardly supplied news to its audience. A program presented in January, 1836, by Albert Koch, the "enterprising proprietor" of the St. Louis Museum, was superior in variety and in part, at least, a good deal more timely as news.[9] His "cosmoramic views" included shots of the Battle of Austerlitz, the French Revolution of 1830, the tunnel under the Thames, and Bonaparte entering Moscow. But best of all in a newsreel was the picture of "the fracas with the gamblers at Vicksburg, with a view of North's house." The trouble referred to had occurred only on the sixth of July previous, and it is quite possible that the picture had appeared in other cities before reaching St. Louis.[10]

During the next decade and a half St. Louisans sat through many newsreels. There was one tremendous exhibit showing "the Battle of Waterloo, the Battle of Genappe, St. Helena and the Funeral of Napoleon, &c., in 12 different views, the movements of which are accompanied by appropriate music." For this presentation a special building was erected, since, the proprietor assured us, there was none obtainable in town big enough for his needs. The *Missouri Republican* was not represented at the opening night (August 25, 1838) of Sinclair's "grand moving panorama," but it discovered from persons who had attended that the exhibition was "every way worthy of the patronage of the public." The notable thing about the show seemed to be that "the view of the several detachments engaged in that memorable conflict, are presented with a distinctness and the scenery is said to be so accurate, that the view gives a complete and faithful idea of the whole fight." During its last week (it closed September 15) the producer added "a representation of the New Longwood House made in England, and sent to St. Helena for Napoleon's Residence, a view of the Governor, Sir Hudson Lowe, Napoleon, &c., in the foreground."[11]

10

Later (December 10, 1840) another impresario brought a GRAND COZMORAMA, OR A PICTURESQUE VOYAGE AROUND THE WORLD. This, the public was respectfully informed, was the largest ever imported from Europe and therefore of great value. It was composed of "ONE HUNDRED magnificent tableaux, of large dimensions, and painted by the first Italian and French artists. It represents towns, public squares, monuments, ruins, landscapes, &c., &c." Though not technically the same sort of show, it filled the function of an educational reel. Just how it was managed the advertisement in the *Republican* does not make clear. "The optic is so well arranged that it leaves nothing to be desired," we are told, "the illusion being so complete that the spectator believes himself transported into the midst of the scene before him. Two persons can at the same time enjoy the view of the same scene, and communicate to each other any remarks that may strike them, or anything concerning what they may have witnessed in their own voyages." With this wise touch, the proprietor abstained from further details, for he wanted his audience to surprise themselves, but he did not fail to say that "this is not only an agreeable recreation, but imparts instruction to all, from the man of the world and the man of letters to the schoolboy, to whose eyes it presents the places described in his geography and ancient and modern history."

The opening program offered six views: "1st. Exterior of the grand Facade, or front, and lateral parts of the magnificent and immense Gothic Cathedral called the Dome, in Milan, Italy. 2d. The Artificial Lake of Moeris, near the Nile and Memphis, in Egypt. 3d. Taking of the Palace of the Tuileries by the people of Paris in the Revolution of July, 1830. 4th. Interior of the immense Library of the Vatican at Rome. 5th. Great Royal Street, called the 'Po,' the most

11

NEWSREEL—
OLD STYLE

magnificent in the world, at Turin in Piedmont. 6th. Grand Review of the Army commanded by Alexander, the Emperor of all the Russias, on the great Square of St. Petersburg." A very fine organ was to play overtures and French and Spanish airs, the pictures were to be changed every week, and the admission charge was to be only ten cents (a very unusual price). The producer of this news show apparently did not flourish very long, for there is no repetition of his advertisement beyond the first week. It is possible, of course, that business was so good that he did not need to advertise.[12]

Next appeared an American painter destined to make himself famous as the artist who produced the first of the "largest pictures in the world." The St. Louis Museum (now under the proprietorship of W. S. McPherson) in March, 1841, advertised an exhibition which presented "*Miss Hayden*, the accomplished *American Sybil*" and also the "Grand Moving Panoramas, of the Cities of Jerusalem and Venice, covering an extent of canvass exceeding 100 [1,000?] square feet, painted by the celebrated artist Banvard; this alone is worth the price of admission [fifty cents]." These reels, which opened on March 17, were still showing in April. The editor of the *Missouri Republican*, a week later, declared that "the Panoramas of Venice and Jerusalem, from the pencil of the distinguished artist J. Bonvard [*sic*], Esq., are replete with interest and instruction; and all who admire fine paintings, and have a taste for the Fine Arts, we would advise to go and view them." It is amusing to think of Banvard keeping the wolf from the door by making pictures of towns he had never seen! On April 12 the museum announced that "the proprietor has the satisfaction to inform the public that he has been able to produce a new and splendid Panorama of the City of St. Louis, which has been in preparation a long time, and painted by the celebrated scenic artist, Banvard, and he trusts his exertions to produce novelty, and to please generally, will not go unrewarded." Apparently this picture continued to show until the end of the month. After that, silence. But to Banvard I shall return.[13]

In the late 1840's there was a deluge of panoramas in St. Louis. A man named Weedon in 1848 presented the first of a famous lot of scenic newsreels. This one was a "mammoth Painting" which opened on the eleventh of May for a short time: "Hudson's Grand Panoramic View of the Hudson River, painted on over 12,000 feet of canvas, representing, with wonderful accuracy, every city, town and landing, (on both sides) from New York Bay to the mouth of the Mohawk river; constituting one of the largest panoramas ever exhibited." Later in the month, the *Republican* informs us, there were "crowds of gratified spectators." The show was so popular that prices were cut and liberal reductions further made for schools, and it was not until May 29 that the positively last week was advertised.[14] It was in this year that Stockwell offered his Mississippi River picture, and in 1849 that Lewis and Pomarède exhibited simultaneously their rival pictures of the river.

Throughout the month of April, 1848, St. Louisans were able to see a "Grand French Dio-Panorama of the Funeral of Napoleon." According to the modest advertisement, "It represents one of the most gorgeous and magnificent spectacles the world ever saw—the whole scenery from St. Helena to Paris—a distance of over 4,000 miles. The Funeral Car, drawn by sixteen horses, and the whole Funeral Procession—including hundreds of military, on horseback and on foot, all march in order, keeping step with the bands of music—as they wend their way from Neuille [*sic*], the residence of the late French King, to the city of Paris, a distance of 9 miles—over 700,000 spectators assembled at Paris to witness the Funeral Ceremonies, all of which are represented." During its last week there was a daily matinee for children.[15]

The variety of these newsreels is further illustrated by two others that appeared in St. Louis in this same year. In mid-July "a beautiful Panorama of some of the most striking scenes and events in the early history of the world" was being shown at the Odd Fellows' Hall. "We had the pleasure," wrote the editor of the St. Louis *Daily Union*, "of witnessing a portion of it last evening. The painting, to say the least of it, is a good one, and does great credit to the artist. The opening scene—a view of the garden of Eden—is gorgeous, and throughout the painting, the scenes are striking and of excellent design. All can see it, young and old." On the same day (July 12) the *Union* carried a detailed description of the parts of this "Grand Historical Panorama of the Antediluvian World." It began with the Creation and ended with the Deluge, according to the proprietors, and consisted of the following sections: "1. Garden of Eden, with Adam & Eve. 2. Temptation. 3. Expulsion. 4. Cain & Abel. 5. Land of Nod. 6. City of Enoch. 7. River Euphrates. 8. Noah's Ark; working figures, &c., of the Animals entering the Ark. 9. The Deluge. 10. Mount Ararat, with the Ark resting." How long the citizens of St. Louis patronized this representation of some of the livelier portions of biblical history I know not, for it seems to have been advertised only once.

In December St. Louis was being entertained by another show, which offered a good deal of variety for the price of one admission. In brief, it was a "Sacred Panorama, Dissolving Scenes, and Bombardment of Vera Cruz." The first part sounds as if it were the July show holding over with additional attractions, but it may quite easily have been a rival biblical piece. "This sublime and magnificent Painting," the advertisement in the *Republican* for December 5 promised St. Louisans, "is intended to illustrate the great work of the CREATION OF THE WORLD, as described in the Book of Genesis, with a Panoramic view from the GARDEN OF EDEN, with all its sublime and beautiful scenery, correctly taken from Scripture, to the awful destruction of the world by the GREAT DELUGE." Following this were offered "dissolving scenes of the SHIPWRECK OF THE MEDUSA, BLACK FOREST IN SPAIN, and the MIDNIGHT MASS IN ROME, with appropriate music, chorus, &c." To top off this varied bill at the Hall of the Mechanics Institute was the "BOMBARDMENT OF VERA CRUZ," which, I suppose, no patriotic American could fail to attend. The price was the usual fifty cents for adults ("front seats reserved for ladies"); perhaps it was not as successful as the proprietors hoped, for the next week the price was reduced to twenty-five cents.[16]

Panoramas continued to flourish and to satisfy or attempt to satisfy all demands that an exacting public could make on an expanding industry. Late in March of 1850 George Brewer offered nine newsreels in one show. Brief they must have been, but consider the subjects they presented. His program included views of Mammoth Cave, "with its immense Halls and Grottoes, extending in various directions, between six and seven hundred miles"; Niagara River and Falls, both summer and winter scenes; a day's journey through the western prairies; Mount Vernon; the Natural Bridge in Virginia; scenery of the Nile; and other views.[17]

Hardly had Brewer closed, when Benjamin Russell opened with a panorama of a whaling voyage; perhaps this can be called one of the first newsreels of an important American business. The editor of the *Republican* (April 19) pointed out that "the spectator fancies himself to start from New Bedford, of which city and neighboring coast there is a beautiful view, bound on a whaling voyage. The Azores, the Cape de Verd Islands, Rio Janeiro, Cape Horn, Pitcairn's Island, the Society Islands, and other islands are successively represented, together with a vast variety of sea scenery, the capture of whales, storms, &c."[18]

In the fall of the year James F. Wilkins brought his *Moving Mirror of the Overland Trail* to Wyman's Hall. Painted from two hundred water-color sketches made "from nature on the spot" (the artist had gone out with the 1849 caravan), the picture was sure to appeal, for most St. Louisans had either been to California or their friends or relatives had. "The spectator, with very little assistance from the imagination," the *Republican* declared, "may fancy himself in an air balloon, overtaking and passing the emigrants on the road, witnessing their distress, and seeing the country and the nature of the obstacles they have to contend with; and all with the safety and comfort of sitting at your own fireside."[19]

The sound establishment of the newsreel business is characteristically demonstrated by the shows offered by a Mr. Gester in September of this same year 1850, which included a "magnificent Diorama" of that favorite old subject, the burning of Moscow. To this he added "experiments in Magic & Ventriloquism" and called the whole thing, appropriately, his "amusement for the millions."[20]

Extraordinary as these pictures may seem in subject and in technical production, astonishing indication that they were of the energy, industry, and enterprise which characterized the producers of instructive entertainment in that day, they

Odd Fellows' Hall,

AMUSEMENT FOR THE MILLION!
FOR ONE WEEK—Commencidg on Monday night, Sept. 23, and continuing every evening during the week.
The Magnificent Diorama of the
Conflagration of Moscow!!
together with experiments in
Magic and Ventriloquism, by Mr. GESTER, will be exhibited as above.
☞ Cards of admission, 25 cents.
☞ Doors open at 7—to commence at 7½ o'clock.
sep23

Advertisement of Gester's Diorama in the St. Louis DAILY UNION, *September 23, 1850*

were mere trifles compared to the supernewsreels made in the West and exhibited to hundreds of thousands of admiring Americans and Europeans a century ago. In the history of the theater there are no productions so nearly incredible as the panoramas of the Mississippi. Five times within the 1840's the Father of Waters sat—or kept rolling along—for his portrait. Five times artists made lengthy, laborious, and expensive trips sketching river scenery and then spent weeks and months transferring those sketches to canvas. The originals are all lost or destroyed, but there is little doubt that they were faithful reproductions and that more than once they caught the very being of the Great River. The history of these pictures makes vivid the art business of panorama-making and re-creates the Mississippi which our ancestors knew.[21]

17

NEWSREEL—
OLD STYLE

CHAPTER 2

JOHN BANVARD

Paints "The Biggest Picture in the World"

"The day was bright, and the setting sun was casting its mellow light over the ever beautiful autumnal foliage of an American landscape, bordering on the noble Mississippi. A tiny skiff was floating upon the mirrored surface of the stream, guided by its solitary occupant, a boy, scarce sixteen, who sat with folded arms, contemplating with wonder and delight the glowing scene around him. That boy was JOHN BANVARD. He had heard and now realized, that America could boast the most picturesque and magnificent scenery in the world and as he glided along by the beautiful shores, the boy resolved within himself to be an artist, that he might paint the beauties and sublimities of his native land."

So the romantic young Banvard discovered the work that was to win him fame and fortune as a newsreel producer. There was always about him a certain epic quality, a youthfulness and zest for living that cast a glow of excitement over all his experiences. From childhood he had been a person

18

THE LOST PANORAMAS
OF THE MISSISSIPPI

with a consuming ambition: he would paint the biggest picture in the world. He knew nothing of the art of painting and he had had no instruction, but these were slight discouragements. The United States was full of self-made painters in that fabulous age of expansion, and a young man with the drive characteristic of Banvard was sure of success. At fifteen this energetic New Yorker was on his own. Young men went west. He traveled to Louisville where he worked as a drug clerk. But chalk tempted him, and his caricatures failed to please his boss.

Free, he tried to paint, but no one wanted his pictures. He obtained an engagement "to ornament and decorate a public garden," but the business failed and again he found himself without job or money. By this time he was sixteen. As a boy he had once "constructed a respectable diorama of the sea, having moving boats, fish, and a naval engagement." Now, finding himself at New Harmony, with some other young men he "got up" some dioramic paintings. These they loaded on a flatboat for a traveling exhibition. But the difficulties of the artist-impresario increased. They had not enough money to fit out their boat properly; not one of the party knew the river, the channel, the sandbars. They almost exhibited at Shawneetown, but they grounded on rocks half a cable's length from shore and could not get loose to meet the audience which their advance publicity had assembled on the wharf. In the night, swells from a passing steamer set them afloat, and they woke up eight miles below Shawneetown on a bar.

The next day they did manage to land at a settlement where they gladly accepted for admission a bushel of potatoes, a fowl, or a dozen eggs. After their exhibition that night they had the first good meal in days, indeed, a "luxurious supper." There were other troubles. The boat was small, and, if the audience crowded too much on one side, the water would come over the gunwales into the exhibition room. Once a wag loosed the boat, and it drifted two miles with the "unconscious spectators" who had to be landed in a cane-brake. At Plumb Point, the young showmen were attacked by the Murrell gang, which they succeeded in fighting off. Finally they reached the Gulf. Banvard had learned something about show business: he "had found the receipts of the floating expedition to be more potatoes than dimes, more eggs than dollars." He sold out.

For a time he painted in New Orleans, Natchez, Cincinnati, Louisville. His biographer declared that he "executed a very fair panorama of the city of Venice"—did it matter that he had never seen the place? He made money by his tour with the picture until he was forced to stop by the sinking of a steamer and the loss of the newsreel. He settled in St. Louis as the proprietor of a museum, but in that business managed to lose all the money he had previously gained. He left town, went to Cincinnati, and started down the Ohio painting portraits at small places. He was able soon to buy a larger boat and peddled produce on the river. He speculated a bit, presently "managed to make during this Quixotic expedition several thousand dollars," and with this capital started on his life work. In the spring of 1840, before he came of age, Banvard began the drawings for his most noted work.

Thus far I have followed the anonymous account entitled *Banvard, or the Adventures of an Artist* published in London in 1849 and obviously inspired by Banvard the impresario.[1] There is about the pamphlet that vagueness concerning time and place characteristic of heroic narrative. The glow of

River Scene. Oil by John Banvard (Minnesota Historical Society)

Title Page of BANVARD, OR THE ADVENTURES OF AN ARTIST, *1852?* (*Minnesota Historical Society*)

imagination was more important to the artist than any literal truth. Regretfully, I find some confusions. The pamphlet implies that he was born in 1819 or 1820; yet he was old enough and active enough to be attacked by the notorious Murrell gang, which was broken up early in 1834. At the time of the attempted holdup he had already been in the West for a year or two, but he was fifteen when he first came to Louisville. Later, according to this booklet, came the adventure with the panorama of Venice and still later the struggle with the museum at St. Louis. All this, we are told, happened before he started on his sketching of the Mississippi in the spring of 1840.[2]

However, in none of the newspaper files extant is there a mention of Banvard in St. Louis before 1841. In March of that year he was booked for the St. Louis Museum along with the "American Sybil," Miss Hayden. At that time his panoramas of Venice and of Jerusalem were presented. W. S. McPherson was then the sole owner of the Museum, for in January of that year he had bought out Albert Koch, who had owned and operated it for at least five years. Banvard could not have been the proprietor of "the St. Louis Museum" between January, 1836, and January, 1841. In April, 1841, he added to his offering a panorama of St. Louis, which no doubt he had painted during that spring season. It was only in the middle of April that his name was associated with that of McPherson as co-proprietor. On the nineteenth of that month these two advertised that "the new and terribly terrific spectacle of the INFERNAL REGIONS is now open, which has undergone entire alterations and improvements, and so constructed as to occupy the whole depth of the building, nearly 100 FEET IN LENGTH, which now makes it undoubtedly the Largest in the Union." With this production, under the immediate direction of Mr. Hedger of Cincinnati, was to be exhibited also the "GRAND PANORAMA OF ST. LOUIS, besides a large collection, both natural and artificial curiosities from all parts of the Globe." The last week of the *Infernal Regions* was advertised on Monday, April 26. On August 19 Banvard took a benefit at the City Theatre, then being run in connection with the Museum. After that the newspapers carried no further mention of Banvard and McPherson or these exhibits until six years later when Miss Hayden returned to St. Louis with her "Polite Illusions or Mysteries of Philosophy" and the panoramas of Venice and Jerusalem—this time, of course, without Banvard, who had bigger fish to fry.[3]

It is not likely, then, that Banvard put himself seriously to work on his preliminary sketches until some time after 1841. He was now determined "to paint a picture of the beautiful scenery of the Mississippi, which should be as superior to all others, in point of *size*, as that prodigious river is superior to the streamlets of Europe—a gigantic idea!— which seems truly kindred to the illimitable forests and vast extents of his native land." Here indubitably was an aspiration worthy of an America. "The idea of gain never entered his mind," we are assured by the anonymous biographer, "when he commenced the undertaking, but he was actuated by a patriotic and honorable ambition, that he should produce the largest painting in the world." No man could hold back from such an irresistible urge. He was ignorant of what the future held for him; he later admitted that "had he been aware, when he commenced the undertaking, of the vast amount of labor it required he would have shrunk from the task in dismay." But he persevered, spurred on in part by the

Stack Island, Mississippi. Pencil Sketch by John Banvard (Minnesota Historical Society)

"assertions of some foreign writers, that 'America had no artists commensurate with the grandeur and extent of her scenery.'" It was a challenge.

What if he had never had an instructor? "Nature was his teacher. Many a time, at the close of a lovely summer's day, after finishing his solitary evening meal, would he sit upon some lonely rock, near the margin of the noble river, when all was still, save the sweet charm of the feathered songsters of the adjacent forest, or the musical ripple of the eddying waters at his feet, and watch the majestic bluff as it gradually faded through the gray twilight from the face of the day unto the darker shades of night. Then would he turn and study the rising moon, as it peered above the opposite shore, ascending the deep blue ether high in the heavens above, casting its mellow light, over the surrounding landscape, and gilding the smooth surface of the river with its silvery hue. It was then and there he studied Nature in its lovely grandeur, and seized those glowing moonlight scenes which now adorn his canvas—so vividly, too, as if painted with a pencil dipped in the silvery beams of the living moon itself."

Innocent and eager, Banvard started off one spring for a trip that was longer and harder than he had expected, but he lost none of the opportunity that it gave him for the exercise of his poetic imagination. What couldn't an advance agent do with the exciting story of the making of this tremendous picture in the wilderness! No publicity man today, writing about a cinema made in the heart of Africa or Asia, could give a better impression of absolute devotion to the public than did John Banvard in describing the difficulties and hardships he encountered in painting "the biggest picture in the world." Listen to him awhile:

One of the greatest difficulties he encountered, was the preparatory labour he had to undergo in making the necessary drawings. For this purpose he had to travel thousands of miles alone in an open skiff, crossing and recrossing the rapid stream, in many places over two miles in breadth, to select proper points of sight, from which to take his sketch; his hands became hardened with constantly plying the oar, and his skin as tawny as an Indian's, from exposure to the rays of the sun and the vicissitudes of the weather. He would be weeks together without speaking to a human being, having no other company than his rifle, which furnished him with his meat from the game of the woods or the fowls of the river. When the sun began to sink behind the lofty bluffs, and evening to approach, he would select some secluded sandy cove, over-shadowed by the lofty cotton wood, draw out his skiff from the water, and repair to the woods to hunt his supper. Having killed his game, he would return, dress, cook, and from some fallen log would eat it with his biscuit, with no other beverage than the wholesome water of the noble river that glided by him. Having finished his lonely meal, he would roll himself in his blanket, creep under his frail skiff, which he turned over, to shield him from the night dews, and the sand of the bar for his bed, would sleep soundly till the morning; when he would arise from his lonely couch, eat his breakfast before the rays of the rising sun had dispersed the humid mist from the surface of the river,—then would start fresh to his task again. In this way he spent over four hundred

25

BANVARD PAINTS
THE BIGGEST PICTURE

Cottonwood Tree in Grandview Reach. Pencil Sketch by John Banvard (Minnesota His-
torical Society)

days, making the preparatory drawings. Several nights during the time, he was compelled to creep from under his skiff, where he slept, and sit all night on a log, and breast the pelting storm, through fear that the banks of the river would cave upon him, and to escape the falling trees. During this time, he pulled his little skiff more than two thousand miles. In the latter part of the summer he reached New Orleans. The yellow fever was raging in the city, but, unmindful of that, he made his drawing of the place. The sun the while was so intensely hot that his skin became so burned, that it peeled off the backs of his hands, and from his face. His eyes became inflamed, by such constant and extraordinary efforts, from which unhappy effects he has not recovered to this day.

At length, the preliminary work all done, he set up a studio in Louisville for the painting of the panorama. Artists, we are reminded, always have a hard time. Even to do the "ordinary labour about his painting room" he could not afford a "menial assistant." He ground his own paint, cut his own wood; to obtain ready money for canvas he did a decorating job for the Odd Fellows. How an artist worked at such a job is pictured in a letter (April 13, 1846) from S. Woodworth, a young naval officer, to George P. Morris of the New York *Home Journal:*

Within the studio, all seemed chaos and confusion, but the life-like and natural appearance of a portion of his great picture, displayed on one of the walls in a yet unfinished state. Here and there were scattered about the floor piles of his original sketches, bales of canvas, and heaps of boxes. Paint-pots, brushes, jars and kegs were strewed about, without order or arrangement, while along one of the walls several large cases were piled containing rolls of finished sections of the painting. On the opposite wall was spread a canvas, extending its whole length, upon which the artist was then at work. A portion of this canvas was wound upon an upright roller, or drum, standing at one end of the building, and as the artist completed his painting he thus disposed of it.[4]

Five months later Banvard was still painting, although he had ventured in July to exhibit a portion of his great work. The Louisville *Courier* in September reported the picture

Bluffs on the Mississippi (Banvard Scrapbook, Minnesota Historical Society)

"nearly completed" and was highly pleased with what he had accomplished.

We have taken occasion to visit his rooms, on several occasions, to view his progress and examine some 'sketches.' The towns, scenery, &c., between New Orleans and Memphis, were eloquently depicted by the artist, but the exceeding beauties of the portion that has been exhibited sink into insignificance, almost, when compared with what Mr. Banvard has recently painted. The romantic scenery, the bold bluffs, the towering hills, and the elevated shot-towers between the mouth of the Ohio and St. Louis, are transferred to the canvass with wonderful force, effect and truthfulness. The artist has here had full scope, and he has shown his capacity and ability to properly perform the great work he has undertaken, in a most effective manner. The view of St. Louis is an admirable one, and our friends in that city would, we know, look on it with no slight satisfaction and pleasure. The picture does credit both to St. Louis and to Mr. Banvard. The entire painting will be finished in the course of three or four weeks.[5]

At last, at last, "the Mississippi is painted." Banvard "now boasts the largest painting in the world"—what a moment in a man's life!

There were some mechanical difficulties before him which do not confront the moving-picture operator today, but they were not insurmountable. Since this was a moving panorama and far larger than those previously shown in the circular halls, it required a different presentation. "The mode of exhibiting it is ingenious," Woodworth had written, "and will require machinery. It will be placed upon upright revolving cylinders, and the canvass will pass gradually before the spectators, thus affording the artist an opportunity of explaining the whole work."[6] There was another difficulty that could be worked out only with the co-operation of the audience. "The painting alternately ascends on the one representation, and descends on the next." Consequently, the program warned, "it will be necessary for the reader, when ascending, to commence at the end of the description, and

Mississippi River Plantation Scene. Oil by John Banvard (Minnesota Historical Society)

follow it back to the beginning." Since, however, each scene
was separately mentioned and properly headed, such a reading backward would bring no great dizziness on the reader.
Probably because he found the scenes more interesting, Banvard made "the views of the painting above the mouth of
the Ohio . . . all on the western shore: below the Ohio, they
are all on the Eastern shore."

The Machinery for Banvard's Moving Panorama (SCIENTIFIC AMERICAN, *December 16, 1848*)

These bits of information are all found in the "program notes" which interested spectators could buy for a small sum at the hall: *Description of Banvard's Panorama of the Mississippi River, Painted on Three Miles of Canvas, exhibiting a View of Country 1200 Miles in Length, extending from the Mouth of the Missouri River to the City of New Orleans, being by far the Largest Picture ever executed by Man.* The pamphlet contained an unexciting, twelve-page listing of scenes that would pass before the eyes of the audience, but it was enriched by an introduction in which the artist gave a history of his activities and of the difficulties under which he had worked. To stimulate the romantic response there was a fervid description of the rise of the Mississippi River as well as a superb sketch of "Life on the Mississippi" (both borrowed from Timothy Flint). The skilfully assembled little book closed with Morgan Neville's version of the Mike Fink legend: "The Last of the Boatmen: A Tale of the Mississippi."[7]

The panorama (1846 version) actually began with a view of the confluence of the Missouri and the Mississippi. The scene, typical of Banvard's whole show and of the other panoramas, gave not merely landscape but sought to introduce all possible human interest; here he had placed "immediately in the foreground, under the shade of some stately elms,—an encampment of Shawnee Indians; the warriors are reclining lazily upon the greensward while their squaws are preparing their rude repast." After a brief glimpse of Bloody Island, famous for its duels, the artist passed to St. Louis, a town built upon the "pleasant elevation" of a double shelf of limestone, with steamboats "seen at all seasons of the year lying in the harbor."

Since the panorama no longer exists, one cannot tell how many places appeared in the "largest picture in the world," but the *Description* of this first exhibit of Banvard's names thirty-six scenes besides the three already mentioned. Plumb Point was included, and the artist did not forget to tell his story of the attack by the Murrell gang. At Palmyra Island below Vicksburg the audience passed the steamer "Uncle Sam," and at this moment Banvard took time to assure those present that all the steamboats introduced into the panorama were correct likenesses. Spanish moss, the palmetto, cypress trees, the pecan tree "tresselled" with the muscadine vine, cotton, sugar—all the usual and the pictorially effective

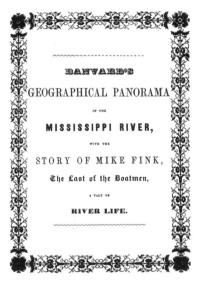

Front Cover of the Banvard Descriptive Pamphlet of 1847 (Minnesota Historical Society)

Banvard's the Seat of the White Fawn, or the Bluffs of Selma (New York WEEKLY ATLAS, *March 5, 1848. Courtesy American Antiquarian Society)*

bits were called to the attention of the reader of the pamphlet and no doubt were specifically mentioned by the artist presiding in person.[8] A note in the program (Boston edition, 1847) informed the readers that Banvard had completed the drawings of the Ohio and would have the panorama of the Ohio ready for exhibition before he left for Europe.

As first exhibited in America the panorama was quite a modest affair, but the newsreel Banvard took to Europe showed considerable growth in the intervening months. The title of the London pamphlet (1849, 1850) indicates the changes: *Description of Banvard's Panorama of the Mississippi, Missouri, and Ohio Rivers, extensively known as the "Three-Mile Painting," exhibiting a view of country over 3000 miles in length, extending from the mouth of the Yellow Stone on the Missouri, and the Little Miami, on the Ohio, to the City of New Orleans, on the Mississippi, being by far the Largest Picture ever executed by Man.*[9] For the benefit of the untraveled spectator the pamphlet carried a fine Banvardic description of the course of the Missouri, which I cannot resist quoting:

At first, the river is a furious mountain torrent, leaping in wildness from rock to rock through deep gorges and dark ravines, rendered still darker by being overshadowed by the almost impervious foliage of terebenthines, firs, pines, and cedars. Then it spreads into a gentle rivulet, with its rippled waters sparkling in the light of midday sun, rejoicing, as it were, in its escape from the rocky embrace of the mountain gorge. Soon it spreads out into a peaceful and gentle stream, with its bosom dotted with romantic and beautiful islands, all covered with the richest foliage, and matted with flowering vines. These, again, overshadowed by lofty peaks of perpendicular rocks, raising their heads to the height of a thousand feet. Among their abrupt terraces, and over their steep precipices, may be seen bounding, in their native wildness, the rocky mountain sheep and nimble antelope.

As it thus glides along, stream after stream enter on either side, contributing their waters to swell its advancing march, until it becomes a large and flowing river. Steep bluffs, of many coloured clays and fantastic shape, range along the shores, some falling perpendicular into the water, others

DESCRIPTION
OF
BANVARD'S PANORAMA
MISSISSIPPI, MISSOURI,
AND
OHIO RIVERS,
EXTENSIVELY KNOWN AS THE
"THREE-MILE PAINTING,"
EXHIBITING A VIEW OF COUNTRY OVER
3000 MILES IN LENGTH,
EXTENDING FROM THE
MOUTH OF THE YELLOW STONE ON THE MISSOURI,
AND THE LITTLE MIAMI, ON THE OHIO,
TO THE
CITY OF NEW ORLEANS, ON THE MISSISSIPPI,
BEING BY FAR
THE LARGEST PICTURE
EVER EXECUTED BY MAN.

LONDON:
PRINTED BY REED AND PARDON, PATERNOSTER ROW.
1852.

4

INDIAN ENCAMPMENT—
And the Sioux, dancing their war dance upon the
GRASSY PLAINS,
Which stretch far away in the distance.
INDIANS HUNTING BUFFALOES.
Large numbers of these animals are taken yearly merely for their hides, which the Indians sell to the white traders.
VILLAGE OF THE DEAD,
Or an aboriginal cemetery. Here will be seen the curious manner the Indians dispose of their dead.
GRAND PRAIRIE—
With its tall waving grass, and myriads of wild flowers— one of the most beautiful sights in nature.
PRAIRIE ON FIRE—
Burning away in the distance, as far as the eye can reach.
INDIAN VILLAGE (by Moonlight)
And the return of the Grand Détour.
KNIFE RIVER,
And the Square Hills. In the fore-ground is Mr. Banvard, seated upon a log, with his rifle by him, and his little skiff moored by the bank of the stream. Upon the gum tree, near him, will be seen one of the gorgeous tints of American foliage.
INDIAN RUINS,
A deserted village of the Mandans, an extinct tribe.
TETON ISLANDS—
And the steamer General Taylor.
BRICK KILNS.
These are some very peculiar cliffs, of different coloured clays, but principally red, which give them the name. The rains are washing them down in many fanciful shapes, not unlike the stalactites of a subterranean cavern.

5

THE MISSISSIPPI RIVER.
Below the "brick kilns" the Missouri empties its waters into the Mississippi.
A short distance above the mouth of the Missouri stands the town of Alton, situated at the base of a beautiful bluff, which rolls in on the river in a graceful outline, clearly defined against the bright sky beyond.
Immediately in the foreground, under the shade of some beautiful trees, is an encampment of Shawnee Indians, the warriors reclining lazily upon the green sward, while their squaws are preparing their rude repast.
Below the junction of the Missouri stands out, in fine relief, some very beautiful islands, clad in the brightest verdure.
We now travel down the Mississippi in a southerly direction, viewing the western bank, until we arrive at the mouth of the Ohio. Below its junction with the Missouri, the Mississippi has no wider channel than above, but its depth and rapidity of current are much increased. Appearing on the opposite bank is the
CITY OF ST. LOUIS.
This is one of the oldest, and first settled towns in the Mississippi Valley. It was settled and occupied by the French, until the country was purchased by the American government. A great number of steamboats, and river craft of all descriptions, bound to all points of the boatable waters of the Mississippi, are seen at all seasons of the year lying at the landing. Miners, trappers, hunters, adventurers, emigrants, and people of all character and languages, meet here, and disperse in pursuit of their various objects, in every direction, some even beyond the remotest points of civilization. Population about 100,000.
UNITED STATES ARSENAL.
It is beautifully situated on a gentle declivity, immediately below the city, at the foot of "the bar." A short distance below the arsenal commence some rocky bluffs, upon which are situated, very prominently, several lofty shot towers; they have a very striking appearance when viewed from the river

Title Page and Pages from DESCRIPTION OF BANVARD'S PANORAMA, *1852 (Minnesota Historical Society)*

receding back from the river, leaving a strip of the richest soil intervening, which nourishes a luxuriant growth of willow and cotton wood, whose varied foliage stand out in strong relief against the light clay bluffs beyond.

The scenery in these remote regions has an aspect of majestic grandeur rarely witnessed upon the globe, perfectly unique in its kind. These bluffs assume a great variety of fanciful shapes, some resembling the ruins of ancient cities, with their domes, towers, and castellated walls, as if nature, in a playful mood, was mimicking the works of man. Beautiful prairies stretch off from the elevated shores like a sea of verdure, until they meet the horizon. Myriads of wild flowers, of every size and hue, are intermingled with the luxuriant grass, "wasting their fragrance on the desert air." Smooth grassy hills at intervals roll, with graceful and uniform shapes, down to the river's edge, relieving the eye, by their graceful curves, from the angular and abrupt forms of the more majestic bluffs above. As it approaches the Mississippi, it is bounded by dark forests and heavily timbered shores, with the banks jagged and broken. Openings in the trees,

33

BANVARD PAINTS
THE BIGGEST PICTURE

and the sound of the axe echoing through the woods, betoken the appearance of civilization. The rude cabin of the settler, with the smoke curving from its chimney, indicates that you have passed the wild regions of the savage, and are now among the abodes of white men. Such is the character of the Missouri, from its source in the rocky mountains, till it discharges its waters into the channel of the Mississippi.

After this lush description of the Missouri, one can proceed to the actual account of the Missouri River views. "The spectator is supposed to be travelling on the left, in a southeasterly direction, going down the stream." He is given a view of the Yellowstone Bluffs, of "Assinnaboin's Bar," then the Domes. "Here," says Banvard, "we have some of the most unique scenery probably in the world. Large clay bluffs, of different coloured clays, rear their heads towards the heavens, the tops are washed away by the rains into circular forms, so that at a distance they resemble immense domes of some gigantic city." This for Banvard is a full and vivid program description of a scene in his panorama. Obviously, however poetic he became in his introductory descriptions of the rivers, he depended upon the excellence of his picture for all the scenes he included.

The next view was of the Grand Detour, where a walk of a mile could save twenty-five or thirty miles of boating. Then followed an Indian encampment, with the Sioux doing a "war dance upon the Grassy Plains which stretch away in the distance." Next, a picture of Indians hunting buffalo, followed by one of the "village of the Dead." Then one saw the Grand Prairie "with its tall waving grass, and myriads of wild flowers—one of the most beautiful sights in nature." A view of the prairie on fire was followed by one of an Indian village in the moonlight. After this the audience saw the Knife River and the Square Hills and with them, as a special touch, a portrait of the artist: "In the foreground is Mr.

John Banvard, 1849 (Courtesy Miss Esther W. Bates)

Banvard, seated upon a log, with his rifle by him, and his little skiff moored by the bank of the stream. Upon the gum tree, near him, will be seen one of the gorgeous tints of American foliage." All that remained before the audience reached the confluence above St. Louis were Indian ruins (a deserted village of the Mandans), the Teton Islands, with the steamer "General Taylor," and some bluffs called the Brick

Kilns. These fifteen scenes, then, if one is to judge from the printed description, formed the principal part, and possibly the entire section, of the panorama devoted to the Missouri River.[10] The Mississippi reel contained the thirty-nine views already mentioned.

The third reel of the finished panorama—the Ohio—to which the audience was taken from New Orleans—offered twenty-three views: the Little Miami River, Cincinnati ("the Panorama gives an excellent view of the city, with its numerous public buildings, as you would see it from a boat on the middle of the river"), the North Bend and the monument to Harrison ("an evening scene shows us a large steamer 'wooding up,' a party of emigrants with their cattle, and a beautiful Forest view," which was a scene in itself), a deadening ("or dead forest; where the trees have been killed by girdling, or cutting a circle or girdle about the trunk with an axe"), a fire in a forest, a moonlight view ("showing on the opposite side the town of Rising Sun"), a log cabin, a snaggy bar, Vevay, Madison, and the mail steamer "Ben Franklin," Twelve Mile Island, a white fog ("several islands and a large steamer are seen in the misty atmosphere"), the town of Jeffersonville, Corn Island, Falls of the Ohio, Goose Island, the Pocket, Sandy Island, the town of New Albany, a floating theater, Blue River Island, and the town of Leavenworth. All of these places are described in the same flat, brief, and prosy fashion; how much Banvard may have added by way of lecture it is impossible to say.

We must return to Banvard and the opening in Louisville. The great work was done; the program was printed; but before the exhibition could begin the producer had to put up double the usual deposit on the gas fixtures and to pay a

Banvard Missouri Views. Above: City of the Dead and Wordum Indian Encampment. Below: The Brick Kilns (PEOPLE'S AND HOWITT'S JOURNAL, *London, April, 1849*)

Banvard Missouri Views. Above: Fur Company's Steamer. Below: Assinaboin Indians and the Domes (PEOPLE'S AND HOWITT'S JOURNAL, *April, 1849*)

special tax levied by the city. The first night was rainy—no one came. In his despair Banvard stumbled upon a clever idea; he gave tickets away among the boatmen. "They were delighted and their wild enthusiasm was raised as one well-known object after another passed by them." The public was convinced and "rushed to see it by hundreds." Ten captains, ten pilots, and more than a hundred others, one of the program jacket blurbs informs us, on October 31, 1846, testified before the mayor of Louisville that the picture was notable for its correctness to nature and truthfulness. Louisville—or, at least, the *Courier*—announced that "this painting now stands the greatest and proudest work of art in the world." The mighty phrases of the voice of the people! The newsreel started on its tour. Banvard set out to conquer the world—and did.[11]

After a visit to New Orleans late in November, "the great artist" departed for the East and tremendous popularity. "So great was the desire to see it," read the modest publicity, "that the railroad companies ran express trains from adjacent towns into the city for the accommodation of the eager throngs who wished to view the greatest achievement of individual enterprise on record."

The panorama reached Boston late in 1846[12] and immediately served to assist the most popular of American poets. On the seventeenth of December Longfellow, who had then finished the first part of *Evangeline*, noted in his journal, "I see a panorama of the Mississippi advertised. This comes very *a propos*. The river comes to me instead of my going to the river; and as it is to flow through the pages of the poem, I look upon this as a special benediction." Two days later he added: "Went to see Banvard's moving diorama of the Mississippi. One seems to be sailing down the great stream, and

39

sees the boats and the sand-banks created with cottonwood, and the bayous by moonlight. Three miles of canvas,[13] and a great deal of merit."[14]

Longfellow was not the only one pleased with the newsreel. The Boston *Herald* declared emphatically that "the painting,—its wild beginning, its difficult progress, and final triumphant completion, stands alone in the annals of art, as a marvelous monument of the patience, daring ambition, and genius of American character." The Boston *Atlas* found it "from the beginning to the end, one of the most living, charmings things, that ever came from the hands of man."[15]

Banvard opened in New York on December 13, 1847, and, except for a week in July, continued to show his picture until late in September, 1848.[16] Four hundred thousand people, Banvard said, attended his show in America; and estimates of his profits ran as high as two hundred thousand dollars.[17] But the best bit of business, for advertising value, was the exhibition in Washington, D.C., and the subsequent resolutions passed in the Senate and the House which declared that these great bodies "regard the Panorama of the Mississippi river, painted by Mr. John Banvard, as a truly wonderful and magnificent production." They expressed in emphatic terms their "high admiration of the boldness and originality of the conception, and of the industry and indefatigable perseverance of the young and talented artist in the execution of his herculean work."[18] With such endorsements—ranging from Ohio River boatmen to Boston newspapers and Congress—Banvard was ready for a European tour.

In the fall of 1848, bearing among others a letter of commendation from Edward Everett, late minister to England, to the president of the Royal Geographical Society, Banvard sailed for Europe.[19] A press notice in the Bristol *Gazette* sum-

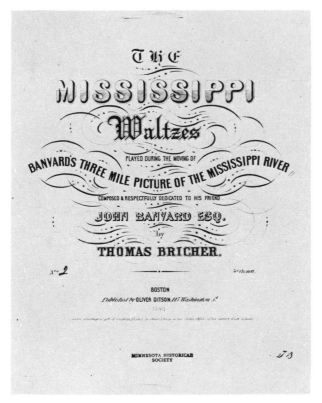

The Mississippi Waltzes (Minnesota Historical Society)

marized the show so vividly that Banvard thought it worth adopting as a blurb.

You pass by, as in a rapid voyage, "temple, tower, and town"; and in an hour and a half's sitting, there is brought vividly before you all the chief incidents of savage and of civilized life, from the wigwam of the Indian and the log hut of the settler, to the lofty domes and graceful spires of the gay and crowded city. You flit by a rice swamp, catch a glimpse of a jungle, dwell for an instant on a prairie, and are lost in admiration at the varied, but ever glorious dress, in which, in the Western world, Nature delights to attire herself.

The White Fawn of the Mississippi (Minnesota Historical Society)

At Christmas time (1848) the panorama was showing at Egyptian Hall, Piccadilly, where "the excitement produced was even greater than in America." The London *Examiner* was not quite so enthusiastic as some other papers. It found Banvard's work lacked the artistic refinement, brilliancy of color, and subtle effects so notable in "those delicate and beautiful pictures by Mr. Stanfield,[20] which used once upon a time to pass before us in like manner." Nevertheless, that journal was much impressed by the statement—accepted without question—that this picture was three miles long and in other respects equally stupendous. Furthermore, "it is a picture irresistibly impressing the spectator with a conviction of its plain and simple beautifullness." In Banvard himself "there is a mixture of shrewdness and simplicity . . . which is very prepossessing; a modesty and honesty, and an odd original humor, in his manner of telling what he has to tell, that give it a peculiar relish."[21]

The *Illustrated London News* (December 9) found that the picture "occupied nearly two mortal hours in unrolling," but the audience liked it and the reviewer was impressed in spite of himself. "It is shown in what is termed the 'dioramic' fashion, with the aid of strong gas light; the picture being inclosed in a sort of dark proscenium; and the apartment in which the audience are seated is alike darkened. Upon a platform is seated Mr. Banvard, who explains the localities as the picture moves, and relieves his narrative with Jonathanisms and jokes, poetry and patter, which delight his audience mightily; and a piano-forte is incidentally invoked, to relieve the narrative monotony." The majority of the scenes was "on the level of scene-work," wrote this critic, but

the river scenery is of greater variety than might have been expected; and its flatness is relieved by many episodal groups which illustrate the manners, customs, and modes of life, of the dwellers on the banks. Now and

What the Poets and Others Said.

Mr. Banvard, in painting the Mississippi, is the *originator and inventor* of this enormous class of Paintings.—*Edward Everett, to the President of the Royal Geographical Society, London.*

We want a national epic, superior to all others, as Banvard's Panorama is to all other paintings—the largest in the world.—*Henry Wadsworth Longfellow, in Cavenaugh.*

Everybody should visit Egyptian Hall, not only to see the beautiful paintings, but to see Mr. Banvard; for in his peculiar manner of illustrating his subjects, he is a greater curiosity than his pictures.—*Charles Dickens, in Household Words.*

Banvard.—In the current number of the People's Journal, we publish the biography of this most wonderful man and his remarkable paintings.—*William Howitt, in People's Journal, London.*

Mr. Banvard is a remarkable man.—*Manchester Guardian.*

We trust our British artists will not be lead away by Mr. Banvard's wonderful success in London, and adopt his "gigantic dodge" in painting enormous pictures—it would certainly create a rise in canvas.—*Punch, London.*

Mr. Banvard is not only a great traveller and lecturer; he is also a poet, a painter and a wit.—*Geo. P. Morris.*

Mr. Banvard has refuted the assertions of foreigners, that America had produced no artist commensurate with the grandeur of its scenery.—*N. P. Willis.*

Windsor Castle, April, 1849.

Her Majesty has directed me to convey to you this slight testimonial of the great delight she experienced on witnessing your great paintings, in St. George's Hall, on Saturday evening last.

Bowles, Master of the Household.

Oh, that I had the skill of a Banvard, that I might depict the glowing scenery of the Nile, as he did of the Mississippi.—*Bayard Taylor, Letter from Egypt.*

Rear Cover of BANVARD, OR THE ADVENTURES OF AN ARTIST, *1852?* (*Minnesota Historical Society*)

then, we have the incident of a steamer upset by "snags," and left an useless log upon the waters; and then, a well-freighted vessel, steaming in all the pride of a river race, with a wonderful prodigality of steam and human life, imparts great animation to the scene. Then we have bluffs, bars, islands, rocks and mounds, points and cliffs, without number, and of fantastic varieties of form; encampments and war-dances; hunting-grounds and burial places, prairies with their giant grasses, perchance burning to the very horizon; log cabins and villages, sometimes nestling in natural amphitheatres, and at others perched upon the rock tops; and a great variety is imparted to the Exhibition by showing it under different influences, as night and daybreak, moonlight and coming storm.

Below Baton Rouge the river was lined with

splendid sugar plantations. . . . Behind the levees we see extensive sugarfields, noble mansions, beautiful gardens, large sugar-houses, groups of negro quarters, lofty churches, splendid villas, presenting, in all, one of the finest views of the United States.

Mr. BANVARD exhibiting and explaining his MAMMOTH PANORAMA OF THE MISSISSIPPI, before the **Queen, Prince Albert,** **the Royal Children, and the Court, at St. George's Hall, Windsor Castle.** At the Close of the Exhibition, HER MAJESTY was pleased to bestow upon Mr BANVARD a distinguished mark of her Royal Approbation.

WILL OPEN MONDAY EVENING, February 9th, 1852

AT THE

ASSEMBLY ROOMS,

GEORGE TAVERN, NORTH SHIELDS.

MR. BANVARD

Has the honor of announcing that his GIGANTIC, ORIGINAL, MOVING PANORAMA of the

MISSISSIPPI

MISSOURI AND OHIO RIVERS,

THE SAME THAT WAS EXHIBITED BY ROYAL COMMAND, BEFORE THE

QUEEN AND COURT, AT WINDSOR CASTLE,

Will be exhibited, as above

FOR FIVE DAYS ONLY.

A Broadside Advertisement Showing Banvard Exhibiting before Queen Victoria (Missouri Historical Society)

As in America, everyone went to watch Banvard's show. The hall was "daily crowded by the nobility and fashion of the metropolis." Those who had traveled in America were hearty in their appreciation. J. S. Buckingham, the lecturer, who had been three years in the United States, commended the picture. Even Charles Dickens wrote the artist-operator approvingly: "I have visited your exhibition of the Missouri and Mississippi Rivers, and cannot refrain from saying that I was in the highest degree interested and pleased by your picture, by its truthfulness, by your account of it, by its remarkable characteristics, by the striking and original manner in which the scenes it represents are plainly presented to the spectator. . . ."[22] Banvard showed excellent judgment in his choice of indorsers and met with the greatest success. The crown of all, of course, was a command performance at Windsor.[23]

After that, all England—Paris—the world were at his feet.

Glenada, the House the Panorama Built (BALLOU'S PICTORIAL DRAWING-ROOM COMPANION, *May 16, 1857*)

JOHN ROWSON SMITH'S
"Four-Mile Painting"

The tremendous popularity and financial success of Banvard were certain to call forth competition. In the London edition of the pamphlet, *Banvard, or the Adventures of an Artist*, the announcement was made that "the public should be on their guard against several spurious copies and incorrect imitations which have been hurriedly prepared by parties of unprincipled persons, who are now [1849] endeavoring to palm them off as being original in various parts of the country; thus robbing Mr. Banvard of the fruits of his years of toil and danger." Banvard had been cautious enough to get Abbott Lawrence, the American minister in London, to certify that he was the sole author of the moving panorama of the Mississippi, and the following year in Paris he received and published the indorsement of the American minister to France, who declared the enterprising painter to be the originator of the idea. It is probable that attempts were soon made to pirate "The Largest Picture ever executed by

Man," and to them Banvard had reason to object. But it is quite possible and even likely that he referred to the panorama of John Rowson Smith, and that was a different matter.[1]

Banvard, who was undoubtedly the first of the Big Five to exhibit, fought for his priority and superiority; but Smith, the nearest rival, had no intention of accepting second place. He had the greatest scorn for the work of Banvard and did not fail to express it in his own (1848) pamphlet. The Smith "Panorama has been painted to show places in their true light, instead of a mere apology from imagination, and to give something like a correct and general character of the Great West. There are few who can compute the labor, time and expense of producing a picture of this description. The Mississippi part of the Panorama covers an area of 20,000 square feet, more than half as large again as Banvard's, and contains 700 miles more of its scenery. The artist has painted this Panorama from personal and minute study and observation, occupying his time for years, to the exclusion of all other pursuits; and he has received the assurances of the best artists in the United States that the Picture is beyond all comparison, better than the smaller panoramic painting called *Banvard's*, and has no equal of its character in the world."

In the London issue of the pamphlet the next year (and was it this that excited Banvard's strong condemnation?), Smith and his partner reiterated their opinion: "A feature that cannot be too strongly dwelt upon in this extensive picture is its completeness and its fidelity. In other attempts to convey to the eye and mind of the spectator a reflex of these grandest works of Nature's hand, there are very many serious drawbacks—putting aside the crude effort of the uncultivated artist—many of the most beautiful views on the banks of the great Mississippi are entirely omitted, and many of the scenes introduced are entirely imaginary. In the work now presented to the public, there is not an inch of attractive landscape omitted—not a patch of inlet—not a rock—nay, scarcely a tree."

Probably the most effective bit in this statement from Smith's point of view was the slur on the "crude effort of the uncultivated artist." John Rowson Smith was the son of John Rubens Smith, painter, engraver, and teacher of the arts. Young Smith had learned his business under proper guidance in his father's school—he was an artist; the self-made were mere awkward amateurs. When he attained maturity, John Rowson Smith devoted himself for years to theatrical work; in his *Description*, he declared he had "long been known as one of the first American Scenic Artists of the Age." He had been "principal artist" for J. A. Caldwell at the St. Charles Theater in New Orleans, he had painted "with distinguished success" at the Princess Theatre in London, and had done the "splendid scenery" for the production of the *Naiad Queen* in Philadelphia. More prophetic, he had "also painted a superb Panorama of Boston, from views taken from the dome of the State House."

The history of Smith's painting of the Mississippi is a bit confused. In 1848 appeared *A Descriptive Pamphlet of Smith's Leviathan Panorama of the Mississippi River! Now Exhibiting at Mason Hall, Philadelphia*. Undoubtedly this was written by Smith himself, or, at least entirely on his authority. The readers were informed that in 1840 Smith had exhibited in Boston (and in Louisville) a panorama of the Mississippi River. This picture, two hundred feet in length, offered "views of the mouth of the Licking River opposite

Cincinnati, Louisville by moonlight, storm on the Mississippi, cotton plantations and New Orleans, together with the conflagration of Moscow."

When a new program guide was issued in London a year later, Smith had taken on a partner who managed to put his own name first: *Professor Risley and Mr. J. R. Smith's Original Gigantic Moving Panorama of the Mississippi River, extending from the Falls of St. Anthony to the Gulf of Mexico, painted by John R. Smith, Esq., Depicting nearly four thousand miles of American scenery, running through nine states of the Union (sixteen degrees of latitude, from the wheat of the north to the orange of the south); Being one-third longer than any other pictorial work in existence; Four miles in Length.* Risley (if he were the author of this issue) declared J. R. Smith the "originator of the moving Panorama in America" and stated that his first Boston exhibition had been in 1839. He said nothing of the length of that first painting, but did say that it was destroyed by fire. The original drawings were saved, but the artist was unable to complete the present picture until assisted by Professor Risley "when new drawings became necessary from the vast increase of towns on the Mississippi." Risley in his own eyes—or in his own words—was a pretty important fellow, but one wonders why he was not mentioned in the first *Description.*

Banvard and Smith both claim precedence for a beginning of the great work, and it is quite possible that they started about the same time. Henry Chapman, a western pilot who saw Banvard's panorama twice in London, testified that he had been with that artist on the Missouri and Mississippi rivers in 1833 and 1834 and "knew him at that time to make drawings of those shores with the intention of executing a panorama." Among other press opinions quoted in Ban-

GRAND AMERICAN HALL,

(LATE MISS LINWOOD'S)

LEICESTER SQUARE.

⁓⁓⁓⁓⁓

PROFESSOR RISLEY AND MR. J. R. SMITH'S

ORIGINAL

GIGANTIC MOVING PANORAMA

OF THE

MISSISSIPPI RIVER,

EXTENDING FROM THE

FALLS OF ST. ANTHONY TO THE GULF OF MEXICO,

PAINTED BY

JOHN R. SMITH, ESQ.,

DEPICTING NEARLY

FOUR THOUSAND MILES

OF AMERICAN SCENERY, RUNNING THROUGH NINE STATES OF THE
UNION (SIXTEEN DEGREES OF LATITUDE, FROM THE WHEAT
OF THE NORTH TO THE ORANGE OF THE SOUTH);

BEING ONE-THIRD LONGER THAN ANY OTHER PICTORIAL WORK IN
EXISTENCE: EXTENDING OVER

FOUR MILES OF CANVASS.

⁓⁓⁓⁓⁓

London:

PROFESSOR RISLEY AND MR. J. R. SMITH,

GRAND AMERICAN HALL,

LEICESTER SQUARE.

———

1849.

Title Page of the Description of
Smith's Panorama, 1849 (Courtesy
Mercantile Library, St. Louis)

51

SMITH'S

FOUR-MILE PAINTING

vard's London (1850) pamphlet was that of the *Kentucky Luminary* to the effect that Banvard had been painting in the cities, or trading with the Indians and settlers on the western rivers for eighteen years. These statements fit reasonably with the known, rather than legendary, date of his birth (November 15, 1815) and with the general array of facts in the *Adventures of an Artist.*

But Smith (born May 11, 1810) was also early in the West. When he first came out to the Mississippi is not known, but in the summer of 1836 he was painting scenery for the new theater of Ludlow and Smith, which opened in St. Louis the following July. The editor of the *Commercial Bulletin* (September 24, 1836) found the ten sets that Smith had just completed "as fine as any of its kind in the United States." They did the artist much credit, "especially the Gothic and Palace scenes. The Wood is also good, and the two little Landscapes, on the wall of the Parlor scenes, are gems of the art." The writer closed his enthusiastic praise by declaring that "the Building Committee have procured through him a source of frequent delight to the future visitors of the new St. Louis Theatre."[2]

Both Banvard and Smith were in the western country in the mid-1830's, and, from the popularity of panoramas as theatrical fare, it is probable that both very soon had the idea of doing a river picture. It is even more probable that neither accomplished much of his serious work before the 1840's; and since Banvard was able to devote more time to the project, his picture was first on exhibition.

According to Frederick C. Coburn, Smith finished his panorama of the Mississippi, falls to mouth, in 1844;[3] but, when we consider the other work he was doing, it seems doubtful that he could have done such a large job at this time. In the autumn of 1842 he was painting scenery for the Park Theatre in New York and appears to have been rather well occupied with such professional work throughout the winter. The next summer he was engaged, with assistants, in decorating Simpson's Theatre in New York, which opened on September 11, 1843. Furthermore, the New York *Spirit of the Times* on November 9, 1844, referred to "a panorama of . . . Boston, painted in sections, by Mr. John R. Smith" which was then being shown at the Chatham Theatre. If his masterpiece had been finished, it would certainly have crowded out the earlier painting. Even as late as September 27, 1847, he was announced as scenic artist for the Broadway Theatre, New York. Probably he did much of his sketching during his years in the West; when he found time for the enormous labor of painting cannot be determined. It appears certain, however, that Smith was not ready to exhibit until 1848.[4]

Possibly the first place of exhibition was fashionable Saratoga. On August 14, the Saratoga *Daily Whig* reviewed the show. "The *Great Panorama of the Mississippi*, now exhibiting at the Pavilion House, was crowded with a brilliant and fashionable audience on Saturday evening, and never has an exhibition given greater satisfaction than this. It is, indeed, the wonder of the age. The immense size of the pictures—the thrilling interest kept up throughout the whole—the burning steamboat, the pilot burnt at the wheel, the captain tearing the planks off the upper deck, the yawl upsetting, and females perishing is a sublime and terrible scene."[5] On the twenty-fifth, Major General Scott attended and admired the faithfulness of the painting. Smith evidently had a predilection for the army. At Troy, on September 8, Major General John E. Wool wrote appreciatively, testifying to the accuracy of the panorama. And three months later, the great Thomas Sully in Philadelphia was pleased to add his commendation. Apparently, in six weeks at Saratoga, his picture earned twenty thousand dollars, and then Smith toured the East.[6]

During this winter, before he left for Europe, he took into partnership Professor Risley. Information concerning this man is somewhat meager. A native of New Jersey, Risley "became a trader among the Indians, and for many years resided with the Powtowattomy tribe, and other roving bands of the great west." When his eldest son was eighteen months old, the "quick eye" of the Professor "detected the extreme elegance of his motions"; he trained the boy, and they traveled in the tropics, "exhibiting their marvelous feats." A second son was added to the troupe. In January, 1842, Risley and his sons appeared in the act of the Polish Brothers at the Arcadian Garden. The next month, with a pupil, he indulged in "terrific gymnastic feats" at the Chatham Theatre. A little more than a year later (May 4, 1843) the New York *Herald* declared that one of the chief attractions at the Park Theatre was Professor Risley and his boy, who had in the meantime "dodged" the Guadaloupe earthquake. The following year they were featured at the opening of the St. James Theatre in London. On October 4, 1847, Professor Risley and sons appeared once more in New York in "classical, aerial and popular exercises" at the Broadway Theatre; this was announced as his first appearance in America in five (*sic*) years. Finally, the Risley family was appearing at Burton's Chamber Street Theatre in New York early in November, 1848. It is likely, then, that the Risley-Smith partnership was not entered into until after this date.[7]

Sometime in this winter the partners left for England where they had to compete with Banvard. They, too, managed to show their panorama by invitation to Victoria at Balmoral and from that happy occasion swept on to huge audiences in London and on the Continent. Forehanded Mr. Smith in Europe prepared a *Panorama of the Tour of Europe* for showing on his return to America.[8]

But the panorama is more exciting than its history. Banvard gives the impression of being the poet, the artist, the dreamer, the man of imagination. Smith, on the other hand, is the realist, the practical man, the one who sees all the value that lies in such a gigantic undertaking as the painting of the course of a great river. He is not willing to give a mere picture; it must be an accurate one, for only so can one give the proper idea of the Mississippi. "We may trace its crooked course upon the map, read animated descriptions of it, but these sink into nothingness in comparison with its faithful representation upon canvass, embodied in the glowing tints of nature. We see, as it were, the living realities before us. In taking the views of Memphis, a separate drawing was made for each house upon the bank of the river; the same may be said of Vicksburgh, New Orleans, and other cities; and it is upon this ground that the Panorama comes before the Public as the only correct representation ever offered to their notice."

The real purpose of this picture, the producers repeatedly insisted, was essentially educational and scientific: the panorama becomes a document of historical value.

In America the country itself is ever on the change, and in another half century those who view this portrait of the Mississippi will not be able to recognize one twentieth part of its details. Where the forest now overshadows the earth, and affords shelter to the wild beast, corn fields, orchards, towns, and villages, will give a new face to the scene, and tell of industry and enterprise, which will stimulate to new and untiring efforts. Places of small population will have swelled their limits, and there will be seen cities where are now beheld hamlets—mansions in the place of huts, and streets where the foot path and deer tracks are now only visible. How much might be gathered of ancient manners and history, had our ancestors bequeathed to us works of a similar description. . . . Let the artists of every clime depict the most attractive portions of their countries on an extent like that now spread before us—they will convey the instruction and delight of reality, and they may rest assured of being hailed with a general welcome by every nation they visit, and reaping that reward without which so many professors of art now languish.

Here was a notable purpose in which the artist was ably seconded by Professor Risley, who, if we are to credit him with the London pamphlet, was certainly an acrobat with words. Banvard's most poetic effort is not superior to the fine phrases of the Professor.

In no other painting in the world is to be witnessed so amply the diversity of the human race nor of the variableness of scenery. Man, from the lordly ruler to the slave, moves before us engaged in the various occupations of life. The swart Indian on the borders of his native river stands in fine contrast with the white captain who rules the floating palace that is steaming by: and to strengthen the effect, the tawny mariners are grouped with visages of Nubian blackness, and thus present to one passing glance every variety of complexion. On land we behold the buffalo, the wild deer, the horse, the ox, the goat, and the peaceful lamb—each subsisting on the spot peculiar to its habits, and carrying the mind of the spectator to the far lands of which it is a denizen. On the water, there is not a species of vessel that may not be seen, from the huge unwieldy raft to the light canoe and the magnificent steamboat. Alligators and other creatures of the deep, of which Europeans only hear and read, are seen sporting in several places: and thus the beholder is constantly reminded that it is of no familiar scene he is the spectator. The habitations are as diversified as the other features of the Panorama. We see man's first dwelling place, the cave, hollowed by the hand of Nature herself—the rude log hut next attracts our admiration by the beauty of its construction, while we inwardly shudder at the bare idea of rheumatic draughts and damps, suggested by its numerous fissures and exposed condition. Floating past this, the Indian wigwam, scarce built with the skill displayed by the beaver in the formation of its home, rears itself in clusters like an emmet's settlement athwart the green sward, and teaches the owner of a palace the superfluity of his possessions. Further on the comfortable farm house, the pleasant cottage and the stately mansion, with warehouses, churches, theatres, and every other description of building, display their architectural peculiarities, and furnish one more proof of man's superiority over the lower animals, the dwellings of which are now constructed with precisely the same form first given them by the original artificers. With respect to the scenery, the same spirit of variety pervades the whole. The wild and the city—the mountains and the plain—the swamp, forest, prairie, cataract, and tributary stream succeed each other in almost endless changeableness, and whilst storing the mind with information never to be effaced the viewer congratulates himself at not being actually exposed to the dangers and inconveniences of so extended a pilgrimage.

This is language beyond anything Smith achieved in the first pamphlet. Obviously Risley was an addition to the firm. Not many could resist a show so elegantly and so vividly present-ed. Not many would avoid instruction when it was so enter-taining, or amusement when it was so instructive.

The Smith panorama was evidently superior to Banvard's both in length[9] and in detail of the Mississippi. Banvard had begun at the mouth of the Missouri and had finished at New Orleans, offering for this region thirty-nine views. Smith started his painting from the Falls of St. Anthony above Fort Snelling and carried his audience to the Gulf. But even for the region the first man had covered, Smith gave more views. Furthermore, Banvard's printed description of places was limited. We gain no vivid idea either of the nature of his panorama or of the river country itself from the program he supplied. Smith had much more to say in his first pamphlet, and this feature the partners continued. His accounts are fuller, have more news value, and are pictorially more effective.

He divided his picture into three reels. The first of these, the "Corn Region," extended from the falls almost to the mouth of the Ohio and offered thirty-two views. The falls, Fort Snelling, Lake Pepin, Prairie du Chien, Dubuque, Galena, passed before the eyes of the spectators. At the last-named place, they were treated to a diversion: they left the town and were carried through twenty miles of rolling hills toward Chicago until they were given a sight of the prairies of Illinois. "A more enchanting scene for above 150 miles in width by 400 in length the eye never beheld. It seems as though its gentle undulating slopes were the work of art, covered with green velvet and masses of flowers, with innumerable flocks of birds of all kinds, prairie hens, grouse, &c." Then, as if afraid that they had become too poetic, the producers gave themselves over to the poetry of practical life. "Here is a post-office in a log-cabin; stage-coach changing horses; home of the Illinois volunteer. Farms can be purchased here for $1.25 the acre, formed by the hand of nature. All that is required is to fence it in, to keep the cattle out, plough up the sod, and plant on the richest soil in the world. By keeping out the fires, which spread over the prairies in the fall of the year, all kinds of forest trees spring up spontaneously. There is an abundance of rock three or four feet beneath the surface, and good well water. This is a greater El Dorado than the mines of California." The prairie states could have had worse press agents than the panorama-producers. The Black Hawk Hills and Rock River; Rock Island, with a view of Fort Armstrong; Davenport, from which ten thousand quail in one season were sent down to St. Louis; and Burlington, Iowa, all come and go. Next we have a clear indication that such a panorama as Smith's did not pretend to be an absolutely complete picture of the river banks: "We must necessarily pass many small towns, as Bloomington,

The Mormon Temple at Nauvoo. View of Smith's Panorama (GRAHAM'S MAGAZINE, *1849*)

Oquawka, Clarksville, Quincy, Warsaw, &c. as they would prove uninteresting to the mass, and present no peculiarities."

Nauvoo, however, where lately the Mormons had proved so upsetting to the good people of the West, was excellent copy, and they made the most of it. It is curious how far the comment goes beyond necessary description, and how much the writer tried to add to news value:

Nauvoo—A Mormon City, and settlement, now deserted. It is one of the finest locations for a town upon the river, it being situated at the second and last rapids below the Falls of St. Anthony, which extend from this place to Keokuk, a distance of 12 miles. The great Mormon Temple stands out conspicuous. [Or "stood," for a footnote adds that "on the 9th of October (since this pamphlet was prepared for the press) this splendid edifice was entirely destroyed by fire."] It is the finest Building in the west, and if paid for, would have cost over half a million dollars. It is built of a white stone, resembling marble, 80 feet front by 150 deep; 200 feet to the top of the spire. The caps of the pilasters represent the sun; the base of them, the half moon with Joe Smith's profile. The windows between the pilasters represent stars. A large female figure with a bible in one hand is the vane. An inscription on the front, in large gilt letters, reads as follows: —"The House of the Lord built by the Church of Jesus Christ of the Latter Day Saints. Commenced April 6, 1841. Holiness to the Lord." There is in the basement of the temple a large stone basin, supported by twelve oxen of colossal size, about fifteen feet high altogether, all of white stone and respectably carved. A stair case leads up to the top of the basin. It is the fount where all the Mormons are baptized. It is seen in the Panorama standing aside the Temple, *but in the basement is its real situation.* The first view is Nauvoo and the Temple in the distance. The next, a large architectural elevation of the Temple, showing all its details.[10]

Enquiries were made from reliable sources by Mr. Smith, and to the credit of the people of the west, the Mormons never were driven forth or molested on account of religious opinions nor spiritual wifeism, but as being living representatives of the "Forty Thieves." They would steal a horse and wagon from some Neighboring town and run it into Nauvoo. The owner pursueing them there would get out a warrant from Joe Smith and a dozen Mormons were ready to swear the horse and wagon had been there for five years, and the stranger would then be fined $100 for false accusation, and if he got off with his life, he was lucky. Cows, horses, pigs, etc., it was impossible to keep in their vicinity. Their doctrine is, the earth is the Lord's and the fulness thereof—*we are the Lord!* Their spiritual wifeism is all true, and a greater set of rascals never met with the just and deserved vengeance of an outraged community. Both parties fought with cannon, about 2000 men of a side. The marks of the balls can be seen among the ruins of the now deserted city; it once contained a population of 18,000.[11]

Leaving Nauvoo, we see the islands near Hamburg, the mouth of the Illinois River and the town of Grafton, the rocky bluffs above Alton, the steamer "Time and Tide," with two barges in tow, and the mouth of the mighty Missouri. The levee at St. Louis had life to it, but principally that commercial vitality of which Risley and Smith were fond: "Some idea may be formed of the business of the place from the droves of carmen, piles of boxes, hogsheads, barrels, lead, hemp, sugar, tobacco, furniture, iron, &c., the whole being the productions of the various parts of the Valley of the Mississippi. Negro carmen beating their horses, as though both parties were fond of it; barrels rolling down the levee, passengers running, boatmen swearing, crowds of Dutch emigrants, and as much bustle as is ever seen in London or New York." For the more romantic there was given next a view of the city from the Illinois shore.

After this came the usual run: Bloody Island, Reed Bush (Vide Poche!) or Carondelet, the American Bottoms, Jefferson Barracks. Now for a diversion, a storm scene near the mouth of the Meramec River and the wreck of the steamboat "Anglo Saxon." The Plateen Rocks; Cornice Island and Cornice Rocks; Herculaneum; Rush Island and Bar "with the splendid new steamer Alek Scott (sixteen feet long on the Panorama)"; Bayley's Island and another wreck, interesting this time because it showed the diving bell at work; the Grand Tower and the Devil's Bake Oven; the lower part of Hat Island, known as the "Graveyard of the Mississippi," twelve boats lost there in one season; and then Ste Genevieve and Cape Girardeau—these views brought the first reel to a close.

The second reel—the "Cotton Region"—began with the mouth of the Ohio and ran on as far as Natchez. The twenty-five scenes were all on the east bank of the river. The first view attempted something Banvard had not thought of. It "commences with a longitudinal section of a steamboat of the first class (fifty feet long on the Panorama). A correct representation of the pilot house, ladies' cabin, social hall, and the main saloon. The lady passengers are seen sitting at the table, while gentlemen who have no ladies under their care remain standing until the steward rings the bell, thus always securing seats for the ladies, no matter how great the crowd. Below the cabins are seen the boilers, and the whole arrangement of a high-pressure engine with the accommodations for deck passengers; the whole being a correct view of the interior of the steamer Magnolia. The steamer General Worth is bow and bow racing with the Magnolia, and about parting company, the one for St. Louis, and the other for Louisville."

After this start we see the mouth of the Ohio and the city of Cairo, the levee of which cost nearly a million dollars; we are also informed that "the Rothschilds are said to have been deeply interested in this city." Now we go swiftly down this stretch of the river, past the Iron Banks, the small town of Columbus, the Chalk Banks ("a mass of potters' clay"), the Madrid bend, Plumb Point bar, the Second Chickasaw Bluffs with the town of Randolph and "in the foreground a large flatboat, loaded with cattle for the New Orleans market," Memphis, Fort Pickering, President's Island "with a small Clump of trees at the head of it . . . called a *tow head.*"

Next follows a moonlight view of the steamer "Saladin" taking wood, and, to balance so romantic a scene, we are treated to some shipping statistics: "She had on board 861 empty barrels on the hurricane roof, eighteen dozen turkeys, 180 dozen chickens, 3,000 sacks of corn, 200 kegs of lard, 40 cows and oxen, 200 live hogs, 25 mules, hay and hemp in bales"; yet she had room for one hundred deck passengers on that run to New Orleans. A view of some islands and island "shutes" and then we are shown the "terrific explosion of the General Brown" near Helena, Arkansas. She had been racing and two hundred lives were lost in the accident. Next we see the Yellow Bend and the plantation of John L. Martin.

Steamboat at General Taylor's Plantation. View of Smith's Panorama (GRAHAM'S MAGAZINE, *1849*)

As we draw down the river towards Vicksburg we overtake a showboat. "Traveling theatres and amusements of all kinds are to be seen on the river," our program reminds us. "The Naiad Queen Theatre is here represented going down stream to gratify the people with some plays, which have been expressly got up, with new scenery, machinery, decorations, and appointments, and without regard to expense." In contrast we see a wood chopper's home and a canebrake. The scenery takes on a southern appearance: "the cypress in gloomy grandeur; large alligator with young ones running over its back; the palmetto; negroes carrying a catfish weighing 100 pounds . . . turtles under logs; paroquets, cranes, &c." Then the mouth of the Yazoo River, the Walnut Hills, Vicksburg, Warrenton, Palmyra Islands and the Grand Gulf, the town of Grand Gulf, Petit Gulf and the town of Rodney, and the home and plantation of General Zachary Taylor bring this section to a close.

Reel Three—the "Sugar Region"—continues down the east bank from Natchez to the Gulf of Mexico. The artist tells us when he was in Natchez once on a Sunday he saw slave women "dressed in gaiter boots, silk bonnets with flowers, and silk cardinals, all of the latest New York fashion." No doubt he put them into his picture. Continuing our education in river ways, we see wharf boats. Then Natchez Island and the wreck of the "Maria." We are shown a traveling blacksmith's shop on a flatboat. At Ellis Cliffs we view the house of a colored slaveowner. And now we come to one of the highlights of the whole exhibition—the burning of the "Ben Sherrod." This had occurred in 1837 and had made a great impression on Smith, for he had booked passage from New Orleans on her and only by chance had not been aboard. The boat caught fire late at night. "Captain Castleman . . . tore up planks from the upper deck and cast them to drowning passengers. . . . The pilot was burnt at the wheel. . . . The Columbia succeeded in rescuing a great number of lives. In this terrific picture the yawl-boats are seen picking up some of those overboard. The glare of the fire from the burning steamer is finely contrasted with the moonlight at Fort Adams, where the boat floated to and sunk." One hundred lives were lost in this catastrophe.

Fort Adams, Red River Cut-Off, and Bayou Sara need hardly detain us. More interesting are a traveling greenhouse on a flatboat, and a family boat, "with a wood-chopper, or a poor farmer, moving his 'plunder,' as a few tin pans, an iron pot, a frying-pan, and his wife and children are called." We slip by Port Hickey and Port Hudson, Prophet's Island, the steamer "Splendid," and Baton Rouge. A crevasse claims excited attention. "The view represents the giving away of a place in the levee. Hundreds of slaves are seen carrying earth,

The Burning of the Steamer "Ben Sherrod" (Risley-Smith Descriptive Pamphlet, 1849. Courtesy Mercantile Library, St. Louis)

trees, &c. to fill up the gap. The negro quarters are washing away. A flatboat is being brought up to sink in the break."

In the heart of this third region are shown the interior of a sugarmill, a field of sugar cane, and the famous Whitehall plantation with three sugar mills, the owner's house, and other buildings. The New Convent; Cantrell Church, College Point, and Louisiana Institute; the large passenger steamer "Missouri"; Mrs. McCutcheon's plantation; Red Church; an English brig taking on a cargo of molasses and sugar; Detrian's (Destrehan's) splendid villa ("foreign plants and oranges are here seen in rich profusion"): Carrollton, at sunset, with a view in the foreground of the racecourse where the Mexican

Above: Montgomery's House, Headquarters of General Jackson at the Battle of New Orleans. Below: The Balize. Views of Smith's Panorama (GRAHAM'S MAGAZINE, *1849*)

War volunteers had camped; the city of La Fayette—this varied and informative succession leads us to New Orleans. Then let us follow Smith down to the Gulf, a journey that Banvard did not make. It need not take long. We pass the back of a villa opposite New Orleans, the steamer "Clay," the convent, the government barracks, and then Montgomery's house, which had served Jackson as headquarters in January, 1815. We stop at the battleground, at Lizardi's plantation, we see rice growing, we round Fort Bend, enter the Southwest Pass, and at last see the Gulf of Mexico.

Before taking leave of Smith—and Professor Risley—let us return for one more look at New Orleans. There the *Description* rises to its highest in more senses than one.

It is one of the most beautiful scenes imaginable to leave New Orleans in a steamer. The bell gives one tap, the gang plank is drawn in, the engine gives a slow revolution, she backs out into the eddy, and some 25 or 30 negro firemen and deckhands stand on the gang-way plank and strike up their songs and choruses; their voices echo as they pass the ponderous wheelhouses of the adjoining boats, and swell in harmonious concert with those negro melodies which are at the present day so much admired. Here was their origin. The boat has now turned her head up stream. Wheugh, wheugh, goes the puff of the engine, and like a race horse, she starts with a full head of steam, and rushes by the panorama of steamboats, flatboats, and the mile of shipping, then by La Fayette, the suburbs, and Carrollton. A person can scarcely realize the view; the moving palace, the complicated machinery, the fierce fires burning beneath, the long perspective of the superb saloons, the crowd of people, the beauty of the landscape on each shore, and then, when the boat meets the powerful current against her in full force and she staggers a moment, then rushes on impetuous and irresistible, you cannot but feel that steam is indeed an almighty power in the hands of many, in the hands of American ingenuity and go-aheaditiveness.

67

SMITH'S
FOUR-MILE PAINTING

CHAPTER
4

SAM STOCKWELL
"Canvasses" the Mississippi

"Ever since the advent of Banvard, this city has been literally over-run with panoramas," wrote a Boston correspondent
of the St. Louis *Reveille* in October, 1849.

I cannot enumerate them all, but there is always two or more open at
the same time. With the exception of "Bayne's Panorama of a Voyage to
Europe," all have lost money. Two *Mexican Panoramas* were failures.
"Champney's Rhine," the "Shores of the Mediterranean," a "Voyage to
California," the "Creation and Deluge," "Ireland and her Shores," Hudson's "Ohio and Mississippi," "A Voyage round the World," "A walk
through the Garden of Eden," are anything but successful. Some of them
are "up the spout," and some "laid by" for the present. The panorama
rage, however, is still high. The Panorama of the "River St. Lawrence and
Falls of Niagara," and another called "American Scenery, embracing all
that is grand and wonderful in America," also, "Stockwell's colossal
Panorama of the Mississippi river," are yet in full blast. "Skirving's overland journey to California" was opened October 1st. "The sketches are
by Col. Fremont, &c., (so announced,) and exhibit his late disastrous trip
over the mountains, etc.''! Stockwell is doing finely, owing to the fact that
as a "Boston Boy" he is very popular, and as an artist greatly admired. His
friends were determined to "put him right tho"—and they have done it.
While the other halls are empty, Stockwell's is full. It has become a "Bos-

ton notion," and will, of course, take. Though successful, Stockwell has not been idle. He was furnished with a beautiful sketch of "St. Louis in ruins," and has transferred it to canvass with peculiar effect. He has not yet given this to the public, but is holding it back for an *occasion*.[1]

Of Samuel B. Stockwell, painter of the third Mississippi panorama, little is known, save that he was trained in the scenic art in Boston and worked in the theaters there for about ten years before making his way to the West. In January, 1843, he is discovered, in the pleasant old stage use of the word, as scenic artist for the Ludlow and Smith St. Charles Theatre in New Orleans and later served in their houses in Mobile and St. Louis. The writer of his obituary in the Boston *Post*, October 7, 1854, spoke of him as "an untiring student of his profession" who "left no superior, and few equals, behind him." Certainly, the elaborate sets he painted for the stage were ample preparation for the production of a super set for the rolling Mississippi.

Since his panorama has disappeared, since his sketches for it have never been found, and since no printed program guide for it has been located, his masterwork is remembered today only because he enjoyed a first-rate press. He was well known and well liked. He was the chief mover in a genuine "western enterprise." He was the first panoramist to exhibit in the home town. For these reasons he was given much space in the St. Louis newspapers, and we are thus able to reconstruct his panorama and its story.

Perhaps the most remarkable fact concerning his picture was the speed with which he executed it. According to a story in the St. Louis *Weekly Reveille* of July 31, 1848, in five months time he had made two long sketching trips and had finished one-third of his actual painting. Like Banvard and Smith, he claimed some antiquity for his intention; the editor (probably Joseph M. Field) vouched for the fact that Stockwell had had the idea for at least seven years.[2] Only of late, however, had he found time to devote to this work. In March, 1848, at last, with only one companion and with sketchbook in hand, he had left St. Louis in the customary open boat to travel to the mouth of the Mississippi. His object, said the *Reveille*, "was to paint, faithfully, the features of the great river, a thing which, no matter what may have been the success of others with the public, *has never yet been done.*"

Amid a multitude of adventures and with considerable hardship, Stockwell had accomplished his purpose. On his return to St. Louis he had taken a steamer to St. Peters at the mouth of the Minnesota River on the Upper Mississippi, sketched the scenery there, and, having procured another open boat, dropped slowly down the river taking views all the way to St. Louis—"thus for the first time [the *Reveille* declared] completing the river from the falls to the Gulf of Mexico." Since his picture was intended to be three times the length of Banvard's, well might he expect a "full triumph" for his truly "herculean labors." If all this story was true, he was a prodigious worker.

Sam was a favorite with the *Reveille* people (Field, one of the editors, had long been a man of importance in the Ludlow-Smith Company), and they took pleasure in recounting some of his adventures on the trip to New Orleans. The stories amused the readers and spread among them the knowledge of Stockwell's work; and, though the narratives were probably touched up considerably by Field, they do picture the impression which a floating artist might make and they present some of the people he might meet.

We can see "our friend Sam Stockwell, the artist," starting out from St. Louis in an open skiff on his sketching voyage to New Orleans. A Dutch boy traveled with him as companion and aid; his "plunder" floated behind in a second boat. In the raw March weather Sam, pencil and sketchbook in hand, "would 'take a point,' then slap his hands, blow on his fingers, and cut a variety of antics to keep his chilled blood in circulation." Sometimes the floating ice would strike his boat; the blow would knock Dutch George over on him and he in turn would nearly go overboard. These annoyances he bore philosophically, but one day as he neared shore some men on the riverbank demanded to know where he was going. "To New Orleans." Why did he have two boats? "For my own convenience," replied Sam shortly. "You are a couple Thieves, and have stolen them boats," shouted one of the questioners, attempting to seize the skiff. Sam and his Dutchman hastily pulled out into midstream, while the men on shore emptied two rifles at them.[3]

All panorama-makers liked to sketch the quaint. They were fond of local color and realized the full theatrical value of both the unusual and the homely. The *Reveille*, in a prose sketch of another "Adventure" on the New Orleans trip, makes it possible to watch the artist at work "taking the Mississippi." One afternoon while he was floating down the river a shower came on just as he was about to sketch the shack of a squatter. "Haul out the old umbrella, and I will try a sketch," he said to George, his boatman. "Perhaps by the time we finish our view, the proprietor will invite us in to take some butter milk with him." There was Sam, working under this umbrella that hung "like a wo-begone sombrero" over him, the "sorriest apology for shelter, ever stretched over a sovereign citizen of the great U. States." While he sketched, a flood of water poured down through "the ill-shaped skylights in its roof."

The scene was too much for the curiosity of the squatter, who called out from the shore: "Look *yur*, you, with that awful ugly hat; what in thunder are you sittin' out thar in the rain for? Who are you? What are you goin' to do?" Sam replied facetiously, "I am going to canvass the Mississippi." The puzzled squatter wanted to know if he was electioneering. "No," said Sam, "I am going to 'take the river.'" "Whar ar you goin to take it to?" "All round the country and over to England." "Well," thought the squatter, "afore you kin do that, you'll hev to get an awful big tub, and sot yourself at the mouth to draw it off." "Oh, no," says Sam, "I am drawing it off, now." Finally, the artist explained that he was painting the Mississippi. The squatter wanted then to be assured that Sam had got his cabin chalked down. "When you show me to them Inglish fellars, jest tell 'em I'm a Massissippi screamer—I kin hoe more corn in a day than any Yankee machine ever invented, and when I hit anythin', from a bullock down to a humin Natur', they gin--erally think lightin' is comin'." They exchanged views on politics. "Do you support Van Buren?" asked the artist. "No, *Sir*," shouted the screamer, "I support Betsy and the children, and it's d——n tight screwin' to get along with them, with corn at only twenty-five cents a bushel."[4] This sort of personal anecdote without doubt went into the lecture accompanying the panorama on exhibition.

On Monday evening, July 31, 1848, the editors of the St. Louis papers were invited to a preview at which the first section of the painting was displayed. The artist had evidently made the most of the characteristic features of the river. The representative of the *Reveille* found it "vivid and life-like in all its features" and was considerably impressed by the news that the remaining portion of the picture would represent the river to the Falls of St. Anthony, *"up one side and down the other!"* Furthermore, he declared, "the grandeur of this work will be appreciated, when it is known that Mr. S. has already covered an amount of canvass equal to the whole of Banvard's exhibition." The *Missouri Republican* was equally enthusiastic. Mr. Stockwell, it asserted, was an artist of "no ordinary merit"; the pleasing effect of the beautiful scenery of the Upper Mississippi, when transferred to canvas by this master hand, would undoubtedly be increased.[5]

Through the early autumn months the panorama was kept in the foreground of news by a succession of stories. On September 10, the *Reveille* declared Stockwell had been at work "night and day upon his panorama of the Mississippi." The announcement was then made that John M. Weston had given up his place in the theater to accompany Stockwell on tour.[6] But the end was not so near as the story implied. Twelve days later, the *Republican* thought it would be gratifying to the numerous friends of the artist to know that he was now rapidly nearing the end of his great work and expressed the thought that it would "far exceed the anticipations of his most sanguine friends." The writer informed interested persons that he had watched the picture in all stages of completion and had been uniformly impressed by it. The numerous boats were facsimiles, and "indeed, in many instances the representations are so life like that the features of some well known captain, who at the time, is snugly ensconced in his berth below, can be easily imagined." On the upper reaches of the Mississippi "the monotony of the scenery has been happily varied by numerous groupings of Indians. They are pursuing their different avocations and in their peculiar way."[7]

The painting was now to be completed in about two weeks; it would require two and one-half hours for exhibition, and Weston would point out and explain the different remarkable scenes. Weston had for some time been a popular figure in St. Louis; he was stage manager of the Ludlow and Smith theater and from time to time an actor. "Everyone is aware of the necessity of selecting a competent person for this position," said the *Republican*, "as in his hands, in a great measure, rests the success of the painting. In Mr. W.'s hands this department will not suffer. He has been assiduously weaving together the numerous legends with which the banks of the Mississippi are so prolific, and we feel confident that his discourses will furnish an agreeable and instructive lesson."[8]

More than three weeks later, in mid-October, the indefatigable Stockwell was reported near "the close of his wonderful labor," and we are full of wonder at the labor he must have done. Among other features of his picture was the representation of more than thirteen hundred different craft and the "likenesses" of more than two hundred well-known steamboats! If this was true, we can well believe that "every object of interest" was embraced in his panorama.[9]

At last, on October 24, the long-expected advertisement appeared. The great painting will be exhibited, for a short time only, at the Planters House. "This Panorama is THREE TIMES THE EXTENT OF ANY PAINTING IN THE WORLD," the notice asserted, "and faithfully represents a view of country THREE THOUSAND FIVE HUNDRED MILES in length. The Drawings were made from actual observation, by MR. STOCKWELL and are *truthful copies of some of the most magnificent scenery in the world*, and include every CITY, TOWN, VILLAGE, and 'LANDING' from the GULF OF MEXICO to the 'FALLS OF ST. ANTHONY.' Innumerable STEAMBOATS, each one *a correct like-*

ness of the *original*, are represented as *under way, wooding, at the landing, burning, snagged,* in *collision*, &c., &c., and countless numbers of other kinds of water craft, will be seen on the river. In the 'Upper Mississippi' will be shown a great number of *Indian Villages* and encampments, with their 'Lodges,' 'Wigwams,' &c., and Groups of Indians in Full Costume, dancing, at *ball play, fishing,* and *equipped for battle.* In short, *no feature* of the mighty 'father [of] waters' has been slightly passed over." In short, at an admission price of fifty cents (children half-price), every spectator would get his money's worth.[10]

Editorially the *Reveille* commended the choice of the hall (the "Grand Saloon" of the Planters House), not merely because it was "commodious and central" but because it was "sure to be comfortable in all kinds of weather." Of the excellence of the picture there could be no doubt: while the painting was in progress "many of the oldest captains and pilots, men who have lived upon the river for the best parts of their lives," had visited the artist and given "high and enthusiastic opinions of the merit of his work." The writer (very likely Joe Field, who had been in Boston in the autumn of 1847), said: "We have seen a panorama of a portion of the Mississippi exhibited in the east, and know that this exceeds that [Banvard's] in *merit* as it does in extent." Everything considered, the news story concluded, Stockwell had done an extraordinary job and had done it alone.[11]

The St. Louis *Daily Union*, too, gave the picture a rousing send-off on the twenty-fifth.

The artist is well known as one of the best scenic painters in the country. . . . We believe this the only panorama which gives a full and accurate view of the Mississippi river from the Gulf to the Falls of St. Anthony. No spot of interest is omitted, and nearly every streamer now running on the river is accurately drawn. The view[s] below New Orleans and on the Upper Mississippi are exceedingly beautiful. . . . The Indian villages, lodges and sports, as well as the romantic scenery about the Falls, the plantations of the coast, the large cities and thriving towns, the wild forests and dark bottom lands, the snagging and collision of steamers, all kinds of river craft, seen by daylight, moonlight and twilight, combine to present a faithful picture of the West at this time. Such a work affords not only gratification to the lover of the beautiful in art, but material for deep study. The river running for about three thousand miles through a fertile valley, as yet but imperfectly cultivated, exhibits on its banks every phase of life, from that of the savage to the bustling scene of commerce, wealth and refinement, stretching through two zones, with all their varieties of productions.

On Saturday evening, October 28, the panorama began moving at seven o'clock before "a most gratified and gratifying assemblage of spectators, notwithstanding the unfavorable state of the weather." It was well applauded by the river men and others attending. The town, we are told, "was awake to its beauties," and it was certain that Europe would soon "endorse the judgment of our 'far west' town of St. Louis." The *Reveille* was quite pleased, too, that this opening performance would be marked "as an era in the fortunes of one of our best artists, and most amiable men that we have had the pleasure of studying and knowing."[12]

The *Daily Union* on Monday gave the new show an excellent review. From it we discover that the depiction of New Orleans occupied one hundred and fifty (linear) feet of canvas, and that the whole work was so large that the exhibition of it took more than three hours "and still only a brief glance was allowed each prominent point." So literal was the picture that, when the Crescent City passed before the audience, the spectators "pronounced the names of prominent buildings, quays, &c." The director was repeatedly "abashed at finding himself anticipated in his descriptions, and his vocation for the moment, rendered comparatively unnecessary." The scenery above Burlington was found especially romantic: "it will compare favorably with the Highlands on the Hudson." Added interest the artist achieved "by placing frequently in the river opposite a prominent point, some steamer whose history is connected therewith, either by a collision, conflagration, race or explosion." It was indeed a work which "must be seen more than once. . . . The artist has achieved his object, and to have his work endorsed here, where nearly every spectator is familiar with each point, is the best test to which he could have submitted his enterprise."

The *Missouri Republican*, too, was impressed with "the immense size as well as the interest" of this panorama and was glad to report that "fashionable and critical audiences" had given it a "decided and unanimous approval." It stressed the visual education appeal of the picture: "An afternoon passed in examining this painting, and listening to the explanations, will give a child more accurate and lasting ideas of the geography and general history of the country than months of study."[13]

Several weeks later Rebecca S. Nichols, a western poet, told how the view of New Orleans stirred up memories of the South. It had been years since her foot had "pressed the yielding soil of that land of sweets and spicery, yet . . . once more we saw the graceful sea-gulls whirling in the air, or skimming along the surface of the waves, like the bright aerial things that crowd the regions of fancy. Once again the little boats, laden with rich and tempting fruits, floated on the waters; while the full, lusty voices of their owners filled the ear with nearly all the languages known to the nimble tongue of man. The illusion was momentary—but it was complete." All the towns and plantations on the lower river were handled with such evocative realism. Above the Ohio Mrs. Nichols thought the artist had taken "vastly more pains" with the natural scenery, which was "bold, grand, and life-like." As the country grew grander, "so did his hand become bolder and truer." However, "the highly wrought and excited imagination of the artist, who [had] sketched while his soul was drunken with the beauties of the landscape, and colored from rosy recollection," had somewhat betrayed him into coloring that was "a little too high" and into "moonlight too golden." After becoming ecstatic over some of the scenes on the upper river, the poet concluded, "How glorious, then, that art, which can thus hold 'the mirror up to nature,' and paint the majestic works of the Almighty's hand!"[14]

At last, after a run of eighteen nights, the show closed. From St. Louis Stockwell and Weston moved to New Orleans, arriving on December 3 and opening on the eleventh. According to a New Orleans *Crescent* story reprinted in the *Reveille*, the picture was viewed there by thousands. A correspondent of the *Reveille* wrote from the southern city on January 16, 1849, that "Stockwell's *Panorama* is now nightly filled with audiences, such as it is a pleasure to look upon." John S. Robb, writing a travel letter to the *Reveille* on February 4, reported that Stockwell "is now doing a fair business, but the cholera has hitherto affected his receipts." The picture continued to draw, however, until it was removed to Mobile on February 17.[15]

According to Weston, their fortnight at Mobile was most agreeable. "They had been fearing the cholera so bad that the assurance of its having taken leave of New Orleans produced a wonderful effect. Business improved, strangers poured in from the country; life, bustle and gaiety resumed its sway with increased zest." From Mobile they went up the

Alabama on the steamboat "Emperor," "a boat that, in size, elegance, comfort and all its appointments, will compare favorably with any of the Mississippi steamboats," even though the Alabama River looked small enough to be one of the younger children of the Father of Waters. After eight or nine days in this capital they went by railroad to Opelika seventy miles away and then by stage on to Columbus, Georgia, twenty-eight miles farther. Next they took stage to Barnesville, another seventy miles, and then to Macon, by railroad, another fifty miles.[16] In May they exhibited in Charleston, South Carolina.[17]

The picture was on view in Baltimore on July 6.[18] By early autumn Stockwell had reached Boston, where he was tremendously received. The *Reveille* of October 1, 1849, quoted a Boston critic, who, after lauding the interest and the beauties of the picture, stressed one feature of the work in particular: "While the artist has labored—most successfully, we think—to give us a beautiful specimen of painting, he has not, to gratify this desire, sacrificed nature but has rather aimed to represent both nature and art beautifully combined. His sunrise and sunset scenes, the foliage of the trees, and the appearance of the cliffs, are pronounced by those who have often journeyed on the Mississippi as being true representations of what may there be seen—and while this is being secured, we are still furnished with a work of art of which, we, as Americans, may well be proud."

One of the local journalist wits was stirred to verse. In a piece of one hundred and thirty-two lines he gave a lively impression of the contents of the panorama, though no great proof of his ability as a poet. One stanza will suffice as illustration:

Now a storm,
 Time for surtouts
 And Cowhide boots,
And something to keep the interior warm.
 Pike's tent and Medicine Rock,
 Where the artist received a shock,
 And nearly a knock,
 For touching a rag
 The red men called their medicine bag!
 Eo nomine, wasn't it shocking,
 Only six arrows wrapped up in a stocking!
Wabashaw Prairie, and now Fort Snelling,
Beneath which Indians encamped are yelling!
 And, a little beyond, which never palls
 You have what an out-and-out sportsman calls
 A crack turn-out of St. Anthony's Falls.[19]

Toward the close of November Stockwell's panorama was still going strong in its fourth month. "He has introduced a prairie on fire, and several other effects, since he first opened here," a correspondent wrote on the twenty-fourth.[20]

Late in the year Weston took the picture down to the West Indies,[21] but the tour there was unsuccessful, for Stockwell had to send money to get the painting back to Boston. In spite of the popularity the picture seems to have enjoyed in St. Louis, New Orleans, and Boston particularly, it was unsuccessful financially. "The little fortune we once had saved by strict economy, was all sunk in that Panorama," Mrs. Stockwell wrote to Sol Smith in 1855, "the last was some stocks in my own name which Sam gave me, was sold at a loss to send it to Cuba, from which we never received *one cent*, and Sam was obliged to pay 50$ to get it back to Boston, two years since it was sold for a small sum."[22] Stockwell now returned to scene painting. No further trace of his picture has been found.

HENRY LEWIS' *"Great National Work"*

Each producer in turn claimed to be the originator of the colossal idea for a travel picture of the mighty Mississippi. Chief among these ambitious workers was Henry Lewis, an Englishman, carpenter by trade, who arrived in St. Louis in 1836. More than a dozen years later Lewis declared that he had told Banvard of his brilliant concept and that the latter had then rushed a picture to completion. However true this may be (there is no way to resolve these conflicting claims), with Lewis we come to a more substantial knowledge of the making of a panorama and of the business arrangements necessary for production.[1]

Like Banvard, Lewis (born in 1819) was a self-made artist. For a number of years he worked as carpenter and cabinet-maker in St. Louis. By the middle 1840's, however, he had certainly set up as an artist, for on March 25, 1845, the *Missouri Republican* referred to him as "a landscape painter of more than ordinary merit." He was then sharing a studio with James F. Wilkins, a portrait painter, who presently was

Henry Lewis. Oil by J. B. Irving, 1856 (Courtesy Mrs. M. B. Chapin)

to paint a panorama of the Overland Trail. A few days later the *New Era* likewise commended Lewis' "very considerable skill as a landscape painter." Toward the end of April the editor of the *Reveille* saw in his Market Street studio "many original pictures of undoubted merit."[2]

Within two years his local reputation was much increased. The *Reveille* declared on March 8, 1847, that his landscapes "are lifting him rapidly to a high rank in his profession." At this time he had in his workroom an oil painting of St. Louis, and, said the *Reveille*, "several of our first citizens have availed themselves of his talent to place upon canvass the semblance of their truly elegant residences near the city." His "correct view of St. Louis as seen from the Illinois shore" was awarded first prize at the Mechanics Fair (such fairs were in a sense the first "shows" by local artists) and elicited the praise of all beholders.[3]

The first detailed comment on the work of Lewis appeared in the *Reveille* a year later. "J. B." had not seen the "originals" of his landscapes and could not therefore "speak of the fidelity of his drawing; but his painting speaks for itself. His views of the Upper Mississippi and St. Croix—Fort Snelling and the Falls of St. Anthony, for example,—have in them the very shades, the very atmosphere, the very glimmer—almost the *mirage*—which we have often, in western wilds, seen in like localities. It is the perfection of coloring to give them their proper effect, without throwing into the picture a gaudiness offensive to the eye; and it is no faint praise to say, that Mr. Lewis has succeeded in accomplishing a part so difficult."[4]

In the same month (May 20) the *Republican* approved of two views of Italian scenery (copies) then in his studio; "rich in color and highly finished," they were worthy of a place in

Falls of St. Anthony in 1848. Oil by Henry Lewis (Courtesy Minneapolis Institute of Arts)

The Mouth of the St. Croix. Lithograph after Henry Lewis (DAS ILLUSTRIRTE MISSIS-
SIPPITHAL)

any gentleman's parlor. But it was the paintings of American scenery that the *Republican* found most admirable—"sketches from nature, taken in a new, wild, and by the landscape painter, unfrequented region of country, where the wild man of the American forest has had his home for untold ages, and has not yet left it." Mr. Lewis, we are told, in the prairie and forest, "has found scenes and landscapes out-rivaling in beauty and grandeur many of the far-famed views of Switzerland and Italy." The writer became even more enthusiastic. He pictured the artist sketching away "at the foot of dashing water-falls," at the "tops of high bluffs, and on the shores of silvery lakes." To all who had traveled in those regions the *Republican* was sure the pictures would be very interesting, and certainly to others they would give an excellent idea of the country. "He has painted, not only the landscapes, but the Indian's hut—the Indian himself—the rocky bluff—the towering hemlock—the oak barrens—the high prairies—the winding river—the steamboat and the canoe—the solitary warehouse—the far distant lone tree, and the white man's cabin—and has thrown around his views a pale blue atmosphere, hard to be painted, and peculiar only to those high northern altitudes." Gentlemen who "fill their parlors and drawing rooms with fancy sketches" were urged to remember that in the work of Lewis they could obtain views which would soon be altered by the progress of civilization. "How pleasing will it be then, and what richer legacy could be left to the future, than the opportunity which these paintings will furnish, of contrasting the past with the present, here in our own West."

The editor of the *Republican*, however, was not concerned merely with a proper recognition of art and Mr. Lewis; he was much impressed by the enterprise that the "rich materials of the Upper Mississippi" suggested to the artist: "*It is the idea of a gigantic and continuous painting of the Mississippi river, from the Falls of St. Anthony to where it empties into the Gulf of Mexico.*" We must remember that no panorama of the Mississippi had yet been displayed in St. Louis, nor had any artist been known to paint the upper river.[5] This was a project, therefore, of great local interest. "It is to be painted on one hundred thousand feet of canvas—and is designed to represent the geological formations along the river, the landscapes, the islands, and, in fact, a truthful view of the river and all the principal objects on its shores the whole distance." The *Republican* felt assured that from "the evidences of energy, taste and talent which Mr. Lewis has given us in the paintings alluded to, and from the further consideration of the fact that he will be aided in this matter by a couple of gentlemen equally capable with himself, we have reason to expect that the contemplated work will prove to be worthy of the Great West."

Late in the spring of 1848, then, Lewis was ready to set to work on his panorama. He had already made sketching tours on the upper river in the summers of 1846 and 1847,[6] but for the travelogue he needed a full and continuous record of the river and river life. His plan was to ascend to Fort Snelling, build himself a special kind of boat in which to float slowly down the river, and stop to sketch "every thing of interest or beauty." He proposed to take "an exact scale for the whole length of the river" and to include not merely prominent objects but "the towns, farms, Indian encampments, &c., along the entire distance."[7]

In the advance announcement he was a little more modest or more accurate than his predecessors, for he informed the

Republican that two other artists were going to work with him. Who these associates were is uncertain. At one time he had arranged to work with Stockwell, but "pecuniary difficulties and a difference of opinion as to the best method of doing the work, finally broke our connection." He did not say when the break came. Possibly it occurred after Stockwell had returned from the southern sketching trip on which he had departed in March, 1848; it is quite as probable, however, that they had parted company before this trip.[8]

With Stockwell out of the picture, Lewis entered into an agreement with Leon D. Pomarède, an artist of long residence in St. Louis. This arrangement was in force until midsummer, 1848, when they likewise fell out. Lewis' side of the controversy we have in the draft of a letter to the French artist.[9]

ON BOARD THE SENATOR July [June] 14th 1848
MESSIUR POMERADE

I was somewhat astonished that I saw nothing of you on Sunday last and still more so when on Monday I started without seeing you. The many duties I had to perform that day render'd it impossible for me to call upon you but I did think you would have been down aboard the boat to have have seen me off. It now seems evident to me that you go into this speculation with much reluctance and as Mr Stagg informs me you tender'd to him your resignation prior to your departure to N York ~~therefore~~ and as I myself have withdrawn I would inform you so far as I am concern'd that you have my full consent to withdraw at once for altho' I have taken upon myself all the labour of this ~~thing~~ expedition I find that behind my back I received nothing but abuse for my pains—it is also evident to me ~~that~~ you wish to carry on your shop at the same time we are painting this picture thus dividing your services contrary to our written agreement and in addition to this as you have in all painting matters been accostom'd to rule absolute—and as I have never lear[n]'d to obey (even as great an a[u]thority as yourself) I foresee nothing but difficulties in our path which would be the death of any such ~~undertaking~~ enterprize therefore after taking all these considerations and giving them due reflection I find it best that we should proceed no further in this matter together I shall pay for this outfit myself and you may settle with Mr Stagg for your trip to N York. Altho' I much regret to part with you still I consider it best for both of us. We are not constituted to get along together—and if you think that painting panoram's is still better than your own business—why the field is still open to you and you have my best wishes for your success.

Yours respectfully
H Lewis

One of the associates referred to in the *Republican* of May 20, 1848, was probably the Rogers who arrived to join the party at Galena on July 21.[10] It is certain that, as early as June 14 when writing to Stagg about the final break with Pomarède, Lewis impressed on his partner at home that they must not lose Rogers "on any acct as his knowledge of sket[c]hing and of the character of the river is imense." As soon as Rogers arrived at St. Louis with the southern sketches, Stagg was to send him upriver to meet Lewis. The arrangement was secret: "dont say a word to any one that we have engag'd him." Apparently Rogers was being enticed away from Stockwell to whom he had been engaged. The word was to be put out casually by Stagg that Lewis had "abandoned the idea of sending a person down south to make sketches." Some trouble from Stockwell was to be anticipated (but probably none developed, for it will be remembered that in none of his publicity did Stockwell ever admit having assistance in his sketching or painting). "Secrecy must be observed" about all plans and progress.[11] The share of Rogers in the Lewis panorama is indicated by his signature on some of the scenes in the 1848 sketchbooks as well as by a statement in the *Republican* on September 11, 1848, that "Mr. Lewis has been assisted in his undertaking by another artist of acknowledged ability, who has sketched the Mississippi from this city to the Balize, faithfully rendering every city, town, village or place of interest, and preserving the whole in a connected view. These views are mostly tinted, and the fidelity will strike every one who has visited the South. The delineation of the cities of New Orleans, Vicksburgh, Natchez, and the sketches of several scenes and landscapes on the river, are eminently successful and accurate."[12]

It will be convenient to summarize here other aspects of the panorama business. From Lewis we learn much more about the work of sketching than we can from the pamphlets of Banvard and Smith. The romantic solitude Banvard described so feelingly was not always a part of panorama-making, for Henry Lewis' picture, at least, was the result of careful organization. Lewis, though originator and director of production, had no hesitation in calling in Rogers as assistant field-artist. On part of the trip down from Minnesota Lewis was accompanied by John S. Robb, whose planned job was possibly to produce a continuity for the show and certainly to promote it by feature-writing in the *Reveille*. Stagg was instructed to "settle everything with Mr Robb [who had not yet left the city] and any thing you do I shall approve of. . . . with his pen and my brush and proper industry and energy it will be singular if we dont make a fortune for the whole of us." Two boatmen were employed for this trip. The business manager of the enterprise was Henry Stagg. The director of the exhibition, in St. Louis at least, was William A. Warner, and Lewis himself is known to have spoken from the platform.

Even this array of names does not include the entire personnel. For the actual painting of the canvas Lewis went to Cincinnati in the fall of 1848. There he had to assist him "Messrs. Leslie, Durang, Johnston, and Laidlaw, the first scenic artists of the country." John Bates, proprietor of the National Theatre in Cincinnati, helped finance and was for a time part owner of the panorama. At the opening in that city the following May, "the oral explanations of the picture" were given by "the gentlemanly George Stanley, who knows the Mississippi, from stem to stern, 'like a book.' " Charles Gaylor of Cincinnati wrote the *Description*, was named on its title page as "Director of Panorama," and for a time was treasurer of the enterprise. Gaylor mentioned in his text that Edmund Flagg then had a work in press "designed to accompany the Panorama." All these people and (if we are to believe the publicity) some fifteen thousand dollars capital were necessary for the production of this "mammoth work of art."[13]

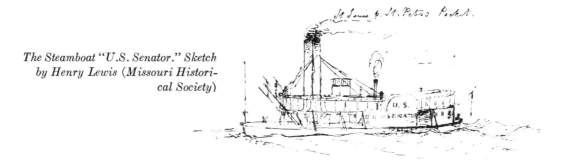

The Steamboat "U.S. Senator." Sketch by Henry Lewis (Missouri Historical Society)

The artist left St. Louis on Wednesday, June 14, 1848, on the steamer "Senator." Most of the upriver trip was uneventful. On the second day they took on board a specimen of frontiersman who interested Lewis. At Galena Henry H. Sibley came aboard, and the painter much enjoyed the company of someone with whom he could talk. The fourth day found them at Dubuque, where Lewis saw a farmer drive aboard with his plow, wagon, eight oxen, and his other belongings, a performance that astonished the artist by its casualness. Just after this they passed the "Highland Mary" with a pleasure

89

Fort Snelling. Lithograph after Henry Lewis (DAS ILLUSTRIRTE MISSISSIPPITHAL)

party returning to St. Louis. The following morning they reached Prairie du Chien, and here they first heard of the troubles over the Winnebago removal. They went next to Stillwater on the St. Croix and then to Fort Snelling.[14]

At the fort they stayed only long enough to unload freight. Lewis, anxious to see what he could of Indian life, went down again immediately to Wabashaw Prairie (present-day Winona) where he arrived at ten o'clock at night. On the way down he wrote for the St. Louis *Missouri Republican* an account of such information concerning the difficulties with the

Indians as he had gathered during his brief upriver stops at the Prairie and at Stillwater—scenes that would furnish exciting passages in his travelogue.

LAKE PEPIN, IN A GALE
June 21st, 1848

MESSRS. EDITORS:

I arrived at Fort Snelling today, after a pleasant run of six days and a half. As there have some events occurred up here which might interest your readers, I take my pencil (not being able to write with a pen)[15] to give you some items.

On our arrival at Wabashaw's prairie, I was some what astonished at meeting Captain Eastman,[16] with troops, encamped on the bank. It seems that the Winnebagoes, which you are aware are being removed to their new home, after having got as far as this spot, refused to go any further, instigated no doubt by some of the traders who live near their old haunts, and who are fearful that they will not be able to get a license to trade among them where they are going. . . . |Many of the Indians| alledge that the sale of their former lands was made without their consent; that the spot the government has given them is not large enough; (it is about twenty-two miles square,) and that they are placed in the war path of two hostile tribes, (the Sioux and Chippeways,) to be murdered. In addition to this, Wabashaw,[17] who is not in very good standing with his own people, (the Sioux,) has offered the Winnebagoes a part of his land if they will remain with him. They have concluded to do so, and the [United States] force with them[,] being totally inadequate to compel them to move, have sent to the fort for reinforcements; and Capt. E. has taken down 25 men and 100 Sioux to counteract the influence Wabashaw has had with the Winnebagoes, and persuade them to move. They hold a grand talk to-day, and should the Sioux brought down by the Captain join with Wabashaw's band in asking the Winnebagoes to remain with them, I believe they will have to stay, as there are not troops enough to force them, being only 125 men, all told, against some eight hundred fighting men the Indians could command. Should the Captain attempt to force them to go against their will, I think a fight is inevitable, and I am now on my way to join them, being anxious to see a little Indian life. I will send you a detailed account, should anything worthy of note occur. . . .[18]

At Wabashaw Prairie there was much to interest Lewis. He was in the midst of everything, even to sharing a tent with Captain Seth Eastman. Especially eager was he to see as much as he could of ceremonials. It was not long, however, before Eastman had accomplished his purpose and was ready to leave.

Lewis did not send down any further details to the *Republican*, but a correspondent of the *Reveille* dispatched an excellent brief account of scenes which the artist had witnessed. The Winnebagos, he reported, were a set of fine, fierce, determined-looking warriors. "Their dresses were mostly beautiful, and far exceeded anything seen among the Dahcotahs [Sioux]." Mounted on splendid chargers, they formed "a formidable, novel, and truly grand appearance, to oppose which the gallant captain appeared to think a trifle." But Eastman had soon constructed

an excellent breast-work, formed with about 100 or 120 wagons, his men placed at intervals of three paces, the dragoons in a good position of defence, the Dahcotahs a little in the rear with stacked arms, ready at a moment to assist; the two field pieces being placed in an admirable position for a *general sweep*—the matches lighted—every eye full of fire— every ear to catch the least sound. To a spectator the sight was beautiful; but still the Winnebagos did not advance—they had, previous to the regulars going, challenged the volunteers. Captain Eastman sent them word he would receive them gladly as friends—or, if they preferred fighting, it was a matter of no consequence to him. But the fierce and bold looking warriors appeared at once to have been struck with astonishment, to see such a defence made against them with the wagons which brought their provisions; and the manner the gallant captain had the troops stationed, evidently, was fast bringing them to their senses; but just at this critical moment, when it was not known but the next day they might be engaged in deadly strife—when all were anxiously anticipating its result—a volunteer, a little the worse for liquor, had, by some means, insulted an Indian (Winnebago). In far less time than it takes me to write this, the Indian had seized a musket and levelled it at the soldier. Quick as thought, and fortunate as quick, Mr. Rice[19] threw his arms around the Indian and prevented his firing; and, I may safely say, also, prevented a most bloody engagement, for, like lightning, every soldier near was ready. Order once more restored, the Winnebagos began to come in one at a time, at first, and made offers to the Dahcotahs to dance to them. . . . Thus did Capt. Eastman,

The Camp of the United States Troops. Lithograph after Henry Lewis (DAS ILLUSTRIRTE MIS-SISSIPPITHAL)

through his coolness and firmness, overcome these wild Winnebagoes, who are notorious for having done more mischief than any other tribes of Indians west. He was enabled to return to his command at Fort Snelling by the Dr. Franklin, with his detachment and the Dahcotahs. . . .[20]

Once more at Fort Snelling, Lewis looked about for canoes and for men to build his floating studio. He found boats but no carpenters. Setting to work himself, in three or four days he produced a serviceable craft. On canoes some fifty feet in length, fastened by beams three feet apart, he laid a platform about eight feet by eleven. On this he built a cabin, rigged the boat with a square sail and a jib, and equipped it

93

Artist's Encampment. Lithograph after Henry Lewis (DAS ILLUSTRIRTE MISSISSIPPITHAL)

with oars. Such a vessel he found quite steady; furthermore, from the top of his cabin he had a vantage point for sketching. He named his boat the "Minnehaha"[21] in honor of the falls and presently was ready to float down to St. Louis.

In the meantime, on the day that Lewis first arrived at Fort Snelling, the "Highland Mary" left St. Louis on another pleasure excursion to the Falls of St. Anthony.[22] Among the passengers was John S. Robb. Exactly what part Robb was intended to play in the finished production is not known; apparently he was to write a continuity in his liveliest style.

The Grand Council. Lithograph after Henry Lewis (DAS ILLUSTRIRTE MISSISSIPPITHAL)

Certainly he was an excellent choice. A collection of his popular stories, *Streaks of Squatter Life*, had been published in Philadelphia the year before; but, more important than that, he was a first-class reporter. Before coming to St. Louis he had served on the *Picayune* of New Orleans, and from December, 1844, he had been on the staff of the *Reveille* where he wrote joyously and often brilliantly over the signature "Solitaire." Although, in the long run, he did not do a descriptive book for the show, the venture received excellent publicity from the accounts he sent back to his editor.[23]

Robb arrived in the North too late to see the little drama

enacted at Wabashaw Prairie, but he saw much of the final act of this particular Winnebago trouble, and he recorded his observations during a week's visit at the fort in a series of letters to the *Reveille* (apparently he was enjoying himself as a roving correspondent).[24] No doubt, what Robb saw, Henry Lewis was also seeing, even though the reporter did not mention the artist in this portion of his correspondence. The first letter, written on the day of Robb's arrival, July 1, 1848, recounted the news and rumors he had picked up at Wabashaw Prairie and the fort. Three days later he described at some length the Indian council being held there: "The whole plain beneath the Fort has been covered with Winnebagoes, and among them our tent was pitched. On the opposite side of the river two bands of Sioux are encamped. . . . Since we have been here it has been a continued succession of dancing, feasting, and visiting."

On July 8—the council had closed three days earlier—came an alarm of a Chippewa attack on the Sioux, and the latter immediately turned out in force to avenge their people. Captain Eastman sent twenty men to prevent a clash between the tribes. Robb, unable to get a horse and join the chase, had to content himself with watching as best he could from the tower of the fort. But it proved a false report and the district quieted down again.

Lewis, too, found lively interest in the agitation caused among the Sioux and the Winnebago by the report of the Chippewa outrage.

At the Fort, just before I left, [he wrote to the *Missouri Republican*] we had quite a stampede among the Sioux, some five or six bands of whom had come on down to eat, drink, and talk with the Winnebagos. News came up from the nearest village, about six miles up the St. Peters, that a party of Chippewas had made their appearance on the bank of the river, had murdered one young man, and had gone off towards the Falls. In ten minutes after the news arrived, every man that had a horse or a gun was on his way towards the Falls. One party was six miles below, at St. Pauls, dancing; an express was sent after them, and it is astonishing to see the rapidity with which they made their canoes fly against the current of the Mississippi. Their ornaments were off, and *they* on the trail in less time than it has taken to tell it. One party crossed the river and dashed into the camp of the Winnebagos which was situated near the Falls of St. Anthony, and two hundred of their young men joined in the hot pursuit. I suppose six hundred warriors were out after those unfortunate twenty Chippewas, and they would no doubt (had they caught them) scalped, skinned and *eaten them*. But the richest part remains to be told: the whole thing was a hoax, got up by a Sioux woman, (you see the women are the same everywhere) and it is said she was put up to it by a chief of her own band, to test the Winnebagos and see whether they leaned more in their friendship towards the Chippewas or themselves.[25]

Robb declared in a very pleasant "bread and butter" letter (even though it was directed to his editor and not to his hosts at Fort Snelling):

I have never passed a more interesting week in my life than during our sojourn at the Fort.[26] We had, daily, opportunities for seeing Indian life. in all its rudeness, for fishing and bathing in the clear adjacent streams, sailing the Mississippi and St. Peters, and last, and what was a gratification ever to be remembered, enjoying the kind hospitality of Capt. Eastman and his amiable and talented lady. I confess I was much surprised at the Fort. Until recently I had known but little of Capt. Eastman, and that little only through samples of his fine historical paintings of Indian life. On encountering him, I soon discovered that my host was not only an accomplished soldier, but an artist of rare excellence, as his collection of original paintings and sketches abundantly testify, and, moreover, learned in Indian history and character. It is true, he had rare opportunities, both in Florida and on the Upper Mississippi, for studying savage life, both in its warlike and peaceful aspects and with the true eye of artistical genius he has gloriously improved them. Nor has he been alone in his labors. Mrs. Eastman, with a mind vividly alive to every thing around her, interesting or romantic, connected with Indian character, has learned from the lips of the Sioux many of their historical legends, and strange superstitions in regard to venerated points on the Upper Mississippi and its tributaries. I have myself listened to her converse in the Dahcotah language with a celebrated old "medicine woman" of the Wah-pe-ton band.

. . . Mrs. E. has gathered material for a legendary work, full of the most curious romance, thrilling incident, and strange superstitions, and which the talented pen of this fair lady will make a standard production to add to our national literature.[27]

Capt. Eastman, to aid him in his artistical illustrations of Indian character, has collected a choice and beautiful cabinet of Indian curiosities, dresses, pipes, ornaments, &c., which, aside from their value to an artist, are invaluable as a collection of an interesting race fast passing away.[28] He is so familiar with every thing relating to the Dahcotah, or Sioux tribe, that he has nearly taught me to read the private history of a chief or brave by the ornaments which decorate his person. . . .

I passed a few hours very pleasantly at the residence of Mr. [Henry H.] Sibl[e]y, the courteous agent of the American Fur Company's post on the St. Peter's. He has been sadly annoyed at times by those vagabondizing scribblers who ascend our streams on *steam boats* for the purpose of making books—who look at a solitary Indian half an hour, bore a fur company agent, an interpreter, or old resident, with innumerable questions, and then write histories of the tribes and early white settlers. . . .[29]

At last the boat was ready, the artist was eager to start down river, and the correspondent had seen all that he wanted of Indian and fort life. After waiting for four or five days for a favorable wind, they "set sail" on Monday, July 10,[30] Robb wrote,

with a pair of oars. . . . We took on board a passenger, named *Weld*, the Indian farmer stationed at Little Crow's village, and that same night quartered in his cabin.[31] It was situated on the bottom below the village, and, for a newly settled spot, was most densely inhabited—with *mosquitos*, of course. In the morning we visited the Indian village, and was, as soon as we entered its precincts, put through a delightful little piece of incident— a naked Indian, beautifully excited—or, as ordinary tourists would say, "beastly drunk"—drove us into "Little Crow's" lodge. The chief, himself, was lying asleep after a previous night's debauch. I happened to be the last one of the party which entered the lodge, and as it had a door on hinges, I closed it on the pugnacious native just as he was reaching out to catch me by the neck. The lodge was well built of bark, its door was made of good solid inch and a half plank, and when I banged it shut against the hand which was put forth to finger my scalp, Mr. Indian gave forth, very suddenly, that native exclamation of "How!" which was followed by either a shriek of pain, or a war whoop, I could not well distinguish which, but it is my opinion it was a little mingling of both, executed as well as his excited state would permit. He tried to force the door, but "Little Crow's" squaw handed me a strong pin of wood, and pointed to a place in the door-post, made for its reception; with this I put an effectual stop to this savage's further progress. They called him "Chun-dah-kee," or *Rattler*. On finding his entrance barred, he *rattled* off, for our private gratification, a very crooked war dance, which he appropriately accompanied with a remarkable blood-thirsty kind of song, and finally he stretched himself upon the ground before the entrance to await our egress. Soon his song grew more and more faint, until at last potent potations and a quiet, reclining position, put a stopper upon it altogether. He went sound asleep, and we stepped out of the lodge over the prostrate body of our naked warrior. Whisky, the spirit-water of the white men, had floored him without further aid—the soldier of the wilderness was helpless as an infant.[32]

On Tuesday they traveled only about fifteen miles. Lewis had sketched Little Crow's village the first night, and the next day made several more drawings while on the water.[33] St. Paul, the mouth of the St. Croix, caves, mosquitoes, rattlesnakes, and beautiful stretches of bluffs were alike of interest to his journalist companion.

I observed [wrote Solitaire] two points upon the river which I think will soon grow into considerable importance; one of these is the town of St. Paul, and the other the mouth of the St. Croix. St. Paul is already doing considerable trade. It lies six miles below Fort Snelling, outside the U.S. Reservation, and is the great whisky mart for the Sioux Indians—it is also the point at which the Selkirk Settlement traders rendez-vous; and it will always be the supply depot for the valley of the St. Peters [the Minnesota], the rich lands above the Falls of St. Anthony, and the district lying west of the Mississippi and near its borders. It may at present be considered the head of navigation on this great river.

The mouth of the St. Croix is the site for a thriving town, and, from its location, will no doubt soon be the supply depot for the pine region above. It is elevated and healthy.[34]

Figure Sketches from Lewis Sketchbooks (Missouri Historical Society)

The travelers visited the two caves, above and below St. Paul, which Nicollet had mentioned in his report.[35] They both ran in under bluffs of unstratified white sandstone, "so soft that with a knife we could carve it into any shape we pleased. A rivulet runs through the first, and when we had penetrated forty yards, the sound of a waterfall was distinctly heard. We penetrated to this fall, and found it a beautiful little cascade, about four feet high, and six wide. This stream has formed the cave. We found names carved there, dating back anterior to the visit of any explorers acquainted with the Roman character, and as the face of the rock is continually wearing away, I question much if any record carved upon its face will continue there much over ten years. The Indians call these caves the 'Cha-do-kah-ska,' or 'White Holes.' "

The night after they passed the St. Croix they camped at a spot called Old Man's Prairie. "The old man was not there," declared Robb, "and before morning I was not surprised that he had raised stakes and departed, for the mosquitos have, at this point, not only established a '*claim*,' but have resolved to hold it against all invaders. We '*jumped*' it for a night, but we *hopped* off it in the morning very suddenly, without even waiting to cook breakfast. They *whispered* their war song about our ears all night, and to them our bar was no bar—they surrounded it, carried it by storm, drove us forth from the tent, and forced us to build a circle of fires, inside of which they made frequent and fierce excursions."

That morning (July 12) they dropped down to Red Wing's village,[36] and there, surrounded by about fifty of the inhabitants, cooked breakfast. "They eyed the feeding operation with grave and silent interest, and when it was concluded, an old chief intimated to us, that they would have no objection to try an imitation of the process we had just gone through—provided we would furnish the material."

Now they climbed the La Grange "mountain,"[37] and enjoyed the kind of view which was a "must" for a panorama.

"Westward the valley of the Mississippi, studded with its thousand islands, and skirted by innumerable hills, stretched away beneath the eye for at least twenty miles; northward rose the lofty bluffs which sheltered the Indian village, beneath the mountain; east, appeared another range, skirted by a beautiful prairie, which lay in solitude, sheltered in the lap of a circle of picturesque hills; and before us, far as the eye could see, danced and glittered in the summer's sun the waters of beautiful Lake Pepin. At the base of the mountain, looking toward the lake, the waters of the great river appeared to wind with all the grace of art, as if its floods had here been trained to run in symmetric curves through the pleasure grounds of some great feudal chief of this mighty wilderness. Eye never looked upon a scene so full of wild grandeur."[38]

Late in this day the party encamped on a beach near the head of Lake Pepin. Of their days on this lake Solitaire wrote:[39]

Many prophesied that our canoe-built craft would never survive the dangers of Lake Pepin—that the sudden squalls and roaring surge of that "great" Mississippi reservoir would swamp us; and they predicted it so confidently, and backed up their opinion with the relation of so many hairbreadth escapes, that, we finally began to grow a little *"skeery"* of this "inland sea." As we approached the entrance, we, by a unanimous vote, concluded to land, pitch our tent, and make an early start next morning upon the waters of the lake. It was then near three o'clock in the afternoon. We encamped upon the beach, just beneath a slight ridge, at the upper entrance, and had no sooner commenced cooking, when the settlers of that region (the *Mosquitos*) came pouring over the ridge into our camp. They soon became so numerous, that to eat in peace was out of the question. I ascended the knoll nearest us to look beyond, and lo! there was the mosquito settlement of the other side, within a few rods of us, in the shape of a swamp about a mile square. We moved—*suddenly!* Our boat had become so filled with them that we had to raise a mosquito bar on board, and here, as we floated broadside into Lake Pepin, we made out to finish a tolerably comfortable dinner.

The meal being ended, our *voyageurs* resumed their oars, I took the helm, and on we journeyed. The lake had smoothed her waters, and lay there lazily lolling beneath the beams of the bright summer sun, while old Sol was brazenly looking into her depths, and reflecting his fiery face from her surface with all the self-sufficiency of an antique dandy. Pointing our prow for a prominent point ahead, which appeared about three miles distant, on the right descending the lake, we there resolved to camp. The oars were plied lustily, and I steered steadily, yet after nearly an hour's progress the point appeared as distant as ever. I was, after another hour's rowing, beginning to conclude that the lofty promontory I had been steering for was an optical illusion, when we gradually came in view of the shore, stretching away on our right. I soon discovered that we had been rounding Point-no-Point, so called because it presents a semi-circle of five miles, which, as you approach from above, appears a sharp "point," jutting out into the lake, but which, particularly in *rowing* round, you find to be *no point at all*, and is accordingly so named. At the base of this great hill, which reared itself five hundred and fifty feet above us,[40] we found a tempting little strip of sand beach which promised to be free from mosquitos, and here we concluded to halt. A few of the vagabonds welcomed us, but heeding them not we proceeded to hurry our culinary preparations, and *then* they came—well, yes they did! I tied my hat down like a bonnet over my ears, put on a pair of gloves, placed myself in the midst of the smoke, curling upwards from our fire, but all of no avail, they poured upon me in millions—they filled my mouth, when I opened it to swallow a little coffee —they almost closed my eyes, and ascending beneath my pants, they attacked my legs, and I commenced an animated and eccentric *Polka* which would have thrown *Capt. Korponay* into dancing fits—it was decidedly unique in style, hurried in time, and vigorous in execution.[41] I finally took refuge under a mosquito bar, and here concluded my meal, with not more than a dozen at a time depleting the small part of my person uncovered. . . .

Our run through "Pepin" will long be remembered by me, as a day of pleasure after a night of torment. We were early aroused in our tent, at the foot of "Point-no-Point," by the noise of the surf rolling in upon the beach —a fresh breeze was blowing down the lake, and making a clean sweep through the cabin of our little craft. We had drawn the bows of the two canoes high up on the beach, and the waves had rolled completely over them, filling both. There was soon a mad rushing to and fro, a casting off of garments, during which in our hot haste, some rents were made, and soon captain and crew, in garden of Paradise costume, were up to their waists in the flood, exerting their utmost to launch the craft. Strength of arm, and consummate skill, soon set her afloat again, and, conveying her into a small cove, protected by some large boulders, we pumped her out, loaded up, and getting hastily under way, were soon scudding before the breeze in a direct line for the "Maiden's Rock." When fairly out from shore, an Indian family, seated in their canoe, shot out from beneath the bluff a mile ahead of us, and as we passed we noticed a part of their lodge poles still standing— they had been our nearest human neighbors during the night. We made a pleasant run to the lofty prominence, where Indian tradition says that "Winona," or "The First Born," a beautiful Sioux maiden, all for love, cast herself headlong down the dizzy steeps. Her resolution must have been strong, and her grief overpowering, or she would have changed her purpose long before she reached the summit. It required all my strength, and a good portion of determination, to climb it for pleasure, that I might feast the eye in looking upon nature—to mount its rugged sides and gaze on death, with a song of sorrow upon the lip, required Indian resolution. I stood upon the spot where it is said Winona cast her griefs behind her, and stepped into the happy hunting grounds, and I looked down where, far below, disappointed love and suicide met earth in a final embrace.[42]

The view from the summit of this rock would tempt any lover of the picturesque and beautiful to linger. Three hundred feet below, the waters of the lake stretched away for miles, its surface ruffled by a gentle breeze. Its shore on the right rose up in lofty hills, covered to their summits with giant trees, while on the left it gradually sunk away to a beautiful prairie, terminating on the shore in a pebbly beach. Beyond, on either side, hill rose above hill, until lost in the blue and hazy distance. Dense masses of foliage everywhere around us greeted the eye, until it wearied with tracing the extent of forest, and gradual indistinctness of outline. The dwellers in cities need go no farther than here to gaze upon solitude—in the whole vast distance, scanned from this height, but one house was visible, and upon the bosom of the lake no bark floated save the single canoe of the savage, which, like a dark line, we could see, indistinctly, close in by the shore on our left. The chirp of the birds fluttering in the trees below, and the low moan of the waters breaking against the shore, were the only sounds which broke the stillness around us. How will it be a century hence? The traveller may then stand upon the same promontory, and look upon the spires of a "*Winona City*," the first born mart of commerce in this now unpeopled wilderness.[42]

I left Lewis here, working away with his pencil, completely wrapt up in the beauty of the scene before him; and taking command of the pinnace, hoisted sail, and bore away for the foot of the lake, some sixteen miles distant. . . . Here, upon a beautiful beach, I pitched our tent, had fire kindled, enjoyed a delicious bath; soon after, Com. Lewis with his double decker hove in sight, on the right shore, descending. He announced his approach by firing a gun to leeward—I answered, and he hove to, came to anchor, and was soon landed alongside the pinnace. No mosquitos troubled us here —we enjoyed our supper in peace. I made a fine cup of Young Hyson tea, fried some potatoes, toasted some bread, opened a box of *potted lobster*, and with an appetite such as, when a harrassed denizen of a populous city, I have often sighed for, I reclined upon my buffalo robe, and feasted most gloriously. The meal ended, we stretched ourselves upon the mats within the tent, threw its front open to the welcome breeze, and watched the moonbeams playing on the waters until the music of the surf, beating upon the shore, lulled us into a sweet and refreshing repose.

On one of these stops the artist took "a couple of beautiful views from the summit" of Maiden Rock (one of these was probably the original of the view of Lake Pepin used in *Das illustrirte Mississippithal*). Because the height of the rock was a matter of general dispute, Lewis dropped a line from the summit to his man François and noted that it was one hundred and twenty-six feet high.[44] He then returned to his boat, sailed after Robb, and sketched as long as the wind lasted.

The next day they stopped at Wabashaw Prairie at the foot of Lake Pepin. Lewis pictured in his journal a typical encampment.

I dont know that I have given you a scene in camp and as I have a little spare time I might as well do so now. As soon as the boat lands Fransuois and John pitch our canvass home[,] two things always being consider'd necessary[,] water and a spot where in case of rain it could not run into our tent another important consideration is to find a location where the musquetoes are not in millions Where they are only in thousands is consider'd a good camping ground. Well, the tent being up—the next thing is to make a fire where the wind will carry the smoke towards the door of our tent to keep off the hungry varment, and heat some water to make the coffee. Whilst this is going on I take a stroll with my gun or fishing rod to look for fresh meat and if unsuccessful why we must take a rasher of broil'd ham or dried beef—and the mattrasses being spread in the tent supper is announs'd in due form by striking a knife on the bottom of the frying pan and we sit down a la Turk and take our time to it in true aristocratic style. This performanse being over next comes the pipes and then the long chat over the events of the day pass'd and the plans for the coming one & then right well fatigued after setting our night lines we turn in and sleep such sleep as is not even dreamt of beneath city shingles.[45]

Here they met again Captain Morgan, who, with his troops, was waiting for the steamboat "Dr. Franklin" to take them up to the fort. The "Minnehaha" excited a good deal of curiosity among the passengers on the steamer; "many were the visits I had to pay to and from the S[t] Boat to show people our floating curiosity shop."[46] By mid-afternoon the panorama expedition was under way once more. It stopped a few miles downstream at Mount Trempealeau.[47] From the top of that well-known bluff Lewis observed opposite a much higher hill from which he took "a birds eye view of as grand a scene as ever eye rested upon." His diary records the effect the scene had on him and on Robb.

Far as the eye could reach could be seen the Missi[ssi]ppi with its thousand islands winding like a stream of silver thro' dense masses of varied green. Mountain o'er mountain rose, forest stretched beyond forest, prairie beyond p[r]a[i]rie until the eye sought releif in the dim purple distance with its broad masses without detail its varied and lengthen'd shadows added a crowning charm to the whole. Yet a feeling of sadness would break over one to think of all this b[e]auty—this adabtation [sic] of natures to mans wants was a *solitude*, vast, and lonely, inhabited only by a few bands of indians now fast melting away and the solitary deer and elk. No smoke from the cabin to remind one of home and its comforts no spires, or domes of cities to tell of commerce or its manufactories, no waving fields of grain to contrast with its golden undulations the vast masses of dark green foliage all all was solitude. . . . As I looked I felt how hopeless art was to convey the *soul* of such a scene as this. . . . But a truce to sentiment here I am with pencil and sketch book ruminating and dreaming when I should be at work so here goes to make an effort if it is only in outline to carry to my friends at home and try and give them some idea of where I have been. There, 'tis done—and now to wake friend Robb who has taken in so much poetry of the scene that together with the climb has quite overpower'd him for you must recollect that we are five hundred and twenty feet nearer heaven than we were an hour ago in our boat, and I

105

HENRY LEWIS'
GREAT NATIONAL WORK

would remark at passing that if the whole road to those delectable regions is as rough as this was it will be a pilgrims progress with a vengeance and an up hill business to boot.[48]

Leaving this "pictiresque" scene, they encamped presently near the mouth of the Black River. The next day (Sunday, July 16) Lewis sketched this location before they made an early departure. During the next fifty miles he "took a great number of sketches." These apparently included views of Prairie Lacrosse, the Upper Iowa River,[49] a "birds eye view of the celebrated bend call'd Coon slue," and others. "The view from the summit of the bluff at the foot of the slue is magnificent," the artist declared, "but almost impossible to draw, in outline." They stopped for a little time at the house of a Mr. Reed (the United States farmer to Wabashaw's band), and here Lewis expected "some stirring narratives," but Reed was absent. They were soon opposite the scene of the Battle of the Bad Axe where in 1832 Black Hawk made his last desperate stand. "I immediately went to work and made a true sketch of the spot," Lewis wrote. Here was dramatic material for the panorama. That night they spent "in an old deserted whiskey dealers cabin. . . . the house was in pretty good repair[,] the huge fire place open'd its hospitable jaws to receive us and soon we had a jolly fire roaring on the hearth."

The next day they made a late start because Lewis had to do the baking, "as our half breeds knew nothing about it." On Tuesday they traveled forty-five miles and camped not far above Prairie du Chien. Lewis made "a great number of sketches" that day. Among other scenes recorded was a bluff they named "the Alter [sic] bluff, for you can see the pulpit the reading desk and the baptismal fount." They marked their names on this bluff. After breakfast on the nineteenth,

Dubuque, Iowa. Lithograph after Henry Lewis (DAS ILLUSTRIRTE MISSISSIPPITHAL)

Lewis took a careful view of Prairie du Chien with its "quaint, old, french chateaux and cottages" and spent the night in this "very picturesque" town.

Leaving Prairie du Chien on the twentieth, they stopped at Dubuque long enough to call on the editor of the local paper and to leave with him "our names and objects, which he said he would notice." The "Minnehaha" now began to pass "many rafts and flats and it was curious to hear them sing out to us—What you got to sell stranger? I would generally

Studies of Boatmen by Henry Lewis (Missouri Historical Society)

answer Elephants turks and Carcassian slaves   then there would be a pause and a talking among themselves. We had ma[n]y a pretty little bit of badinage of this kind as we pass'd the shore or rafts." That night they encamped near Fever River.

The next morning there was some difficulty in finding the true mouth of this stream, but finally they managed to get up to Galena. Now they enjoyed meeting friends, including a Mr. Snyders with whom Lewis had roomed at Fort Snelling. "Our boat became as great as [an] object of curiosity as before

View on Fever River. Lithograph after Henry Lewis (DAS ILLUSTRIRTE MISSISSIPPITHAL)

and Rob[b] and myself did nothing else that day but walk down with little parties some to look at the boat, some at my drawing, and some to take a chat and a glass with us." Here, too, they were joined by Rogers, "a gentleman, I had been anxiously looking for, to assist me in making sketches." Before they started early the next morning, Rogers made a "very pretty sketch" of the Fever River encampment and in it included a portrait of the "Minnehaha."[50]

A brief stop was made at "the beautifully situated town of Bell[e]vue. This is a scattering little town of some 150 inhabitants, but of cour[s]e it is *going* to be a city some day."[51] Here there had recently been some lynchings of murderers, horse thieves, and counterfeiters, and the inhabitants were suspicious of the sketching party, who "expected to be brought ashore by the crack of half a dozen of their rifles to be examin'd but they let us go on unmolested."

Late in the day they were forced by a heavy rainstorm to seek the only available shelter in an old log cabin guarded by large dogs whom Lewis put to flight by suddenly opening his umbrella in their faces. The owner was got out of bed by his "very lady like" wife "(this was Sunday you must remember and he was fulfilling the commandment which we were not, by making a day of rest of it)." The host, a Scotchman named Jackson, a former British naval officer and a rebel in the Canadian revolution of 1837, "now farming on a low bottom which is surrounded by water one half of the year, and selling wood to the steam boats for a living," provided with "his intelligent lady a very pleasant ev[en]ing."

The next day they passed the towns of Fulton, Illinois, and Lyons, Iowa. Now, the artist observed, "the signs of civilization began to increase the pioneers log hut began to give place to the comfortable log house and the small and poorly-cultivated fields, which necessity alone compels the pioneer to labour on, gives place to larger farms and more smiling meadows and fields." In the back country, he was told, "little rival towns (between whom the most christian and city like hatred existed) were beginning to flourish."

On the twenty-fourth they stopped at the upper end of Rock Island, and, while Lewis went hunting, Rogers made a "sketch of the beautifully situated town of Moline." They dropped down a little lower for their camp. "The count[r]y above and along the rapid," wrote Lewis in his journal, "is beautiful in the extreme, highly cultivated and with its numerous fields of ripe grain and dark green meadow, told plainly that the labourer was rewarded for his toil, and that an all bou[n]tiful providence had smil'd upon his efforts. But it was a country that the pencil could not convey, the idea of utilitarian plenty and comfort predominated and altho' ma[n]y a rude log hut and smiling cottage with its flowers train'd about its tresilated porch giving good promise that fair forms dwelt within would have made separately good a[nd] pleasing pictures still as a whole they were wanting in bold strong features like the country I had pass'd thro'. I however with Mr Rogers made many sketches and we took also all the little towns we pass'd some of which were very prettily situated."

While Lewis and Rogers were engaged the next day in making sketches of the "two beautiful towns on opposite shores of the river," Robb went into Rock Island City to inquire for letters and papers. The whole party then had dinner in Davenport at the La Clare House with Mr. Stout of St. Louis, and again they spent some time satisfying the curious with a sight of their boat and the sketches already made. After a pleasant hour they put off once more, encamping for the night on a willow island below the towns. There "with the rain pattering on my tent, I am stretch'd on my mattrass writing this, by the light of a gas lamp, Friend Robb being asleep on one side and Rogers on the other reading Domb[e]y and son while my two voyagers are silently sleeping at each end."[52]

July 26 found them at Bloomington (soon to be renamed Muscatine), Iowa. "This place was so picturesque that I was induc'd to take three views of it, one from above, one panoramic view and a view over looking it from the bluffs by which it is back'd." Here along the river were beautifully cultivated farm lands: "the people were gathering in their wheat harvest and the scene was one of great animation. . . . and the yellow fields and busy hands, the loaded teams and happy, healthy-looking children form'd altogether a picture which Thompson would have lov'd to contemplate."[53]

Burlington, Iowa. Lithograph after Henry Lewis (DAS ILLUSTRIRTE MISSISSIPPITHAL)

The next day for fourteen miles they skirted the Muscatine prairie to Port Louise. Eight miles more along a densely wooded bottom—"the river very wide and cover'd with numerous and thickly wooded islands"—brought them to New Boston, Illinois.[54] On the summit of the steep sand bluff were "three warehouses at equal distance of the same size and same style of architecture, if a hugh [*sic*] square frame bu[i]lding with three windows and a door can be said to have any style about it."

Just at sunset they arrived at Oquawka, also on the east bank, and camped below the town on a beautiful prairie, where they made a "very fine sketch." At "Drew's Pra[i]rie" he sketched a farm scene with an eye to effective detail: "1 waggon with harvesting machine at wark   A number of hands round it and a pile of bags on the shore full of wheat— extreme distanse very blue—Island of willow in right hand corner—"[55] They stopped next at Burlington, where Lewis drew a view "approaching Burlington," noting particularly "1. old house in ruins   2. chimney of a mill or furnace." This "fine thriving town," Lewis wrote in his journal, "beautifully situated on a gradually rising slope surrounded by very picturesque hills . . . will make a fine view for our panorama."[56] They now passed three or four smaller towns, but, except for Dallas, Iowa, Lewis found no place of interest until they came to Fort Madison.

The sketching procedure of a panorama artist is well illustrated by the drawings made at Fort Madison. Four double pages were required for a reproduction of the whole length of this sprawled-out river town. Here use was made of washes: pinkish shade for red brick buildings, and gray probably for stone. On the first left page, signed "V Rogers," a note mentioned "Rafts," and on the right were indicated the Eagle Hotel and the Courthouse. Such notes of public and semi-public buildings obviously were made in order that the commentator could point them out properly to the audiences. On the next double the town sketch was continued. The Madison House was named on the right-hand page, and at the top of this fourth section was written a historical note: "The old fort with a small garrison was here surrounded—by the Indians—and being closely pressed had to mine himself [*sic*] out to the bank of the river and left in the night in his boats."

113

HENRY LEWIS'
GREAT NATIONAL WORK

The third double showed the outskirts of the town; only a few buildings were pictured. On the fourth spread, although it too is given the name of the town, no buildings were shown; the left page was a view of the "Hog back bluff."

At sunset on the twenty-ninth the sketching party stopped at the "celebrated city" of Nauvoo. Lewis immediately "hurried up to take a look at the [Mormon] temple and see it by sun set." He was much impressed and remarked, "Taking into consideration the circumstances under which it was built it is a wonderful building and considering too that it is of no particular style it dones [does] not in the least offend the eye by its uniqueness like all most all innovation[s] from old establish'd standards do. . . . It bears a nearer resemblance to the Bysantium of [or] Roman Greecian style than any other altho' the capitals and bases are entirely unique still the cornices are grecian in part."

The next day the entire party returned to the town in order to explore the interior of the Temple, and Lewis called on Joseph Smith's widow, who "is now again married to a man by the name of Bideman but she is always call'd the widow Smith." Lewis described her as "a remarkably fine looking woman I should judge of some 35 or 40 years of age with a strongly mark'd tho' kind and inteligent face on whose surface are the marks of much care and suffering." He added that she "supports herself and family by keeping one of the largest and best hotels in the place and seems to be doing a thriving business." Lewis stayed at this uncommon town long enough to sketch "Nauvoo from Above," and to draw the detail of the "shape of the mouldings" and of the "exterior and cornice" of the Temple as well as a view of the baptismal font in the basement. Nauvoo and the Mormons were still "news."[57]

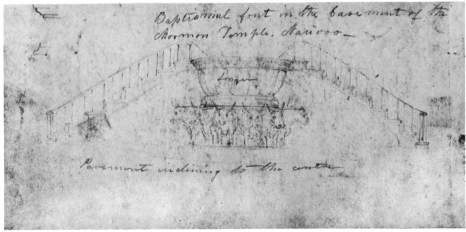

Above: *Nauvoo, Illinois. Lithograph after Henry Lewis* (DAS ILLUSTRIRTE MISSIS-SIPPITHAL). Below: *Baptismal Font in the Mormon Temple. Pencil Sketch by Henry Lewis* (*Missouri Historical Society*)

Quincy, Illinois (Lewis Sketchbook, Missouri Historical Society)

The next day at the rapids (Keokuk), "Mr. Robb whose duties at home [had] been long urgent and who by the by was getting pretty well tired of the trip," left them to return to St. Louis on the steamboat "Kate Kearny."[58]

From Nauvoo to Quincy, Lewis noted, most of the little towns "were beautifully situated and apparently thriving."[59] The camp of July 29, Churchville (Missouri), the mouth of the Des Moines, Tully (Missouri), were all recorded in the sketchbook. Presently they arrived at Canton, also on the west bank, where Lewis made note that "2 mile below here 25 years ago lived a man by the name of White he was the last

settler in the northwest at that time—Since that time all
these towns above have been built." On the same day he
sketched "Lone Tree Prairie [with] La Grange in the distance[,] looking up [river]." Here he observed that the "bank
of the prairie next the river appears with a bright line of green
on the top showing the height of the grass [?]—the bluffs beyond break dark against this line of a dark blackish green
without detail."[60]

That evening they encamped on the upper end of a densely
wooded island, below and in view of Quincy, Illinois. The
town, declared Lewis, "looks more like Cincinnati than any

other town only it is cleaner and that is paying it a great compliment."[61] The next morning he made a sketch of the encampment. Two double pages in his sketchbook he gave over to a detailed view of the town.

On the following day—which proved a "regular roaster"—they made forty-six miles and stopped that night on the land of a farmer, who "having a barn[,] 2 ruined sheds, which he call'd wharehouses[,] and his cabin besides a bridge over a slue of the most fever and auguish aspect, he dignified by the name of *Gilgal*." He charged them fifteen cents for a quart of milk. Lewis did not bother to sketch Gilgal but quickly left that place where even the trees "shook with but little wind like one who had the ague. the dogs were sneaky and lank and *yellow* and look'd as tho' they might have had the ague. the children had all white hair . . . and were shaking away bravely."[62]

He took a view of an island above Marion City, another of that town looking down river on the west side ("houses all frames and unpainted"), and a third looking up from a mile below. The same day sketches were made of the bluffs at Hannibal, a view from the landing there, and three more double-page drawings of the town itself. The second of these carried a note: "The first man who settled here was a blacksmith by the name of John S. Miller—in 1823." Here, as in the Quincy sketches, the brick houses are washed with pink. Severton, Illinois, looking up river ("Haskel was the founder of this place"), and the bluffs above Louisiana, Missouri, were also recorded on this busy day.

Five miles rowing the next day brought them to "the prettily situated town of Louisiana in Missouri," but they pushed on two miles below Clarksville for their camp. Views of both towns were garnered for the sketchbook. In the latter

Quincy, Illinois. Lithograph after Henry Lewis (DAS ILLUSTRIRTE MISSISSIPPITHAL)

Clarksville, Missouri, by Moonlight. Lithograph after Henry Lewis (DAS ILLUSTRIRTE MISSISSIPPITHAL)

place "the houses were mostly going to decay. . . . a mill in ruins at the upper end of the town stands boldly out and make[s] the place look quite picturesque." In his journal Lewis regretted that he failed to take a view of this night's camp; he had pitched his tent under a tree thirty-four feet in girth which "would have made a splendid study."[63]

The "Minnehaha" was now just one hundred miles from St. Louis. Lewis was hopeful of reaching that day (August 3) the home of a friend forty-five miles down river from the Clarksville camp. The wind was fair and the men fresh. "The men," he wrote, "are singing at their oars. Mr Rogers is devouring Domby and Son." He stopped once to inspect a great tree which had been struck by lightning in the last night's storm. They reached Hamburg, Illinois, a thriving German settlement, but there the strong current and a side wind kept him from getting a very good view of the place. Next they came to Westport, Missouri, "such a wee place I did not sketch it—besides it had no picturesque features." By and by they approached Bailey's Landing or Cap au Gris on the Missouri side, "a poor wretched place with most of the people that I saw sooking [looking] decidedly fever and aguish."[64]

An hour later Lewis landed at the house of his friend Poppleton and found waiting him two other friends, James F. Wilkins and George I. Barnett, who had come up to meet the artist.[65] "It is needless to say," Lewis wrote, "we made a night of it here. I pitched the tent and after supper over a bucket full of excellent egg-*nogg* which our hospitable host had prepar'd for us I recounted my adventures to them." He was invited to make a real visit, but his anxiety to get back to St. Louis made him push off the next morning with his St. Louis friends as passengers.[66]

Above: The Piasau Rock near Alton, Illinois. Below: Alton, Illinois. Lithographs after Henry Lewis (DAS ILLUSTRIRTE MISSISSIPPITHAL)

Gen Washington - St Louis & Pittsburg packet - see next page - Bright blue stripe round
guards - "Regular Pittsburg packet" in front gilt letters - steps in front - Pilot house ver
high - with Washington on a dark red ground on the top picture of Washington from
Stewart on Wheel house - green blinds.

Paris - Regular passenger Pittsburg packet" on the side - PARIS in front in large Bold
under the hurricane deck - double pilot house with gothic windows and guards round
and second story also round hur'n deck - Pittsburg and St Louis Packet. Paris - on the top
house in red letters - Blinds dark yellow - Chimneys plain - double engine - no steps in f
Hamilton - Upper Miss packet - White with pale yellow blinds - Alexander Hamilton on
Wheel house in black letters - Chimneys plain - small one story pilot house - five Wind
Amaranth - 2 story pilot house - plain Chimneys - New Orleans packet -
Wyandott - 1 do do do - Green blinds - plain Chimneys
Fort Wayne - double pilot house - Short Chimneys plain US Fort Wayne Black fancy lette
shaded with blue : Green blinds double engine - loaded with military stores - front of Lowe
deck cover'd with Gun carriages, heavy mortans and Ramon
Edward Bates - Pale yellow blinds - double Pilot house double engine very light draught
fancy Chimney tops with the name cut in the iron | Winding single otter in front
lettures on wheel house

...inois fancy Chimneys ( ) Plain in front — Black letters on Wheel house
...Orleans Packet — double Pilot house — green blinds
...rick Henry — Plain Chimney — double pilot house double engine — in...
Southern trade — Time and Tide — a small Illinois river packet — It's small packet
...and Tide — on Wheel house in black letters — Cotton — large first Class N. O. Boat
...ck letters on Wheel house — Green blinds — short Chimneys — Common Pilot houses.
. Autocrat. Large N. O. Packet. 2 story Pilot house. very high scape pipes
ornamented on top — as well as the chimneys. pale yellow blinds and yellow
doors Wheel houses come high above the hurricane deck

Above: A Page of Notes about Steamboats. Left: The Steamboat "Alec Scott." Right: The Steamboat "Illinois" (Lewis Sketchbook, Missouri Historical Society)

Alton, Illinois. Northern Section of Three (Lewis Sketchbook, Missouri Historical Society)

Though Lewis had written in his journal on August 3 that there would not be much to draw between Clarksville and Poppleton's house, he and Rogers did make quite a number of sketches. One double page shows a view of Hamburg; on the lower right corner is the alarming and cryptic notation: "Edward Bates blown up." Another sketch of "Hamburg from above," however, carries the explanation: "scene of the explosion of the Ed Bates—on the shore a party hail the boat to put on board one of their wounded, he is in a litter—large quantities of chord wood on shore—with several flats—the gable ends of several houses painted red—the rest mostly

white. St Boat Senator in the foreground."[67] Other sketches in this area showed islands below Hamburg and a series picturing Cap au Gris. On one of these he noted a "large Wharehouse to come in next to the tavern on the bank—90 feet fronting on the river—an old fort used to be here." Last in this group was a view of a rock on which appear the names "Leslie, Johnson, LEWIS & ROBB." Finally, the encampment was pictured.

The day after leaving Poppleton's was a hot and busy one. There was much sketching to do. Now were recorded a view "20 miles above the mouth of the Illinois" which featured a

Alton, Illinois. Middle Section of Three (Lewis Sketchbook, Missouri Historical Society)

woodyard; "Grafton looking up with the mouth of the Illinois," ("the colour of these rocks is a bluish grey limestone with parts [?] in veins of sand stone of the to[ne?] of a very warm green almost yellow—and very even or like velvit"); then more sections of bluff below Grafton ("Bluffs of this character continue from Grafton to Alton on the E side distance 11 miles—the character of the rock is the same all the way—blue limestone capped by yellow sand stone in layers"); a view of the "Staircase Bluffs opposite Portage de Sious." It was late in the afternoon when Lewis reached Alton, and "the sketch of that place taking a long time to make," they

were forced to camp there. An elaborate view of Alton was spread on three double pages in the sketchbook, the buildings in wash colors with greens and blues used also. A "Village adjoining Alton," a drawing of the mouth of the Missouri, and another simply labeled "Mississippi River" were the last ones made before the "Minnehaha" tied up at St. Louis at 4:00 P.M. on August 5.

Once home, Lewis made a few more local sketches. The principal ones were of Cardondelet, showing the Catholic College, Montesano House (a resort), and a shot tower; of the Illinois shore opposite Carondelet; and of Jefferson Barracks.

Alton, Illinois. Southern Section of Three (Lewis Sketchbook, Missouri Historical Society)

Now or at some earlier time Lewis and his assistants made sketches of the steamboats "Scott" and "Illinois" and penciled notes on many others that undoubtedly appeared in the panorama: the "Gen. Washington," "Paris," "Hamilton," "Amaranth," "Wyandott," "Fort Wayne," "Edward Bates," "Patrick Henry," "Alton," "Time and Tide," "Autocrat," "Montauk."

At last a sufficiently large and varied portfolio, including Rogers' sketches of the lower river,[68] had been collected and the actual painting of the panorama could begin. Nearly six weeks after the return of the sketching party, the *Missouri*

Republican (September 11, 1848) in an interview stated that "Mr. Lewis will shortly leave for the east to commit his labors to the canvass, and in the accomplishment of this object, he will be assisted by one or more artists of eminent reputation, and thus securing not only accuracy, but beauty and interest of a finished painting." His friend Robb of the *Reveille* gave him parting praise: "We are ourselves cognizant of the faithful manner in which he sketched the imposing scenery of our great 'Father of Waters,' and our recollection of many of the pleasing incidents connected therewith makes us wish him every success which can attend merit."[69]

129

HENRY LEWIS'
GREAT NATIONAL WORK

Carondelet, Missouri (Lewis Sketchbook, Missouri Historical Society)

It was to Cincinnati that Lewis went to do his painting—probably because he could there more easily obtain the assistance of such men as "Leslie, Durang, Johnston, and Laidlaw,"[70] whereas he had fallen out with the other scenic artists in St. Louis (Stockwell and Pomarède, who were busy painting panoramas of their own). Lewis started painting on September 20, 1848. One section of the picture was finished and on exhibition at the Apollo Hall before the middle of May, 1849, but the fear of cholera apparently kept the houses small.[71]

From Cincinnati the panorama moved across the river early in June for a twelve-day showing in Louisville. The

newspapers acclaimed it, but the artist was a little worried about business. Receipts were $429, but the expenses had been heavy. Besides his treasurer, Gaylor, who drew $20.00 a week (he wrote press notices as an additional duty), the working crew consisted of two carpenters at $23.00 a week for the pair, three doorkeepers at $6.00 each a week, and three other assistants behind who were paid $16.00 a week in all. Such a payroll did not include anything for Lewis who "described" the picture to the audience, nor did it take into account traveling expenses. So far, the prospect of profits was not great.[72]

Then back to Cincinnati, and, while he was "lying on his

St. Louis in 1846. Oil by Henry Lewis (Courtesy City Art Museum of St. Louis)

oars" waiting for the cholera epidemic to subside, Lewis, with Leslie and Rogers, worked away on the painting of the lower river. Toward the end of July he wrote to his brother that "the other panorama is nearly finish'd there being only about 50 yds to paint." Special pains were being taken with the "dioramic view of the great fire in St L. [which] will take some time to complete and it may be some 3 weeks before I am finish'd. I wish to show this under 3 effects—namely, the sun setting on St Louis as it was—the moon rising—and then the first boat taking fire and communicating to all the others and the grand conflagration will finish the spectacle. It will make a grand finalé."[73]

On August 18 Lewis exhibited for the first time his "splendid picture of the Lower Mississippi" (the two rivers were never shown on the same night).[74] The new panorama commenced

GREAT NATIONAL WORK

LEWIS'
MAMMOTH PANORAMA
of the
MISSISSIPPI RIVER.

· AT THE LOUISVILLE THEATER,
Southeast corner of Green and Fourth streets.

THIS GREAT PICTURE will remain on exhibition for one week at the Theater. It is painted on 45,000 SQUARE FEET OF CANVAS, and represents a view of the MISSISSIPPI from the city of St. Louis to the beautiful and romantic Falls of St. Anthony. It was originally designed and has been perfected by Mr. H. LEWIS, assisted by Messrs. LESLIE, JOHNSON, and DURANG, and is now presented to the public with the assurance that it is all it purports to be—*a beautiful Work of Art and a correct delineation of the "Great Father of Waters."*

☞ The doors will open at 1 to 9 and the Panorama commence moving at 8¼ precisely.

Prices of Admission.
Dress Circle and Parquette......................... 50 cents.
Second Tier of Boxes............................. 25 "
Boxes for Colored Persons......................... 50 "
Gallery for Colored Persons....................... 25 "
☞ Box office open from 10 A. M. to 4 P. M., where seats may be secured on application to CHARLES GAYLOR, acting Manager and Director.
N. B. Liberal arrangements made for the admission of Schools.   16 d4

Louisville Advertisement for Lewis' Panorama (Lewis Press Book, City Art Museum of St. Louis)

with a view of the Gulf and of two of the mouths of the River celebrated as the North-West and South-West Passes—next the Pilot Station—next Fort Jackson upon one side of the river, and Fort Plaquemine, an old Spanish Fort, opposite—the "English Bend" where the British fleet had to stop in 1814, 45 miles below the city, and which saved New Orleans—the plains of Chalumet, 12 miles below New Orleans, stretching from the river back to an impassable swamp, and across which Gen. Jackson threw up an embankment, where the British were met on the 8th of January, the Plains appearing now as then—the Military Station two miles below New Orleans, and where the troops for the Mexican War, awaiting transport, were encamped—views of Plantations below New Orleans, and which in the richness, variety, luxuriance, and we might say magnificence of beauty, open a new field to the vision of the Northerner,—next New Orleans itself, exhibiting with complete fidelity, the street upon the levee and the immense congregation of ships, steamboats, &c., at their respective positions, the famous Markets where the French take the morning cup of coffee, (they say, the only coffee in the world)—next Carrollton, the residence of wealthy men from the city, and which presents a landscape which for beauty of outline and affluence of verdure and foliage must be *seen* by Northern eyes to be appreciated—next a view of the Missouri, a first class

133

Cotton Plantation and Memphis, Tennessee. Lithographs after Henry Lewis
(DAS ILLUSTRIRTE MISSISSIPPITHAL)

river steamer, 312 feet in length—Bayous, which drain the interior of Louisiana—Convent of the Sacrament, a large and splendid edifice—Baton Rouge, the capital of Louisiana, where we meet the appearance of Bluffs on the River—the celebrated Flat Boats of the Mississippi, with their jolly crews fiddling, playing cards, or dancing the break-down upon the hencoop—next Bayou Sara—representation of the explosion of the steamboat "Clipper" two years and a half ago—the mouth of Red River—the White Bluffs or Ellis Cliffs, just below Natchez, strikingly bold, wild and picturesque—next "Natchez under the Hill," the city proper being situated back of the high Bluffs, to compensate for which the view is wild and beautiful—the Plantation of Gen. Taylor between Natchez and Vicksburgh, a very plain affair—next Vicksburgh, which is built upon the side of a high and comparatively bold, rugged Bluff, which gives to the town, seen at one view, an air of singular boldness and beauty—next the Walnut Hills, fine scenery—the town of Napoleon and the mouth of the Arkansas—view of "Cut-offs" by which the River is shortened—next the city of Memphis, which shows splendidly from the River, as it comes out plump to the edge of the almost perpendicular Bluff 40 or 50 feet high, on which the city is built, also a view of the Memphis Navy Yard—New Madrid—Mills Point, in Tennessee, a high, beautiful, cultivated Bluff, the termination of the stage road from Nashville—the iron Banks or Bluffs, so called, just below the mouth of the Ohio—Cairo and Ohio city, and the mouth of the Ohio—steamboats "wooding" at night—town of Geradeau—a stretch in the river called "grave yard" of the Mississippi, from the number of steamboats injured and lost in it—the vast Rocky Bluffs, in castellated form, which occasionally skirt the margin of the river on the Missouri side, some of them singularly like works of art—the immense pile of rocks, called the Grand Tower, in the river, where a fleet of steamboats is represented as passing—a steamboat race—town of Commerce, a remarkably romantic looking place, the scenery diversified, wild and beautiful—town of St. Genevieve, settled in 1695 [*sic*], and where they used to have "mysterious knocking" in an old unfinished Convent, which still stands—Bluff of Rocks on the banks which form natural Shot-Towers—town of Herculaneum—Jefferson Barracks, which is one of the most beautiful localities in the world, and can only be said to be equalled by the old French settlement of "Gorondola [Carondelet]," seven miles below St. Louis, this single view being worth the cost of admission to see this magnificent work. Next, and lastly, we have a view of the great fire of the 18th May, 1849, painted from accurate drawings made the day after the fire, the filling up of the scene, being from memory as an observer of that terrible conflagration.[75]

On August 30 Lewis returned to St. Louis with his panorama, which, declared the *Weekly Reveille*, "has been much talked about and concerning which the liveliest curiosity exists in our city." At a preview the following day the *Missouri Republican* decided that "the artist has preserved with great fidelity the actual scenic effect of the river shores, and the delineation of towns and prominent objects."[76] And now, at last, on Saturday, September 1, 1849, at half-past seven in the evening, the "GREAT NATIONAL WORK" was opened to the public.

The picture was well received. Evening performances drew good audiences. Admission was fifty cents, children halfprice, and "liberal arrangements" were made for schools. On Thursday, the fifth, an afternoon exhibition was held for families and schools, and soon thereafter regular three o'clock matinees were given twice a week.

All the papers were praising the picture. The *Daily Union* found it "a beautiful delineation of the principal natural features and the most striking points upon the river." It was correctly drawn, and skilful coloring heightened the effect. "The mouth of the Missouri, as a scenic painting, is very beautiful." The *Missouri Republican* declared, "the architectural view of the Nauvoo Temple is a magnificent work . . . as also the views of Galena, city of Dubuque, Prairie du Chien, Rock Island, Muscatine Prairie and the Falls of St. Anthony." The *Reveille* was certain that "Lewis can impart a more extensive and more accurate knowledge of the country in one hour than the books will teach in a month."[77]

Citizens began writing to the *Missouri Republican* to express their admiration. "G" was enthusiastic: "By happy groupings of picturesque scenery, by the introduction of incidents and characters of historical importance, and especially

Cairo, at the Mouth of the Ohio. Lithograph after Henry Lewis (DAS ILLUSTRIRTE MIS-SISSIPPITHAL)

by throwing over and around them all the brightest tints and the most beautiful colorings of the pencil, the artist has succeeded in imposing on the senses of the beholder and inducing him to believe that he is gazing, not on canvass, but on scenes of actual and sensible nature. . . . The pleasure of a visit is also greatly increased by the recital of numerous Indian legends and romantic incidents connected with the various localities of the picture. These are briefly and effectively told by the talented young artist, in his own modest, natural and peculiar manner . . . a rare intellectual feast."[78]

"B" (quite possibly George Barnett), who had known Lewis "when the grand idea first popped into his head," thought his success wonderful. "His twelve hundred yards of

Steamboat Wooding at Night. Lithograph after Henry Lewis (DAS ILLUSTRIRTE MISSISSIPPITHAL)

canvas are literally covered with glowing ideas, with dashing water falls, with clear and silvery lakes, with verdant isles dipping their luxuriant branches into the bright waters of rivers, with wide-spread prairies, beautiful bluffs, cultivated fields, towns, and cities." The writer declined to pass on figures and on the costumes of Indians and the like, but declared "his landscapes are beautiful."[79]

It was the illusion of steamboat travel that most struck the fancy of the papers. "Captain" Lewis, taking a pleasure party to the Falls of St. Anthony—so common an experience for St. Louisans—had stepped out of the old panorama routine of following up one side of the river and down the other. "By an almost magic power," the *New Era* felt, he had "drawn before you both banks, and you have, at a single glance, the enchanting and life-like scenery as it appears on both sides." The editor of the *Herald of Religious Liberty* said "the painting 'rounds to,' like a graceful steamer, wherever there are towns or beautiful views on both sides, or some rich island scenes, or a lovely river view, so as to show it as the traveller sees it." Here were "the best scenes only from the most striking point of view." Now, a vista up the river for several miles. Again, where a town could barely be sighted from the river, the artist "takes you to an adjacent hill, where, in a bird's eye view, you are presented with the town and country." Then once more the spectator is gliding upstream, passing a keelboat or a raft or a steamboat.[80]

The absolute fidelity of the artist was attested to repeatedly. One of the earliest testimonials to the panorama's "magic realism" had been reported earlier by the Louisville *Courier:* "We were amused at a respectable old gentleman from the country, in the vicinity of Rock River; of which a beautiful view is given in this picture, who sat apparently

139

wrapt in the contemplation of the ever changing scenes, giving utterance occasionally to some commendatory remark. When all at once he burst out, 'well, who'd a thought it,—if they haven't got my very house right down here on this picture, yes,—that's the place—barn—the big walnut tree,—the old gate'—and as the picture came more fully into view—'if there ain't old Bally and the white mare, well, it *is* surprising how the mischief he come to get it so natural I don't know, *stop the boat and let me get out.*' "[81]

The merit of Lewis' picture lay not merely in the skill with which he had selected and arranged his scenes and the fidelity of his copy, but in the painting of it. Alfred E. Waugh, a local artist who had had some training in Dublin, wrote: "The landscape charms the beholder with its varied character. Shadows from passing clouds, lend their richest effect to hill and dale, making the picture one of the finest artistic illusions" he had ever seen. The great variety of skies throughout

is among the happiest efforts of genius, from the clear blue of peaceful day to the terrific grandeur of storm and rain. . . . A close observation of the character of clouds is every where apparent; no rapid change from day to night, shocks your idea of propriety with their *"presto"* like magic, but in accordance with the course of nature, the evening shades follow the light of day with easy strides, and are succeeded by soft twilight soothing your feelings with the world into repose and peace. Presently the stars twinkle in the blue vault of heaven, and a faint and silvery light illumines the horizon —*"Avant couriers"* of the orbed moon, who rises with queen-like majesty to smile upon the earth. With the same calm dignity as she arose, does she take her departure, darkness for a space prevails, when at length "aurora" ushers in the day and the great luminary presides over the scene; all is naturally and beautifully executed.

Only one small criticism did Waugh permit himself: Lewis should "soften the smoke from some of his steamboats" and "take away the rigidity of the waves" disturbed by the wind.[82]

The Great Fire in St. Louis. Lithograph after Henry Lewis (DAS ILLUSTRIRTE
MISSISSIPPITHAL)

The *Republican*, too, praised Lewis' skill in drawing clouds
and giving the painting the natural appearance of the river
scenery. It noted with passing objection, however, that
"above the muddy Missouri, the houses and sun mirror their
shadows in the water." This certainly showed the labor and
skill of the artist, but it "rather confuses the view of the
spectator, and does not, it seems to us, add to the beauty of
the painting." The *Herald of Religious Liberty*, on the other
hand, asserted that the painter "shows his genius . . . in his

Handbill for Lewis' Panorama at Montreal (Courtesy Mrs. Emilie Greenough)

SALLE ST. ANDREW,
RUE ST. PIERRE, MONTREAL.

POUR UNE SEULE SEMAINE.
GRAND
PANORAMA
DU MISSISSIPI,
PAR Mr. LEWIS.

L'exhibition commence par une belle représentation de la VILLE de St. LOUIS.

Comme elle paraissait avant le feu du 17 Mai 1849, et se termine par deux magnifiques vues du *SAULT ST. ANTOINE*, montrant toutes les cités, villes, villages, et l'aspect de la route entière, ou l'on verra tous les établissements fondés par les Canadiens Français sur une distance de plus de 1,000 milles.

Une Particularité caractéristique et Originale de cette œuvre,

est qu'*elle représente les deux cotés du fleuve à la fois*, donnant une belle perspective de plusieurs milles en même temps, — la beauté principale de toutes les scènes du fleuve.

Cette peinture a été universellement,

recommandée de tous ceux qui l'ont vue, et est reconnue par les artistes et les connaisseurs comme le Panorama le plus grand et le mieux élaboré qui ait jamais été exhibé au public Américain.

Pour représenter les Scènes,

avec toute l'exactitude possible, un bateau a été construit pour cette fin, au Sault St. Antoine, et l'Artiste (Mr. Lewis) a passé deux étés à les prendre et à les perfectionner autant que possible, représentant non seulement le fleuve, mais l'aspect du pays avoisinant tel qu'on le voit du sommet des Coteaux et des Montagnes sur les rives; ce qui est un caractère nouveau ajoutant beaucoup à la beauté de la peinture.

Passant sur notre route les Villes,

agréablement situées de Alton, Hannibel, Keokuk, Quincy, Burlington, Muscadine, deux magnifiques vues de Rock Island, la belle Cité de Galena, Dubuque et la prairie du Chien avec toutes les villes intermédiaires; nous arrivons enfin dans.

Le pays Sauvage,

et nous avons une représentation complète de la vie de l'homme Rouge. On le voit dans son village, son wigwam solitaire, ses excursions de chasse et de pêche et dans ses combats orageux. Dans la belle représentation du transport des Winnebagoes, plus de

Trois milles Figures,

sont représentées telles quelles paraissaient dans leur grand Campement de la *PRAIRIE DE WABASHAW*, ou le gouvernement des E. U. eut beaucoup de difficultés à les faire rendre à leur nouvelle habitation, audelà de *CRO-WING RIVER*. Cette scène fut prise sur le lieu par l'Artiste qui était campé sur cette prairie durant ces scènes d'agitation. Un grand Conseil des SIOUX est aussi représenté avec une représentation d'Indiens pour signer un Traité avec le gouvernement. En réalité, dans la section supérieure de cette peinture le spectateur voit au naturel les manières et les coutumes des sauvages sur le Mississipi.

Une lecture intéressante et explicative accompagne l'exhibition, à mesure que la peinture se déroule devant le spectateur, donnant dans l'espace de deux heures une connaissance plus générale de cette partie très intéressante de notre pays qu'on ne pourrait l'acquérir par une autre méthode dans autant d'années.

water shadows." The *Daily Organ*, too, found the water "excellent; the light or shade of the night or day, by sunshine or cloud, is beautifully and artistically preserved. . . . it looks more like the Mississippi than painted canvass." The *Organ* pointed to another excellence: "Unlike many of its predecessors, the eye is not offended by its glaring coloring; the grass is not an eternal mass of emerald green, but subdued and natural; the houses do not *all* look as if they had just received a coat of red or white paint, but are suffered to look a little smoke dried like the originals."[83]

After much praise and a very successful run, the Lewis panorama finally closed in St. Louis on Wednesday night, September 26,[84] and went on an extended tour. It was exhibited in Illinois. "The Peoria papers speak of it in the highest terms," reported the St. Louis *Daily Union* on October 15. Chicago gazed on it for ten days. Milwaukee had it for a week early in November. Then Detroit and Rochester and Buffalo. On one Saturday in January in the latter town Lewis "had upwards of fourteen hundred children filling the theatre from pit to dome. It was a beautiful sight and yealded us nearly ninety dollars."[85] Syracuse and Utica had the pictures in their turn (generally Lewis showed one panorama in one town while his partner King[86] exhibited the second in some nearby place).

Through most of April and May, 1850, the painting was being unrolled at the Odd Fellows' Hall in Washington, with a two weeks' side trip to Richmond. Late in the summer Lewis was at Salem, Massachusetts, and then moved on to Maine. During the winter months he penetrated Canada— Hamilton, Halifax, Toronto, Kingston, Quebec had the opportunity to learn of the beauties and importance of the Mississippi Valley. In October, 1851, he displayed the picture in

Boston and later that year took it to Europe. Berlin in January, 1853, was appreciative: "It is one of the most pleasing features of this painting, to see the artist from time to time himself, now on the stream and again on one of the many beautiful islands engaged upon his arduous task."[87] At last, European showings exhausted, Lewis settled down in the art colony at Dusseldorf about 1853 and presently sold his picture to a planter who carried it out to the East Indies. Of it we hear no more.

Portrait in Oils by POMARÈDE

On September 13, 1849, an advertisement in the St. Louis *Missouri Republican* announced that "POMAREDE'S ORIGINAL PANORAMA of the Mississippi River and Indian life, Painted in Oil, will be Exhibited at the Odd Fellow's Hall, commencing on Monday Evening, the 17th September. The painting comprises four sections, embracing Indian Scenery, War Dances, Buffalo Hunts, Dog Feasts, &c., &c., Dissolving and Moonlight Views, Prairies on Fire, Steamboats and Mechanical Moving Figures of Steamboats, Flat Boats and Indians. The fourth section will conclude with a beautiful dissolving view of the Great Fire at St. Louis, on the night of 17th May, representing that awful and terrific conflagration in all its fury, as it appeared to the distracted citizens. Gradually the devouring element subsides, and daylight appears, like a messenger from God, to stay the wreck of destruction. The river is seen gorged with half sunken wrecks and charred remains of 23 steamboats, and the district presents a sad spectacle, blackened and broken walls, and tottering chimnies rearing their summits, ghastly gloom over the smouldering ruins."

The creator of this impressive show was even more a St. Louis artist than Henry Lewis. Born in Tarbes, France, about 1807, Leon Pomarède arrived in New Orleans in 1830. Two years later he painted a view of St. Louis as seen from the ferryboat landing on the Illinois side. His readiness to turn his hand to any kind of painting is shown by his work on the newly built cathedral at St. Louis in 1834: he painted the interior walls and ceilings, the galleries, the altars, he marbled the columns and gilded the sanctuary, he painted altar pieces (including a Rubens "Descent from the Cross"), he made ten transparencies for the windows and painted views (later lithographed) of the interior and exterior of the church. He presently returned to New Orleans, where he decorated the Church of St. Patrick and married the daughter of Antonio Mondelli, a local scenic artist. By 1843 he was once more settled in St. Louis, where for almost fifty years he painted theater scenery, advertising signs, landscapes, city scenes, Indian genre pictures, and portraits, in addition to decorating in fresco many churches and public buildings.[1]

It cannot be determined when Pomarède first thought of doing a panorama of the Mississippi. The popularity of this kind of show, the reports of fortunes earned by Banvard and John Rowson Smith, were enough to interest any man who made his living by the brush. During the spring of 1848, we have already seen, Pomarède worked for a time in partnership with Henry Lewis, but the Frenchman, who had had training in French art schools, and the self-taught English artist could not agree, and each went on to paint his own panorama.[2]

Pomarède was in New York at the time Lewis wrote to him, but he was soon back in St. Louis and promptly went north to the Falls of St. Anthony. T. E. Courtenay, compiler of the program guide issued for the panorama a year later, declared that when the artist first beheld the scenery of the upper Mississippi, he was struck with awe, "doubting in his own mind whether he had the capacity of doing justice to the magnificent works of nature so profusely presented to the eye." But he took courage, for "he had seen the miserable attempts of others who had preceded him, to transfer to canvass the glorious spectacle; their failure was his hope. The Great Valley of the Mississippi and its peculiarities had yet to be painted, and had yet to be unfurled, truthfully and faithfully delineated before the world. Nerving himself with hope and a reliance upon his ability to accomplish with success the great task, he went steadily on, neither hurrying or slighting the work in the least, determined to produce a painting that would outlive the Mammoth, Gigantic, and Monster daubs, which are scattered at home and abroad." His object was to provide for the amusement and information of the world a picture that "would stand for ages in the scale of truth and excellence, and when the changes of another century will have taken place, and millions of civilized beings inhabit and adorn the wilderness of the forest and prairie after their fashion, then will his work be referred to as a portraiture of its grandeur in its primeval state, where the buffalo, elk and deer, found shelter in its fastnesses."

Whether or not he was stirred as much as his script writer declared, the painter settled down to work. A correspondent of the *Missouri Republican*, in a letter dated St. Peters (mouth of the Minnesota River), August 1, 1848, reported that he was then "engaged in a faithful manner, sketching in oil colors, the beautiful picturesque country which lies above us, from the Falls of Anthony. . . . [His] intention is to get up a panorama . . . *four yards wide and three thousand long*, tak-

Leon Pomarède (Courtesy Missouri Historical Society)

147

PORTRAIT IN OILS
BY POMARÈDE

ing in the whole valley of the Mississippi, from the Falls of St. Anthony down to New Orleans."

We are to picture him, then, in a "very comfortable boat," floating downstream by day and laying up at night, painting "from nature every object worthy of notice . . . not missing town, village, bluff, rock, Indian encampment, or a single object of interest." Others before him, his friendly admirer wrote, "imagine that it is enough to sketch the magnificent scenes and views of nature, with a crayon and paper only. . . . [But] how are they to catch the rich tints and colorings of nature; the beautiful skies at sunrise and sunset, and of moonlight; the rich and variegated foliage of the forests, and the cultivated works of man; the color of the land, bluffs and rocks which rear their monster castle-like peaks, and frown with solitary indifference upon the mighty flood of waters rolling along their base. All these glorious sights . . . must be painted by brush and colors, on the spot"—just as Pomarède was doing them.[3]

This panorama no longer exists, but from St. Louis newspaper reports we can reconstruct many of its scenes. The artist returned to the city probably in the early fall and settled down to hard work in his painting room, assisted by his business partner Charles Courtenay (and possibly by young Charles Wimar, who is said to have had his first lessons in painting from Pomarède).[4] The *New Era* on January 11, 1849, reported that the Frenchman was "getting on finely with his stupendous painting." By this time he had finished his canvas from St. Louis up the west bank of the river as far as Burlington, Iowa.

Six weeks later, according to the *Missouri Republican*, his "beautiful and truthful panoramic view of the Mississippi, with the towns, land-marks, hills and dales, scenery and

148

THE LOST PANORAMAS
OF THE MISSISSIPPI

View of St. Louis from Illinois Town in 1832. Oil by Leon Pomarède (Courtesy Arthur Ziern and the City Art Museum of St. Louis)

The Law of the Tribe. Oil by Leon Pomarède (Courtesy Jefferson National Expansion Memorial, St. Louis)

points of note and interest" was fast progressing toward completion. The writer had only praise for the portion of the painting then to be seen in Pomarède's workroom. "So accurate and complete has the artist transferred the whole to canvass . . . it will admit of close, critical, and minute study —not more in reference to the fidelity of the picture than in the elaborately finished style of the painting, with all the perfection of drawing—beauty of light and shade—grandeur of perspective—and the tints and trees of landscape, that nature herself presents when arrayed in her most favorable attire."

The artist had now reached as high as Prairie du Chien and Fort Crawford. These places, with the mouth of the Wisconsin, presented "a splendid view." Here was afforded an interesting field for the artist's skill: "Anyone who has visited the country, will recognize the accurate and even the minute fidelity of the sketch. Those who have beheld this scene lit up by the first blush of the rising sun—who have stood upon the steamboat's deck, and seen the hills and the islands, with their rich livery of green mirrored in the peluccid waters of the river—will admire the clear and natural tints, the blending of colors, and the happy manner in which the artist caught nature in the first, rich, modest, glowing burst of a summer morning."[5]

In April a newly completed section of the panorama showed "Wa-ba-sha prairie, with the gathering of the tribe at that spot."[6] Late that month a staff writer for the *Reveille* reported enthusiastically that he had just examined in Pomarède's studio "a choice portion of his great painting" including views of Fort Snelling, the town of St. Peters, and a stretch of river scenery below. These he described in some detail:

Fort Snelling, the military post of the north west, with its stone walls, and its crescent battery commanding both sides of the Mississippi, situated as it is on a steep bluff, presents a very imposing aspect.

On the river bank, a little distance below the fort, are a deputation of Sioux Indians paying their annual visit in quest of hunting and wearing apparel due them by the Government. They are in the act of landing from their canoes, and the manner in which they point towards the rocky heights above them, indicates that they have reached their point of destination. Immediately at the foot of the bluff, is a correct likeness of the fine little steamer Senator. She has landed and her hands are on the point of rolling the freight ashore.

The whole scene possesses a finish which we have never seen equalled on any panoramic painting. The light of the sun as it falls on the roofs of the buildings, and just tinges the side of the bluff; the scant vegetation endeavoring to force its way through the sandy soil immediately surrounding the fort, the limpid waters below, and the fine well-timbered country that

PORTRAIT IN OILS
BY POMARÈDE

surrounds it, are copied not only with striking fidelity, but with an artistic effect which brings the prominent points immediately under the notice of the spectator.

The town of St. Peters is also represented with great accuracy. Sibley's large warehouse, and others, will be immediately recognized by those who have visited the town. Indian encampments, steam boats, rafts, and Indians in their canoes, have been judiciously placed at various points along the river, giving the scene an air of life and animation.[7]

Pomarède enjoyed an excellent press at home; hardly a week went by without a story concerning his work. The *Reveille* on May 1 announced that his view of Brown's Falls (much better known now as Minnehaha Falls) was just finished.

The stream leaping over the bluffs; the huge time-worn rocks that cradle it on either side; the overhanging trees; the thick mist at the base of the cliff, hiding the waters as they descend, and a bright sun bringing out in bold relief the brow of the bluff—all contribute to render the scene strikingly romantic. [Next in sequence came the Falls of St. Anthony. In July, 1848, this had been a spot of much interest when the whole plain had been] covered with lodges of the Winnebagoes, who, having been brought up from the Wabasha Prairie on steam boats, stopped here awhile on their way to their new homes. The artist represents these Indians spread in thousands over every part of the vast prairie. In one scene is presented a group around their chief, Wa-ba-sha,[8] who is in the act of haranguing them on the subject of their journey. In the foreground are seen the high conical-shaped wigwams. Swarthy Indians, in fantastic costumes, are seated in small parties upon the ground, or loitering from one lodge to the other. The women, with their young papooses stowed securely upon their backs, and boys gambolling carelessly upon the ground, ignorant and indifferent to the great change which has occurred in their fortunes, have not been omitted.

The scope of the panorama is indicated when the reporter adds that this scene occupied sixty-five linear feet of canvas.

Early in August the *New Era* reported that the picture would be ready in three or four weeks. Some of the delay in its completion, said the *Reveille*, had been caused by the sickness and death of several employed in constructing the machinery. The panorama itself was now quite finished and extended over "*five thousand four hundred feet of canvass.*" When the reporter entered the studio he found "Mr. Pomarede giving the finishing touches to a beautiful proscenium, executed *en style de la Renaissance,* one of the most striking features of which, is the very appropriate and venerable figure of Machcha-ce-bet, the father of Waters. This portion of the work is forty feet by twenty-one, giving a double view at a single glance, of twenty by twenty-one feet of the picture behind."[9]

Three subjects were now singled out by the *Reveille* for special comment—St. Louis in flames and ruins, Dubuque by moonlight, and a prairie on fire:

The first is a record of our own disasters—St. Louis as it appeared on the memorable night of the 18th [17th] May.[10] The scene represents a long line of steamers wrapped in flames. The air above is filled with showers of bright sparks, casting a strong, red light on the house tops and elevations of the adjoining streets. Men and women are seen, some fleeing in consternation from the destroying element, others endeavoring with the determination of despair, to arrest its progress. In the background, a heavy mass of black clouds, looking more sullen from the contrast, lowers threateningly over the city. After a revelation of all the horrors attending that event, by an ingenious arrangement of the light, the strong glare fades away, houses, boats &c., are lost sight of, and the darkness of night again shrouds the city. Then follows morning, revealing, magically enough, a totally different scene, a view of "St. Louis *in ruins,*" wherein a mass of charred wrecks choking the harbor, whole blocks of blackened and tottering walls, groups of citizens surveying their own ruins &c., &c., form the principal features. The whole catastrophe, we would briefly state, is truthfully recorded, and must reflect credit on the genius and skill of the artist. The second scene, which we would in advance, place before the public, is a moon-light view of the town of Dubuque. The town is but indistinctly visible, until, as gradually the clouds sweep from a round bright moon *which is shining above,* a clear space occurs in the skies, and a rich flood of light breaking over the whole scene, houses, river bank, and hills are all brought out in strong relief. A third subject, "the prairie on fire," gives in connection with a preceding scene, a view of an "Indian encampment in open prairie." After the

153

setting in of night, as the last object fades from view, a small steady light appears in the distance. Suddenly it commences to spread, broader and broader, nearer and nearer, until as far back as the eye can reach, the prairie presents a sheet of living flames, leaving but a small unburnt space near the edge of a precipice, the site of the Indian encampment. Here affrighted horses and buffalo are madly leaping over to certain destruction, wildly accoutred Indians standing on the edge of the chasm, with desparing [sic] countenances, are awaiting the approaching doom, and women with children pressed to their bosoms, are running distractedly to and fro. The subject, indeed, is one calculated to call forth the highest resources of the artist, and, in this instance, it seems to have been most successfully delineated.

At the beginning of August *A Guide to Pomarede's Original Panorama of the Mississippi River, from the Mouth of the Ohio River, to the Falls of St. Anthony* came off the press.[11] This pamphlet performed the customary duties of explaining how and why the artist undertook the project, devoted half a dozen pages to the description and history of St. Louis, and reprinted Matt Field's poem "The Chouteau House." It makes clear that Pomarède abandoned his original intention of doing the river down to the Gulf, for he found that his picture would then be too long for proper exhibition during an evening.[12] He contented himself, therefore, with a four-reel show that moved north from the mouth of the Ohio along the west bank as far as the Falls and then in the last section returned to St. Louis through a number of views on the east bank. The scenes listed in the *Guide* (presumably a full list of scenes represented) were:

Section First: Mouth of the Ohio River; Cairo, Illinois; Ohio City, Missouri; Commerce, Missouri; Cape Girardeau, Missouri; Graveyard of the Mississippi; Grand Tower; St. Genevieve; Bluffs of Selma, Missouri; Herculaneum, Missouri; Jefferson Barracks, Missouri; Carondelet, or Vide Poche, Missouri; United States Arsenal, Missouri; City of St. Louis; The Chouteau House; Mouth of the Missouri River; Cap au Gris, or Portage des Sioux, Missouri; New Hope, Missouri; Clarkesville, Missouri; Louisiana, Missouri; Hannibal, Missouri.

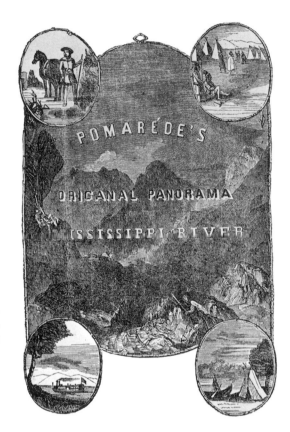

Decorative Title Page for
A GUIDE TO POMARÈDE'S
PANORAMA (*Courtesy Historical and Philosophical Society of Ohio, Cincinnati*)

Section Second: Marion City, Missouri; La Grange, Missouri; Tully, Missouri; Churchville, Missouri; Mouth of Des Moines River; Keokuk, Iowa; The Lower Rapids; Nashville, Iowa; Montrose, Iowa; Fort Madison, Iowa; Burlington, Iowa; Mouth of Iowa River; Bloomington, Iowa; Davenport, Iowa; Rock Island; Stevenson, Illinois; Upper Rapids; Cammanche, Iowa; Prairie Pomme de terre, Iowa; Charleston, Iowa; Belleview, Iowa; Dubuque, Iowa; The Little Makoqueta; Turkey River; Pike's Tent; Wisconsin River; Prairie du Chien; The Painted Rock; Cap à Lail.

Section Third: Prairie la Crosse; Black River; Lester's Bluffs; La Montaigne que trempe à l'eau; King and Queen Mountains; Wa-pa-sha Village and Prairie; Eagle Rocks; Five Point Bluffs; Red Oak Point; Lake Pepin;

155

PORTRAIT IN OILS
BY POMARÈDE

The Maiden's Rock; Story of the Indian Maiden; Red Wing Village; Little Crow Village; Mouth of St. Croix River; Saint Paul's; St. Peter's, River and Town; Fort Snelling; Falls of St. Anthony; The Story of the Indian Wife; The Indian Wife's Lament; Prairie Lands.

Section Fourth: Bad Axe River, Rock and Battle; Cassville; Mouth of Fever River; Galena; Water-power Mills on the Upper Rapids; New Boston, Illinois; Nauvoo, The Mormon City; Warsaw, Illinois; Quincy, Illinois; Hamburg, Illinois; Mouth of Illinois River; Grafton; Bluffs above Alton; Alton; Bloody Island; Conflagration of St. Louis.

Most of the entries in the *Guide* were brief and informative but not exciting; few of them indicated anything about the painting itself. Hannibal was represented by a "moonlight dissolving scene." The "montaigne que trempe à l'eau,"[13] readers were informed, was so named by the Indians because, they said, "on a certain day each year it *sinks* a little into the earth." A very brief account was given of the Winnebago removal troubles of 1848. The author reached his greatest powers in his pages on the grandeurs of Lake Pepin at sunset and then wandered off on a lengthy retelling of the inevitable Winona legend. At last, however, the sun rose beyond the mouth of the St. Croix, and the reader found himself looking upon Fort Snelling at high noon.

Now the author indulged in another Indian legend. An Indian princess fell in love with one Florimond de Rancé, once of Quebec; years later he deserted her and returned to civilization, taking with him their young lady daughter but leaving a son, six-year-old Louis. Overcome by grief, his "Startled Fawn" of a wife leaped with the boy into the water, and the two were carried over the Falls of St. Anthony. After many pages of this narrative in prose, it was recapitulated in verse.[14] No doubt it was popular.

While the reader was in the neighborhood, he was treated to some scenes of Indian life on the prairie. Finally, after stopping at several towns on the east bank, he found himself once more at St. Louis, and the panorama came to a dramatic close with the dissolving scenes of the Great Fire. None of this is presented with the detail and effectiveness of the news reports about the painting.

From the *Guide*, too, we learn something of the special machinery employed in showing the panorama. Here Pomarède was credited with "a new invention [which exhibited] a great portion of the water craft moving . . . distant and apart from the canvass. The majestic Steamers are made to move against the mighty flood, their engines in motion, and emitting smoke and steam from the chimneys and escape pipes. The hardy Flatboatsman and his cumbersome charge, float down the current guided by the brawny arms of the oarsmen, the motion being as natural as life; and on the Upper Mississippi where the works of civilized man are rarely to be seen, the Indians in their shallow and easily overturned canoes, are paddling in life-like motion on the placid waters that bear the frail thing."

The newspapers of September 13, 1849, carried the first advertisement of the panorama, which had cost sixteen months' labor and six thousand dollars capital to produce. It was promised to open four days later, but the non-arrival of Mr. Brough, the lecturer, caused a postponement to Wednesday, the nineteenth. On the opening night the "saloon" of the Odd Fellows' Hall[15] was crowded—"many retired from the door unable to gain admission."[16] The *Reveille* three weeks earlier, on August 30, announcing the arrival in town of Henry Lewis with his panorama, had declared that, when Pomarède opened, "between the *two* 'rivers' we shall have a rise which will make the whole town turn out." So they did. For a week St. Louisans had the opportunity to compare the

157

two pictures—and to enjoy the war of words in the daily press. But Lewis, after a run of nearly four weeks, left the town to Pomarède.

The French painter was a good showman. Changes, improvements, additions kept the people pouring in. On October 4 the *Republican* announced that "Mr Pomarede is adding new attractions to the beauty and interest of his Panorama. . . . He has supplied a defect, in the absence of smoke and steam issuing from the pipes of the steamers, and they now get along in a very lifelike manner." A new "Illustrator, very essential to a proper appreciation of works of this kind," also made his appearance; he was expected to introduce "many interesting anecdotes of Indian life." In addition, "a splendid Piano, with Eolian Accompaniment, will be used while the Painting is moving." About a week later St. Louisans were told that "A splendid painting of a BUFFALO HUNT has just been finished by Mr. Pomarede, and will be exhibited for the first time." A museum of Indian curiosities was open for two hours every morning—admittance free of charge—where costumes and equipment of the Blackfeet, Crees, Sioux, and Assiniboins could be examined at leisure.[17]

Advantage was taken of every special occasion to attract crowds to the exhibition room. A benefit was held for the Catholic Orphan Asylum on the eleventh. Although the show was advertised to close on October 13, St. Louisans woke to discover that "the proprietors had been induced to exhibit their splendid Panorama of the Mississippi one week longer, for the gratification of the many strangers in attendance at the Railroad Convention." A benefit held for the Protestant Orphan Asylum on the twenty-fifth brought three hundred dollars to that institution. The picture was still being held over as late as October 27.[18]

*Western Landscape with Indians. Oil by Leon Pomarède (Courtesy Chicago Historical So-
ciety)*

Just when the panorama closed in St. Louis is uncertain. Early in November Pomarède left for New Orleans to make preliminary arrangement for exhibition there.[19] The picture opened in the Armory Hall on Camp Street on November 26 and drew crowds for five or six weeks. This "pupil of our eminent resident artists, Mondelli and Davelle," was well received by the *Daily Picayune*.[20] In January, 1850, Pomarède started to move to the eastern seaboard cities with the intention eventually of taking his picture to Europe,[21] but his road tour was cut short in little more than a year, for his panorama was destroyed by fire in Newark, New Jersey, in November, 1850.[22] Of his huge picture no fragment remains today save only a few woodcuts by another hand used to illustrate the *Guide*.

EPILOGUE: *The Fate of the Pictures*

The public must have grown tired of exclaiming over the wonders of the moving pictures of the great Mississippi. After Pomarède we find no more of them. Five tremendous likenesses had been taken.[1] The bluffs and the entering streams, the islands, the grass waving on the prairie, the tall trees on the river bank, the cotton fields and the wheat harvest, the cities, towns, villages, and lonely houses, the log huts and the mansions, the flatboats and the steamboats, the farmers and the soldiers, the Indians and the Negroes, the jolly flatboatmen and the notables, the forts, the fires, the wrecks in the river—every aspect of life along this mighty stream had been recorded that posterity might be fully informed how the father of rivers looked and behaved in the fabulous forties a century ago.

They are gone now beyond trace, these portraits of the Mississippi that so interested and delighted our great-grandparents. The Banvard panorama after its many years of exhibition and revival was eventually carried to Watertown, South Dakota, where the artist retired in 1883. A grandson remembers playing on it in the basement of the artist's home. Banvard's youngest daughter said that some portion of the picture was cut up for scenery and that "years and years of being wound on a cylinder ruined what was left . . . so that it was finally discarded." An editor in Watertown heard a rumor that the panorama was on the wall of a building in that town [three miles—or even four hundred yards of it?], covered with "varnish, paper, and possibly other layers of wall covering." But no one can speak with assurance of having seen any fragment of it in the last sixty years.[2]

Of the fate of the Smith panorama there is no information whatsoever following the news of its showing in 1853 on Smith's return from Europe. Stockwell's picture, after its unsuccessful tour of the West Indies in 1851, was brought back to Boston, sold there in 1853, and heard of no more. Henry Lewis in Düsseldorf sold his painting in 1857 to a planter returning to Java: after collecting with difficulty a portion of the purchase price he finally let the buyer sail with it for Calcutta four years later. Only for the Pomarède painting is there absolute assurance of permanent disposal, since it was burned during exhibition in New Jersey in November, 1850. But there is little hope that even a fragment of any of the others will ever be found.

With the disappearance of the panoramas it is certain no art masterpieces were lost. Huge areas of canvas covered by several hands in a race against time are not likely to prove masterworks except in magnitude. Nevertheless, the Mississippi pictures were probably a good deal superior to the crudely primitive work of panoramists like John J. Egan and

John Stevens[3] (out of hundreds or thousands produced in the nineteenth century their slight and crude panoramas alone remain for comparison today). Of Stockwell's ability we can say nothing, for we have not a single specimen of work by which to judge. But the others left enough to qualify them as serious artists. Smith, trained in his father's drawing academy, was good enough to exhibit miniature views and crayon sketches in the Boston Athenaeum Gallery before he turned west as a scenic artist. Banvard's pencil sketches and oils of Mississippi River subjects show that he was not without skill in landscape. Some of Lewis' early oils are evidence that even in his beginning years his work had feeling and depth beyond the ephemeral demands of scene painting. A view of St. Louis and some Indian genre subjects demonstrate Pomarède's command of oils.

The skill of these painters in their studios tells us nothing, of course, about the quality of their extended canvases. The panorama calls for a technique far different from that of the easel picture. After all, it is a gigantic backdrop, displayed a portion at a time for the convenience and comfort of the viewers. Designed to be looked at by four or five hundred people seated in a hall, each scene passing from view after brief exposure, succeeded by another and another and another, it has no need or use for the subtleties of fine landscape work. Its values are theatrical. Its effects must be achieved quickly and boldly. Its success will depend upon its striking yet familiar subjects, upon the faithfulness of detail, upon the fulness of report, not upon its depth of emotional experience; upon the appearance of reality, not upon the essence. But even so, from what we have discovered of these painters, we can judge that within this special genre their work was likely enough above average, that their pictures unrolling before the spectators may have at moments achieved something of the illusion of art.

But the real loss in their disappearance is not their disputable value as art, but their indisputable importance as representation, their literal statement of another time and place. They were the documentaries of a day and a manner and condition of life that is gone. The record of the great river so laboriously made, faithfully portraying not every inch of the river landscape as was sometimes enthusiastically declared but the towns and villages that have grown into cities or disappeared into history and all the phases of life up and down the valley—this vivid, pictorial record that would today be so revealing to us in rubbed away in time, despite the plans and efforts and aspirations of the painters.

From crude engravings in newspapers, pamphlets, and magazines, from a few loose sketches and studies by Banvard, from the sketchbooks of Henry Lewis and the lithographs made after his paintings, from the elaborately detailed descriptions so admiringly and so admirably written by newspapermen, we can learn much about the choice of subject and the arrangement of composition, about the details recorded and the faithfulness of the record. We can reconstruct the pictures and assert confidently that they were effective facsimiles of life on the Mississippi a century ago—and we can lament their passing.

THE LENGTH *of the Panoramas*

To arrive at any precise knowledge of the length of these panoramas is impossible. The little available data are too much colored by the press-agent qualities of the producers for us to accept them easily. For the first three paintings, at least, the claims are simply in the tradition of tall tales. A brief consideration of these statements will be sufficient.

Banvard declared that his panorama was three miles long (it is, perhaps, significant that later he merely said it was "extensively known as the three-mile painting"); yet the Bristol *Gazette* in a review, which Banvard used as a blurb, said that one and one-half hours were necessary for the exhibition of the picture. At this rate of two miles an hour, 176 feet of canvas passed before the eyes of the spectator every minute. Such a speed cannot easily be reconciled with the time necessary for the close examination of scenery of which the reports all speak, nor do they allow for any kind of detailed remarks by the commentator. How, for instance, could Banvard have told his favorite story of the attack by the Murrell gang while the picture passed at the rate of three feet per second?

The Smith-Risley panorama was announced as the four-mile painting. The *Daily Saratoga Whig* of August 14, 1848, according to the panorama proprietors, made reference to the two hours in which it passed rapidly along. Were these statements both true, it must have moved just as fast as Banvard's—with equal dissatisfaction to an audience. In their London pamphlet (1849) the proprietors declared that "the great difficulty of moving so extensive a piece of canvass has just been accomplished after years of experiment," and they boasted of the twenty thousand square feet which the Mississippi section of their panorama contained. Not merely did they say their picture was a mile longer than Banvard's, but they claimed this section alone covered more than half again as much space as Banvard's. But a four-mile-long painting containing twenty thousand square feet would be something less than one foot high. Eighteen hundred or two thousand linear feet is much more likely to have been the actual length of a picture of so many square feet, and even that was probably an exaggeration.

From the advertisements of Stockwell and the interviews with him we get no more satisfactory statements. He announced that his picture was three times the length of Banvard's, that the section from the Gulf to the Ohio was as extensive as the whole panorama of the first producer. Did he actually wish people to believe it nine miles long? In an early announcement we read that he expected to need two and one-half hours for the showing; one of the reports on the opening night declared that "the size of the work causes more than three hours to be spent in unfolding it, and still, only a brief glance was allowed each prominent point." A writer in Boston in October, 1849, spoke of the two hours necessary for this canvas to move. Brief, indeed, must have been the glances if the picture were nine miles long!

The size of Lewis' "magnificent work of art" has been recorded with more precision than Banvard or the Smith-Risley partnership thought necessary or advisable, but there is still uncertainty as to its actual dimensions. Lewis planned a travelogue using 100,000 square feet of canvas. News stories and advertisements in the Cincinnati and St. Louis papers in 1849 declared that the completed panorama covered 45,000 feet—at 12 feet high, the picture was then 1,250 yards long. Although the published statements are sometimes confusing, it seems certain that both sections, upper and lower, were included in this figure. The unknown person who wrote the article on Lewis' panorama for the *Western Journal* (October, 1849) declared that Banvard's picture was 440 yards in length, Stockwell's 625 yards, and Pomarède's about the same length as Stockwell's—the length of Smith's he did not give. Lewis' panorama was here described as in two sections: the upper river 825 yards and the lower 500, a total of 1,325 yards in length by 12 feet in height. Since the two pictures were not exhibited on the same night and the showing time of the upper river was given as two hours, the figures for the Lewis paintings are within reason. According to a Bath, Maine, newspaper (1850), 22 feet of Lewis' picture could be seen at one time.

There remains Pomarède's panorama. An early announcement informed the public that he would paint a picture three thousand yards long by four high. When he was nearly ready for exhibition, the *Reveille* spoke of the fifty-four hundred feet of his production. The phraseology is not clear, but the paper must have meant linear feet. We would have then a painting of eighteen hundred yards. Allow for paternal exaggeration and say that his canvas may have been half as long as claimed. Since none of these panoramas is known to exist today, we can speak of length only with hesitance.

Nevertheless, though there may be wide differences between claimed and actual length, these pictures were yet quite long enough to be considered prodigious. Their newsreel value and their educational range were not diminished by the overstatements in their sales publicity.

Three Other "Mississippi" PANORAMAS

HUDSON'S MISSISSIPPI PANORAMA

In the first chapter, I mentioned an exhibition at St. Louis in 1848 of *Hudson's Grand Panoramic View of the Hudson River*. This Hudson was also the enterpriser responsible for *Hudson's Great National Painting of the Ohio and Mississippi Rivers! Executed on over Twenty Thousand Feet of Canvas, Showing Nine Different States, and delineating an extent of over 1400 miles of river scenery* (so reads the title page of a descriptive pamphlet printed in New Haven in 1848). The latter painting won no space in the St. Louis newspapers of that day, nor has Odell recorded it in his *Annals of the New York Stage*. As described in the pamphlet it consisted of Ohio River views only.

The opening scene was Pittsburgh. Then followed views of Alleghany City, Economy, Beaver Town, Wellsville, Steubenville, Martinsburg, Wheeling Island, the Mound Scene, Marietta, Point Harmar, Hocking Port, Blennerhassett's Island, Coal Port, Gallipolis, Hanging Rock by Moonlight, Jackson Furnace Landing, Portsmouth, Manchester Bar and Islands, Aberdeen, Maysville, Ripley, Cincinnati and nearby spots, Rising Sun, Big Bone Lick,

Vevay, Madison, New London, Jeffersonville (with the Falls of the Ohio), New Albany, the Haunted Mill at Brandenburg, Leavenworth, An Encampment by Moonlight, Rock Island Bend, Evansville, Wabash River, Shawneetown (showing also a tobacco plantation, a field of hemp, eight slaves at work, Cave-in-Rock, and other features of this region), Metropolis, America, and Cairo. The last entry in the description is a summary headed "Mississippi River": "Here for many miles we find the low, distant shores of Missouri and Arkansas, with their forests of cotton wood, sycamore, and ash. The numerous islands and dangerous passes, the noted iron banks; the famous chalk banks of Kentucky; the Spanish moss; the town of New Madrid, which was once partially destroyed by an earthquake, and where the bed of the river rose in its co[n]vulsions so high that the river's current was turned up stream for miles.

"The most dangerous pass on the Mississippi River, Plumb Point Bar, with its Snags and wrecks.

"The Chickasaw Bluffs, or the Old Counsel [sic] Bluffs, situated in the state of Tennessee, with an Encampment of Indians on a visit to the graves of their fathers, as is their annual custom." The Preface informed the public that another strip of the painting was then in process of completion so that his work would presently give the entire route from Pittsburgh to New Orleans.

The producer, according to his own account, had undergone the customary arduous exertions in preparing his work.

The first sketch of this gigantic undertaking was commenced in the year 1838. Three sections of it were completed in April, 1848. The artists have completed the sketches of Mississippi above the falls of St. Anthony, and they had to endure almost endless privations in taking their sketches, being many times obliged to encamp upon the hard ground near a fire, over which they cooked their frugal supper, which was supplied by the inhabitants of the *Western Wilds*. During the day they were constantly employed in rowing their skiff and taking the sketches. No one can form an idea of their privations but those who have traveled through these wilds, or commenced a settlement in the Western forests; but the task was cheerfully performed, with the prospect of producing the FIRST and *largest Painting of the kind in the world;* the last of which has already been realized, and with the hope that the enlightened citizens of our country would extend to the artists a degree of patronage and approbation, they have presented it to our citizens in the form of an exhibition, and for a *small fee*, they may obtain a view of a Painting, representing a country that would cost them hundreds of dollars, and much time, and many dangers to visit.

The pamphlet closes with five pages of testimonials. From them we discover that Wm. R. Vance, mayor of Louisville, had witnessed with great pleasure the exhibition of this work and on April 21, 1848, had certified that the views were "wonderfully accurate." The mayor of Cincinnati was also quoted as testifying to its excellence. Masters and captains of river steamers, together with a United States surveyor and a United States inspector, made affidavit to the "astonishing accuracy" of the picture as well as to its "great beauty as a work of Art." Newspapers in Louisville, Cincinnati, Baltimore, and New York were all quoted as lauding this *"Chef d'œuvre* of Panoramic Art." In October, 1849, the picture was showing in Boston (see p. 68 above). A year later it was still on tour, for Henry Lewis, writing to his brother from Bangor, Maine, November 1, 1850, referred to "Cassidy's Panorama of the Ohio and Mississippi . . . got up by a taylor in Boston by the name of Hudson."

From this scant array of facts we can see that Hudson's panorama was on display later than Banvard's but earlier than Smith's and Stockwell's. That it was completed late in 1848 has now been established by Joseph Earl Arrington.[1] Available details, however, add little to this story of the painting of the Mississippi.

THE DICKESON-EGAN PANORAMA
OF THE MONUMENTAL
GRANDEUR OF THE MISSISSIPPI VALLEY

One of two extant examples of a moving panorama on a Mississippi Valley subject is now owned by the City Art Museum of St. Louis, but it is not, properly speaking, a panorama of the Mississippi. My first knowledge of this work came from a handbill which Dr. J. Alden Mason, the curator of the American section of the Museum of the University of Pennsylvania, sent me in 1941. Later (January, 1942) Dr. Mason contributed to the *Pennsylvania Archaeologist* an account of this work and its authors, which was reprinted in *Minnesota History*, XXIII (December, 1942), 352–54. From these sources I have made the following summary.

Dr. Montroville Wilson Dickeson (1810–82), archeologist from Philadelphia and one-time professor of medicine there, spent twelve years opening Indian mounds, studying the geology, mineralogy, and botany of the western country, and meditating on the antiquities and customs of the "unhistoried" Indian tribes. From more than one thousand mounds opened during his exploration of the whole valley of the Mississippi he had collected forty thousand relics. Based on all this, he had prepared a lecture which was accompanied by a "magnificent *Scenic* Mirror, covering 15,000 feet of canvass, illustrating the Monumental Grandeur of the Valley, with Splendid Scenes that occur upon the *Father of Rivers.*"

The painting was by I. J. (or John J.) Egan. "Each view and scene," we are told, was "taken from drawings made on the spot" by Professor Dickeson. Actually this canvas was not intended as a continuous picture of the river and, consequently, is not another "portrait." It was rather a series of pictures which derived unity from the lecture. The scenes included such diverse geographical views as Marietta, Ohio, Natchez, and the Rocky Mountains (seen beyond St. Charles, Missouri!), historical subjects as De Soto's burial, Lewis and Clark's camping grounds, and the slaughter of the French at Fort Rosalie in 1729 (all painted on the spot?), as well as of contemporary matter. The handbill gives a full description of the scenes:

SECTION I.

Marietta Ancient Fortification—A grand view of their Walls, Bastions, Ramparts, Fossa and Walls, with the relics therein found—Circleville Aboriginal Tumuli—Cado Chiefs in full costume—Youths at their war practice—Hanging or Hieroglyphical Rock—Colossal Bust at lower water mark, used as a metre by the Aborigines—Portsmouth Aboriginal Group, in a Storm—Cave in the Rock, Stalagmitic Chamber and Chrystal Fountain, Desecated and Mummied Bodies in their burial places—Magnificent effects of Crystalization—Terraced Mound in a snow storm at sunset—Twelve gated Labyrinth, Missouri—Indians at their piscatory exploits.

SECTION II.

Bon Hom Island Group—Distant view of the Rocky Mountains—Encamping Grounds of Lewis and Clark—Louisiana Swale Group, with extensive Walls—Lakes and Sacrificial Monuments—Natchez Hill by Moonlight—Indian Encampment—Distant view of Louisiana—Indians preparing Supper—The Tornado of 1844—Destruction of Indian Settlements—Horrid loss of Life—Louisiana Squatter pursued by Wolves—Humorous Scene—Prairie, with Buffalo, Elk, and Gigantic Bust on the ledge of a Limestone Rock—Spring Creek, Texas—Fort Rosalie—Extermination of the French of 1729—Grand Battle Scene—Mode of Scalping.

SECTION III.

Chamberlain's Gigantic Mounds and Walls—Natchez above the Hill—Indians at their Games—Baluxie Shells, Mounds—Ferguson Group—The Landing of Gen. Jackson—Lake Concordia and Aboriginal Tumuli—Huge Mound and the manner of opening them—Cado Parish Monument—De Soto's Burial at White Cliffs—Mammoth Ravine—Exhuming of Fossil Bones—Temple of the Sun by sunset.

According to Dr. Mason the Dickeson-Egan panorama was exhibited in Philadelphia in 1851; it was still on display there as late as January 31, 1852 (Philadelphia *American Courier*). Probably during the next year or two it traveled extensively about the United States.

In 1949 the picture was unrolled as a moving panorama by the City Art Museum of St. Louis in its notable show of western Americana and has since been acquired by that museum. It measures seven and one-half feet by three hundred and forty-eight (not quite the advertised size of the original!), painted in tempera on muslin sheeting. For a further account of the picture and of Dr. Thomas T. Hoopes's work in staging it, see Rathbone, *Mississippi Panorama*, pp. 13–16, 127–35 (the ten illustrations include seven scenes from the panorama).

JOHN STEVENS' PANORAMA OF THE SIOUX WAR

John Stevens' newsreel of the Sioux War in Minnesota (1862) is a Mississippi River panorama only in the sense that it reports events and scenes in Minnesota, but as one of the very few extant moving panoramas it is worth a glance. Like the Egan picture it is a primitive painting and very small in comparison to the five Mississippi "portraits." Two of four versions have been preserved, with all the machinery for exhibiting them, one in the Gilcrease Museum, the other in the Minnesota Historical Society. The latter has recently been displayed.

Stevens, born in Utica, New York, moved to Minnesota in 1853 and became one of the original settlers of Rochester. Farmer, hotel-keeper, sign-painter, he was stirred to paint the adventures of the Murray County settlers shortly after the Sioux massacre at Lake Shetek. In 1865 he set to work on a more elaborate panorama which was displayed in 1868. Presently he turned out two more versions of his newsreel and was still exhibiting one of them as late as 1878.

The Gilcrease panorama consists of thirty-six panels, many signed by Stevens and dated Rochester, 1870. The reel opened with a view of Minnehaha Falls followed by a picture of Washington welcoming Lafayette. Next came more than twenty Sioux War pictures, and "at the end is what may be described as a newsreel recording ten events of the day." The Minnesota Historical Society panorama, also of thirty-six panels, each six feet high by seven wide, has an over-all length of almost two hundred and twenty feet. It begins with a view of Lincoln and his cabinet and, besides the Sioux War scenes, includes views and events in the Black Hills, Yellowstone Park, and other places of the Far West.

The history of the Stevens pictures has been ably reported by Bertha L. Heilbron in her "Documentary Panorama."

NOTES

[Note: The complete citation for each reference will be found in "Sources Consulted," pp. 197–204 below.]

CHAPTER 1

1. Bapst, *Essai sur l'histoire des panoramas et des dioramas*, pp. 7–10, 13–17. Philip de Loutherbourg as early as 1781 opened to the English public his *Eidophusikon*, but this was no more than "a sort of panoramic moving peepshow," not comparable to the Barker-type panorama (Waterhouse, *Painting in Britain*, p. 234).

2. Bapst, pp. 19–22. For Daguerre's share in the development of these forms see, particularly, Gernsheim, *L. J. M. Daguerre*, pp. 5–6, 13–45.

3. For a discussion of these effects see Williams, *Transparency Painting on Linen*, pp. 42–44 (effects of distance) and 44–52 (painting and lighting of dioramas). He said in part: "The sky and distance being seen through two transparent surfaces have their tints modified and softened, insomuch, that a surprising aerial effect is obtained. The objects also, on the second surface, being seen through the first, maintain their tone of middle distance, and the boldness of the foreground objects on the front surface, secures for the combined subject a powerful and truthful appearance." In Germany three surfaces were used, foreground, middle distance, and extra distance and sky. "By such arrangements, very successful effects of moonlight, of winter scenery, and of fire, are obtainable. In some instances, portions of the middle and back surfaces are cut away, in such forms as will admit of light being thrown on particular spots on the front surface, in order to

secure at those places the highest points of light. Thus, in employing two surfaces, we may, by cutting from one, or both surfaces, the quantity corresponding with the extent of the light, throw a bright light upon foreground figures, buildings, or other near objects, and communicate to them a striking reality of relief and brilliancy. Moonlight scenes, with reflection on water, sharp bright lights on the trees, and the ruined tower, all enhanced by the contrast of an expanse of sombre tone and shade, are subjects well adapted for this treatment."

4. New York *Mirror*, VII (April 17, 1830), 322–23, quoting from Dr. Arnott's *Physics*. Another moving panorama exhibited about the same time in London presented "the latter part of Bonaparte's career." This was quite possibly the Napoleon picture shown in New York in 1831 mentioned below.

5. John Rowson Smith, *Descriptive Pamphlet of Smith's Leviathan Panorama of the Mississippi River*. Charles Dickens, through his character Mr. Booley, expressed a similar opinion: "It is a delightful characteristic of these times, that new and cheap means are continually being devised, for conveying the results of actual experience, to those who are unable to obtain such experiences for themselves; and to bring them within the reach of the people—emphatically of the people. . . . New worlds open out to them, beyond their little worlds, and widen their range of reflection, information, sympathy, and interest" ("Some Account of an Extraordinary Traveller"). Percy Fitzgerald (*Memories of Dickens*, p. 172) credited the unsigned article to Dickens; the tone is certainly Dickensian. Mr. Booley, a Londoner advanced in life, suddenly "closed the door of his house behind him at one o'clock in the afternoon of a certain day, and immediately proceeded to New Orleans." Returning from this trip, he traveled to New Zealand, Australia, up the Nile, to India, and to the polar region. We discover, of course, that he has been spending his afternoons at the panorama halls.

6. Odell, *Annals of the New York Stage*, I, 286, 398; II, 460; III, 73, 541; IV, 110, 419–20. Victor von Hagen ("Mr. Catherwood's Panorama") thinks that Catherwood's *Jerusalem* (1838) was the first moving panorama to be shown in the United States; it must give place apparently to this giant picture of Napoleon's last years. Vanderlyn's *Versailles* is now (1957) on exhibit at the Metropolitan Museum, New York (see Gardner, *Vanderlyn's Panorama of Versailles*).

7. I find two earlier announcements of panoramic shows in St. Louis; the second was possibly a repetition of the first. In a mixed exhibition, of which the feature was the mummy of an Egyptian queen, the townspeople were offered "Panoramic Views of the different cities of Europe"

along with paintings and wax figures; the show lasted more than two weeks (*Missouri Republican*, May 27, June 10, 1828). On August 29, 1829, the St. Louis *Beacon* carried the advertisement of an enterprise calling itself the "St. Louis Museum." The exhibits there included a marvelous newly invented musical instrument known as the "Grand Pan-Harmonicon," some eighty statues "as large as life," an "electric machine," and a "Grand Panorama: Representing more than Fifty correct views of Cities, Palaces, Castles, Churches, Bridges, Naval and Land Battles, &c. &c. &c." The whole thing was offered from 9:00 A.M. to 10:00 P.M. for twenty-five cents and was still advertised as late as December 23. I found no editorial comment, no communications from readers further describing this show (McDermott, "Museums in Early Saint Louis," pp. 134–35).

8. Antonio Mondelli, an Italian-born New Orleans painter, served as scenic artist in the St. Louis Theatre in the summer season of 1830. In an advertisement of entirely new scenery for *Masaniello* (*Missouri Republican*, July 20, 1830), the following scenes were announced for the last act: "Grand Eruption of Mount Vesuvius. Terrific Explosion!! Forked Lightenings Rend the Sky! The Burning Lava Impetuously flows down the side of the Mountain, and the whole country becomes awfully illuminated!!! Fenella plunges into the sea; Grand Display of Fire Works; Popular Tumult, and Death of Masaniello." It was this sort of work, obviously, that prepared so many scene-painters for their careers as panoramists. The naval piece was actually painted in New Orleans earlier this season. Mondelli has a further connection with this story, for he was the friend and father-in-law of Leon Pomarède.

9. *Commercial Bulletin*, January 27, 1836. For Koch, consult McDermott, "Dr. Koch's Wonderful Fossils."

10. On July 4, 1835, the citizens of Vicksburg (having had much trouble with gamblers) in a mass meeting warned such persons to leave the city within twenty-four hours. Notices were posted the next day and many left immediately. On the sixth the military corps accompanied by several hundred citizens made the rounds of the place. At North's house they forced the door; a citizen was shot. Thereupon the attackers rushed the house, seized North and four others, and hanged them. An account of this affair can be found in Howard, *The History of Virgil A. Stewart*, pp. 263–68.

11. *Missouri Republican*, August 22, 27, 31, September 10, 15, 1838; *Missouri Argus*, September 15, 1838. Can this twelve-reeler be the London panorama of 1829 (nn. 4 and 6 above) and the New York show of 1831?

12. *Missouri Republican*, December 10–18, 1830.

13. Banvard's connection with the St. Louis Museum is discussed in the next chapter.

14. *Missouri Republican*, May 2, 9, 24, 29, 1848. Hudson at this time was engaged on a panorama of the Ohio and Mississippi rivers; for a brief discussion of it see Appendix B.

15. *New Era*, April 21, 1848; *Weekly Reveille*, April 3, 1848.

16. *Missouri Republican*, December 12, 1848.

17. *Ibid.*, March 27, April 8, 1850.

18. *Ibid.*, April 15, 19, 1850.

19. McDermott, "Gold Rush Movies," pp. 32–38.

20. *Missouri Republican*, September 25, 30, 1850.

21. General accounts of panorama-painting in the West are scarce. The form is discussed in: Butts, *Art in Wisconsin*, pp. 51–65; Heilbron, *Making a Motion Picture in 1848*, pp. 1–19; McDermott, "Newsreel—Old Style"; Born, "The Panoramic Landscape as an American Art Form" and *American Landscape Painting*, 75 ff.; and Schick, *The Early Theater in Eastern Iowa*, pp. 134–41 (the latter contains an interesting summary of panorama shows in Davenport, Iowa, between 1852 and 1862). Well known, of course, is Mark Twain's description of a panorama lecturer whom he met on a Mississippi steamboat (*Life on the Mississippi*, chap. lix). Writings about specific panoramas will be noticed in the pertinent places.

CHAPTER 2

1. For a discussion of the various editions of this pamphlet and the earlier forms in which much of the material was published see my "Banvard's Mississippi Panorama Pamphlets." Miss Heilbron, editor of *Minnesota History*, informs me that the Minnesota Historical Society has an 1848 edition of the *Adventures;* I have not seen it.

2. Miss Edith Banvard confirmed to me the date given by the *Dictionary of American Biography* for her father's birth: November 15, 1815. J. P. Frankenstein sketched him at Louisville, 1834. In a lecture before the American Geographical Society (New York) in 1862 Banvard declared that he had spent sixteen years in the West (that is, 1830–46) and he placed one incident on the Mississippi River in 1842.

3. This summary of the museum under the proprietorship of W. S. McPherson and Banvard is based upon news items and advertisements in the *Missouri Republican*, March 17, 22, 24, 29, April 12, 20, 21, 26, 1841; St. Louis *Pennant*, August 19, 24, 1841. For the return engagement of Banvard's pictures see the St. Louis *New Era* for September 22, 29, 1847. What I have said does not prove that Banvard did not have a museum in

St. Louis before 1841; it merely makes clear that the "St. Louis Museum" was not his, and from lack of specific evidence in the many extant newspaper files it is probably safe to assume that he was not active there in a museum way before the spring of 1841.

4. The Woodworth letter was quoted both in the *Adventures* and the *Description* pamphlets. The midshipman was the son of Samuel Woodworth, the poet, an old friend of the Banvard family.

5. The Louisville *Courier* as quoted in the St. Louis *Weekly Reveille*, September 30, 1846, p. 1021. As will be seen below, the exhibition of the completed picture was opened late in October.

6. The actual machinery used was described at length in the *Scientific American*, IV (December 16, 1848), 100: "We here present an engraving of the machinery employed by the renowned artist Banvard in operating his wonderful Panorama of the Mississippi. The mechanical devices employed are very simple but answer the purpose in an admirable manner. The canvass is wound upon one large vertical roller while it is being unrolled from the other.—This is done by bevel gearing A and B. As there is a great extent of canvass spread at once, which being painted is very heavy, it is very important to hold it up between the rollers and prevent it from what is technically termed *sagging*. To accomplish this object well, there is a cross beam erected in which there are set a double row of pulleys C C C. The manner in which this is done will be better understood, however, by examining fig. 2, which is an end section. A is a beam running along above B B, in which the pulleys C C C are erected. These two pulleys C C, are fixed in B B, so as to receive the panorama canvass between them—therefore the edge of the canvass is only seen in this view. On the upper edge or it may be called "a selvage," there is sewed a thick cord or small rope D, and as this rope rests on part of both pulleys—running along the tops of the whole of them in the like manner—the canvass is rolled up along the whole length of the line without any sensible dropping of it at one place more than another. This is a very ingenious way to hold up the canvass and yet allow it to be wound freely on the large rollers." When Banvard passed through customs at Liverpool (October 13, 1848), the panorama was on four cylinders, for which he was charged only four pence duty (Diary).

7. Published at Boston, 1847, this was the first of many issues; for an account of them see my "Banvard's Mississippi Panorama Pamphlets." The Flint passages are from his *Condensed Geography and History of the Western States*, I, 131 ff., 229 ff. The Neville story, first published in 1829, was here reprinted without acknowledgment. The last pages and the rear cover were filled with testimonials and critical comments from steamboat captains and pilots, the mayor of Louisville, the secretary of the Kentucky

Historical Society, and Louisville and Boston newspapers. Some of the pamphlets describing Mississippi panoramas were sold for a bit, some for a dime.

8. The Boston edition (1847) listed the following places: Missouri River, Bloody Island, St. Louis, U.S. Arsenal, Vide Pouch [Poche] (or, in English, Empty Pocket), Jefferson Barracks, Plateen Rocks, Herculaneum, Bluffs of Selma, Rush Island, Mouth of the Ohio, Cairo, Iron Banks, Chalk Banks, Mills Point, Indian Mounds and Island Number Twenty-five, Plumb Point, Fulton, Randolph, Memphis, Fort Pickering, President's Island, Commerce, Stack Island, Vicksburg, Warrenton, Palmyra Island, Grand Gulf, Petite Gulf, Natchez, Ellis's Cliffs, Fort Adams, Bayou Sara, White Cliffs, Prophet's Island, Baton Rouge, Carrolton, La Fayette, New Orleans.

9. The British Museum Catalogue lists an 1848 London edition which I have not seen. The description of the Missouri now added may have been "borrowed" but it is so much in tone with the *Adventures of the Artist* that it earns a place here.

10. Further description of the Missouri River section can be found in "Mr. Banvard's Panorama of the Mississippi," the *People's and Howitt's Journal* (London), VII, 26–28, 281. These reports, published in January and April, 1849, were accompanied by four woodcuts here reproduced. Another review appeared in the *Illustrated London News*, XIII (December 9, 1848), 364–65.

11. Opinions of newspapers and indorsements by individuals in the remainder of this chapter (except as otherwise credited) are drawn from the Banvard pamphlets.

12. Dondore ("Banvard's Panorama and the Flowering of New England") says that it was on exhibition in Boston as early as December 15, 1846, and showed there for seven months.

13. None of the contemporary accounts seemed to question the "three miles of canvas," although that was a completely impossible size. The length of this panorama, and of the others as well, is discussed in Appendix A.

14. Samuel Longellow, *Life of H. W. Longfellow*, II, 67–68. It was in the second section of Part II of *Evangeline* that the poet described the Mississippi.

15. "Fred," a regular correspondent of the St. Louis *Weekly Reveille* (in a letter dated Boston, December 26, 1846, and published January 18, 1847, p. 1144) declared that he had visited the panorama several times and was much impressed by it.

16. The New York *Weekly Atlas* (December 12, 1847) advertised that Banvard's painting of the Mississippi from the mouth of the Missouri to New Orleans would open on Monday the thirteenth at the New Panorama Building on Broadway adjoining Niblo's Garden. Admission fifty cents; children one-half; the painting to start moving at seven o'clock. Five feature stories, illustrated with woodcuts after the painting, appeared in the *Atlas* during the first half of 1848 (January 30, February 20, March 5, June 10, July 23). The "last week" of the St. Louis-to-New Orleans picture was announced on July 23. The show then closed for a short time but reopened August 2 as "Banvard's New Panorama of the Missouri and Mississippi Rivers," showing a country of twenty-three hundred miles. This (the larger version?) commenced moving at 8:00 P.M. The "positively last week" was announced on September 17, the artist intending to leave for London on the twenty-seventh.

17. The St. Louis *New Era* (September 29, 1847), when the painting was only eleven months old, declared the artist had cleared fifty thousand dollars by his tour in the East. The New York *Home Journal* (G. P. Morris' paper) on December 18, 1847, stated that the picture has been "exhibited to crowded audiences for nearly a year in Boston, where the worthy and singularly gifted artist realized about seventy thousand dollars profit!" That there was a snug profit is clear from the twenty-four-room house, Glenada, that Banvard built at Cold Spring Harbor on Long Island after his return from Europe. In 1862 Banvard revived the Mississippi panorama, cutting the Missouri and Ohio sections and inserting a "war section" featuring scenes of current interest.

18. I find nothing in the index to the *Descriptive Catalogue of Government Publications, 1794–1881* to support Banvard's claim; such a resolution may, however, have been passed.

19. Banvard, his wife, and secretary sailed from New York on the steamer "Europa" on September 27, 1848 (Diary). At least two pieces of advance publicity for the Banvard panorama appeared in British periodicals in 1847: (1) "A Painting Three Miles Long," *Chambers's Edinburgh Journal*, VII (1847), 395–98, reprinted in *Littell's Living Age*, XIV (September 25, 1847), 594–96; (2) "John Banvard's Great Picture," *Howitt's Journal* (London), II (September 4, 1847), 145–48, reprinted in *Littell's Living Age*, XV (December 11, 1847), 511–15. A piece from the Boston *Bee* was reprinted under the title, "A Story about Banvard," in *Howitt's Journal*, III (April 1, 1848), 211–12.

20. Clarkson Stanfield (1793–1867), marine and landscape painter. He

served first in the merchant and naval service and later (1818) for years as a painter in the theater (*Dictionary of National Biography*, LIII, 476–77).

21. "The American Panorama," December 16, 1848.

22. These quotations are among those printed in blurb fashion in the London, 1850, edition of the *Description*. Dickens' much longer report in *Household Words* has already been mentioned, n. 5, chap. i above; the "travels" of Mr. Booley began with a visit to Banvard's panorama, which is described at some length and for the most part with approval.

23. Henry Lewis, visiting Europe in his turn a few years later, picked up a copy of the handbill Banvard had struck off following the command performance. It is reproduced here from the Henry Lewis Papers of the Missouri Historical Society.

CHAPTER 3

1. Something of this is indicated in the secondhand remarks of "O. P. Q.," a correspondent of the *Weekly Reveille*, in a letter dated Boston, October 9, 1849, and published in the *Reveille* on October 22): "I saw a letter yesterday from a gentleman in London, who says, 'Banvard and Risley have both lost money by their Mississippi Panoramas, and yet each has got out a duplicate for the provinces. Banvard made money at first, and might have made more instead of losing it, if he had not made it a point to attack Risley and Smith, and their Panorama, and they in turn proved that B.'s was not correct, &c. The result was, that the public became tired and sick of both, and were exceedingly doubtful whether either were faithful representations of the river." About a year later Henry Lewis wrote to his brother from Bangor, Maine (November 1, 1850) that "Banvard is in Paris with *one* of his panoramas. The other he sent to Germany where his bitter enemies Risley and Smith are now exhibiting."

2. See also *Missouri Republican*, June 29, 1837; Carson, *The Theatre on the Frontier*, pp. 171–72.

3. *Dictionary of American Biography*, XVII, 306–7.

4. Odell, *Annals of the New York Stage*, IV, 611; V, 1, 114, 329. A man named Smith (without initial) did the scenery for the *Devouring Ogre* (opened at Welch's Olympic Circus, New York, February 1, 1843); this job included "The Frozen Ocean, with floating icebergs, the Steel Castle, the Castle of Skeletons, a Horrid Repast of Cannibals, and others, the locale shifting, with pantomimic inconsequentiality, through the East Indies, England, Italy, Germany, Switzerland and Central America," says Odell (IV, 614). Explanation of delay between completion and exhibition may possibly lie in a statement in the Risley edition of the *Description:* "Owing

to a disagreement in contract it [the panorama] has been involved in a suit in the Supreme Court [*sic*], and damages laid at 50,000 dollars. It has recently been amicably settled by paying several thousand dollars." Indexes to Supreme Court cases, both for the United States and for New York and Massachusetts, fail to show record of this very interesting case; probably the matter was handled in one of the lower courts, but the case is spoken of so vaguely that it is practically impossible to trace it.

5. This was the "Ben Sherrod" disaster of May 5, 1837; an account of it will be found in *Niles Weekly Register*, LII (May 27, 1837), 203.

6. Indorsements are from pamphlet blurbs.

7. Odell, IV, 566, 589, 619; V, 333, 438; New York *Weekly Atlas*, October 17, 1847 (reprinted from the London *Pictorial Times*).

8. Odell (VI, 412, 501) reports that Smith's "One Hundred Views of Europe" and "Siege of Sebastopol" were showing in New York through the season of 1854–55 at the Empire Hall and that they continued through the next season as well. Sabin (*Dictionary of Books Relating to America*, XX, 298) lists the following title: *Descriptive Book of the Tour of Europe, the largest moving panorama in the world. Now exhibiting at the Chinese Rooms, Broadway, New York. Painted on thirty thousand square feet of canvass, from views taken on the spot, and at an expense of ten thousand dollars, by J. R. Smith, artist of the celebrated panorama of the Mississippi, which has been exhibited with distinguished success in the United States, London, Dublin, Edinburgh, Paris, Brussels, Rouen, Berlin, Antwerp, Vienna, etc. Pianist: Mr. Aylwin Field* (New York: Pettiner & Gray Printers, 1855, 48 pp.). Smith's partner also brought back a picture from Europe; who did the painting of it I do not know. Odell (VI, 263) says that Risley's panorama of the Thames opened in New York January 6, 1853. It appears that Risley must have become sole proprietor of the Mississippi panorama on its return to America and continued to exhibit it, for Sabin (XX, 299) lists a *Great National Painting, Professor Risley's original gigantic moving panorama of the Mississippi River* (Philadelphia, 1853, 32 pp.).

9. For discussion of length see Appendix A.

10. Four views from the panorama were engraved by permission expressly for *Graham's Magazine*, XXXIV (1849), 56, 206, 257, 336: the Balize, General Zachary Taylor's cotton plantation, the Mormon Temple at Nauvoo, and Montgomery's house, the headquarters of General Jackson at the Battle of New Orleans. They are reproduced here.

11. The artist evidently referred to the troubles of 1846. With the departure of the Mormons the town shrank greatly but it was not a "deserted city." The finished temple had been dedicated in April, 1846, and was burned October 9, 1848.

CHAPTER 4

1. *Weekly Reveille*, October 22, 1849, p. 3072, date of letter October 9. The last reference is to the St. Louis fire of May 17, 1849.

2. Actually, Henry Lewis had asked Stockwell to work with him on a panorama, but they fell out (see p. 86 above) and Stockwell undertook one alone.

3. *Weekly Reveille*, August 7, 1848, p. 1786.

4. *Ibid.*, September 10, 1848, p. 1825.

5. *Ibid.*, August 7, 1848, p. 1786; *Missouri Republican*, August 1, 1848.

6. John M. Weston as early as September, 1844, was stage manager at St. Louis for the Ludlow-Smith organization and continued as late as 1846–47 to serve in their Mobile and New Orleans theaters as well. In 1850–51 he was once more a member of the company, appearing at New Orleans. The *Missouri Republican* of May 9, 1851, carried a letter by Weston about a proposed new theater in St. Louis. A Boston publisher in 1856(?) brought out his *Lucretia Borgia: A Drama in Three Acts. Adapted from the French of Victor Hugo* (of which the University of Michigan owns a copy). The last mention of Weston by Ludlow concerns the opening of Weston's Chicago Museum in July 1863 (Ludlow, *Dramatic Life*, pp. 606, 640, 660, 661, 715, 732). Consult also Carson, *Managers in Distress*, p. 254 and *passim*.

7. *Weekly Reveille*, September 10, 1848, p. 1826; *Missouri Republican*, September 22, 1848.

8. *Missouri Republican*, September 22, 1848; *Weekly Reveille*, September 24, 1848, p. 1845.

9. *Weekly Reveille*, October 15, 1848, p. 1868.

10. *Ibid.*, October 29, 1848, p. 1888; *Missouri Republican*, October 24, 1848.

11. *Weekly Reveille*, October 29, 1848, p. 1882.

12. *Ibid.*, p. 1884.

13. *Missouri Republican*, October 30, November 1, 1848.

14. *Weekly Reveille*, November 19, 1848, p. 1905. This letter was signed "R. S. N." but another issue of the *Reveille* describes its writer as "Mrs. R. S. Nichols, a daughter of the west, and one whose mind and eye have equally been devoted to its scenes of beauty and grandeur" (November 16, p. 1907). Rebecca Nichols contributed verse and prose to the St. Louis newspapers, a good deal over the signature "Moina." Sabin (XIII, 338) lists one book for her: *Bernice; or the Curse of Minna, and other Poems* (Cincinnati, 1844).

15. *Weekly Reveille*, February 5, 1849, p. 1995; March 5, 1849, p. 2031; New Orleans *Picayune*, December 3, 12, 1848; February 16, 1849; McDermott, "Gold Fever," p. 125.

16. *Weekly Reveille*, April 30, 1849, p. 2090—letter signed "Jenks" and dated Macon, Georgia, April 9.

17. Charleston *Courier*, May 5–29, 1849, as cited by Rutledge, *Artists in the Life of Charleston*, p. 149. Pomarède was there at the same time.

18. According to the New Orleans *Picayune* of July 15, 1849, the Stockwell panorama arrived in Baltimore on July 6; it stayed there only a few days.

19. *Weekly Reveille*, October 15, 1849, p. 3040 [3070].

20. *Ibid.*, December 10, 1849, p. 3133. Was it Stockwell's panorama or Lewis' that Thoreau, in the beginning of his 1851 journal, mentioned having seen (*Writings*, Walden ed., VIII, 146–47)? I am indebted to Mr. Walter Harding, secretary of the Thoreau Society, for calling my attention to this passage.

21. So said Joseph M. Field in the *Missouri Republican*, May 8, 1851.

22. Mary S. Stockwell to Sol Smith, May 22, 1855, Sol Smith Papers. Stockwell had returned to theater work in 1852 and died in Savannah, Georgia, in September, 1854. J. Earl Arrington has also traced the history of this picture in "The Story of Stockwell's Panorama."

CHAPTER 5

1. For twentieth-century accounts of Lewis and his work consult: Bay, "Henry Lewis (1819–1904)," in *Das illustrirte Mississippithal*, pp. iii–xii; Squires, "Henry Lewis and His Mammoth Panorama of the Mississippi River," pp. 244–56; Heilbron, *Making a Motion Picture in 1848;* McDermott, "Henry Lewis and His Views of Western Scenery," pp. 332–35. Contemporary materials, including those of the artist, will be noticed in the course of this chapter.

2. *New Era*, March 29, 1845; *Weekly Reveille*, April 27, 1845, p. 836.

3. *Weekly Reveille*, March 8, 1847, p. 1198; *New Era*, April 10, 1847. This view of St. Louis (1846) has recently been acquired by the City Art Museum of St. Louis.

4. *Weekly Reveille*, May 8, 1848, p. 1685. These paintings were the result of his last season's tour. The *Missouri Republican*, December 1, 1847, reported that he then had "on his easel a large number of landscapes, taken by himself during the last summer and fall, of scenes and prominent places on the upper Mississippi. Even the drawings we recognize as faithful."

The *Republican* of May 20, 1848, named six of these subjects as finished: two views of the Falls of St. Anthony, one each of Fort Snelling, Lake St. Croix, the falls of the St. Croix, and the gorge of the St. Croix. Of the latter two the Minnesota Historical Society possesses oil sketches; in 1948 the Minneapolis Institute of Art acquired the finished paintings (they are twenty inches by thirty inches). Location of the other landscapes is unknown.

5. Smith had painted the upper river, but his picture was not exhibited until August, 1848, and then not in the West. In the extensive files of St. Louis newspapers I have found no reference to sketching trips by Banvard or Smith or to their work-in-progress otherwise.

6. "I had been up, the two previous summers [previous to 1848], reconnoitering the country, and making drawings from Fort Snelling to Prairie du Chien, and exploring the tributaries that empty into the Mississippi between these two points" (letter from Lewis quoted in "Lewis's Panorama of the Mississippi," p. 70). In 1847 he traveled for a time with the party of David Dale Owen, the geologist, who was exploring in Wisconsin, and possibly from him Lewis acquired interest in geological formations. A view of a "natural wall of sandstone" near the Kinikinick River, a tributary of the St. Croix, Owen in his official report credited to Lewis (Senate Document 57, plate 12). See also Owen, *Report of a Geological Survey of Wisconsin*, p. 70. A passage from Lewis' 1847 journal (August 18) was quoted in *Das illustrirte Mississippithal*, p. 76. See also *Missouri Republican*, September 11, 1848.

7. So reported in an interview in the *Missouri Republican*, September 11, 1848.

8. "Lewis's Panorama of the Mississippi"; Heilbron, *Making a Motion Picture in 1848*, p. 7.

9. "Lewis's Panorama of the Mississippi"; Heilbron, *Making a Motion Picture in 1848*, pp. 7, 9. The draft of the letter to Pomarède was found by Miss Heilbron in the back of the Lewis diary. The correct date is June 14, not July, for it was on June 14 that Lewis left St. Louis aboard the "Senator."

10. Heilbron, *Making a Motion Picture in 1848*, p. 42

11. Draft of a letter to Henry Stagg, written on board the "Senator," preserved in the back of the Lewis diary.

12. Rogers later made sketches for an Ohio River reel which apparently was never completed. John A. Lewis, nephew of Henry, has a sketchbook of scenes from the mouth of the river to Cincinnati. One hundred and thirty-six places from Cairo to Pittsburgh were indicated for the attention

of the field-artist and thirteen were marked as of special importance. On the opening page Lewis gave particular instructions to his assistant: "The towns marked with a star are all places of importance—you will therefor take them with extra care—and if [you] possibly can without injuring the picture take the views of all places *looking up*—and where there are two towns opposite make a distant one from below taking in both at once—you will also try and bring foregrounds wherever you can—and make some few *bird* eye views from prominent points of important places as you have in your Burlington &c—If you can find time make a few studies in *oil* of the forest shore—and a few islands &c—so that we can have the character— We shall find these of much [value?]." Nowhere in his diary or letters did Lewis give this artist's first name. Although some of the drawings in the Lewis "Sketch Book No. 1" (Missouri Historical Society) appear to be signed "V Rogers," I am strongly inclined to identify this man as Charles Rogers from New Hampshire. Among other paintings exhibited by this artist at the Western Art Union, Cincinnati, 1849, was a view of "Floating Mountain [Mount Trempeleau], Upper Mississippi." In January, 1851, he was at St. Louis painting a panorama of the Land Route (Overland Trail) to California (*Missouri Republican*, February 1, 1851).

13. *Missouri Republican*, May 31, September 1, 1849; Heilbron, *Making a Motion Picture in 1848*, pp. 11–12; undated Cincinnati newspaper clippings in the Henry Lewis Papers, Missouri Historical Society; letters of Henry Lewis to his brother George, private collections. Charles Gaylor's little book with a big title, *A Description of Lewis' Mammoth Panorama of the Mississippi River, from the Falls of St. Anthony to the City of St. Louis; containing an account of the distances, and settlements of the country; the names and population of the various cities, towns and villages on the river, with historical remarks, &c. Compiled from various authentic sources* (Cincinnati, 1849), is a very odd piece of work. It opens with a four-page account of "The Upper Mississippi," descriptive and historical, much of which is borrowed word for word (and without acknowledgment) from Edmund Flagg's *Far West*. Next comes a section headed "Far West, Vol. 1st. II" in which not fewer than sixty-seven scenes from the Falls of St. Anthony to St. Louis are listed with comment. The last section of the pamphlet is entitled "The City of St. Louis, XV"; this is devoted to brief remarks about the city. In addition to views of St. Louis before and after the great fire of May, 1849, the panorama, according to the *Description*, offered pictures of Bloody Island and Illinois Town (East St. Louis). There is no more. Gaylor (or Gayler), lawyer, journalist, and playwright (1820–92) was editor of the Cincinnati *Evening Dispatch* in 1846 (*Dictionary of American Biography*, VII, 198).

14. Unless otherwise credited all details of the sketching trip are from Lewis' "Journal of a Canoe Voyage from the Falls of St Anthony to St Louis" (cited hereafter as *Journal*), so ably edited by Bertha L. Heilbron in *Making a Motion Picture in 1848;* the original diary is in the Minnesota Historical Society. For other accounts of the Winnebago trouble at Wabashaw Prairie see Neill, *History of Minnesota*, pp. 483–87 (his version is based on a manuscript by George Culver and a conversation with Henry M. Rice, both concerned in the Winnebago removal), and Bushnell, *Seth Eastman*, pp. 9–10. Pomarède also featured this "news story" in his panorama.

15. Because of the vibration of the steamboat.

16. Seth Eastman (1808–75), officer and artist. Consult Bushnell, *Seth Eastman*, and Heilbron, "Seth Eastman's Water Colors." Lewis was indebted to Eastman for one or two of the sketches used for lithographs in *Das illustrirte Mississippithal.*

17. For chiefs of this name consult Willson, "The Successive Chiefs Named Wabasha"; Hodge, *Handbook of American Indians*, II, 91. Hodge spells the name "Wapasha." See also Mrs. Eastman's sketch, "Wabashaw," in her *Dahcotah*, pp. 81–91.

18. *Missouri Republican*, June 26, 1848.

19. Henry Mower Rice (1816–94). See n. 14 above.

20. *Weekly Reveille*, July 31, 1848—letter dated St. Peters, June 23, and signed "Dahcotah" (possibly H. H. Sibley, who signed contributions to the New York *Spirit of the Times* "Hal, a Dahcotah").

21. I use the standard spelling. Lewis wrote it variously: Mine-ha-ha, Mine-ha-hah, Mene-ha-hah, Mine-ah-ah, Menehaha. The boat was destroyed in the great fire at St. Louis, May 17, 1849. Consult *Missouri Republican*, September 11, 1848; Heilbron, *Making a Motion Picture in 1848*, pp. 28–29.

22. The "Highland Mary," Atchison master, was scheduled to leave St. Louis on Wednesday, June 21, at 4:00 P.M. (St. Louis *Daily Union*, June 20, 1848).

23. The fullest account of Robb's life will be found in the introduction to my "Gold Fever," pp. 115–21.

24. For the full text of the letters here summarized see my article, "A Journalist at Old Fort Snelling: Some Letters of 'Solitaire' Robb."

25. *Missouri Republican*, July 27, 1848; the letter was dated "Prairie du Chien, July 20th 1848."

26. Fort Snelling for many years was the chief point of interest on Upper Mississippi River excursions; Robb was only one of many travelers to enjoy

his experience there. Consult Blegen, "The 'Fashionable Tour' on the Upper Mississippi"; Hansen, *Old Fort Snelling*, pp. 159–75.

27. Mrs. Mary Eastman's *Dahcotah*, published a year later, is especially interesting for its introduction and preliminary remarks, pp. i–xxxi.

28. Captain Eastman was presently to illustrate Henry Rowe Schoolcraft's *Information respecting the History, Condition, and Prospects of the Indian Tribes of the United States: Collected and Prepared under the Direction of the Bureau of Indian Affairs, per act of Congress of March 3d, 1847* (6 parts; Philadelphia: Lippincott, Grambo & Co., 1851–57). After his brief visit, Robb was certain that it would "be hard to find [another] man possessed of the same artistical ability, who combined with it a thorough knowledge of Indian character" to qualify for the then-unfilled post of illustrator (*Weekly Reveille*, July 31, 1848, p. 1777).

29. Henry Hastings Sibley (1811–91), one of the most interesting and important of the early settlers of Minnesota; he had been in charge of this post for fourteen years (consult Solon J. Buck in *Dictionary of American Biography*, XVII, 144).

30. Lewis' dates in his journal are often incorrect. He wrote that they left Captain Eastman's on "Monday afternoon 27 July" (Heilbron, *Making a Motion Picture in 1848*, p. 29). Robb, however, in a letter dated "On the 'Mine-Ha-Ha,' Raccoon slough, July 17th 1848," stated that "one week ago we set *sail*" (*Weekly Reveille*, July 31, 1848, p. 1777).

31. Eben Weld, then government farmer at Kaposia, on the site of South St. Paul (Heilbron, *Making a Motion Picture in 1848*, p. 29, p. 18).

32. *Weekly Reveille*, July 31, 1848, p. 1778. Little Crow's village, according to Lewis, consisted of fourteen or fifteen lodges (Heilbron, pp. 29–30).

33. The most important by-product of Lewis' work for the panorama was his book *Das illustrirte Mississippithal* published in Germany half a dozen years later. Illustrated with seventy-eight colored lithographs after paintings or sketches by Lewis (and Rogers?), it is one of the most attractive and pictorially valuable pieces of nineteenth-century Americana. For its history see the articles by Bay, Heilbron, and McDermott in Sources Consulted. The plates probably represent scenes in the Lewis panorama, but as small book-illustrations the treatment of views necessarily is far different from that in the panorama. Compare, for example, the sketch and the litho of Carondelet and those of Quincy, reproduced here. The lithographs were captioned variously in German and English or both; in the following list of Upper Mississippi scenes I give them all in English: St. Louis; Steamboat Grand Turk Wooding at Night; Indian Deputation; Fort Snelling; The Falls of St. Anthony; The Rolling Prairies; The Valley

of the St. Peters (Minnesota); The Little Falls (Minnehaha); St. Paul's in Minnesota Territory; Little Crow's Village; Red Rock Prairie; Medicine Bottle's Village; The Mouth of the St. Croix; Red Wing's Village; The Indian Cemetery; Lake Pepin; The Maiden Rock; The Grand Council; The Camp of the United States Troops; The Indian Camp; Travelling Hunting Party; Dog Dance; Prairie on Fire; Battle of the Bad Axe; Indians Spearing Fish; Hunting the Deer by Moonlight; Scalping Scene on the Mississippi; Prairie du Chien, Wisconsin, in 1830; Mouth of the Chippeway, Wisconsin; Mouth of the Wisconsin from Pike's Hill; Cassville in 1829; The Indian Look-Out; Dubuque, Iowa; Tete de Mort River; Galena, on Fever River in Illinois; View on Fever River; Bellevue, Iowa; Savannah, Illinois; Port Byron, Iowa, and Berlin, Illinois; The Rapids; Fort Armstrong; Fort Armstrong on Rock Island; Muscatine, Iowa; Great Muscatine Prairie, Iowa; Burlington, Iowa; Fort Madison, Iowa; Nauvoo, Illinois; The Mormon Temple; Artist's Encampment; Warsaw, Iowa; Quincy, Illinois; View on the Mississippi near Quincy (Illinois); Keokuk, Iowa; Hannibal, Missouri; The Town of Louisiana, Missouri; Clarksville, Missouri; The Piasa Rock near Alton, Illinois; Ballustrade Bluffs with the Grand Staircase; Alton, Illinois; Mouth of the Missouri; The Great Fire in St Louis May 17th 1849; Carondelet or Vide-Poche, Missouri.

34. *Weekly Reveille*, July 31, 1848, p. 1778, letter dated "Below the 'Bad Axe,' July 18, 1848." Details through Robb's impression of La Grange "mountain" are from this letter.

35. Nicollet, *Report Intended to Illustrate a Map of the Hydrographical Basin of the Mississippi River*, p. 72. Seymour (*Sketches of Minnesota*, pp. 130–34) said that Carver's Cave, which had been open the previous summer, he found blocked in 1849.

36. Site of the present city of Red Wing.

37. Barn Bluff, near Red Wing.

38. Lewis found the views so beautiful that he made "a panoramic series of sketches embracing the whole horizon" (*Journal*, p. 31).

39. Letters dated July 24 and 25, 1848, *Weekly Reveille*, August 7, 1848, p. 1785.

40. Point-no-Point is on the Minnesota shore nearly opposite the Maiden's Rock.

41. Korponay was a Hungarian exile who had arrived in St. Louis in 1845 and made a living by teaching the polka and the mazurka. During the Mexican War he raised and commanded a company of mounted volunteers.

42. One of the many versions of this story is to be found in Mrs. East-

man's *Dahcotah*, "The Maiden's Rock or Wenona's Leap," pp. 165–73. On these legends see G. Hubert Smith, "The Winona Legend."

43. The town of Maiden Rock, Wisconsin (nearest to the scene), in 1950 had a population of 269.

44. Lewis must have meant the height of the rock itself? In Gaylor's *Description* Lewis is said to have found the height of the rock 165 feet. Seymour (*Sketches of Minnesota*, p. 82) gave the height of the rock as "about 200 feet" and the total height above the lake as "409 feet."

45. *Journal*, pp. 33–44.

46. *Journal*, p. 35.

47. Mount Trempeleau is about halfway between Winona, Minnesota, and Lacrosse, Wisconsin, on the Wisconsin side of the river. It was so called because it rose abruptly from the water.

48. *Journal*, pp. 35–36.

49. Enters the Mississippi from the west about halfway between Lacrosse and Prairie du Chien, not to be confused with the Iowa River.

50. For Rogers see chap. v, nn. 12 and 68.

51. Bellevue, Iowa, by 1950 had increased to the great size of 1,932 people.

52. *Dombey and Son* was published in England in parts between October, 1846, and April, 1848. Rogers might possibly have been reading the first London edition in covers (1848), more probably the first American edition, 20 parts in 19, 1846–48.

53. James Thomson's *The Seasons* was still a favorite with many readers.

54. Opposite the mouth of the Iowa River. It never quite rivaled Old Boston, for by 1950 it had only 767 people.

55. Lewis' "Sketch Book No. 1" (Missouri Historical Society) records the whole length of the river from Oquawka, Illinois, above Burlington, to St. Louis; the drawings are dated and many are accompanied by notes. The page of the sketchbook measures $5\frac{1}{8}$ inches by $9\frac{5}{8}$; generally the double-page spread was a continuous view. The sketches are in pencil, some of them washed with water color.

56. Sketch Book No. 1; *Journal*, p. 49.

57. *Journal*, pp. 51–52; Sketch Book No. 1. Smith was killed June 27, 1844; his widow, Emma Hale Smith, married Lewis G. Bidamon in 1847 and died in Nauvoo in 1879.

58. It is well no great matter turns on Henry Lewis' dates, for those of his Sketch Book No. 1 and his *Journal* do not agree, just as some of the *Journal* dates do not fit the calendar. It is likely that Robb left on the

twenty-ninth rather than the thirtieth (as in the *Journal*), for the "Kate Kearny" was listed among arrivals at St. Louis by the *Missouri Republican* on Monday, July 31.

59. *Journal*, p. 53.

60. Quotations are from Sketch Book No. 1.

61. *Journal*, p. 53.

62. *Ibid.*, pp. 53–54.

63. *Ibid.*, pp. 54–55.

64. *Ibid.*, pp. 55–56. Cap au Gris had been laid out in November, 1845, on land belonging to David Bailey. Now it is only a name.

65. For several years Lewis had shared a studio in St. Louis with James F. Wilkins, English-born portrait painter. Wilkins caught the panorama fever, too, for eight months later he went out with the California caravan to make sketches for a *Moving Mirror of the Overland Trail* (see chap. i). George I. Barnett, also English, was to become one of the leading architects of St. Louis.

66. *Journal*, p. 57.

67. The "Edward Bates," headed for Keokuk, blew up one mile below Hamburg at 4:00 A.M. on August 12 (*Missouri Republican*, August 14, 1848); the notation was added later to remind Lewis of an important "action" shot for the panorama.

68. See p. 109 above. The following lithographs in *Das illustrirte Mississippithal* were probably based upon the Rogers sketches (Lewis is not known at any time to have made a trip down the river to New Orleans): Herculaneum, Missouri; Cairo, Mouth of the Ohio; New Madrid, Missouri; Memphis, Tennessee; Mouth of the Arkansas; Vicksburg; Cotton Plantation; General Taylor's Plantation; Natchez, Mississippi; Mouth of the Red River; Bayou Sara, Louisiana; Convent du Sacrement (and the Sinking of the Steamboat *Brilliant*); Baton Rouge, Louisiana; New Orleans (double plate); Pilots Station (Balize); Mouths of the Mississippi.

69. *Weekly Reveille*, September 17, 1848. Robb left St. Louis for California in January, 1849; he therefore never saw Lewis' panorama in any stage of production.

70. John R. Johnston, portrait painter and panoramist, born Cincinnati, March 10, 1826, went to St. Louis in the summer of 1848 to paint on Stockwell's panorama and returned in December to paint on Lewis', doing "figures, boats, and cities." A bit later in Cincinnati, with Edwin F. Durang he painted a panorama of biblical scenes. In 1856 he moved to Baltimore. Thus far, the *Cosmopolitan Art Journal*, III, 176–78. But note in Lewis' Sketch Book No. 1, a view of a "rock near Cap o Gris Augt 1"

on which appear the names "Leslie, Johnson, LEWIS & ROBB" without explanation. There is nothing in the *Journal* to show that Johnston or Leslie were with Lewis at this time, but there is nothing to show that Lewis did not meet Johnston in St. Louis. At least one steamboat picture in the Lewis sketchbook is signed by Johnston and among some loose leaves is a portrait sketch of the Cincinnati artist. John Leslie was scenic artist at the National Theatre, Cincinnati. Laidlaw had recently come from the Drury Lane Theatre, London, according to press references.

71. *Missouri Republican*, May 31, September 1, 1849; *Western Journal and Civilian*, III, 70; Henry Lewis Press Book. The Upper Mississippi was on "three stretches of canvass" (undated clippings from the Cincinnati *Daily Dispatch* in the Henry Lewis Papers, Missouri Historical Society).

72. Henry Lewis to George F. Lewis, Cincinnati, July 11, 1849; Lewis Press Book.

73. Henry Lewis to George F. Lewis, Cincinnati, July 29, 1849; Cincinnati *Daily Dispatch*, August 15, 1849, in Lewis Press Book.

74. Cincinnati *Daily Dispatch*, as in Lewis Press Book.

75. Syracuse *Star*, February 18, 1850, Lewis Press Book. The St. Louis fire was featured in both upper and lower river paintings. According to the Cincinnati *Daily Dispatch*, August 18, 1849, "Mr. Laidlaw, the talented artist of the Polyorama, has added to the [lower] Panorama a striking and very effective representation of the late terrible conflagration at St. Louis" (Lewis Press Book). Laidlaw may have made the second painting of the fire from Lewis' first. It is, of course, impossible to give exact credits for any part of this immense enterprise.

76. *Weekly Reveille*, September 3, 1849, p. 3018; *Missouri Republican*, September 1, 1849.

77. *Daily Union*, September 3, 1849; *Missouri Republican*, September 15, 1849; *Weekly Reveille*, September 6, 1849. Reference by the latter paper to "one hour" was figurative; showing time, according to many press notices, was two hours.

78. September 8, 1849.

79. *Missouri Republican*, September 13, 1849.

80. *Weekly Reveille*, September 5, 6, 8, 1849; *Daily Union*, September 15, 1849; *New Era*, September 3, 1849; *Herald of Religious Liberty*, September 13, 1849—some of these notices are in the Lewis Press Book.

81. June 12, 1849, as in Lewis Press Book.

82. Waugh's letter was published in the Rochester *American* on December 12, 1849 (Lewis Press Book); it probably was reprinted from a St. Louis paper. The *Missouri Republican* (September 15, 1849) reported that

the artist had devoted "all space from St. Louis to Quincy in showing various changes from sunset to sunrise."

83. *Missouri Republican*, September 2, 1849; *Herald of Religious Liberty*, September 13, 1849; *Daily Organ*, September 3, 1849.

84. *Daily Union*, September 24, 26, 1849; *New Era*, September 26, 1849. Much of what follows is drawn from the Lewis Press Book and the unpublished letters of the artist to his brother George.

85. Henry Lewis to George F. Lewis, Buffalo, January 8, 1850. Judging from the receipts Lewis must have meant to write *four*, not *fourteen* hundred.

86. John Bates, the original co-owner, apparently sold his interest before the panorama left Cincinnati. On its departure from St. Louis, Washington King was co-proprietor; he probably accompanied Lewis to Europe. King (1815–61) was in the mercantile business in St. Louis, 1844–49. He returned to the city in 1852 and was elected mayor in 1855.

87. *Berliner Nachrichten*, January 22, 1853, as quoted in *Missouri Republican*, April 11, 1853. The panorama, showing at the Hotel de Russie, was that of the upper river: "the picture begins at St. Louis and carries us along that stream upwards to the Falls of St. Anthony."

CHAPTER 6

1. Pomarède died in St. Louis in 1892. For a detailed account of his career see my articles "Leon Pomarède, 'Our Parisian Knight of the Easel' " and "Portrait of the Father of Waters: Leon Pomarède's panorama of the Mississippi." J. Earl Arrington has also written an account of the panorama: "Leon D. Pomarède's Original Panorama of the Mississippi River."

2. See pp. 86–87 above.

3. *Missouri Republican*, August 21, 1848.

4. Courtenay (*Guide to Pomarede's Panorama*, Introduction) said that the artist was "accompanied only by his co-partner in the enterprise, Mr Charles Courtenay." Helmuth fifteen years later declared that Pomarède had with him Charles Wimar, then a boy, and that that painter had his first instruction from the Frenchman (*The Arts in St. Louis*, pp. 38–39).

5. *Missouri Republican*, February 26, 1849.

6. *Weekly Reveille*, April 2, 1849, p. 2058.

7. *Ibid.*, April 30, 1849, p. 2091.

8. A journalist's slip of the pen: Wabasha was a Sioux chief, not a Winnebago. This episode was reported to the *Reveille* by John S. Robb; see my article, "A Journalist at Old Fort Snelling."

9. *New Era*, August 4, 1849; *Weekly Reveille*, August 6, 1849, p. 2184.

10. On the very day after the fire Pomarède made his sketch of the ruins, according to the St. Louis *Daily Union*, May 19, 1849.

11. St. Louis, 1849 (Preface dated August 1). It was published over the initials "T. E. C." but the author was almost certainly Thomas E. Courtenay, life insurance agent in St. Louis, and in all probability a brother of Pomarède's partner, Charles Courtenay.

12. Apparently in New York the next year his picture was linked with a copy (?) of Banvard's. At least there is in the Theatre Collection of the Museum of the City of New York a complimentary ticket for a "Seven Mile Panorama. The Continuation by Pomarède, of BANVARD's Original Panorama of the MISSISSIPPI RIVER. At Panorama Hall, 398 Broadway, (corner of Walker St.)." It bears the signature of "A. A. Parker, Treas."

13. Mount Trempeleau. See chap. v, n. 47.

14. Pomarède was not alone in introducing such sentimental stories Banvard had a "White Fawn" who watched from the bluffs of Selma (below St. Louis) the slaying of her father and all his warriors in bitter battle. After seeing her fiancé die, the very last man of the tribe, "There lonely she sits from morning till night / Until her sad spirit from earth takes its flight," declared Banvard in the poem he composed about the "romantic Indian legend" (New York *Weekly Atlas*, March 5, 1848). In London, Banvard's poem was set to music by Madame Schwieso.

15. The Odd Fellows' Hall, Fourth and Locust Streets, had been dedicated October 27, 1846. On completion its first floor was taken by the Washington Saloon and the second (thirty-seven feet by seventy) was leased to Korponay, the dancing master. This room was "unequalled alike for the splendor of its decoration and style." Upper floors were reserved for the Order. Seating capacity of the hall was four hundred (*Missouri Republican*, October 26, 1846; October 14, 1849).

16. *Missouri Republican*, September 17, 21, 1849.

17. *Ibid.*, October 7, 14, 1849. The new illustrator (lecturer) was A. A. Parker. More than thirty of these "curiosities," from a bark needle-and-thread case to a large bark canoe, were listed in the Courtenay *Guide*.

18. *Daily Union*, October 8, 26, 1849; *Missouri Republican*, October 14, 21, 25, 26, 1849; *New Era*, October 26, 27, 1849.

19. *Weekly Reveille*, November 12, 1849, p. 3098.

20. November 24, 27, December 16, 26, 1849, January 3, 1850.

21. His picture was advertised in Charleston, South Carolina, papers in May, 1849 (Rutledge, *Artists in the Life of Charleston*, p. 241).

22. St. Louis *Intelligencer*, November 29, 1850. The painting had been insured for six thousand dollars. Arrington has traced the travels of the

panorama in greater detail than I have ("Leon D. Pomarède's Original Panorama of the Mississippi River," pp. 268–73).

CHAPTER 7

1. A sixth picture (of the Ohio and lower Mississippi only), prepared in 1848, is briefly described in Appendix B.

2. Letters of Miss Edith Banvard, Miss Esther Willard Bates, James G. Banvard, Robert C. Albrook to me, 1946.

3. For these panoramas see Appendix B.

APPENDIX B

1. "Samuel A. Hudson's Panorama of the Ohio and Mississippi Rivers," *Ohio Historical Quarterly*, LXVI (October, 1957), 355–74. I received a copy of his excellently thorough article from Mr. Arrington while I was reading page proof.

SOURCES *Consulted*

MANUSCRIPTS
AND SKETCHES

Banvard Collection (fragment of a diary, 1848, and notes by Banvard, some sketches, press notices, and an important collection of Banvard pamphlets), Minnesota Historical Society, St. Paul, Minnesota.

Henry Lewis Papers and Sketchbooks, Missouri Historical Society, St. Louis, Missouri.

Henry Lewis Press Notices relating to his Panorama, 1848–50, Curator's Office, City Art Museum of St. Louis.

Henry Lewis, unpublished letters to his brother George, 1849–76, private collections.

Henry Lewis, Ohio River Sketchbook, private collection.

Sol Smith Papers, Missouri Historical Society, St. Louis, Missouri.

NEWSPAPERS

Boston *Post*, 1854.
New Orleans *Daily Picayune*, 1841, 1848, 1849.
New York *Weekly Atlas*, 1847, 1848.
New York *Home Journal*, 1847.
New York *Mirror*, 1830.

New York *Spirit of the Times,* 1844.

St. Louis *Beacon,* 1829.

St. Louis *Commercial Bulletin,* 1836.

St. Louis *Daily Organ,* 1849.

St. Louis *Daily Union,* 1848, 1849, 1850.

St. Louis *Intelligencer,* 1850.

St. Louis *Missouri Argus,* 1838.

St. Louis *Missouri Republican,* 1828, 1830, 1837, 1838, 1840, 1841, 1845, 1848, 1849, 1850, 1851, 1852.

St. Louis *New Era,* 1845, 1847, 1848.

St. Louis *Pennant,* 1841.

St. Louis *Weekly Reveille,* 1845–49 (since this file is numbered, page references have generally been used to facilitate finding sources).

BOOKS AND ARTICLES

[NOTE: Anonymous contributions including the panorama pamphlets have been entered under the name of the artist concerned.]

ARRINGTON, JOSEPH EARL. "Destruction of the Mormon Temple at Nauvoo," *Illinois State Historical Journal,* XL (December, 1947), 414–25.

————. "Leon D. Pomarede's Original Panorama of the Mississippi River," *Missouri Historical Society Bulletin,* IX (April, 1953), 261–73.

————. "The Story of Stockwell's Panorama," *Minnesota History,* XXXIII (Autumn, 1953), 284–90.

[BANVARD]. "The American Panorama," London *Examiner,* December 16, 1848; reprinted in *Littell's Living Age,* XX (February 17, 1849), 314–15.

————. *Banvard, or the Adventures of an Artist: An O'er True Tale.* London: Chapman, 1849.

————. *Banvard, or the Adventures of an Artist! A Biographical Sketch.* London: Reed & Pardon (1852?).

————. *Banvard, ou les aventures d'un artiste.* Paris: Typographie Dondey-Duprè, 1850.

————. "Banvard's Panorama," *Scientific American,* IV (December 16, 1848), 100.

————. "Banvard's Panorama of the Mississippi and Missouri Rivers," *Illustrated London News,* XIII (December 9, 1848), 364–65.

————. "Banvard, the Artist," *Scientific American,* III (June 3, 1848), 291.

————. *Description of Banvard's Panorama of the Mississippi River, Painted on Three Miles of Canvas, exhibiting a View of Country 1200 Miles in Length, Extending from the Mouth of the Missouri River to the City of*

New Orleans, Being by far the Largest Picture ever executed by Man. Boston: Putnam, 1847.

———. *Description of Banvard's Panorama of the Mississippi & Missouri Rivers, extensively known as the "Three-Mile Painting," exhibiting a View of Country over 3000 Miles in Length, extending from the Mouth of the Yellow Stone to the City of New Orleans, being by far the Largest Picture ever executed by Man.* London: Golbourn, 1849.

———. *Description of Banvard's Panorama of the Mississippi, Missouri, and Ohio Rivers, extensively known as the "Three-Mile Painting," exhibiting a View of Country over 3000 Miles in Length, extending from the Mouth of the Yellow Stone on the Missouri, and the Little Miami, on the Ohio, to the City of New Orleans, on the Mississippi, being by far the Largest Picture ever executed by Man.* London: P. P. Thoms, 1850.

———. [Title same as last]. London: Reed & Pardon, 1852.

———. *Description of Banvard's Geographical Painting of the Mississippi River, extensively known as the "Three Mile Picture," with new additions of the Naval and Military Operations on that River, exhibiting a View of Country 1,500 Miles in Length, from the Mouth of the Missouri to the Balize.* New York: Biglow, 1862.

———. *Description of Banvard's Pilgrimage to the Holy Land.* London, 1852.

———. "John Banvard's Great Picture," *Howitt's Journal* (London), II (September 4, 1847), 145–48; reprinted in *Littell's Living Age*, XV (December 11, 1847), 511–15.

———. "Mr. Banvard's Panorama of the Mississippi," *People's and Howitt's Journal* (London), VII (January and April, 1849), 26–28, 281.

———. "A Painting Three Miles Long," *Chambers's Edinburgh Journal*, VII (1847), 395–98; reprinted in *Littell's Living Age*, XIV (September 25, 1847), 594–96.

———. "A Story about Banvard," *Howitt's Journal* (London), III (April 1, 1848), 211–12; reprinted from the Boston *Bee*.

BAPST, GERMAIN. *Essai sur l'histoire des panoramas et des dioramas, extrait des rapports du jury international de l'exposition universelle de 1889.* Paris: Imprimerie Nationale, 1891.

BAY, J. CHRISTIAN (ed.). *Das illustrirte Mississippithal.* New ed.; Leipzig: H. Schmidt & C. Günther; Florence: Otto Lange, 1923.

BLEGEN, THEODORE C. "The 'Fashionable Tour' on the Upper Mississippi," *Minnesota History*, XX (December, 1939), 377–96.

———. "Review of *Das illustrirte Mississippithal*," *Minnesota History*, V (May, 1924), 446–48.

BORN, WOLFGANG. "The Panoramic Landscape as an American Art Form," *Art in America*, XXXVI (January, 1948), 3–10.

————. *American Landscape Painting*. New Haven: Yale University Press, 1948.

BOWERMAN, SARAH G. "John Banvard," *Dictionary of American Biography*, I, 582–83.

BUCK, SOLON J. "Henry Hastings Sibley," *Dictionary of American Biography*, XVII, 144.

————. "Henry Mower Rice," *Dictionary of American Biography*, XV, 540.

BUSHNELL, DAVID I. *Seth Eastman: The Master Painter of the North American Indian*. ("Smithsonian Miscellaneous Collections," Vol. 87, No. 3.) Washington, D.C., 1934.

BUTTS, PORTER. *Art in Wisconsin*. Madison: Madison Art Association, 1936.

CARSON, WILLIAM G. B. *Managers in Distress: The St. Louis Stage, 1840–1844*. St. Louis: St. Louis Historical Documents Foundation, 1949.

————. *The Theatre on the Frontier*. Chicago: University of Chicago Press, 1932.

Catalogue of the [Boston] *Athenaeum Gallery*, 1829, 1831, 1859.

COBURN, FREDERICK C. "John Rowson Smith," *Dictionary of American Biography*, XVII, 306–7.

C[OURTENAY], T. E. *A Guide to Pomarede's Original Panorama of the Mississippi River, from the Mouth of the Ohio River, to the Falls of St. Anthony*. St. Louis, 1850.

[DICKENS, CHARLES]. "Some Account of an Extraordinary Traveller," *Household Words*, I (April 20, 1850), 73–77.

DONDORE, DOROTHY ANNE. "Banvard's Panorama and the Flowering of New England," *New England Quarterly*, XI (1938), 817–26.

EASTMAN, MRS. MARY. *Dahcotah; or, Life and Legends of the Sioux around Fort Snelling*. New York: John Wiley, 1849.

FITZGERALD, PERCY. *Memories of Charles Dickens with an Account of Household Words*. Bristol: J. W. Arrowsmith, 1913.

FLINT, TIMOTHY. *A Condensed Geography and History of the Western States, or the Mississippi Valley*. 2 vols. Cincinnati, 1828.

GARDNER, ALBERT TEN EYCK. *Vanderlyn's Panorama of Versailles*. New York: Metropolitan Museum of Art, 1956.

GAYLOR, CHARLES. *A Description of Lewis' Mammoth Panorama of the Mississippi River, from the Falls of St. Anthony to the City of St. Louis: containing an account of the Distances and Settlements of the Country; the names and population of the various Cities, Towns and Villages on the*

River, *with historical remarks, &c. Compiled from various authentic sources.* Cincinnati, 1849.

GERNSHEIM, HELMUT and ALISON. *L. J. M. Daguerre (1787–1851).* Cleveland: World Publishing Co., 1956.

Green's St. Louis Directory for 1845, 1847, 1851.

HAGEN, VICTOR VON. "Mr. Catherwood's Panorama," *Magazine of Art,* XI (April, 1947), 143–47.

———. *Frederick Catherwood Arch^t.* New York: Oxford University Press, 1950.

HANSEN, MARCUS L. *Old Fort Snelling, 1819–1858.* Iowa City: State Historical Society of Iowa, 1918.

HEILBRON, BERTHA L. "Henry Lewis' 'Das illustrirte Mississippithal': A Contemporary Advertisement," *Bibliographical Society of America Papers,* XLIII (3d Quarter, 1949), 344–45.

———. "Documentary Panorama: John Stevens and His Sioux War Pictures," *Minnesota History,* XXX (March, 1949), 14–23.

———. "Henry Lewis in English," *Bibliographical Society of America Papers,* XLV (4th Quarter, 1951), 359–62.

———. "John Banvard's New York," *Antiques,* LVI (August, 1949), 108–9.

———. "Letter to the Editor regarding Banvard's Mississippi Panorama Pamphlets," *Bibliographical Society of America Papers,* XLIII (2d Quarter, 1949), 245.

———. "Lewis' 'Mississippithal' in English," *Minnesota History,* XXXII (December, 1951), 202–13.

———. *Making a Motion Picture in 1848: Henry Lewis' Journal of a Canoe Voyage from the Falls of St. Anthony to St. Louis.* St. Paul: Minnesota Historical Society, 1936.

———. "Seth Eastman's Water Colors," *Minnesota History,* XIX (December, 1938), 419–23.

HELMUTH, WILLIAM T. *The Arts in St. Louis.* St. Louis, 1864.

HODGE, FREDERICK W. *Handbook of American Indians North of Mexico.* 2 vols. (Smithsonian Institution, Bureau of American Ethnology, Bulletin 30.) Washington, D.C., 1910.

HOWARD, H. R. *The History of Virgil A. Stewart . . . and the Execution of Five Professional Gamblers . . . at Vicksburg.* New York: Harper & Bros., 1836.

"John R. Johnston," *Cosmopolitan Art Journal,* III (September, 1859), 176–78.

LEWIS, HENRY. *Das illustrirte Mississippithal dargestellt in 80 nach der Natur aufgenomenen Ansichten vom Wasserfalle zu St. Anthony an bis zum*

Golf von Mexico (eine Entfernung von ungefähr 2300 englischen Meilen) von H. Lewis, Landschaftsmaler aus St. Louis, in Missouri. Nebateiner historischen und geographischen Beschreibung der den Fluss begränzebden Länder, mit besonderer Rücksicht auf die verschiedenen den obern Mississippi bewohnenden Indianerstämme. (Deutsch und englisch.) Von George B. Douglas. Dusseldorf: Arnz & Co., 1854. (So runs the title page of the first issues of this work in parts. The title of the complete work [1858] was altered to read after the word "Indianerstämme": *Von H. Lewis, Landschaftsmaler aus St. Louis, in Missouri. Nach dem engl Original-Text von H. Lewis deutsch bearbeitet von George B. Douglas.*) See also J. Christian Bay above.

LEWIS, HENRY. *Journal.* See Heilbron, *Making a Motion Picture in 1848.*

[LEWIS]. "Lewis's Panorama of the Mississippi River," *Western Journal and Civilian,* III (October, 1849), 70.

LONGFELLOW, SAMUEL. *The Life of Henry Wadsworth Longfellow.* 3 vols. Boston: Houghton Mifflin Co., 1886.

LUDLOW, NOAH. *Dramatic Life as I Found It.* St. Louis: G. I. Jones & Co., 1886.

MCDERMOTT, JOHN FRANCIS. "Banvard's Mississippi Panorama Pamphlets," *Bibliographical Society of America Papers,* XLIII (1st Quarter, 1949), 48–62.

———. "Dr. Koch's Wonderful Fossils," *Missouri Historical Society Bulletin,* IV (July, 1948), 233–56.

———. "Gold Fever: The Letters of 'Solitaire,' Gold Rush Correspondent of '49," *Missouri Historical Society Bulletin,* V (January, April, July, 1949), 115–26, 211–23, 316–31; VI (October, 1949), 34–43.

———. "Gold Rush Movies," *California Historical Society Quarterly,* XXXIII (March, 1954), 29–38.

———. "Henry Lewis and His Views of Western Scenery," *Antiques,* LXI (April, 1952), 332–35.

———. "Henry Lewis's *Das illustrirte Mississippithal,*" *Bibliographical Society of America Papers,* XLV (2d Quarter, 1951), 152–55.

———. "A Journalist at Old Fort Snelling: Some Letters of 'Solitaire' Robb," *Minnesota History,* XXXI (December, 1950), 209–21.

———. "Leon Pomarède, 'Our Parisian Knight of the Easel,'" *Bulletin of the City Art Museum of St. Louis,* XXXIV (Winter, 1949), 8–18.

———. "Museums in Early Saint Louis," *Missouri Historical Society Bulletin,* IV (April, 1948), 129–38.

———. "Newsreel—Old Style," *Antiques,* XLIV (July, 1943), 10–13.

———. "Portrait of the Father of Waters: Leon Pomarède's Panorama of the Mississippi," *Bulletin of the Institut Français of Washington*, N.S. No. 2 (December, 1952), pp. 46–58.

MONKHOUSE, COSMO. "Clarkson Stanfield," *Dictionary of National Biography*, LIII, 476–78.

MUNSON, SAMUEL B. *A New Map of the Western Rivers, or Travellers Guide, Exhibiting the Mississippi, Missouri, Ohio, and Illinois Rivers, with all the Principal Towns, Islands & Distances*. 1845.

MUSICK, JAMES B. "A Picture of Old St. Louis [by Henry Lewis]," *Bulletin of the City Art Museum of St. Louis*, XXVIII (October, 1943), 30–31.

NEILL, EDWARD DUFFIELD. *The History of Minnesota*. Philadelphia: J. B. Lippincott & Co., 1858.

NICOLLET, J. N. *Report Intended to Illustrate a Map of the Hydrographical Basin of the Mississippi River*. (26th Cong., 2d sess., Senate Doc. 237.) Washington, D.C., 1843.

ODELL, GEORGE C. D. *Annals of the New York Stage*. Vols. I–VI. New York: Columbia University Press, 1927–31.

OWEN, DAVID DALE. *Report of a Geological Reconnaissance of the Chippewa Land District of Wisconsin*. (30th Cong., 1st sess., Senate Executive Doc. 57.) Washington, D.C., 1848.

————. *Report of a Geological Survey of Wisconsin, Iowa, Minnesota*. Philadelphia: Lippincott, Grambo & Co., 1852.

RATHBONE, PERRY T. *Mississippi Panorama; The Life and Landscape of the Father of Waters*. St. Louis: City Art Museum, 1949.

RUTLEDGE, ANNA WELLS. *Artists in the Life of Charleston*. ("Transactions of the American Philosophical Society," Vol. XXXIX, Part 2.) Philadelphia, 1949.

SABIN, JOSEPH, EAMES, WILBERFORCE, and VAIL, R. W. G. *A Dictionary of Books Relating to America*. New York: Bibliographical Society of America, 1868–1936.

SCHICK, JOSEPH S. *The Early Theater in Eastern Iowa*. Chicago: University of Chicago Press, 1939.

SEYMOUR, E. S. *Sketches of Minnesota, the New England of the West, with Incidents of Travel in that Territory during the Summer of 1849*. New York: Harper & Bros., 1850.

SMITH, G. HUBERT. "The Winona Legend," *Minnesota History*, XIII (December, 1932), 367–76.

[SMITH, JOHN ROWSON]. *Descriptive Pamphlet of Smith's Leviathan Panorama of the Mississippi River!* Philadelphia, 1848.

[SMITH, JOHN ROWSON]. *Professor Risley and Mr. J. R. Smith's Original Gigantic Moving Panorama of the Mississippi River, extending from the Falls of St. Anthony to the Gulf of Mexico, painted by John R. Smith, Esq., depicting nearly Four Thousand Miles of American Scenery, running through Nine States of the Union (sixteen degrees of latitude, from the wheat of the north to the orange of the south); being one-third longer than any other pictorial work in existence: Four Miles in Length.* London: John K. Chapman, 1849.

———. *Descriptive Book of the Tour of Europe, the largest Moving Panorama in the World. Now exhibiting at the Chinese Rooms, Broadway, New York. Painted on Thirty Thousand Square Feet of Canvass, from views taken on the spot, and at an expense of Ten Thousand Dollars, by J. R. Smith, artist of the celebrated Panorama of the Mississippi, which has been exhibited with distinguished success in the United States, London, Dublin, Edinburgh, Paris, Brussels, Rouen, Berlin, Antwerp, Vienna, etc. Pianist:— Mr. Aylwin Field.* New York: Pettiner & Gray, Printers, 1855.

———. *Great National Painting, Professor Risley's Original Gigantic Moving Panorama of the Mississippi River, etc.* Philadelphia, 1853.

———. "Views from Mr. J. R. Smith's Celebrated Panorama of the Mississippi River," *Graham's Magazine*, XXXIV (1849), 56, 206, 257, 336.

SQUIRES, MONAS N. "Henry Lewis and His Mammoth Panorama of the Mississippi River," *Missouri Historical Review*, XXVII (April, 1933), 244–56.

TAYLOR, J. N., and CROOKS, M. O. *Sketch Book of Saint Louis.* St. Louis: George Knapp & Co., 1858.

THOREAU, HENRY DAVID. *Journal, 1851,* in *Writings.* Walden ed.; Boston: Houghton Mifflin Co., 1949. Vol. VIII.

TWAIN, MARK. *Life on the Mississippi.* Boston: James R. Osgood, 1883.

WATERHOUSE, ELLIS K. *Painting in Britain: 1530–1790.* Baltimore: Penguin Books, 1953.

WEMYSS, F. C. *Twenty-Six Years, or the Life of an Actor and Manager.* 2 vols. New York: Burgess, Stringer & Co., 1847.

WILLIAMS, W. *Transparency Painting on Linen: for Decorative Purposes, Panoramic and Dioramic Effects, Ornamental Blinds, &c., with Instructions for the preparation of the linen, the combination and transfer of ornamental designs, combined surfaces, &c.* London: Winson & Newton, n.d.

WILLSON, CHARLES C. "The Successive Chiefs Named Wabasha," *Minnesota Historical Society Collections*, XII (1905–8), 503–12.

INDEX

PRINTED IN U.S.A.